Research Methods:

Texts and Cases

Arunangshu Giri
Debasish Biswas

PUBLISHERS & DISTRIBUTORS (P) LTD

7/22, Ansari Road, Darya Ganj, New Delhi
Tel.: +91-11-4077 5252, 2327 3880
E-mail: orders@atlanticbooks.com
Web: www.atlanticbooks.com

Published by Atlantic Publishers & Distributors (P) Ltd 2024

Previously Published by SAGE Publications in 2019

Printed & bound in India by Atlantic Print Services

To

Our Beloved Students

Contents

Detailed Contents

List of Figures, Tables and Exhibits

Figures

Tables

Exhibits

Foreword

Research Methods: Texts and Cases is of great importance in different disciplines in the galaxy of social sciences. Social sciences are not exact science like physical sciences. It deals with human beings. It is difficult to see the underlying uniformities in the diversity of complex human behaviour. This is due to the fact that human activities and environmental changes create complexity in life as well as challenges, but these challenges demand answers for fundamental questions such as what, where, who, why and how. Therefore, interested groups such as researchers, academicians and practitioners need guidance on committing researches. The fields of social science research are unlimited and the materials of research are endless. Every group of social phenomena, every phase of human life and every stage of past and present developments are materials for the social scientists.

Research methodology is a way to solve a research problem systematically. It may be understood as a science of studying how research is done scientifically. It includes studying the various steps that are generally adopted by a researcher in studying his/her research problems along with the logic behind them. It is necessary for the researcher to know not only the research techniques but also the methodology. Researchers not only need to know how to develop certain indices or tests and how to apply a particular research technique, but they must also know which of these methods or techniques are relevant and which are not and what would they mean and indicate and why. The researchers must also understand the assumptions underlying various techniques, and they need to know the criteria by which they can decide that certain techniques and procedures will be applicable to certain problems and others will not be applicable. All these mean that it is necessary for the researcher to design a methodology that suits his/her problem as methodology differs from problem to problem.

Why a research study has been undertaken, how the research problem has been defined, in what way and why the hypothesis has been formulated, what data have been collected and what method has been adopted, why a particular technique of analysing data has been used and a host of similar other questions are usually answered when we talk of research methodology concerning a research problem in social sciences.

I personally know Dr Arunangshu Giri and Dr Debasish Biswas since many years. Both of them are prolific researchers as well as academicians in the field of social sciences. They have made a deliberate attempt to deal with the most important subject in the present volume. Both of them deserve commendation for their proposition of authoring this book on Research Methods: Texts and Cases.

The book is very comprehensive and all chapters have been discussed in a very simple and lucid language so as to make the subject easily understandable to all the stakeholders. My sincere greetings to Dr Arunangshu Giri and Dr Debasish Biswas, and my best wishes for the book.

Debabrata Mitra

Professor and Head, Department of Commerce, University of North Bengal;
Former Dean, School of Professional Studies, Sikkim University (A Central University)

Preface

The aim of the book is to share scholarly knowledge about research methodology in its complexity. This book can be used to train the basics and techniques involved in doing inquiries from different perspectives. Globalization has had a great impact in all aspects of social science research. Organizations are always focusing on the global market due to different compelling factors. When they want to grab the opportunities in the international market, there is a need for relevant and prompt information from the global market for research study. If an organization or marketing research firm tries to involve global research instead of domestic research, different set of approaches and initiatives are required for this purpose. The book tries to identify a family of approaches towards various research situations and distinguish their outcomes.

Our sincere and deliberate efforts have been to give the book a comprehensive form. All chapters have been discussed in a very simple and lucid language so as to make the subject easily understandable to our beloved students. We have incorporated relevant numerical examples with the latest research practices of the industry and related fields. This book emphasizes statistical software (SPSS and AMOS) and their uses through different examples of statistical tests step by step, minimizing computational hassles. It has tried to cover all the dimensions of the research which can help a beginner researcher to learn research methodology easily.

We feel great pleasure in presenting the first edition of this book to our esteemed readers. It is the outcome of a great deal of encouragement from our colleagues and request from students. This book is appropriate for students, researchers and academicians, and corporates in the field of social sciences. We welcome suggestions from all the stakeholders for enrichment and improvement of the book in the future.

Acknowledgements

First of all, we would like to express our sincere gratitude to Professor (Dr) Debabrata Mitra, Department of Commerce, North Bengal University, who has been our motivator since the beginning of our write-up. He provided us with many helpful suggestions, important advices and constant encouragement during the course of this work.

A special note of appreciation is due to Professor Susanta Mitra, professor of Commerce, Kazi Nazrul University, West Bengal, for his valuable contributions towards enhancing the standard of the book.

We are grateful to the esteemed teachers who always provided us with their valuable suggestions from time to time. We are thankful to our students who have always shown a keen interest in our publication. We offer our heartfelt congratulations to Atlantic Publishing Group for their untiring effort and support in bringing out this book.

We also thank Professor Swagata Sen, Hon'ble Vice Chancellor, University of Gour Banga, West Bengal, for extending his help in conducting the task.

The responsibility for errors remains with us alone.

About the Authors

Arunangshu Giri is presently serving as an Associate Professor in the School of Management and Social Science, Haldia Institute of Technology, West Bengal. He is also a visiting professor at Vidyasagar University, one of the eminent universities of India. He is working as a study counsellor of different MBA subjects (research methodology, marketing research and others) at Indira Gandhi National Open University (IGNOU). He was awarded a PhD degree in management on 4 June 2015 by IIT-ISM, Dhanbad. His topic of research was 'Awareness and Impact of Effective Marketing Initiatives of Yoga and Ayurveda in Indian Urban Market: A Study'. Dr Giri obtained his MBA (marketing) from ICFAI University in the year 2009 with first class. He has postgraduate teaching experience of more than eight years. His areas of specializations are marketing, marketing research, statistics, production and operation management. He has authored 31 research papers in national and international journals of repute. He acted as a resource person and chairperson in different national and international workshops and seminars. He also received the Best Business Academic of the Year Award 2016 (gold medal) at the 69th All India Commerce Conference, organized by Lucknow University, Lucknow, on 13 November 2016. He has reviewed many reputed books such as *Management: Principles, Processes, and Practices* by Anil Bhat and Arya Kumar and also edited chapters in several books. He is one of the editors of the journal *International Journal of HIT Transaction on ECCN*.

Debasish Biswas is presently serving as an Assistant Professor in the Department of Business Administration, Vidyasagar University, West Bengal, since April 2012. He is also serving at EIILM, Kolkata, one of the eminent management institutes of India. He is a visiting professor at State Labour Institute, Government of West Bengal. He was awarded a PhD degree in commerce on 7 September 2011 by the University of North Bengal. His topic of research was 'Productivity & Industrial Relations: An Empirical Study on Tea Estates in Dooars Region of West Bengal'. Dr Biswas obtained his MCom from the University of Burdwan in the year 2000 and also his MBA (HR) with first class from the same university in 2002. He has a diploma in labour laws (DLL) from Annamalai University in 2003 and a postgraduate diploma in hospital management (PGDHM) from the same university in 2006. He also obtained a postgraduate diploma in marketing management (PGDMM) and a postgraduate diploma in entrepreneurship again from Annamalai University in 2015 and 2016, respectively. Dr Biswas qualified UGC NET in the field of human resource management in 2008. He was awarded MPhil in commerce from Periyar University in 2008. Dr Biswas served as a full-time lecturer in the Department of Management, University of North Bengal, West Bengal, from 27 July 2010 to 31 March 2012. He served as a lecturer of management at Gyan Jyoti College,

Siliguri, affiliated to the University of North Bengal, for 5 years. His areas of specializations are accounting and financial management, human resource management, industrial relations and quantitative techniques. Dr Debasish Biswas is a prolific researcher. He has contributed 65 research papers in different interdisciplinary areas of management in different national seminars and conferences. He has authored 35 research papers in national and international journals of repute. He has been a resource person and chairperson in different national and international seminars in different parts of India. He is a life member of Indian Commerce Association, International Business Studies Academia (IBSA, Durgapur) and All India Accounting Association, Kolkata. He has authored five books titled *Management Information System*, 2016; *Fundamentals of Financial Management*, 2014; *Industrial Relations & Labour Welfare*, 2013; *The Romance of Human Resource Management*, 2013; and *Relationship between Productivity and Industrial Relations*, 2012 with Professor Debabrata Mitra, Department of Commerce, University of North Bengal, West Bengal.

He has co-edited a book titled *Dynamic Evolution of Management Paradigm*, 2017 with Dr Sudin Bag.

Dr Biswas has also developed study materials for MBA course for the distance education wing of Tezpur Central University, Assam, and has developed study materials for MCom course for the distance education wing of Vidyasagar University, West Bengal. He received the Best Business Academic of the Year Award 2016 (gold medal) at the 69th All India Commerce Conference, organized by Lucknow University on 13 November 2016.

CHAPTER

1

Introduction

LEARNING OBJECTIVES

After studying this chapter, you should be able to

- Visualize the meaning and features of good research.
- Understand the concept, nature, scope, types and time dimension of social science research.
- Learn the decision-making role in social science research.
- Appreciate the factors influencing social science research.
- Understand the global and ethical aspects in social science research.

1.1. MEANING OF RESEARCH

Research is the method of enquiry that uses systematic scientific techniques such as experimental, quasi-experimental and non-experimental. These techniques are used to collect secondary and primary information regarding a topic (Kothari 2004). On the other hand, Merriam-Webster (2012) described a research as hierarchy of actions towards investigation for the purpose of knowledge gain from new facts. Thus, it takes a systematic search and testing of new facts through existing theories to resolve identified problems/improve a certain situation.

Either Zikmund (1997) added that this systematic investigation can be on either existing or new knowledge, whereby the knowledge found can be used to lay a foundation to prove facts or to contribute to expansion on results of previous works and resolve existing problems. Likewise, the process supports confirmation of existing theorems as well as developing new theories. Also, a study can be conducted to test instrument validity and research process, prior to beginning a project to justify the available gap from the previous research work.

1.2. CONCEPT AND DEFINITION OF SOCIAL SCIENCE RESEARCH

Sciences are broadly divided into natural (physical) sciences and social sciences. Social sciences are not exact science like physical sciences. It deals with human beings. Human nature and man's environment are so complex that it is more difficult to comprehend and predict human behaviour than the physical phenomena. It is difficult to see the underlying uniformities in the diversity of complex human behaviour.

Social science is a generic term covering the scientific study of man. It is a discipline or branch of science that deals with the sociocultural aspects of human behaviour. Social sciences include various disciplines dealing with human life, human behaviour and institutions.

Social sciences generally include cultural anthropology, economics, geography, history, political science, sociology, criminology, management and social psychology.

According to P.V. Young (1960), we may define social research as 'the systematic method of discovering new facts and verifying old facts. Their sequences interrelationship, causal explanations and the natural laws govern them'.

1.3. NATURE AND SCOPE

Nature: In contrast to physical science, social science lacks the power of exact prediction; this is attributed to the 'erratic', idiosyncratic and irregular nature of human behaviour. Social scientists point out that the low predictable potential in social science is due to our limited knowledge of relevant variables operative in the group, such as customs and traditions. The cause and effect are difficult to be segregated clearly. The present state of development of social science is far behind physical science. Merton advises to social scientist against their despair; it is possible to develop border applicability.

Scope: The scope of social science research is unlimited and the materials of research are endless. Every group of social phenomena, every phase of human life and every stage of past and present developments are materials for the social scientist. The area of research in various social sciences provides vast scope for research in the field.

The main scope of social research is as follows:

1. Social research provides new insight into the organized society and its social structure.
2. Social research also provides new horizon in scientific explanation, advances and tests principles of procedure and suggests new concepts.
3. Another scope of social research is that it is exemplified by studies and attempts to test or challenge existing theories and revise them in the light of new evidence.
4. Social research helps to establish new theory and techniques of exploration.
5. Social research also contributes to the existing stone of fruitful ideas, methodology and basic understanding of social life and control of its problems.

1.4. TYPES OF RESEARCH

Most research can be divided into three different categories—exploratory, descriptive and causal. These have been discussed as follows:

1. Exploratory research

Exploratory research is an important part of any marketing or business strategy. Its focus is on the discovery of ideas and insights as opposed to collecting statistically accurate data. That is why exploratory research is best suited as the beginning of your total research plan. It is most commonly used for further defining company issues, areas for potential growth, alternative courses of action, and for prioritizing areas that require statistical research.

When it comes to online surveys, the most common example of exploratory research is in the form of open-ended questions. Think of the exploratory questions in your survey as expanding your understanding of the people you are surveying. Text responses may not be statistically measureable, but they will give you richer quality information that can lead to the discovery of new initiatives or problems that should be addressed.

Exploratory research is conducted in order to determine the nature of a problem. It is intended to explore research questions, but its intent is not to offer final and conclusive solutions to existing issues. Exploratory research provides researchers with a better understanding of the problem, but the results of exploratory research are typically not useful for decision-making alone. Exploratory research can provide significant insight into a given situation, as the objective is to gather preliminary information that will help define issues and suggest hypotheses.

Exploratory research can be used in a variety of research methods, including trial studies, pilot studies, interviews, case studies, focus groups and various experiments. Exploratory research takes the form of open-ended questions—questions where participants can leave responses in the format of open text comments. Text comments may not be statistically measureable (unless properly coded), but they will give you richer, more quality data that can lead you to uncover new initiatives or issues that should be addressed.

2. Descriptive research

Descriptive research takes up the bulk of online surveying and is considered conclusive in nature due to its quantitative nature. Unlike exploratory research, descriptive research is pre-planned and structured in design so that the information collected can be statistically inferred on a population.

The main idea behind using this type of research is to better define an opinion, attitude or behaviour held by a group of people on a given subject. Consider your everyday multiple-choice questions. Since there are pre-defined categories a respondent must choose from, it is considered descriptive research. These questions will not give unique insights on the issues like exploratory research would. Instead, grouping the responses into predetermined choices will provide statistically inferable data. This allows you to measure the significance of your results on the overall population you are studying, as well as the changes of your respondent's opinions, attitudes and behaviours over time.

The objective of descriptive research, also known as statistical research, is to describe situations; for example, to describe things such as the market potential for a product or the demographics and attitudes of consumers who buy a certain product or service.

Unlike exploratory research, descriptive research is methodically planned, designed and formatted to collect quantifiable data. Grouping responses into set choices will provide statistically conclusive data. This allows you to measure the significance of your results on the overall population, as well as track the changes of your respondents' opinions, attitudes and behaviours over time.

3. Causal research

Like descriptive research, causal research is quantitative in nature as well as pre-planned and structured in design. For this reason, it is also considered as conclusive research. Causal research differs in its attempt to explain the cause and effect relationship between variables. This is opposed to the observational style of descriptive research, because it attempts to decipher whether a relationship is causal through experimentation. In the end, causal research will have two objectives: (a) to understand which variables are the causes and which variables are the effects and (b) to determine the nature of the relationship between the causal variables and the effect to be predicted (Table 1.1).

1.5. FEATURES OF GOOD RESEARCH

Every research study, irrespective of its type, should have some features so that it can be classified as a good research. Let us discuss some of these features.

1. One of the important features of a good research is that the purpose of the research is clearly defined. A research study with a clearly defined purpose finds wider acceptance and acknowledgement within the research community.
2. Second important characteristic of a good research is that the research method should be defined in a clear manner with sufficient detail. This will allow the repetition of the study in future for further advancement, while maintaining the continuity of what has been done in the past.
3. The third thing to remember is that any limitations and assumptions made by the researcher during the course of the study should be clearly highlighted in the research. This will support the findings of the research study, in case someone tries to validate the findings.
4. The fourth thing to remember is that, as far as possible, the research design should be planned in a way that the results generated are as objective as possible. This will provide an easier understanding about the findings of the research.
5. Another thing to be considered by the researcher is that there should be sufficient data to investigate the research topic and the researcher should carefully check the reliability and validity of the data.
6. Further, in order to deliver a good research, a researcher should confine the conclusions to those justified by the data.
7. Lastly, a good research depends a great deal on the integrity, commitment and ethical norms of the researcher.

1.6. TIME DIMENSION OF RESEARCH

1. Cross-sectional research

One-shot or cross-sectional studies are those in which data are gathered once, during a period of days, weeks or months. Many cross-sectional studies are exploratory or descriptive in purpose. They are designed to look at how things are now, without any sense of whether there is a history or trend at work.

2. Longitudinal research

Research carried out longitudinally involves data collection at multiple points in time. Longitudinal studies may take the following forms:

a. Trend study: It looks at population characteristics over time, for example, organizational absenteeism rates during the course of a year.
b. Cohort study: It traces on sub-population over time, for example, absenteeism rates for the sales department.

TABLE 1.1
Comparison: Exploratory, Descriptive and Causal Research

Types of Research	Exploratory Research	Descriptive Research	Causal Research
Degree of problem definition	Key variables not defined	Key variables are defined	Key variables and key relationships are defined
Possible situations	Quality of service is declining and we do not know why.	What have been the trends in organizational downsizing over the past 10 years?	Which of two training programmes is more effective for reducing labour turnover?

Source: Authors.

3. Panel study

It traces on the same sample over time, for example, graduate career tracks over the period 1990–2000 for the same starting cohort.

While longitudinal studies will often be more time-consuming and expensive than cross-sectional studies, they are more likely to identify causal relationships between variables.

1.7. DECISION-MAKING ROLE IN SOCIAL SCIENCE RESEARCH

For effective decision-making in social science research, the researchers should emphasize on the relevant and accurate information regarding internal and external environment of the organization. The main aim of social science research is to provide significant and timely information to the higher management, so that they can plan and implement effective decisions. Social science research in any organization goes through few important stages. They are as follows:

1. Problem identification

Identification of problems means monitoring and inspecting the internal and external environment of the organization in social science research. This step helps the researchers to execute SWOT analysis (strength, weakness, opportunities and threats) of the organization to understand different environmental trends. It involves exploring the analysis to have a better insight about the situations. In this stage, different information regarding problems and opportunities are collected. For example, an Indian garment company that wants to enter the overseas market should emphasize on different research such as trend analysis of the market, brand awareness, consumer behaviour and competitor analysis. Any delay in problem identification may become very harmful to the organization.

2. Problem prioritization and selection

After identification of problems, the researchers should focus on prioritization of problems because it is impossible for an organization to give attention to all in one shot. Prioritization and selection of the problem depend on the influences of the problem on organization and time factor. Top priority is given to those problems which have a key influence on the organization and demand attention in a short-term period. At this stage, detailed information is collected about the top-priority problems to gain better clarity about the situation. Basically this stage helps the researchers to prioritize the problems and spot the right opportunities. Here, quantitative and qualitative researches are used for this purpose. The related activities of this stage are to provide the real insight about opportunities identification.

3. Problem resolution

This stage helps to decide the path to solve the problem and make use of the prospect. Two steps are followed in this stage: (a) developing the alternatives and (b) evaluating them. Depending on the problems and corresponding solutions, alternative courses of actions are defined by the researchers. These alternatives are evaluated on account of different criteria for getting the best course of action. For example, an organization has three different advertising programmes from among which it has to select the best programme. By customer survey, the researchers can select the best option.

4. Explore the solution

In this stage, a theoretical model may be developed by the researchers with the help of extensive literature review. From the problem statements, hypotheses are formulated. Then sample size and sample techniques are determined. After that, a well-designed questionnaire as a survey instrument is used to collect data for social science research. For analysing the data, statistical techniques are used and findings from statistical results are recorded at last.

5. Implementation

After selecting the best alternative with theoretical and empirical evidence, the organization has to implement it effectively and efficiently. Here, research is used to monitor and control the implemented courses of action. Decision-makers describe findings in the light of their decision range. In some situations, decision-makers may face some limitations for their own constraints. At first, they analyse all these constraints for taking appropriate decisions.

6. Evaluate the decision-making process

In this stage, performance research is executed to measure the performance of the courses of action, so that it can be easily compared with the goals set for each activity. Decisions may be right or wrong in different cases. So the decisions should be systematically examined by the organization's management in terms of time, cost and other resources. Organizations also monitor each activity continuously so as to recognize the opportunities and identify the issues in early stages. In this stage, the organization can alter its plans as per the situational requirement.

1.8. FACTORS AFFECTING SOCIAL SCIENCE RESEARCH

Different social science researches provide many advantages to the organizations, but it is not the ultimate solution of the problems which are faced by them. However, a social science research includes cost, time and effort. So organizations take their decisions on their research considering different affecting factors. These factors are discussed further.

1. Time restraint

It is an important factor which has a huge impact on an organization's decision regarding whether to conduct the research study or not. In some cases, time limitation influences the organization to take any decision without conducting any research. Quick internal and external environmental changes such as frequent alteration of competitor's strategies, market environment and government regulations need immediate action.

2. Resource availability

It also influences the organization's decision of conducting a research or not. Here, the resources indicate financial resources and human resources. Research study cannot be conducted in the absence of proper budgetary allocation of the organization. Absence of financial resources leads to inaccurate research because organizations have to compromise many activities in the research process such as taking smaller sample size instead of large sample size as per the research project requirement and using cheaper data collection techniques and data analysis methods, which are important for proper social science research. So organizations should get insight about the financial resources before conducting a research. On the other hand, unavailability of skilled and qualified personnel negatively influences data collection and analysis process in research which may lead to improper sample selection and collection of data and inaccurate analysis and interpretation of results. So organizations should recruit qualified and skilled employees for this purpose.

3. Information types

Types of information affect an organization's decision of conducting research or not. If the required information in research can be generated from the internal sources of the organization or previous studies by the organization, then new research study is meaningless as well as waste of time and efforts. In some cases, the experiences of management professionals and their intuition are sufficient to take a decision without conducting any research study.

4. Cost-benefit analysis

Research always provides some benefits, but it requires sufficient amount of money for its execution. The management of the organization should prepare a cost-benefit analysis before taking the final decision of conducting a research. If the research benefits are more compared to the cost involved and research results would improve the quality of the management decisions, then only the research proposal should be accepted.

1.9. GLOBALIZATION AND SOCIAL SCIENCE RESEARCH

Globalization has had a great impact on all aspects of social science research. Organizations are always focusing on the global market due to different compelling factors. When they want to grab the opportunities from the international market, there is a need for relevant and prompt information from the global market for research study. If an organization or marketing research firm tries to involve global research instead of domestic research, different set of approaches and initiatives are required for this purpose. Few points should be emphasized by the organizations for global social science research. First of all, the research must be closely associated with global market growth opportunities. This research requires some new creative tools to understand the global markets. Technological advancement should be adopted by the researchers to make the research process efficient. Multinational organizations should always focus on potential emerging global markets rather than on the saturated market where providing time and efforts are insignificant. Conducting research in the global market needs innovative approaches than usual approaches. Usually, the literacy rate is low in those emerging markets. So researchers must be conscious while they design and prepare the research survey instruments. Generally, qualitative research study is more effective in comparison to quantitative research study for the emerging international market. For understanding the consumer behaviour, cultures, preferences and views of these markets, some innovative techniques such as videotaping through observation methods, using focus group, analogies, metaphor, psycho drawing, using technologies like internet, computer-assisted telephone interviewing and computer-assisted personal interviewing can be used by the researchers for efficient and effective global research.

1.10. ETHICS IN SOCIAL SCIENCE RESEARCH

Social researchers should focus on ethical clearance when conducting research involving human subjects. They should keep in mind to (a) show respect to the people involved in research, (b) provide maximum benefit to the research and (c) minimize issues and challenges involved in it. So ethical behaviour in social science research should be essential for all researchers. Voluntary participation of people must be accepted in social science research, which means that people should not be forced into participating in research. Informed consent is required from respondents in the process of gathering information. It indicates that research participants should be fully informed about the process and threats involved in research. Furthermore, researchers do not any right to push participants into a risky situation by disclosing any data about them. Harm may be either in physical form or in psychological form. It may happen at the time of conducting research like generating mental distress. On the other hand, ethical issues may evolve from the publication of research output. Therefore, ethical standards for social science research should emphasize on protecting the privacy of all participants in the research process and maintaining their confidentiality. They should be assured about the restriction of disclosing information to outsiders who are not directly engaged in the research. All the relevant ethical issues should be considered at the time of formulating the research plan in the earlier stage. Researchers should be very careful about utilizing collected information without permission regarding individuals who are not direct participants of the research. At the time of interviews or in surveys, instruments like inappropriate questions in questionnaire should be avoided for restricting the damage to the dignity or image of the respondents or innocence of the subject. An ethics committee should be formed for a large research project to address the ethical issues. This committee must review the research plan considering the ethical implications and take a decision whether any action is required for the purpose of safety and rights of participants. The committee members should be from different disciplinary backgrounds and free from any outside influences.

1.11. INTRODUCTION TO SPSS IN DATA PRESENTATION AND ANALYSIS

Basically, one of the objectives of this book is to provide the readers the step-by-step instructions required to execute the data analysis using SPSS (previously 'Statistical Package for the Social Science', later on 'Statistical Product and Service Solution') for Windows. In the late 1960s, this software was developed by three Stanford graduate students. Now, SPSS, a Chicago-based firm, has been established as the world's largest statistical software company. It provides a very strong platform for data analysis. For handling the software operation, users must have access to a computer that has Microsoft Windows XP or Vista installed and SPSS for Windows installed. The main purpose of using this software is to clarify the users about the fundamentals of most types of data analysis. There are three basic activities associated with data analysis through SPSS that should be known to the users. First of all, users must type the data, organize and format it into the computer. Then users must identify the data according to their types and implement to SPSS. Lastly, users must know how to interpret the SPSS output. To start SPSS, select 'Start → Programs → SPSS Inc → Statistics (Version) → SPSS Statistics (Version)'. For the execution of the first basic activity, numeric data must be entered in the Data Editor window (Exhibit 1.1) which will appear on the screen first after starting the software. Data Editor has two parts: (a) Data View and (b) Variable View. Data and variables can be defined by the 'Data View' window and 'Variable View' window, respectively. These views are located at the bottom of the 'Data Editor' windows. For example, a user wants to create two variables—age and gender. After clicking the 'Variable View' (Exhibit 1.2), user should type 'Age' in the first row of the first column and type 'Gender' in the second row of the first column. Now, the user should click on the 'Data View' (Exhibit 1.3). Then, two variables are observed as the headings for the first two columns of 'Data View'. After that, user can start entering the data into it. For different statistical operations, different menu bars can be used such as 'Data', 'Transform', 'Analyze' and 'Graph'.

EXHIBIT 1.1
Data Editor Window

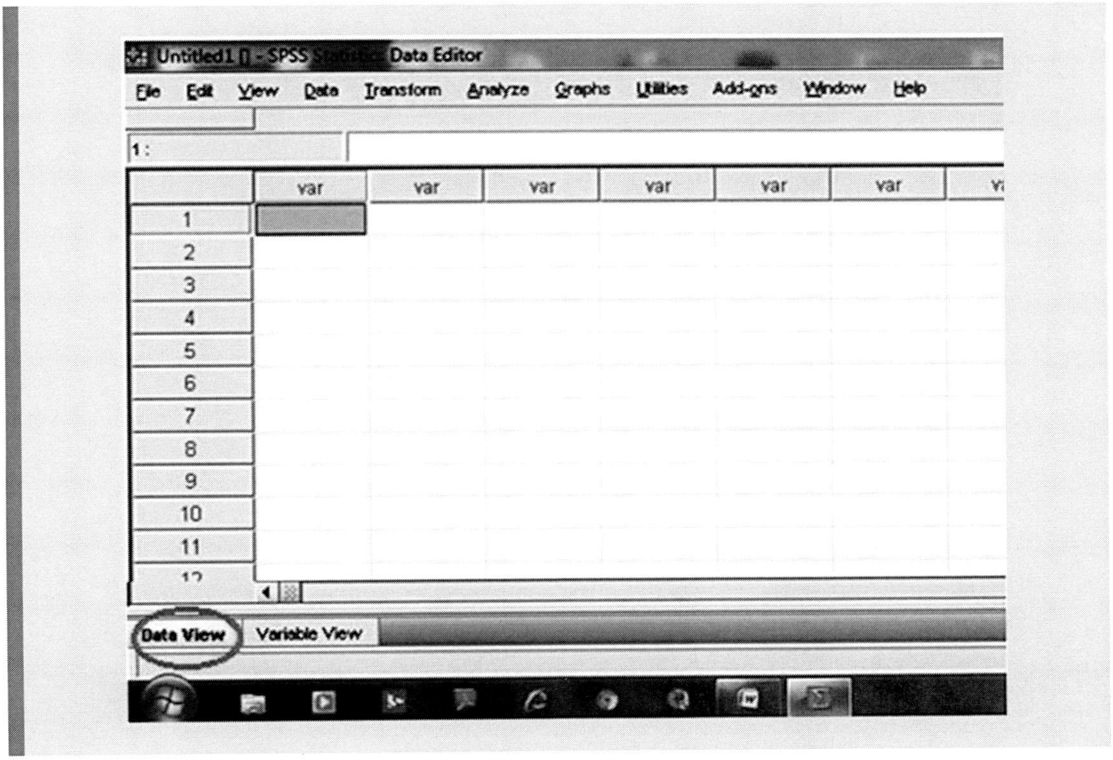

EXHIBIT 1.2
Variable View

Example.sav [DataSet1] - SPSS Statistics Data Editor

File Edit View Data Transform Analyze Graphs Utilities Add-ons Window Help

	Name	Type	Width	Decimals	Label	Values	Missing	Columns	Align	Measure
1	AGE	Numeric	8	0	Age group	{1, less tha...	None	8	Right	Nominal
2	GENDER	Numeric	8	0	Gender	{1, Male}...	None	8	Right	Nominal
3										
4										
5										
6										
7										
8										
9										
10										
11										

Data View | Variable View

EXHIBIT 1.3
Data View

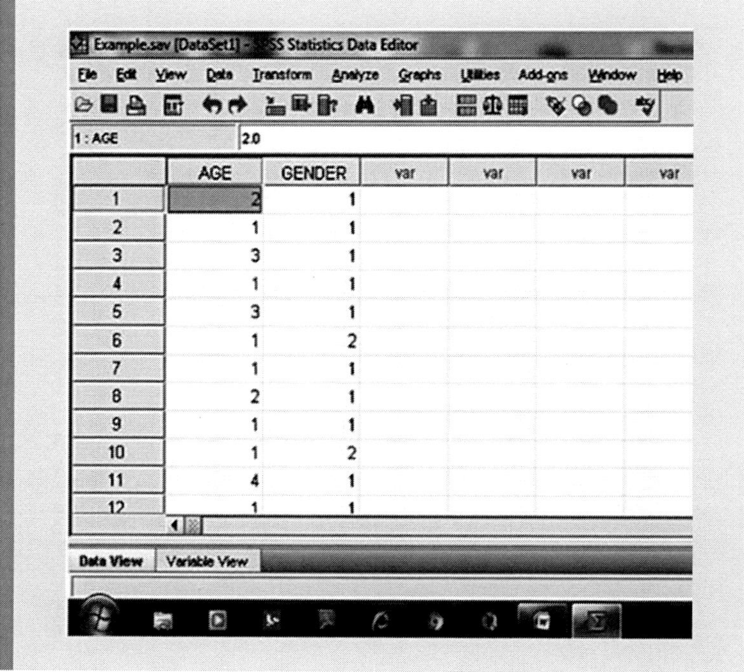

Example.sav [DataSet1] - SPSS Statistics Data Editor

File Edit View Data Transform Analyze Graphs Utilities Add-ons Window Help

1 : AGE 2.0

	AGE	GENDER	var	var	var	var
1	2	1				
2	1	1				
3	3	1				
4	1	1				
5	3	1				
6	1	2				
7	1	1				
8	2	1				
9	1	1				
10	1	2				
11	4	1				
12	1	1				

Data View | Variable View

SUMMARY

Research is the method of enquiry that uses systematic scientific techniques such as experimental, quasi-experimental and non-experimental. On the other hand, social science research deals with human beings. Most research can be divided into three different categories—exploratory, descriptive and causal. On the basis of time dimension of research, cross-sectional, longitudinal and panel data may be the basis for the research. Factors such as time restraint, resource availability, information types and cost-benefit analysis affect the social science research.

KEY TERMS

research (1)
exploratory research (3)
descriptive research (3)
causal research (3)
cross-sectional research (4)
longitudinal research (4)
trend study (4)
cohort study (4)
panel study (5)

EXERCISES

1. Define the term research.
2. What are the nature and scope of social science research?
3. What do you mean by social science research?
4. Classify different types of research.
5. Describe the factors affecting social science research.
6. State the features of good research.
7. Discuss the ethical aspects in social science research.
8. How are globalization and social science research related?
9. Describe the decision-making role in social science research.
10. Make a comparative study of exploratory, descriptive and causal research.
11. Distinguish between longitudinal and panel data analysis.

CHAPTER

2

Literature Review and Data Collection

LEARNING OBJECTIVES

After studying this chapter, you should be able to

- Describe the reasons for reviewing the available literature during the preparation of a research proposal.
- Describe the sources of information and types of review.
- Understand primary and secondary data.
- Know the role of different statistical organizations.
- Learn how the statistical data will be presented.
- Know the important data sources.

2.1. CONCEPT OF LITERATURE REVIEW

A literature review is a survey of sources within a field of study and is an integral part of a research project. A literature review includes both 'summary' and 'synthesis' and provides the reader with an overview of the scholarly work that has been done on a particular topic.

A literature review is not an annotated bibliography. The author must show what has been written in a particular field and prove how his or her research is going to add to the body of knowledge.

A literature review is both a summary and explanation of the complete and current state of knowledge on a limited topic as found in academic books and journal articles.

A literature review should be considered as one part of the overall argument of your research paper or project. It is your opportunity to describe what is already known about your topic, gaps in the body of knowledge and how your research tries to fill the research gaps.

2.2. PURPOSES OF LITERATURE REVIEW

Literature review serves the following purposes:

1. It prevents you from duplicating work that has been done before by the researchers.
2. It increases your knowledge on the problem you want to study and this may assist you in refining your 'statement of the problem'.
3. It gives you confidence why your particular research project is needed.
4. You will be familiar with different research methods applied in the related research works.
5. It will help to identify the research gaps in the particular field of study.
6. It provides a constructive analysis of the methodologies and approaches of other researchers.

2.3. KEY POINTS OF A LITERATURE REVIEW

Researcher can obtain three important things from the review of existing literature. These are theory, methodology and research gap.

Theory tells to the researcher what the previous research says. Researcher can also know the research methodology, that is, how the previous researchers carried out their research in a particular field of study. Researcher can also identify the research gap in the existing literature.

2.4. SOURCES OF INFORMATION

Primary literature sources are the first occurrence of a piece of work. These mainly include (a) reports, (b) conferences and proceedings and (c) theses.

1. Reports include market research reports, government reports and the likes.
2. Conference proceedings refer to any symposia that are often published as unique titles within journals or as books. Most conferences will have a very specific theme.
3. Research papers contain details of research done on a particular topic. It is a good source of detailed information and further reference.

Secondary literature sources mainly include (a) journals, (b) books and (c) newspapers.

1. Journals are also known as periodicals which are published on a regular basis.
2. Books are written for specific audiences. The material in books are presented in a more ordered and accessible manner than in journals.
3. Newspapers are a good source of topical events, developments within the business and government as well as recent statistical information.

Tertiary literature sources are also called 'search tools' which are designed either to locate primary and secondary literature or to introduce a topic. They include indexes and abstracts as well as encyclopaedias and bibliographies. For example, subject catalogues of libraries, list of books and publishers, bulletins and so on.

2.5. TYPES OF LITERATURE REVIEW

For the purpose of research, there are three main types of literature review. These are as follows:

1. Evaluative review

Evaluative review is a type of literature review which focuses on providing a discussion of the literature in terms of its coverage and contribution to knowledge in a particular area. It is often used to directly compare research findings of a project with those from other projects, when findings are directly available.

2. Exploratory review

This type of literature review seeks to find out what actually exists in the academic literature in terms of theory, empirical evidence and research methods as they pertain to a specific research topic and its related wider subject area.

3. Instrumental review

This type of literature review seeks to find out how to conduct some research on a highly specific research problem.

2.6. ORGANIZATION OF INFORMATION ON INDEX CARDS

The index cards should contain the following:

1. Key words
2. A summary of the contents of books or articles which is relevant to one's own study
3. A brief analysis of the content, with comments such as 'How information from that particular study could be used in one's own study'
4. Information obtained from key persons could also be summarized on the index card

After collecting the required information on index cards, the investigator should decide in which order he/she wants to discuss the previous research findings:

1. From global to local
2. From broader to focused
3. From past to current

In conclusion, while reviewing a literature, all what is known about the study topic should be summarized with the relevant references. Overall, the literature review should be adequate, relevant and critical. In addition to this, appropriate referencing procedures should always be followed in research proposals as well as in research reports. While reviewing a literature, emphasis should be laid upon both positive and negative findings and any distortion of information to suit your own study objectives should be avoided.

Finally, after an exhaustive literature review, summarize the findings and write a coherent discussion by indicating the research gap which supports the undertaking of your study.

2.7. DATA COLLECTION

Data collection plays a very crucial role in statistical analysis. In research, there are different methods used to gather information, all of which fall into two categories, that is, primary data and secondary data. As the name suggests, primary data is one which is collected for the first time by the researcher while secondary data is the data that has already been collected or produced by others.

2.8. DEFINITION OF PRIMARY DATA

Primary data is data that originates for the first time by the researcher through direct efforts and experience, specifically for the purpose of addressing the research problem. It is also known as the first-hand or raw data. Primary data collection is quite expensive, as the research is conducted by the organization or agency itself, which requires resources such as investment and manpower. Data collection is under direct control and supervision of the investigator.

The data can be collected through various methods such as surveys, observations, physical testing, mailed questionnaires, questionnaire filled and sent by enumerators, personal interviews, telephonic interviews, focus groups and case studies.

2.8.1. Merits and Demerits of Primary Data

Merits of primary data collection are as follows:

1. Addresses specific research issues

It allows the organization to address specific issues to their own situation. Primary research is designed to collect the information that the organization wants to acquire and report it in ways that benefits the organization. For example, while information reported with secondary research may not fit the organization's needs, in primary research, the organization controls the research design.

2. Greater control

It enables the organization to have a higher level of control over how the information is collected. In this way the organization can decide on issues such as size of project, location of research and time frame for completing the project.

3. Efficient spending for information

Primary data collections focus on specific issues to the researcher. Hence, research funds are spent efficiently.

4. Proprietary information

Information collected by the organization using primary research is their own and is generally not shared with others. Thus, information can be kept hidden from competitors and potentially offers an 'information advantage' to the organization that undertook the primary research.

Demerits of primary data collection have been discussed further.

While primary data collection is a powerful method for acquiring information, it does pose several significant problems including the following:

1. Cost

Primary data may be very expensive since there is a great deal of organizational involvement and the expense in preparing and carrying out research can be high.

2. Time-consuming

Primary data collection takes much longer than secondary data collection.

3. Feasibility

Primary data collection is not always within the reach of an organization. For instance, it would not be practical for an organization to take interview of every customer who visits their stores on a certain day as it requires employment of a huge number of researchers.

2.8.2. Methods of Primary Data Collection

There are several ways of collecting primary data. For the selection of an appropriate method, the objective, nature and scope of study, the availability of time and funds, and the level of precision required are to be taken into consideration.

These have been discussed as follows:

1. Observation method

In the observation method, the information is sought by the way of investigator's own direct observation without asking anything from the respondent. The main advantage of this method is that it is free from subjective biasness, as it is free from respondent's willingness. It is, however, an expensive and time-consuming method. Moreover, the information provided by this method is very limited.

2. Interview method

Primary data may be collected either through personal interviews or through telephonic interviews.

a. In personal interviews, the interviewer asks questions generally in a face-to-face interaction. Personal information can be obtained easily under this method. It is, however, a very expensive and time-consuming method, especially when a large and widely spread geographical sample is taken into consideration. Certain types of respondents, such as officials, executives or people of high income groups, may not be easily accessible.
   In this method, the respondents may give wrong and imaginary information. For an effective interview, there should be a good rapport with the respondents which is often very difficult to develop.
b. In telephonic interviews, contact is made with the respondents through telephone.
   The main merits of telephonic interviews are as follows:
   i. It is more flexible and faster than other methods.
   ii. It is cheaper and a less time-consuming method of data collection.
   iii. Recall is easy and replies can be recorded without causing embarrassment to respondents.
   iv. Access can be made to respondents easily.
   v. Wider representation of sample is possible in this method.

This method also has several weaknesses. For example, the surveys are restricted to respondents who have telephonic facilities, and little time is given to respondents for their answers. It is not suitable for intensive surveys where comprehensive answers are required for various questions.

3. Questionnaire method

In this method, a questionnaire is mailed to the person concerned with a request to answer the questions and return the filled questionnaire. This method is most extensively applied in various researches in social science.

The merits of this method are as follows:

a. There is low cost even when the universe is large and is widespread geographically.
b. It is free from bias of the interviewer as answers are respondent's own words.
c. Respondents, who are not easily approachable, can also be reached conveniently.
d. Moreover, respondents are given enough time to give well thought answers.

The demerits of this method are as follows:

a. Low rate of return of the duly filled questionnaire.
b. It can be used only when the respondents are educated and cooperative.
c. The control of the questionnaire may be lost once it is sent.
d. It is difficult to know whether willing respondents are truly representative.
e. This method is also very time-consuming.

4. Schedule method

This method of data collection is very much like the collection of data through questionnaires, with little difference that lies in the fact that schedules (pro forma containing a set of questions) are being filled in by the enumerators who are specially appointed for this purpose. Enumerators explain the aims and objectives of the investigation and also remove the difficulties which any respondent may feel in understanding the implications of a particular question.

This method is very useful in extensive enquiries and can lead to fairly reliable results. It is, however, very expensive and is usually adopted in investigations conducted by governmental agencies or by some organizations. Population census all over the world is conducted through this method.

2.9. DEFINITION OF SECONDARY DATA

Secondary data implies second-hand information which is already collected and recorded by any person other than the user for a purpose not relating to the current research problem. It is the readily available form of data collected from various sources such as census, government publications, internal records of the organization, reports, books, journals, articles and websites.

2.9.1. Merits and Demerits of Secondary Data

Merits of secondary data collection are as follows:

1. It is easily available.
2. It saves time and cost of the researcher.

Demerits of secondary data collection are as follows:

1. Since the data are gathered from secondary sources, it is neither relevant nor accurate.
2. Moreover, the objective and the method adopted for acquiring data may not be suitable for the current situation.

2.9.2. Methods of Secondary Data Collection

Secondary sources can be classified into two categories, namely, published and unpublished sources.

1. Published sources of secondary data are as follows:

   a. Government publications: The Central Statistical Organisation (CSO) and various state governments collect, compile and publish data on regular basis. Some of such important publications have been listed further.
      i. Indian trade journals
      ii. Reports on currency and finance
      iii. Indian Customs and Central Excise Tariff
      iv. *Statistical Abstract*, India
      v. *Reserve Bank of India Bulletin*
      vi. *Labour Gazette*
      vii. Agricultural statistics of India
      viii. *Bulletin of Agricultural Prices*
      ix. Indian foreign statistics
      x. *Economic Survey*

   b. International bodies: All foreign governments and international agencies publish regular reports of international significance. These reports are regularly published by agencies such as
      i. United Nations Organization
      ii. World Health Organization
      iii. International Labour Organization
      iv. Food and Agriculture Organization
      v. International Bank for Reconstruction and Development
      vi. World Meteorological Organization

   c. Semi-government publications: Semi-government organizations, municipalities, district boards and others also publish reports in respect of birth, death and education, sanitation and many other related fields.

   d. Reports of committee and commissions: Central government, or state government, sometimes appoints committees and commissions on matters of great importance. Reports of such committees are of great significance as they provide invaluable data. Some examples of such reports are Shah Commission Report, Sarkaria Commission Report and Finance Commission Reports.

   e. Private publications: Some commercial and research institutes publish reports regularly, for example, Institute of Economic Growth, stock exchanges, National Council of Education Research and Training (NCERT) and National Council of Applied Economic Research (NCAER).

   f. Newspapers and magazines: Various newspapers as well as magazines also collect data in respect of many social and economic aspects. Some of them are:
      i. *The Economic Times*
      ii. *The Financial Express*

   iii. *Hindustan Times*
   iv. *Indian Express*
   v. *Business Standard*
   vi. *Economic and Political Weekly*
   vii. *Main-stream*
   viii. *Kurukshetra*
   ix. *Yojana*

g. Research scholars: Individual research scholars collect data to complete their research work which is further published with their research papers.

2. Unpublished source

There are certain records maintained properly by governments, agencies, private offices and firms. These data are not published.

2.10. DIFFERENCES BETWEEN PRIMARY AND SECONDARY DATA

There are many differences between primary and secondary data, which are discussed as follows:

1. The term primary data refers to the data produced by the researcher for the first time. Secondary data is the already existing data, collected by the investigator agencies and organizations earlier.
2. Primary data is a real-time data, whereas secondary data is one which relates to the past.
3. Primary data is collected for addressing the problem at hand, while secondary data is collected for purposes other than the problem at hand.
4. Primary data collection is a very involved process. On the other hand, the secondary data collection process is rapid and easy.
5. Primary data collection sources include surveys, observations, experiments, questionnaire, personal interview and so on. On the contrary, secondary data collection sources are government publications, websites, books, journals, articles, internal records and so on.
6. Primary data collection requires a large amount of resources such as time, cost and manpower. Conversely, secondary data is relatively inexpensive and quickly available.
7. Primary data is always specific to the researcher's needs, and the researcher controls the quality of research. In contrast, secondary data is neither specific to the researcher's need, nor the researcher has control over the data quality.
8. Primary data is available in the raw form, whereas secondary data is the refined form of primary data. It can also be said that secondary data is obtained when statistical methods are applied to the primary data.
9. Data collected through primary sources are more reliable and accurate as compared to those collected through secondary sources.

2.11. TRIANGULATION

Researchers need to consider the sources on which to base and confirm their research and findings. They have a choice between primary data and secondary sources and the use of both, which is termed triangulation or dual methodology.

2.12. DIFFERENT STATISTICAL ORGANIZATIONS

1. Central Statistical Organisation (CSO)

The CSO was set up in 1951. The important functions performed by the CSO are the following:

a. Coordination of statistical activities in the country, laying down and maintaining norms and standards, providing liaison with central, state and international statistical agencies;
b. Dissemination of information on the structure and activities of the official statistical system to the public, especially data users;
c. Shouldering the responsibility for preparation of national accounts, promotion of regional accounts at state district levels, generation of industrial statistics, conduct of economic censuses (ECs), follow-up surveys (FuSs) of ECs, family income and expenditure surveys, development of statistics on prices, human development, energy and the environment, dissemination of statistics on socio-economic aspects of life and so on; and
d. Organization of annual 'Conference of Central and State Statistical Organization' (COCSSO) to deliberate matters relating to the development of statistical data on aspects of socio-economic life of the country focusing in particular on the technical and developmental issues.

2. Indian Statistical Institute (ISI)

Founded by Professor P.C. Mahalanobis in Kolkata on 17 December 1931, the ISI gained the status of an Institution of National Importance by an act of the Indian Parliament in 1959.

The headquarters of the ISI are located in Kolkata. Additionally, there are four centres located in Delhi, Bengaluru, Chennai and Tezpur. Research in statistics and related disciplines is the primary activity of the Institute. Teaching activities are undertaken mainly in Kolkata, Delhi and Bengaluru.

3. National Sample Survey Organization (NSSO)

The NSSO was established in 1950 to conduct national surveys to assist the planning exercises on a scientifically designed sample basis in the country.

The main functions of the NSSO are as follows:

a. Design and conduct of socio-economic surveys;
b. Undertaking research on survey techniques and methodology;
c. Organization of field work for ASI (Annual Survey of Industries) and FuSs of EC;
d. Conducting the sample checks on area estimation and crop estimation surveys;
e. Developing urban sampling frames; and
f. Collection of price data and analysis.

4. International Institute of Population Sciences

In 1956, the United Nations, the Government of India and the Sir Dorabji Tata Trust, jointly established the institute to serve as a regional centre for teaching, training and conducting research in the area of population studies in the Economic and Social Commission for Asia and the Pacific (ESCAP) region.

2.13. MODES OF CLASSIFICATION

There are the following four types of classifications:

1. Qualitative classification

It is done according to attributes or non-measurable characteristics such as social status, sex, nationality and occupation. For example, the population of the whole country can be classified into four categories as married, unmarried, widowed and divorced. When only one attribute, for example, sex, is used for classification, it is called simple classification. When more than one attributes, for example, deafness, sex and religion, are used for classification, it is called manifold classification.

2. Quantitative classification

It is done according to numerical size like weights in kg or heights in cm. Here we classify the data by assigning arbitrary limits known as class limits. The quantitative phenomenon under study is called a variable. For example, the population of the whole country may be classified according to different variables such as age, income, wage and price. Hence, this classification is often called 'classification by variables'.

a. Variable: A variable in statistics means any measurable characteristic or quantity which can assume a range of numerical values within certain limits, for example, income, height, age, weight, wage and price. A variable can be classified as either discrete or continuous.
   i. Discrete variable: A variable which can take up only exact values and not any fractional value is called a 'discrete' variable. Number of workmen in a factory, members of a family, students in a class, number of births in a certain year, number of telephone calls in a month and so on are examples of discrete variables.
   ii. Continuous variable: A variable which can take up any numerical value (integral/fractional) within a certain range is called a 'continuous' variable. Height, weight, rainfall, time and temperature are examples of continuous variables. Age of students in a school is a continuous variable as it can be measured to the nearest fraction of time, that is, years, months, days and so on.

3. Temporal classification

It is done according to time, for example, index numbers arranged over a period of time, population of a country for several decades and exports and imports of India for different Five-Year Plans.

4. Spatial classification

It is done with respect to space or places, for example, production of cereals in quintals in various states and population of a country according to states.

2.14. PRESENTATION OF STATISTICAL DATA

Statistical data can be presented in three different ways. These have been listed as follows:

1. Textual presentation

This is a descriptive form. Presentation of data about deaths from industrial diseases in Great Britain in 1935–39 and 1940–44 is an example of descriptive form of textual presentation.

2. Tabular presentation or tabulation

Tabulation may be defined as the systematic presentation of numerical data in rows or/and columns according to certain characteristics. It expresses the data in concise and attractive form which can be easily understood and used to compare numerical figures. Before drafting a table, you should be sure what you want to show and who will be the readers.

Example: The total number of accidents in Southern Railway in 1960 was 3,500, and it decreased by 300 in 1961 and by 700 in 1962. The total number of accidents in the metre gauge section showed a progressive increase from 1960 to 1962. It was 245 in 1960, 346 in 1961 and 428 in 1962. In the metre gauge section, 'not compensated' cases were 49 in 1960, 77 in 1961 and 108 in 1962. 'Compensated' cases in the broad gauge section were 2,867, 2,587 and 2,152 in these three years, respectively.

3. Graphical presentation

Quantitative data may also be presented graphically by using bar charts, pie diagrams, pictographs, line diagrams and so on.

2.15. SECONDARY DATA SOURCES

Secondary data is data collected by someone other than the user. Common sources of secondary data for social science include censuses, surveys, organizational records and data collected through qualitative methodologies or qualitative research.

Secondary data are those which have already been collected and analysed by someone else. There are two major sources of secondary data. They have been discussed further.

1. The first major source is published source. These are the following sources of published data:
    a. Official publications of central and local governments, for example, CBS, NRB, different ministries and so on.
    b. Official publications of semi-government statistical organization, for example, Tribhuvan University, Nepal Bank Ltd, NIDC, Nepal Telecom, NEA and so on.
    c. Official publication of foreign government or international bodies such as the UNO, World Bank, ADB, WTO, UNESCO and so on.
    d. Reports and publications of trade unions, chamber of commerce, commercial banks, cooperatives, stock exchange and so on.
    e. Reports submitted to economists, research scholars, universities and various educational and research institutions.
    f. Reports of various committees and commissions appointed by government.
    g. Newspapers and periodicals.
2. The second source is unpublished source. Statistical data need not always be published. There are various sources of unpublished statistical materials such as the records maintained by private firms, business enterprises, scholars and research workers. They may not like to release their data to any outside agency.

2.16. IMPORTANT DATA SOURCES

Indiastat.com is the mother site of a cluster of 51 websites delivering socio-economic data about India and its states covering various sectors.

Nineteen sites are sector-specific and are listed as follows:

- Indiaagristat.com
- Indiachildrenstat.com
- Indiacrimestat.com
- Indiademographics.com
- Indiaeconomystat.com
- Indiaeducationstat.com
- Indiaenergystat.com
- Indiaenvironstat.com
- Indiahealthstat.com
- Indiahousingstat.com
- Indiaindustrystat.com
- Indiainfrastat.com
- Indialabourstat.com
- Indiaruralstat.com
- Indiascststat.com
- Indiatourismstat.com
- Indiaurbanstat.com
- Indiawelfarestat.com
- Indiawomenstat.com

The remaining 31 sites are state/union territories specific and provide comprehensive information on Indian states and its union territories covering socio-economic aspects of the concerned states. These are listed as follows:

- Indianationalstat.com
- Andhrapradeshstat.com
- Arunachalpradeshstat.com
- Assamstat.com
- Biharstat.com
- Chandigarhstat.com
- Delhistat.com
- Goastat.com
- Gujaratstat.com
- Haryanastat.com
- Himachalpradeshstat.com
- Jammuandkashmirstat.com
- Jharkhandstat.com
- Karnatakastat.com
- Keralastat.com
- Madhyapradeshstat.com
- Maharashtrastat.com
- Manipurstat.com
- Meghalayastat.com
- Mizoramstat.com
- Nagalandstat.com

- Orissastat.com
- Punjabstat.com
- Rajasthanstat.com
- Sikkimstat.com
- Tamilnadustat.com
- Tripurastat.com
- Uttarakhandstat.com
- Uttarpradeshstat.com
- Westbengalstat.com

The available data sources are also important to identify the relevant variables to be included in the study and to frame the research questions properly.

2.17. REPORTS AND PUBLICATIONS FROM GOVERNMENT SOURCES

Government reports and publications cover a wide range of data sources with different topics. They include reports from committees or commissions of government departments and agencies published in regular or irregular issues. Following websites are examples of government data sources:

http://mospi.gov.in
http://censusindia.gov.in
http://dgciskol.mospi.nic.in
http://rbi.org.in
http://planningcommission.gov.in
http://labourbureau.nic.in

SUMMARY

Literature review is essential to understand what has already been done on the specific topic. It helps to understand the background of the specific topic which the researcher intends to research, methodology of research done by previous researchers and research gaps. It is an ongoing process from selection of research problem to report writing. There is a specific structure for noting literature in a research paper.

Data collection plays a very crucial role in statistical analysis. In research, there are different methods used to gather information, all of which fall into two categories, that is, primary data and secondary data. As the name suggests, primary data is one which is collected for the first time by the researcher while secondary data is the data already collected or produced by others.

KEY TERMS

literature review (12)
evaluative review (14)
exploratory review (14)
instrumental review (14)
primary data (15)
observation method (16)
interview method (16)
questionnaire method (17)

schedule method (17)
secondary data (17)
triangulation (19)
Central Statistical Organisation (20)
Indian Statistical Institute (20)
National Sample Survey Organization (20)
International Institute of Population Sciences (20)
variable (21)
discrete variable (21)
continuous variable (21)
temporal classification (21)
spatial classification (21)
textual presentation (21)
tabulation (22)

EXERCISES

1. What is literature review?
2. What are the purposes of literature review?
3. Explain different types of literature review.
4. Discuss the methods of primary data collection.
5. Distinguish between primary data and secondary data.
6. Distinguish between discrete variable and continuous variable.
7. Write the functions of the CSO, ISI and NSSO.
8. How can data be presented?
9. Write a note on 'triangulation'.
10. Distinguish between questionnaire and schedule.

CHAPTER

3

Sampling

LEARNING OBJECTIVES

After studying this chapter, you should be able to

- Understand the meaning of sampling.
- Describe different types of sampling methods and their usage and implications in research field.
- Understand the concept of sample size determination.
- Learn the process of sample size calculation.

3.1. SAMPLING CONCEPTS

The process of selecting small number of elements (sample) from larger identified group of elements (population) is called sampling. Here, the sample (small group) should be the representative of the population (large group). Before discussing in detail about sampling technique, we should be familiar with some fundamental terms under the sampling concept, such as population, population element, sampling frame, sample, sampling unit, sampling error and non-sampling error. Population refers to the total number of units or items desired in any survey research. Population element refers to a single member of the population. Sampling frame contains properly identified population elements which are available for the researcher at any stage of the sample elements selection process. Sample contains some elements of the population and sampling unit is a single member of the sample. Sampling error occurs when a sample is not properly representing the population characteristics. Non-sampling error occurs due to inaccurate answers from the respondents (inability or unwillingness error), recording error by interviewers, data analysis error, questioning error, sampling frame error, respondent selection error and so on.

3.2. CLASSIFICATION OF SAMPLING TECHNIQUES

Basically, there are two types of sampling methods: (a) probability sampling and (b) non-probability sampling (see Figure 3.1).

FIGURE 3.1
Classification of Sampling Techniques

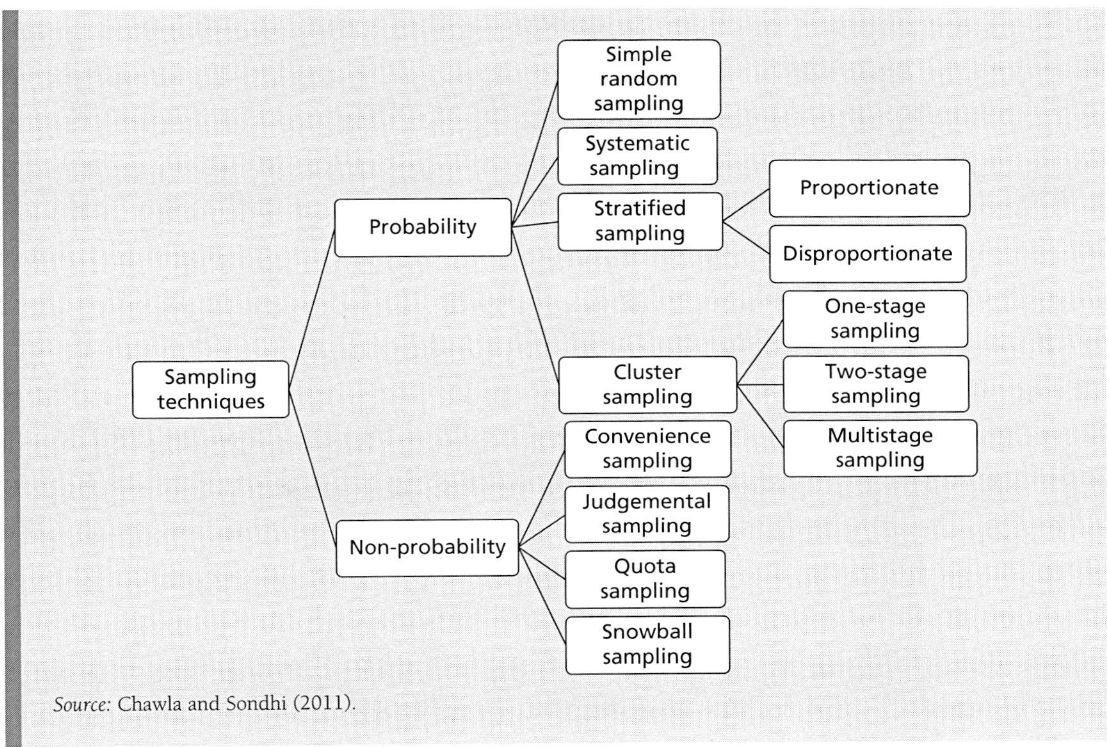

Source: Chawla and Sondhi (2011).

3.2.1. Probability Sampling

Probability sampling is an unbiased method. Sampling units are selected randomly in probability sampling where each population element has the fixed probabilistic chance of inclusion in the sample. The sample units are selected as per the selection schemes of units and the probability sampling process does not depend on the preferences or discretions of the researchers. Probability sampling is classified into four different methods, discussed as follows:

1. Simple random sampling

In simple random sampling process, every sample element is selected independently and randomly from the population. It allots equal probability of selection to each unit of the population (see Figure 3.2).

Here, the sample can be chosen both with and without replacement. In the case of simple random sampling with replacement, every population unit has an equal probability of $\frac{1}{N}$ to be included in each of the n units of the sample, if the population consists of N units. In the case of simple random sampling without replacement, the nth unit of sample is selected with the probability of $\frac{1}{N-n+1}$. Table 3.1 shows the random sampling number table which is the collection of digits generated through the probabilistic technique.

FIGURE 3.2
Simple Random Sampling

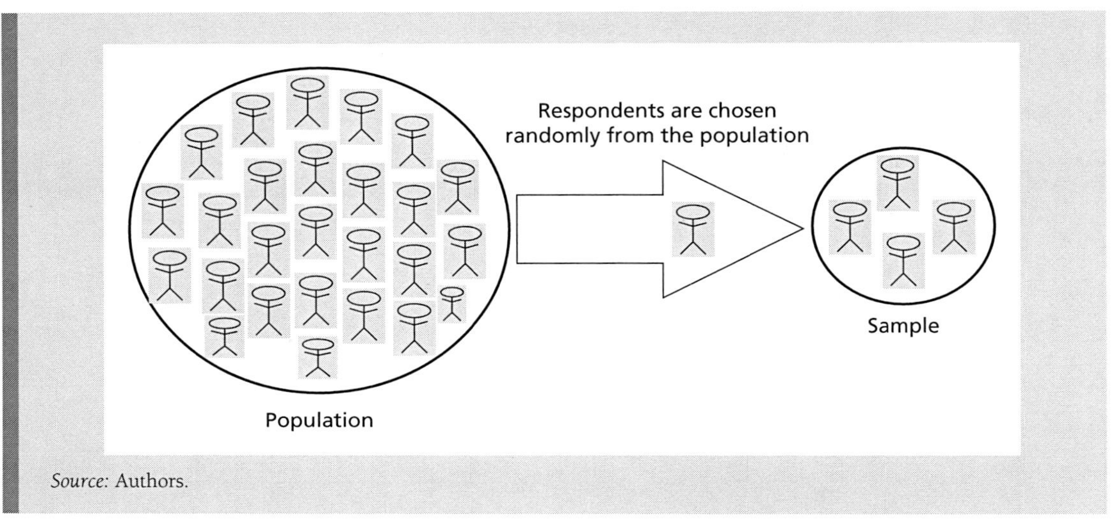

Source: Authors.

TABLE 3.1
Random Number Table

13962	70992	65172	28053	02190	83634	66012	70305	66761	88344
43905	46941	72300	11641	43548	30455	07686	31840	03261	89139
00504	48658	38051	59408	16508	82979	92002	63606	41078	86326
61274	57238	47267	35303	29066	02140	60867	39847	50968	96719
43753	21159	16239	50595	62509	61207	86816	29902	23395	72640
83503	51662	21636	68192	84294	38754	84755	34053	94582	29215
36807	71420	35804	44862	23577	79551	42003	58684	09271	68396
19110	55680	18792	41487	16614	83053	00812	16749	45347	88199
82615	86984	93290	87971	60022	35415	20852	02909	99476	45568
05621	26584	36493	63013	68181	57702	49510	75304	38724	15712
06936	37293	55875	71213	83025	46063	74665	12178	10741	58362
84981	60458	16194	92403	80951	80068	47076	23310	74899	87929
66354	88441	96191	04794	14714	64749	43097	83976	83281	72038
49602	94109	36460	62353	00721	66980	82554	90270	12312	56299
78430	72391	96973	70437	97803	78683	04670	70667	58912	21883
33331	51803	15934	75807	46561	80188	78984	29317	27971	16440
62843	84445	56652	91797	45284	25842	96246	73504	21631	81223

(Table 3.1 Continued)

(Table 3.1 Continued)

19528	15445	77764	33446	41204	70067	33354	70680	66664	75486
16737	01887	50934	43306	75190	86997	56561	79018	34273	25196
99389	06685	45945	62000	76228	60645	87750	46329	46544	95665
36160	38196	77705	28891	12106	56281	86222	66116	39626	06080
05505	45420	44016	79662	92069	27628	50002	32540	19848	27319
85962	19758	92795	00458	71289	05884	37963	23322	73243	98185
28763	04900	54460	22083	89279	43492	00066	40857	86568	49336
42222	40446	82240	79159	44168	38213	46839	26598	29983	67645

Source: Authors.
Note: Collection of digits generated through probabilistic mechanism.

Example: Find the sample of 10 respondents out of 105 respondents (population) with replacement from random sampling numbers.

Solution: Each respondent is identified separately by a serial number from 1 to 105. Since 105 is a 3-digit number, we have to take the groups of 3 numbers from the random sampling number table. So serial number 1 is identified with random table number '001', serial number 2 is identified with random table number '002' and so on. If the random table number is '106', then serial number 1 will be selected (remainder 1, as we divide 106 by 105). It will continue up to 945, the highest multiple of 105 and less than 1,000 (4 digits). '000' and '946–999' will be rejected. First of all, a starting position should be selected to continue and choose numbers from the random table. In this problem, we will start selecting 3-digit numbers from the beginning row (see Table 3.1). Table 3.2 shows the selection of 10 sample elements with replacement.

TABLE 3.2
Selection of Sample Elements with Random Numbers

Sample Number	Random Number Selected	Remark	Selected Respondents (Serial Number)
1	139	Accept	34
2	627	Accept	98
3	099	Accept	99
4	265	Accept	55
5	172	Accept	67
6	280	Accept	70
7	530	Accept	05
8	219	Accept	09
9	083	Accept	83
10	634	Accept	04

Source: Authors.

FIGURE 3.3
Systematic Sampling

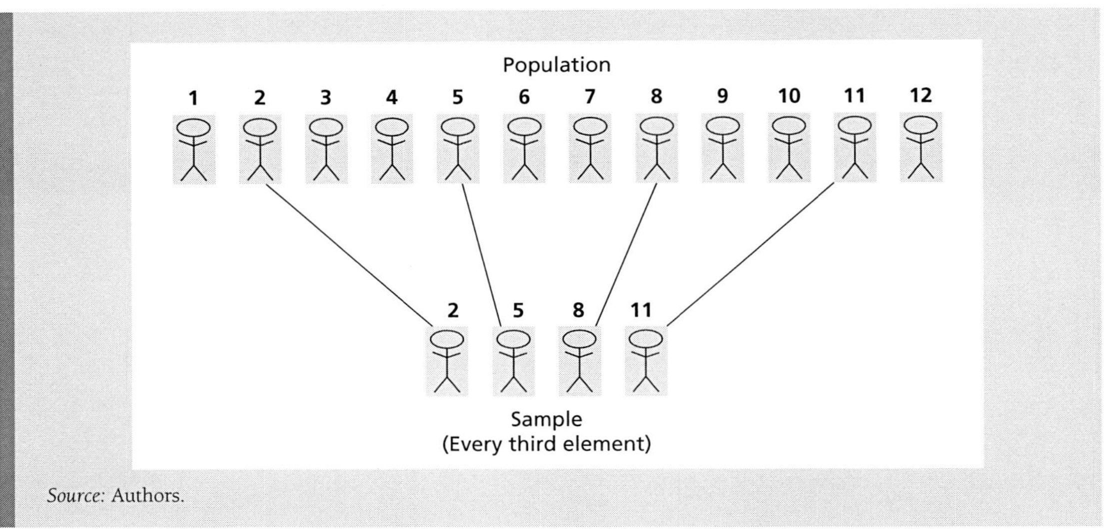

Source: Authors.

Here, 'no serial number' has been selected more than once. Therefore, the concept of 'with replacement' is not applicable here.

2. Systematic sampling

In this probabilistic sampling process, sample elements are selected by picking a random starting point and then choosing every *i*th element consecutively from the population. Here, the sample interval (i) is calculated by $\frac{N}{n}$, where N = population size and n = sample size desired. After calculation, if we get any fraction value, that must be rounded to the nearest integer value. Generally, this process is used in internet and telephonic survey research (see Figure 3.3).

3. Stratified sampling

This probabilistic sampling process is executed in two steps. In the first step, population is divided into different strata. The elements within a stratum should be homogeneous and the elements in different strata should be heterogeneous. In the second step, sample elements are chosen from each stratum randomly (see Figure 3.4).

Stratified sampling is classified into two different methods on the basis of sample elements taken from each stratum: (a) proportionate and (b) disproportionate stratified sampling. In the case of proportionate stratified sampling, sample elements chosen from each stratum are proportionate to the relative stratum size under population. It is calculated by the following formula:

$$n_i = n \times \frac{N_i}{N},$$

where n_i = number of sample elements from strata-i, n = number of total sample elements, N_i = number of elements under strata-i and N = number of total population element.

FIGURE 3.4
Stratified Sampling

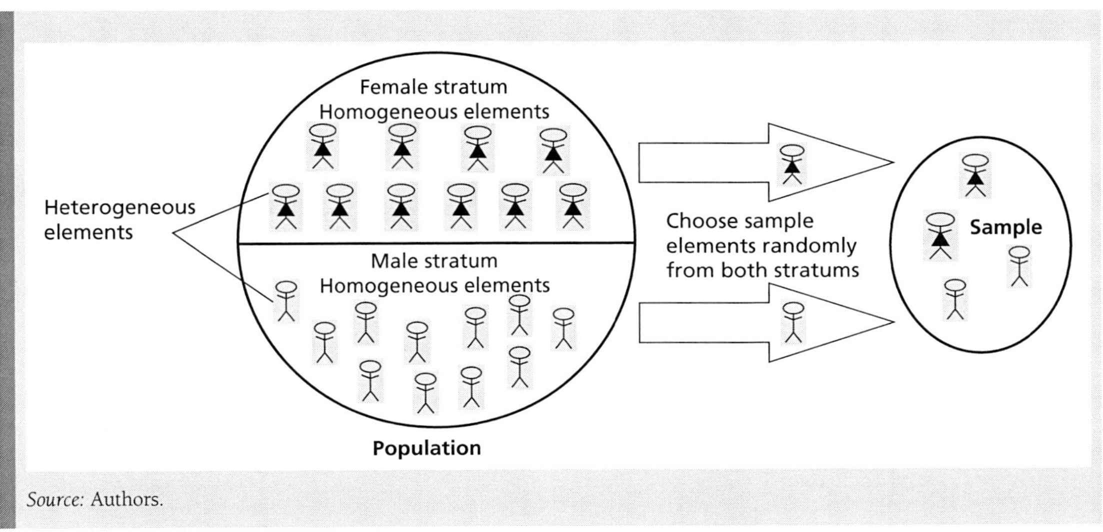

Source: Authors.

In the case of disproportionate stratified sampling, sample elements selected from each stratum are proportionate to the relative stratum size as well as standard deviation of the elements under that stratum. So we can easily understand that more sample elements should be selected from larger strata with larger standard deviation for better accuracy of the sampling technique.

4. Cluster sampling

This probabilistic sampling process is conducted by three steps. In the first step, population is divided by different clusters. A cluster is a group of elements that are made up of individual units that represent mutually exclusive and exhaustive subsets. The elements within a cluster should be heterogeneous and the elements in different clusters should be homogeneous. It is just opposite of stratified sampling for forming strata. In the second step, a simple random sampling technique is used for the selection of a random sample of clusters from population. In the third step, either all elements of each selected cluster are incorporated in the desired sample or sample of elements from each selected cluster is chosen randomly (see Figure 3.5).

Cluster sampling is classified into three different methods on the basis of selection criteria of sample elements: (a) one-stage sampling, (b) two-stage sampling and (c) multistage cluster sampling. In the case of one-stage cluster sampling, all elements of each selected cluster are incorporated in the desired sample. In the case of two-stage cluster sampling, sample of elements from each selected cluster is chosen randomly. In the case of multistage cluster sampling, more than two stages are followed for the selection of sample elements. An example of multistage cluster sampling is area sampling where clusters consist of different geographic areas (see Figure 3.6). In some cases, area sampling may be two-stage cluster sampling.

3.2.2. Non-probability Sampling

In non-probability sampling, selection of sample unit depends on the personal judgement or opinion of the researcher. This selection process does not use the probabilistic mechanism. So sample estimates may not

FIGURE 3.5
Cluster Sampling

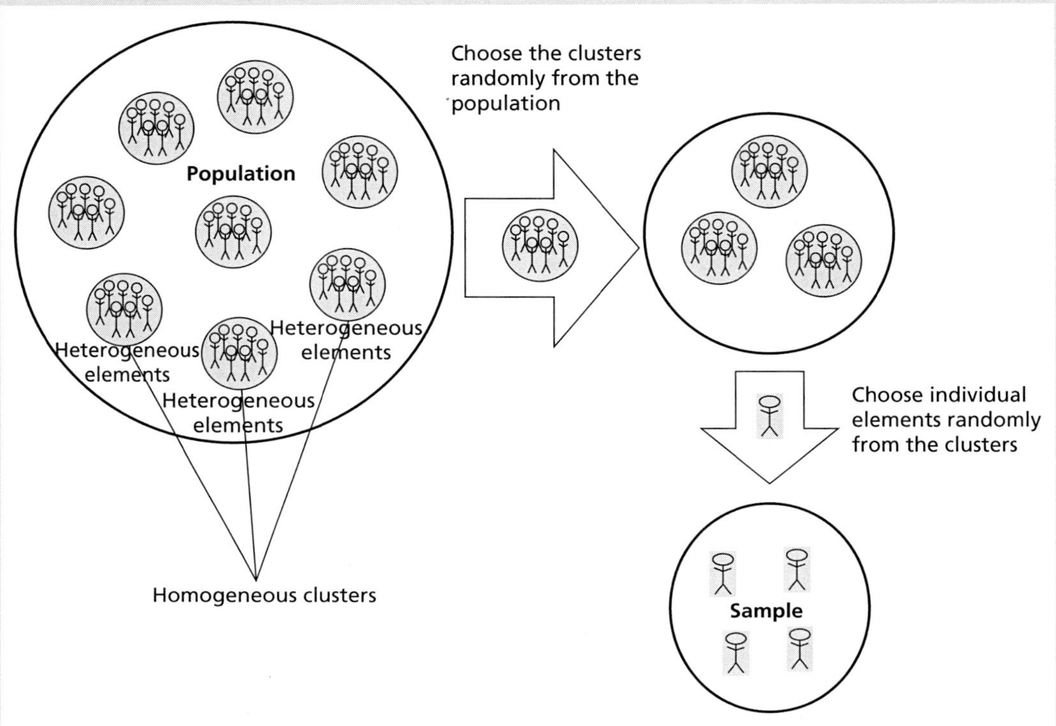

Source: Authors.

be statistically projectable to the population in some cases. Here, biasness is present in the sample elements selection process. Non-probability sampling is classified into four different methods discussed as follows:

1. Convenience sampling

In this non-probabilistic sampling technique, interviewers collect the sample with convenient elements which are readily accessible. These are called convenient elements as selected respondents are present at the right place at the right time. It is a less expensive and least time-consuming sampling process. The examples of convenience sampling are the interviews of people in departmental stores, mall or on the street for survey research (see Figure 3.7).

2. Judgemental/Purposive sampling

In this non-probabilistic sampling technique, sample elements are purposively chosen on the basis of researcher's judgement. Here, the researcher thinks that his/her selected sample elements are appropriate and the actual representative of the population according to his/her expertise and judgement for the research (see Figure 3.8).

FIGURE 3.6
Area Sampling

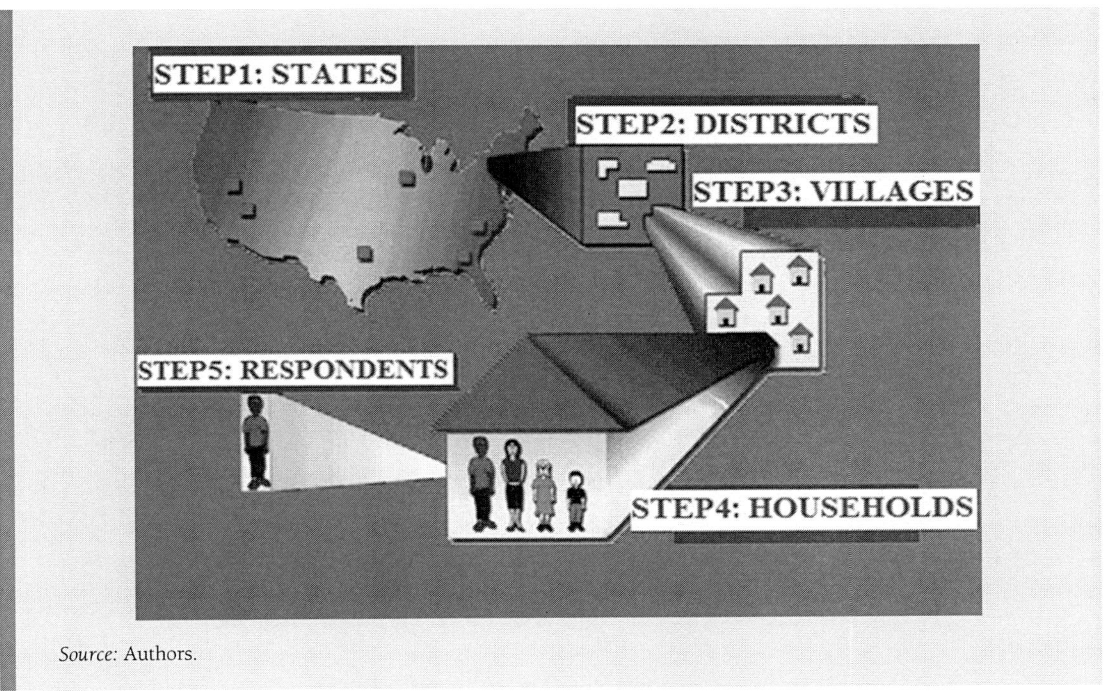

Source: Authors.

FIGURE 3.7
Convenience Sampling

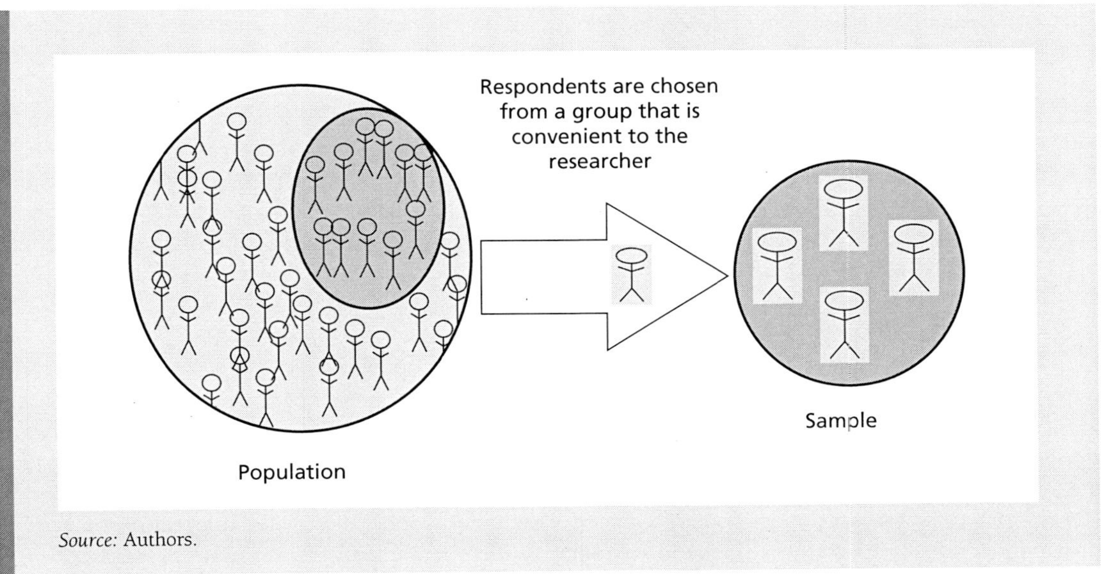

Source: Authors.

FIGURE 3.8
Judgemental/Purposive Sampling

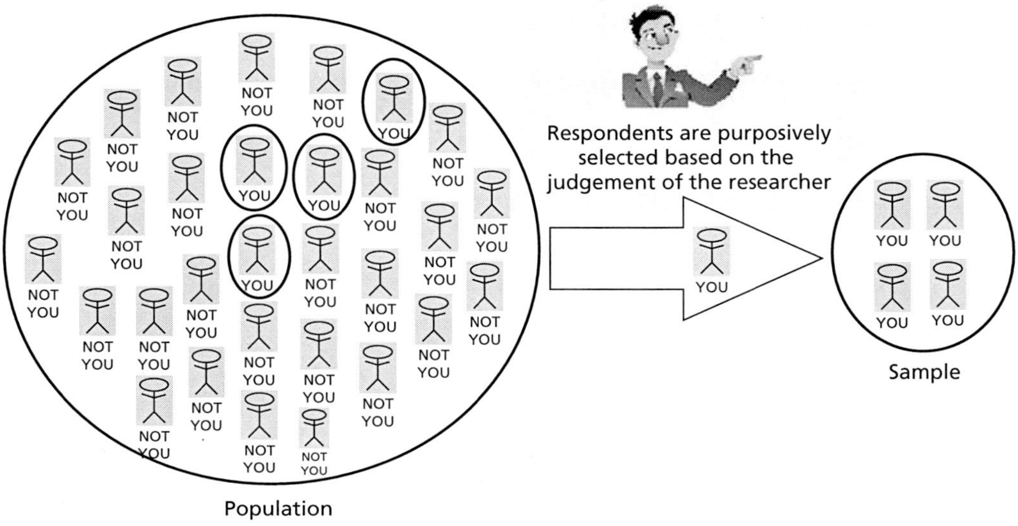

Respondents are purposively selected based on the judgement of the researcher

Population

Sample

Source: Authors.

3. Quota sampling

This non-probabilistic sampling process is conducted in two steps. In the first step, population is divided by different control categories or quotas. These control categories are gender, occupation, income level, age and so on. Different quotas are implemented in the population based on the judgement of the researchers. The proportion of different characteristics of a quota (e.g., age group 21–30 years, 31–40 years and 41–50 years) in the sample elements is the same as the proportion in the population elements with these control characteristics. In the second step, sample elements are chosen from each control characteristic on the basis of convenience or judgemental sampling (see Figure 3.9). It is a less expensive sampling process which provides greater convenience to the interviewers in survey research.

4. Snowball sampling

In this sampling technique, at first, an initial group of respondents is chosen randomly from population. In the second step, other respondents are chosen on the basis of the reference given by the initial respondents. Basically, the first step follows the probability sampling technique and the second step follows the non-probability sampling technique. These referrals-to-referrals process continues till the accumulation of all sample elements with similar types of demographic and psychographic characteristics as per the research requirement (see Figure 3.10). Here, sample estimates always provide low sampling variance. Snowball sampling is also a less expensive sampling process.

FIGURE 3.9
Quota Sampling

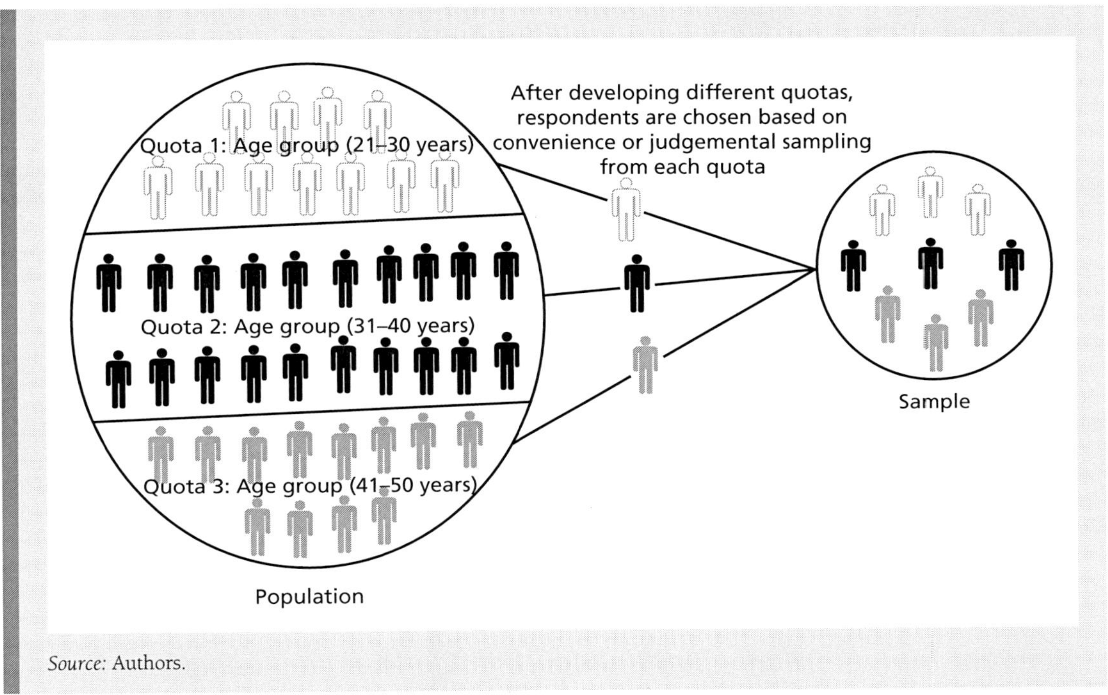

Source: Authors.

3.3. CONCEPT OF SAMPLE SIZE DETERMINATION

It is an important task to determine the sample size in a research study. If an arbitrary number is taken for sample size, anyone can the question as to why that particular arbitrary number was chosen and why not other numbers. Few techniques are used to solve this problem. As recommended by Hair et al. (2003) and Field (2009), the range of 'item to response' ratios should be within 1:4 to 1:10, depending on the nature of the research. In a research study, the sample size (responses) will be 100 if the number of variables (items) is 10 and ratio is 1:10. However, the sample size should be of an optimum size (not so large, not too small). Determination of sample size depends on different factors such as (a) nature of the research, (b) nature of the population, (c) sampling technique, (d) accuracy standard with confidence level and (e) availability of fund for the research study.

FIGURE 3.10
Snowball Sampling

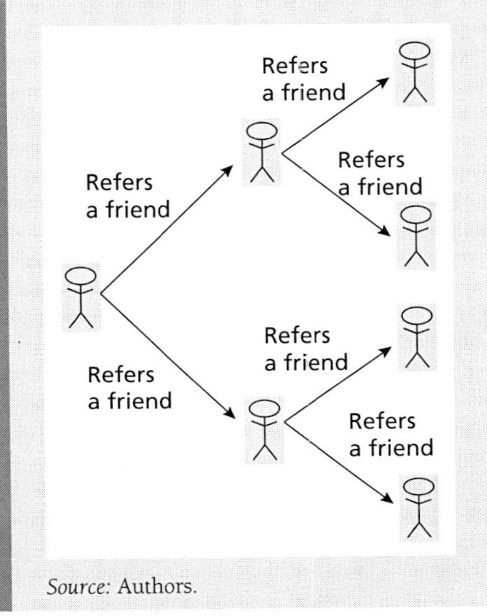

Source: Authors.

3.4. SAMPLE SIZE DETERMINATION THROUGH STANDARD ERROR

3.4.1. Calculation of Standard Error

Standard error is measured by the standard deviation of a sampling distribution. Basically, it helps to understand the accuracy and reliability of a sample. It also helps to determine whether there exists any difference between expected and observed data and specify the limits within which the population parameters lie with a given confidence level. Standard error is calculated in the following situations:

1. Standard error of mean (for infinite population and known population standard deviation):

$$\sigma_{\bar{X}} = \frac{\sigma_p}{\sqrt{n}},$$

where σ_p = population standard deviation and n = number of elements in the sample.

2. Standard error of mean (for infinite population and unknown population standard deviation):

$$\sigma_{\bar{X}} = \frac{\sigma_s}{\sqrt{n}},$$

where σ_s = sample standard deviation.

3. Standard error of proportion (for infinite population):

$$\sigma_{p,q} = \sqrt{\frac{(p * q)}{n}},$$

where p = probability of success in each event, q = probability of failure in each event and n = number of events in each sample.

4. Standard error of mean (for finite population):

$$\sigma_{\bar{X}} = \frac{\sigma_p}{\sqrt{n}} \times \sqrt{\frac{(N-n)}{(N-1)}}$$

where N = number of elements in the population.

5. Standard error of proportion (for finite population):

$$\sigma_{p,q} = \sqrt{\frac{(p * q)}{n}} \times \sqrt{\frac{(N-n)}{(N-1)}}.$$

Basically, confidence level is the expected percentage level where the actual value will fall under the stated accuracy limits.

3.4.2. Different Methods of Calculating Sample Size under Standard Error

1. In the case of population mean estimation for infinite population, the acceptable error (e) within confidence limit is

$$e = z \times \text{S.E.}$$

$$e = z \times \frac{\sigma_p}{\sqrt{n}}.$$

From this formula, we can easily calculate the sample size (n):

$$n = \frac{z^2 \times \sigma_p^2}{e^2}.$$

Example: Determine the sample size in a survey research on the basis of acceptable error within ±3 of the sample mean at 99% level of confidence. (Given, population std. deviation (σ_p) is 3.6 from the past records.)

Solution: In this problem, we have the following information:
Population std. deviation (σ_p) = 3.6
Acceptable error (e) = ±3
Z (table value for 99% level of confidence) = 2.58 (see Table 3.3)

We know, $n = \dfrac{z^2 \times \sigma_p^2}{e^2}.$

Hence, sample size (n) $= \dfrac{(2.58)^2 \times (3.6)^2}{(3)^2} = 9.59 \cong 10.$

2. In the case of population mean estimation for finite population, the acceptable error (e) within confidence limit (see Table 3.4) is

$$e = z \times \text{S.E.}$$

$$e = z \times \frac{\sigma_p}{\sqrt{n}} \times \sqrt{\frac{(N-n)}{(N-1)}}.$$

TABLE 3.3
Calculation of Limits at Different Confidence Levels

Significance Level	Confidence Level	Z (Table Value)	Confidence Limits
1%	99%	2.58	±2.58 S.E.
5%	95%	1.96	±1.96 S.E.
10%	90%	1.65	±1.65 S.E.

Source: Kothari (2004).
Note: S.E.—standard error.

TABLE 3.4
Estimation Formula for Different Situations

Estimation	Infinite Population	Finite Population
Population mean (known population std. deviation)	$\bar{X} \pm z \times \frac{\sigma_p}{\sqrt{n}}$	$\bar{X} \pm z \times \frac{\sigma_p}{\sqrt{n}} \times \sqrt{\frac{(N-n)}{(N-1)}}$
Population mean (unknown population std. deviation and $n > 30$)	$\bar{X} \pm z \times \frac{\sigma_s}{\sqrt{n}}$	$\bar{X} \pm z \times \frac{\sigma_s}{\sqrt{n}} \times \sqrt{\frac{(N-n)}{(N-1)}}$
Population mean (unknown population std. deviation and $n \leq 30$)	$\bar{X} \pm t \times \frac{\sigma_s}{\sqrt{n}}$	$\bar{X} \pm t \times \frac{\sigma_s}{\sqrt{n}} \times \sqrt{\frac{(N-n)}{(N-1)}}$
Population proportion (unknown p and $n > 30$)	$p \pm z \times \sqrt{\frac{(pq)}{n}}$	$p \pm z \times \sqrt{\frac{(p \times q)}{n}} \times \sqrt{\frac{(N-n)}{(N-1)}}$

Source: Kothari (2004).
Note: $\bar{X}$ = Sample mean.

From the mentioned formula, we can easily calculate the sample size (n):

$$n = \frac{z^2 \times N \times \sigma_p^2}{(N-1)e^2 + z^2 \times \sigma_p^2}.$$

Example: In a marketing research survey, determine the sample size for 1,000 population on the basis of acceptable error within 0.6 of the sample mean at 95% confidence level. (Given, population std. deviation (σ_p) is 3.)

Solution: In this problem, the following information is available for finite population:
Population size = 1,000
Population std. deviation (σ_p) = 3
Acceptable error (e) = 0.6
Z (table value for 95% level of confidence) = 1.96

We know, $n = \frac{z^2 \times N \times \sigma_p^2}{(N-1)e^2 + z^2 \times \sigma_p^2}.$

Hence, sample size (n) $= \frac{(1.96)^2 \times 1000 \times (3)^2}{(1000-1) \times (0.6)^2 + (1.96)^2 \times (3)^2} = 87.70 \cong 88.$

3. In the case of population proportion estimation for infinite population, the acceptable error (e) within confidence limit is

$$e = z \times \text{S.E.}$$

$$e = z \times \sqrt{\frac{(p \times q)}{n}}.$$

From the mentioned formula, we can easily calculate the sample size (n):

$$n = \frac{z^2 \times p \times q}{e^2}.$$

Example: Find the sample size in a survey research with customers where 80% of customers were attracted by the advertisement of a product as per the past record. The acceptable error should be within 2% of the true value with 99% confidence level.

Solution: In this problem, we have following information:
Acceptable error (e) = 0.02
Z (table value for 99% level of confidence) = 2.58
p-value = 0.8 (being the proportion of customers attracted by the advertisement in the population)
q-value = 1 – p-value = 0.2.

We know, $n = \dfrac{z^2 \times p \times q}{e^2}$

Hence, sample size (n) $= \dfrac{(2.58)^2 \times 0.8 \times 0.2}{(0.02)^2} = 2662.56 \cong 2663.$

4. In the case of population proportion estimation for finite population, the acceptable error (e) within confidence limit is

$$e = z \times \text{S.E.}$$

$$e = z \times \sqrt{\frac{(p \times q)}{n}} \times \sqrt{\frac{(N-n)}{(N-1)}}.$$

From the mentioned formula, we can easily calculate the sample size (n):

$$n = \frac{z^2 \times N \times p \times q}{(N-1)e^2 + z^2 \times p \times q}.$$

Example: Find the sample size in a survey research with customers where 60% of customers satisfied the service delivery of a hotel chain from a population of 5,000 as per the past record. The acceptable error should be within ±3% of the true value with 95% confidence level.

Solution: In this problem, the following information is available for finite population:
Population size = 5,000
Acceptable error (e) = 0.03
Z (table value for 95% level of confidence) = 1.96
p-value = 0.6 (being the proportion of customers satisfied with service delivery in the population)
q-value = 1 – p-value = 0.4.

We know, $n = \dfrac{z^2 \times N \times p \times q}{(N-1)e^2 + z^2 \times p \times q}.$

Hence, sample size (n) $= \dfrac{(1.96)^2 \times 5000 \times 0.6 \times 0.4}{(5000-1) \times 0.03^2 + (1.96)^2 \times 0.6 \times 0.4} = 850.38 \cong 850.$

SUMMARY

The process of selecting small number of elements (sample) from a larger identified group of elements (population) is called sampling. Before understanding the sampling technique, we should be familiar with some fundamental terms under the sampling concept such as population, population element, sampling frame, sample, sampling unit, sampling error and non-sampling error. There are two types of sampling methods: (a) probability sampling and (b) non-probability sampling. Probability sampling is classified into four different methods, namely, (a) simple random sampling, (b) systematic sampling, (c) stratified sampling and (d) cluster sampling. Non-probability sampling is classified into four different methods, namely, (a) convenience sampling (b) judgemental sampling (c) quota sampling and (d) snowball sampling. Also, different methods of determining sample size are discussed with the help of examples in this chapter.

KEY TERMS

sample (26)
population (26)
population element (26)
sampling frame (26)
sampling unit (26)
sampling error (26)
non-sampling error (26)
probability sampling (27)
non-probability sampling (31)
simple random sampling (27)
random number table (28)
systematic sampling (30)
stratified sampling (30)
cluster sampling (31)
convenience sampling (32)
judgemental sampling (32)
quota sampling (34)
snowball sampling (34)

EXERCISES

1. What is sampling?
2. What do you mean by sample and population?
3. What is the difference between probability and non-probability sampling technique?
4. Discuss different probability and non-probability sampling techniques by giving their merits and demerits.
5. Discuss the significance of standard error in sampling analysis.
6. Differentiate between cluster sampling and stratified sampling.
7. Differentiate between quota sampling and stratified sampling.
8. Find the sample size in a survey research with customers where 75% of customers satisfied the service delivery of a hospital from a population of 4,000 as per the past record. The acceptable error should be within ±3% of the true value with 99% confidence level.
9. Determine the sample size in a survey research on the basis of acceptable error within ±2 of the sample mean at 95% level of confidence. (Given, population std. deviation (σ_p) is 2.8 from the past records.)

CHAPTER

4

Questionnaire Design

LEARNING OBJECTIVES

After studying this chapter, you should be able to

- Visualize the meaning of a questionnaire.
- Understand the questionnaire design process.

4.1. CONCEPT AND DEFINITION

A questionnaire consists of set of questions designed to obtain responses from the potential respondents. Questions in the questionnaire reflect the research objective under investigation. For example, suppose a researcher wants to measure consumer attitude for a product and is in the process of designing a questionnaire. To measure the consumer attitude, the researcher has to first quantify the consumer attitude, which inherently is a feeling. The researcher has to collect relevant statements from the review of the existing literature and then convert them to the form of questions to quantify feelings such as the consumer's attitude. Finally, he/she prepares a set of questions that reflect various dimensions of consumer's attitude rated on a rating scale. The summated score obtained from each respondent is the consumer attitude score for the concerned respondent.

At the time of constructing a questionnaire, a deep thought process is required to select an appropriate survey technique in order to collect the data from the field of enquiry.

On the modus operandi of administration, the researcher may conduct personal interview, telephonic interview, mail interview or electronic interview.

4.2. QUESTIONNAIRE DESIGN PROCESS

Designing of the questionnaire consists of the following steps. Remember that there is no hard and fast rule regarding the number of steps which would be taken into consideration at the construction stage of a questionnaire.

The following steps are generally involved in the questionnaire design process:

1. Specify the information needed: The first and the foremost step in designing the questionnaire is to specify the information needed from the respondents such that the objective of the survey is fully fulfilled. The researcher must completely review the components of the problem, particularly the hypothesis of the study, research questions and the information required.
2. Define the target respondent: At the very outset, the researcher must identify the target respondent from whom the information is to be collected. The questions must be designed keeping in mind the type of respondents under study. Such as, the questions that are appropriate for serviceman might not be appropriate for a businessman. The less diversified respondent group shall be selected. If the group is more diversified, then it will be very difficult to design a single questionnaire that is appropriate for the entire group.
3. Interviewing method: The next step is to identify the way in which the respondents are reached. In personal interviews, the respondent is presented with a questionnaire and interacts face-to-face with the interviewer. Thus, lengthy, complex and varied questions can be asked using the personal interview method. In telephone interviews, the respondent is required to give answers to the questions over the telephone. Here, the respondent cannot see the questionnaire and hence this method restricts the use of small, simple and precise questions.

   The questionnaire can be sent through mail or post. It should be self-explanatory and contain all the important information such that the respondent is able to understand every question and give a complete response. The electronic questionnaires are sent directly to the mail ids of the respondents and are required to give answers online.
4. Determine the content of individual questions: Once the information needed is specified and the interviewing methods are determined, the next step is to decide the content of the questions. The researcher must decide on what should be included in the questions such that they contribute to the information needed or serve some specific purpose.
5. Overcome respondent's inability and unwillingness to answer: The researcher should not presume that the respondent can provide accurate responses to all the questions. He must attempt to overcome the respondent's inability to answer. The questions must be designed in a simple and easy language such that it is easily understood by each respondent. In situations where the respondent is not at all informed about the topic of interest, the researcher may ask filter questions—an initial question asked in the questionnaire to identify the prospective respondents and to ensure that they fulfil the requirements of the sample.
6. Decide on the question structure: The researcher must decide on the structure of questions to be included in the questionnaire. The question can be structured or unstructured. Unstructured questions are the open-ended questions which are answered by the respondents in their own words. Open-ended questions are extremely useful for an exploratory research. In addition, these questions provide the respondent an opportunity to freely express his/her feelings and provide an insight into the problem in hand. These questions are also called free response or free-answer questions.

   On the other hand, structured questions are called closed-ended questions that pre-specify the response alternatives. These questions could be dichotomous (yes or no) questions, multiple-choice questions or a scale.

   a. Dichotomous questions: When a question has two possible responses, we consider it dichotomous. Surveys often use dichotomous questions that ask for a Yes/No, True/False or Agree/Disagree response.

Researchers ask this type of question to understand the demographic profile of the respondents. For example, a medical insurance company has launched a new policy with special features for the children. To understand the response, the company may ask the following dichotomous questions:

1. Please specify your gender.

   Male ☐ Female ☐

2. Is it an attractive policy for children?

   Yes ☐ No ☐

3. Do you want to purchase this policy in this year?

   Yes ☐ No ☐

4. Do you have any other policy for children?

   Yes ☐ No ☐

b. Multiple-choice questions: Here, the researcher presents various answer choices to a respondent and the respondent is supposed to select any one from the available options. These questions are easy to code and analyse. These types of questions are also known as multichotomous questions. Following is an example of a multiple-choice type question:

   For what time period will you be investing in a fixed deposit scheme in a bank?

   - Less than 1 year
   - 1 year to 3 years
   - 3 years to 5 years
   - 5 years to 8 years

c. Scaled questions: Scaled questions are used to measure people's attitudes, opinions, lifestyles and environments. There are many different types of scaled questions, but the most commonly used are Likert and slider scales. The main difference between the two is that a Likert scale consists of ordered categories, whereas a slider scale allows respondents to make a mark indicating their response anywhere along a scale. As a result, a Likert scale-type question will give you data that are measured at an ordinal level, while a slider scale will give you data that are measured at an interval level.

   Likert scales are usually limited to a five-category scale, as it is often difficult to clearly display a larger number of categories.

7. Determine the question wording: The desired question content and structure must be translated into words which are easily understood by the respondents. At this step, the researcher must translate the questions into easy words such that the information received from the respondents is similar to what was intended.

   In case the question is written poorly, then the respondent might refuse to answer it or might give a wrong answer. In case the respondent is reluctant to give answers, then 'non-response' arises which increases the complexity of data analysis. On the other hand, if the wrong information is given, then 'response error' arises due to which the result would be biased and ultimately it will mislead the researcher.

   The following tips will help you prepare a good questionnaire for your study:

   a. Negative wording of questions discourages the respondents and reduces the response rate. Therefore, we will try to avoid the negative wordings in questions.

   b. Questions must be simple and easy to understand and they must contain direct words.

      For example, instead of asking

      'What is your perception about the new advertisement campaign?'

A researcher should frame the same question as
'What is your view about the new advertisement campaign?'

c. Ambiguous or vague words must be avoided.
   For example,
   In a year, how much will you spend on shopping of books?
   - Very much
   - Much
   - Reasonably well
   - Less
   - Very less

   A better way of asking the same question is in the following way:
   In a year, how much do you plan to spend on shopping of books?
   - Less than 1,000
   - Less than 2,000
   - Less than 3,000
   - Less than 4,000
   - Less than 5,000

d. Double-barrelled questions must be avoided. In these types of questions, a respondent may agree to one part of the question but not to the other part.
   For example, instead of asking a question such as,
   'On weekends, would you like an outing with your lover and which is your favourite spot in the city?'
   The question should be:
   Question 1: On weekends, would you like an outing with your lover?
   Question 2: If yes, then which is your favourite spot in the city?

e. Avoid loading and loaded questions. This is a biased way of presenting a question to get the desired answer. For example, a leading question can be presented as follows:
   'Are not you satisfied with the new feature of the product?'
   More specifically, the question should be
   'Are you satisfied with the new feature of the product?'

f. Avoid using overstated words.
   Wrong question: A survey revealed that hepatitis cases are increasing in India due to dirty water drinking. Have you any intentions to purchase a water purifier in the coming six months?
   Right question: Have you any intentions to purchase a water purifier in the coming six months, which can protect you from many waterborne diseases?

g. Implied assumptions must be avoided.
   Wrong: Do you think Company A should continue with its incentive scheme on bulk purchase?
   Right: Do you like a discount scheme on bulk purchase, as provided by Company A?

h. Respondent's memory should not be overstated.
   Wrong: In the previous month, how many times you have eaten ice-cream of Brand X with your lover?
   Right: How many times have you enjoyed ice-cream parties with your lover in the previous month?

i. Any type of estimation must be avoided.
 Wrong: What is the average per person consumption of pulses by your family in the past six months?
 Right: What is the consumption of pulses by your family in past six months?
 How many members are there in your family?

8. Determine the order of questions: At this step, the researcher must decide the sequence in which the questions are to be asked. The opening questions are crucial in establishing respondent's involvement and rapport, and therefore, these questions must be interesting and easy. Usually, the open-ended questions are asked to the respondents for their opinions because people like to express their opinions. Questions should be in a logical order. They may follow three techniques, namely, funnel technique, work technique and selection technique. In funnel technique, questions are presented from general to specific. In the work technique, complicated questions should be placed later. In the selection technique, questions are placed in different sections.
9. Identify the form and layout: The format, positioning and spacing of questions has a significant effect on the results. The layout of a questionnaire is specifically important for the self-administered questionnaires. The questionnaire must be divided into several parts, and each part shall be numbered accurately to clearly define the branches of a question.
10. Reproduction of a questionnaire: Here, we talk about the appearance of the questionnaire, that is, the quality of paper on which the questionnaire is either written or printed. In case the questionnaire is reproduced on a poor-quality paper, then the respondent might feel that the research is unimportant due to which the quality of response gets adversely affected.

    Thus, it is recommended to reproduce the questionnaire on a good-quality paper having a professional appearance. In case the questionnaire has several pages, then it should be presented in the form of a booklet rather than the sheets clipped or stapled together.
11. Pretesting: Pretesting means testing the questionnaire on a few selected respondents or on a small sample of actual respondents with a purpose of improving the questionnaire by identifying and eliminating the potential problems. All the aspects of the questionnaire must be tested such as question content, structure, wording, sequence, form and layout, instructions and question difficulty. The researcher must ensure that the respondents in the pretest should be similar to those who are to be finally surveyed.

    Thus, the questionnaire design is a multistage process that requires the researcher's attention to many details.

SUMMARY

A questionnaire consists of a set of questions designed to obtain responses from the potential respondents. Questions in the questionnaire reflect the research objective under investigation. At the time of constructing a questionnaire, a deep thought process is required to select an appropriate survey technique in order to collect the data from the field of enquiry. Remember that there is no hard and fast rule regarding the number of steps which would be taken into consideration at the construction stage of a questionnaire.

KEY TERMS

questionnaire (41)
dichotomous question (42)
multiple-choice questions (43)
scaled questions (43)
Likert scale (43)
pretesting (45)

EXERCISES

1. What do you mean by a questionnaire?
2. Describe the questionnaire designing process.
3. What is the purpose of pretesting?
4. Write a note on the Likert scale.
5. What is the meaning of a dichotomous question?

CHAPTER

5

Measurement and Scaling

LEARNING OBJECTIVES

After studying this chapter, you should be able to

- Understand the concept of measurement and scaling.
- Understand different types of basic scales.
- Learn the technique of identifying appropriate scaling method for different data sets.
- Know the use of different scales in the SPSS window.
- Understand different types of measurement scales.

5.1. CONCEPT OF MEASUREMENT AND SCALING

The first step of measurement process is to spot the area or concept that is related with our research study. A concept can be described as a general idea developed from definite instances or occurrences in related research study. When a concept has been understood, the researcher can focus on construct development. Constructs can be defined as certain types of concepts which explain properly the overall research study and contain the thoughts at different directions to clarify the complex research study. Basically, constructs are constructed for theoretical evidence and clearly explain the research study. Moreover, a scale can be explained as a set of numbers or symbols created in a specific manner to help the research maintain certain rules. Actually, scaling develops a continuum on which measurements are located. In some cases where parameters can be measured quantitatively such as profitability of a firm, parameters of a particular product and productivity of the employees, scale development is easier. In other instances, it is difficult to measure qualitative parameters (psychological properties) through scaling such as acceptance level and attitudes of the customers about a product and motivational levels of the employees. Researcher should always remember that research quality depends on the adopted measurement technique which must be the best fit in the prevailing research study.

5.2. DIFFERENT FORMS OF MEASUREMENT SCALES APPLIED IN SOCIAL SCIENCE RESEARCH

There are four different forms of measurement scales. These are nominal, ordinal, interval and ratio scale. All scales along with their properties are summarized in Table 5.1 and described elaborately in this section. Basically, research data cannot be analysed in the similar statistical pattern because different research entities are represented by different numbers. It means that numbers represent different meanings in different cases. Therefore, researchers need appropriate knowledge about the basic scale of measurement through which data are to be analysed. On the other hand, design of the scale depends on the research objectives and statistical calculation predicted by the researchers.

5.2.1. Nominal Scale

Numbers and letters are used in nominal scale to identify different research entities. Categorizations are executed to segregate the data into different classes which are mutually exclusive and collectively exhaustive. Numbers which are assigned to individual classes do not indicate any quantitative value. So it is not possible to do any mathematical operation (addition, subtraction, multiplication, division) with those numbers. For example, measurement of gender and educational qualification through nominal scale may be designed in the following manner:

Gender:

Male	1	Female	2

Educational Qualification:

10th Standard	1	12th Standard	2	Graduate	3	Postgraduate	4

In these examples, the numbers 1, 2 for Gender and 1, 2, 3, 4 for Educational Qualification indicate labels for different class. So researchers cannot execute any mathematical and statistical operations with those numbers. A nominal scale never indicates the association among variables. It only provides the frequency of entities under each class. This means the number of people in Male or Female categories under the Gender category and number of people in 10th Standard and so on.

5.2.2. Ordinal Scale

In an ordinal scale, entities can be arranged and ranked according to a definite order. For example, a person secured the second place in a race (Table 5.1) and then we can say that there are other people who achieved first and third places in the ranking order. An ordinal scale only provides the data regarding relative positions of the entities. But it does not provide any data regarding absolute magnitude

TABLE 5.1

Different Forms of Measurement Scales and Their Properties

Measurement Scales		Symbol in SPSS	Common Diagrammatic Explanation	Data Type (SPSS Format)	Examples in Social Science	Statistics and Graphs (Generally Applied)
Nominal (classification and attributes are only named)			Gender	**Qualitative** (alphanumeric)	Gender, social security numbers, age group, occupation, ethnicity, marital status, educational qualification, zip codes	Non-parametric tests (Chi-square test, Sign test, Friedman test, The U test, the runs test, the Kruskal–Wallis H test etc.)
Ordinal (attributes are in order)			4th 3rd 2nd 1st Ranking in a race	**Qualitative** (string and numeric)	Social class ranking, preference ranking, top 10 movies in box office, bestselling books	Bar chart as graphs
Scale	**Interval (distance is meaningful)**		Temperature Performance rating	**Quantitative** (numeric)	Opinions, attitudes, IQ test, most psychological measures	Parametric tests (t-test, Z-test, F-test etc.)
	Ratio (absolute zero)		Time 0 \$100 \$200 \$300 \$400 \$500 Income level	**Quantitative** (numeric)	Time, distance, weight, height, income level	Line graph and histogram as graphs

Source: Authors.

of the difference between different positions. For example, in any questionnaire consumers are asked to provide opinions on a product quality through various statements. These statements can be judged by five given options in a Likert scale (discussed in this chapter later on) as follows:

Statement: Quality of the product 'A' is excellent

Strongly agree (5)	Agree (4)	Neither agree nor disagree (3)	Disagree (2)	Strongly disagree (1)

We can easily rank these options according to their level and assign numeric values to these attributes. Here, '5' is used for 'Strongly agree', '4' is used for 'Agree' and so on. For the convenience of the interpretation of statistical techniques, rankings are set as per the discretion of the researchers. In general cases, the highest number is used for the highest ranking (Strongly agree: same opinion of customers for the statement by researcher) and the lowest number is used for the lowest ranking (Strongly disagree: different opinion of customers for the statement by researcher). We never say that the intervals between different ranking points are equal.

5.2.3. Interval Scale

In the interval scale, the distances between the points on the scale are equal. Fahrenheit and Celsius scales which are used to measure temperature are the perfect examples of an interval scale. In these scales, the distance between 45° and 55° is the same as the distance between 30° and 40°. Here, zero base points are not available for these scales. Another example, mentioned later, is taken for better understanding of an interval scale. An interval 10-point scale is designed with points placed at equal distance of 1 point:

(10)............(9)............(8)............(7)............(6)............(5)............(4)............(3)............(2)............(1)

Here, respondents are asked to place skincare products of Hindustan Unilever Limited (Ponds, Fair & Lovely and Vaseline) on the scale of 10–1. If 'Ponds' is allocated the 8th point, 'Fair & Lovely' the 6th point and 'Vaseline' the 4th point, we can comment that the value difference in preference level is 2 among three entities. In this case, we cannot say that the preference of 'Ponds' is twice the preference level of 'Vaseline' because of the unavailability of zero base point in the interval scale. From this scale, we can understand that a respondent prefers 'Ponds' to 'Fair & Lovely' and 'Vaseline'.

5.2.4. Ratio Scale

Ratio scales have equal intervals and also have zero base point. This scale permits the comparison of two variables assigned on the scale. A perfect example of ratio scale is distance. In this case, we can say that the distance between 3 km and 6 km is the same as the distance between 6 km and 9 km. Also, we can say that 6 km is twice as long as 3 km. Here, zero base point is common in distance (km) as well as age, height, weight, money and the likes. However, the collected data which are called metric data or quantitative data can be processed for different types of mathematical operations such as addition, subtraction, multiplication and division.

'Variable View' and 'Data View' in SPSS with different types of measurement scales (nominal, ordinal and scale) are shown in Exhibits 5.1 and 5.2.

EXHIBIT 5.1

Variable View with Different Types of Measurement Scales (Nominal, Ordinal and Scale)

	Name	Type	Width	Decimals	Label	Values	Missing	Columns	Align	Measure
1	GENDER	Numeric	8	0	Gender	{1, Male}...	None	8	Right	Nominal
2	OCCUP	Numeric	8	0	Occupation	{1, student}...	None	8	Right	Nominal
3	AGE	Numeric	8	0	Age group	{1, less than 25}...	None	8	Right	Nominal
4	EDU	Numeric	8	0	Educational Qualification	{2, 10th std.}...	None	8	Right	Nominal
5	q1	Numeric	8	0	question 1	{1, SD}...	None	11	Right	Ordinal
6	q2	Numeric	8	0	question 2	{1, SD}...	None	11	Right	Ordinal
7	q3	Numeric	8	0	question 3	{1, SD}...	None	11	Right	Ordinal
8	q4	Numeric	8	0	question 4	{1, SD}...	None	11	Right	Ordinal
9	SOCI.CUL	Numeric	8	0	Socio-Cultural Issues	None	None	11	Right	Scale
10	LEG.ISSU	Numeric	8	0	Legal Issues	None	None	11	Right	Scale
11	ETH.ISSU	Numeric	8	0	Ethical Issues	None	None	11	Right	Scale
12	FUT.PROS	Numeric	8	0	Future Prospect	None	None	11	Right	Scale

EXHIBIT 5.2

Data View with Different Types of Measurement Scales (Nominal, Ordinal and Scale)

	GENDER	OCCUP	AGE	EDU	q1	q2	q3	q4	SOCI.CUL	LEG.ISSU	ETH.ISSU	FUT.PROS
1	1	1	1	4	4	4	4	4	3	5	4	4
2	1	1	1	2	4	4	4	4	2	4	5	3
3	1	1	1	2	4	3	3	3	1	3	3	3
4	1	1	1	2	3	2	2	1	3	3	4	2
5	1	1	1	4	4	3	3	3	3	3	4	4
6	1	1	1	2	4	3	3	4	2	4	4	4
7	1	1	1	2	4	3	3	4	3	3	4	3
8	1	1	1	3	4	5	5	4	2	5	5	4
9	1	1	1	3	4	3	3	5	2	4	4	4
10	1	1	1	2	5	5	5	3	1	5	5	5
11	1	1	1	2	3	2	2	4	3	3	4	3

5.3. TYPES OF MEASUREMENT SCALES

There is always a debate among business researchers on the appropriateness of measurement through the rating scales (like ordinal versus interval scale) in different research problems to measure theoretical constructs and variables. Researchers use various scales depending on the dimensions of the research problem. It may be a comparative scale or non-comparative scale. Comparative scale is a direct comparison technique which deals with ordinal data. On the other hand, non-comparative scale deals with interval or ratio data. In this section, various types of scales have been discussed focusing upon the entities included in the scale. Different types of measurement scales are shown in Figure 5.1. These are as follows:

1. Single-item scale
2. Continuous rating scale
3. Multiple-item scale

FIGURE 5.1
Types of Measurement Scale

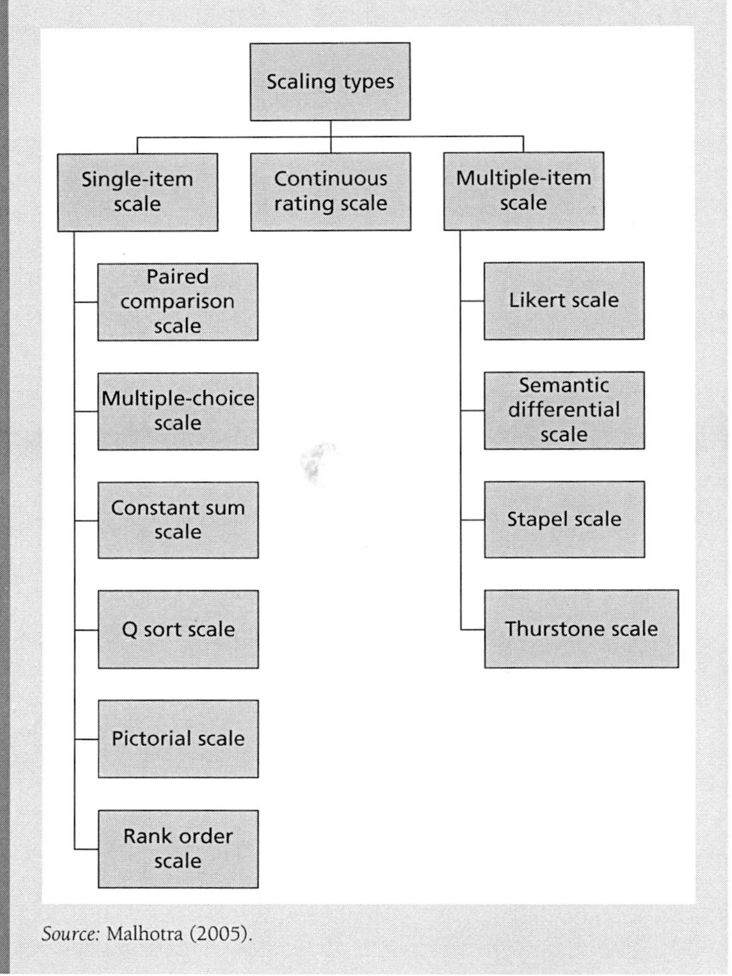

Source: Malhotra (2005).

5.3.1. Single-item Scale

A construct or a variable is measured through only one item. Sometimes, it is difficult to analyse the problem statements through a single-item scale because many items may not be covered using it. In social science research, the commonly used single-item scales have been discussed further.

1. Paired comparison scale

In this technique, respondents compare a pair of objects at a time according to some attributes. Ordinal data are observed here. Basically, for n objects, $[n(n - 1)/2]$ paired comparisons are needed to cover all possible combinations. Table 5.2 represents the paired comparison scale. Here, respondents are asked to indicate the preferable soap brand (Lux, Lifebuoy, Liril, Dove and Pears) under Hindustan Unilever Limited for an individual pair. From the total number of paired preference, the most favoured brand can be evaluated.

2. Multiple-choice scales

Here, researchers provide a single question with multiple alternatives. For collecting demographic or nominal type data, this scale is used. The researcher codes a different number to different alternatives for statistical research analysis. It can be observed from the following examples:

Q1: Specify your gender.

Male [1] Female [2]

TABLE 5.2
Paired Comparison Scale

Brands	Lux	Lifebuoy	Liril	Dove	Pears
Lux		0	0	1	0
Lifebuoy	1		1	1	0
Liril	1	1		1	0
Dove	0	0	0		0
Pears	1	1	0	1	
Total no. of paired preference	3	2	1	4	0

Source: Authors.
Notes: 1. 1 means 'brand in the column' is preferred to 'the brand in the corresponding row'.
2. 0 means 'brand in the row' is preferred to 'the brand in the corresponding column'.

Q2: What is your occupation?

Student	1	Service holder (man)	2	Service holder (woman)	3	Housewife	4	Self-employed	5

Q3: Specify monthly household income (in ₹).

Less than 15,000	1	15,001–30,000	2	30,001–45,000	3	45,001–60,000	4	More than 60,000	5

3. Constant sum scales

In constant sum scale, the respondents are asked to assign points to two or more characteristics based on their preferences such that the total points remain the constant sum of usually 100 or 10. The following example represents the eight attributes of supermarket:

Example: Please specify your points by dividing 100 as per your relative preferences for the attributes of supermarket.

Solution: Constant sum scales

Attributes	Points
Huge range of products	10
Conveniently located	7
Affordable price	31
Cooperative sales person	26
Securities facility	5
Pleasing ambiance	13
Car parking facilities	4
Sufficient billing counters	4
Total points	100

4. Q sort scale

Q sort scaling is used when ranking is tiresome for the large number of rated characteristics. Here, respondents sort out different attributes that are being compared into different groups (pre-defined number of categories/piles, usually 11, ranging from Most Strongly Agree to Most Strongly Disagree) which follow normal distribution. Here, each attribute is printed on a separate card. The number of cards should not be less than 60 and these are presented to respondents who sort them into categories/piles.

Example: Each respondent is asked to rate 100 (n) products with different tastes and preferences by segregating the cards into 11 piles.

Solution: Q sort scale

	Most Strongly Agree	....	....	....	....	....	....	....	....	........Most Strongly Disagree	
Each pile no.	10	9	8	7	6	5	4	3	2	1	0	
No. of cards	8	6	14	13	18	11	2	7	4	12	5	N = 100

5. Pictorial scale

In pictorial scale, respondents are asked to rate the attributes on a pictorial scale from agreement to disagreement. Researchers have to be very careful in developing the pictorial scale so that it is easily understandable by the respondents. This scale is usually used for illiterates and children. Following smiling faces are an example of a pictorial scale:

Example: You like this chocolate (verbal instruction)

Solution: Pictorial scale

6. Rank order scale

Here, the respondents are asked to rank different attributes or entities from a presented list. This scale generates ordinal data. Following is an example of a rank order scale:

Example: Please rank the skincare brands according to your preference (put 1 for the most preferred brand, 2 for the next preferred brand and so on).

Solution: Rank order scale

Brands	Ranking (By Respondent 1)
Olay	2
Proactiv	6
Neutrogena	7
Lotus Herbals	3
L'Oréal	1
Nivea	4
Avon	5

5.3.2. Continuous Rating Scale

In a continuous rating scale, respondents are asked to mark at a proper place on a line scale depicted by two extreme points. Because of a complicated scoring process in continuous rating scale, it is hardly ever used in social science research. Following is an example of a continuous rating scale:

Example: Please rate the overall service of Big Bazaar on a continuous scale ranging from 0 to 100 points.

Best-------------------------*--Worst

100	90	80	70	60	50	40	30	20	10	0

5.3.3. Multiple-item Scale

Generally, these scales are used when researchers require evaluating people's behaviour depending on more than one attribute. In many cases, it is difficult to figure out the overall picture of the research through one-item scale. Different multiple scales, ranging from most favourable to least favourable, have been developed on various issues related to attributes. These are Likert scale, semantic differential scale, Stapel scale and Thurstone scale.

1. Likert scale

Likert scale is commonly used by the researchers for evaluating the attitude of people. It contains different attributes, expressed by a series of statements. Respondents put their opinion for those statements in the form of degree of agreement or disagreement. Here, individual item has five rating categories including 'Strongly Agree', 'Agree', 'Neither Agree nor Disagree', 'Disagree', 'Strongly Disagree', respectively or vice versa. Researchers generally use 5–1 rating scale for 'Strongly Agree' to 'Strongly Disagree' in most of the cases. But in few cases, –2 to +2 (–2, –1, 0, +1 and +2) rating Likert scale has been observed in social science research. In some approaches under the Likert scale, the sum and average are calculated across the scale items for all the respondents. For this reason, the Likert scale is also called a summated scale. This approach is widely used in social science research.

Example: Questionnaire for assessing stress (please put a 'tick mark' in one box on each line according to your answer)

Solution: Likert scale

	General Stress-related Questions	Strongly Agree	Agree	Neither Agree nor Disagree	Disagree	Strongly Disagree
GEN_1	You are not suffering from stress in your daily life.					
GEN_2	You can easily handle excessive workload.					
GEN_3	You have a daily peaceful sleep.					
GEN_4	You can easily maintain your work-life balance.					
GEN_5	You never smoke or drink to avoid stressful situation.					

2. Semantic differential scale

This scale is used to describe a person's attitude or belief towards a product, brand or organization. The respondents are asked to rate multiple items on a 5- or 7-point bipolar multiple-item scale. The scale is bounded by positive and negative adjectives or phrases placed on the two extreme points, and the mid-point indicates a neutral point. After collecting the responses, a graph can be plotted from the rated points. This graph can easily determine the issues and strength of the entities of the research topic. When researchers design a semantic differential scale, they should make sure that all negative or positive adjectives do not appear on one side for avoiding the 'halo effect'. Respondent tend to follow equal rated point reluctantly when negative or positive adjectives appear on one side. This halo effect should be eliminated by keeping some negative and positive adjectives on both sides.

Example: Please tick your preference about the services of your bank through a 7-point scale.

Solution: Semantic differential scale

	1	2	3	4	5	6	7	
Reliable	-	-	-	-	-	-	-	Unreliable
Unorganized	-	-	-	-	-	-	-	Organized
Unpleasant	-	-	-	-	-	-	-	Pleasant
Informal	-	-	-	-	-	-	-	Formal
Careful	-	-	-	-	-	-	-	Careless
Aggressive	-	-	-	-	-	-	-	Submissive
Favourable	-	-	-	-	-	-	-	Unfavourable

Example: Please tick your preference for comparing three washing powder brands (Surf Excel—S, Wheel—W and Rin—R)

Solution: Semantic differential scale

		S	R	W				
Expensive	-	-	-	-	-	-	-	Inexpensive
	S	W	R					
More cleaning power	-	-	-	-	-	-	-	Less cleaning power
	S&R	W						
Good fragrance	-	-	-	-	-	-	-	Bad fragrance
				W	R	S		
More shrinkage	-	-	-	-	-	-	-	Less shrinkage

3. Stapel scale

Stapel scale is similar to the semantic differential scale with a single pole and one adjective. It is constructed by placing a single adjective in the centre of an even number, generally 10-scale ranging from –5 to +5. There is no neutral point (zero) in the staple scale. This scale can properly depict the positive and negative intensity of the respondent's attitude.

Example: Measuring the attitude of the employees of an organization

Solution: Stapel scale

+5	+5	+5
+4	+4	+4
+3	+3	+3
+2	+2	+2
+1	+1	+1
Job satisfaction	Good salary	Good working environment
−1	−1	−1
−2	−2	−2
−3	−3	−3
−4	−4	−4
−5	−5	−5

4. Thurstone scale

In this scale, researchers choose a group of 80–100 entities pointing out different levels of favourable attitudes towards a product, brand, services and the likes under a research study. After selecting the items/entities, a group of judges categorize them according to their favourability. Here, judges maintain equal intervals between categories. At last, the items which have no consensus from the judges are eliminated. For understanding the attitudes towards a particular concept, the outcomes are distributed uniformly on a scale. However, it is a time-consuming process as it follows the two-stage method.

5.4. FACTORS EFFECTING SCALE CONSTRUCTION TECHNIQUES IN SOCIAL SCIENCE RESEARCH

It a great problem for the researcher to decide a particular scale to be used in his research. There are different factors which affect the selection of an appropriate scale. Research objective is one of the main factors in this process. In social science research, we generally investigate consumer attitude and behaviour, purchase intention, customer satisfaction level and post-purchase behaviour. Therefore, every perspective is different and has an influence in scale construction. On the other hand, predicted data types (nominal: *demographic data*; ordinal: *ranking data* and scale: *rating data*) also help in deciding the suitable scale for the research. Here, rating scale can be used in different continuums, that is, 1–3, 1–5, 1–7, 1–9 rating scales depending on the research requirement, where 1 represents strongly disagree and 3 or 5 or 7 or 9 represents strongly agree. In some cases, a single-item scale may not be sufficient to collect the data in a particular context. In that scenario, a multiple-item scale can be appropriate to fulfil the objective. A scale generally includes a neutral point (no opinion) but it can be avoided by the researcher's choice. In some situations, unbalanced scales (favourable and unfavourable categories are unequal in nature) are also used as per the research requirement. Except these factors, nature of the respondent plays a vital role in this context. For example, pictorial representation can be used in the scale for illiterate respondents. However, scale construction techniques are finally dependent on the researchers' decisions on the basis of their wisdom and knowledge.

SUMMARY

Scale can be explained as a set of numbers or symbols created in a specific manner to help the research in maintaining certain rules. Actually, scaling develops a continuum on which measurements are located. Researcher should always remember that research quality depends on the adopted measurement technique which must be the best fit in the prevailing research study. There are four basic scales of measurement. These are nominal, ordinal, interval and ratio scale. There is always a debate among business researchers on the appropriateness of measurement through the rating scales (like ordinal versus interval scale) in different research problems to measure theoretical constructs and variables. Researchers use various scales depending on the dimensions of the research problem. In this chapter, different types of scales (single-item scale, continuous rating scale and multiple-item scale) have been discussed focusing on the entities included in the scale.

KEY TERMS

scale (47)
nominal (48)
ordinal (48)
interval (50)
ratio scale (50)
single-item scale (52)
paired comparison scale (52)
multiple-choice scale (52)
constant sum scale (53)
Q sort scale (54)
pictorial scale (54)
rank order scale (54)
continuous rating scale (55)
multiple-item scale (55)
Likert scale (55)
semantic differential scale (56)
Stapel scale (56)
Thurstone scale (57)

EXERCISES

1. What do you mean by scaling?
2. Discuss the importance of scaling in research.
3. Explain different types of basic scales.
4. Distinguish between ratio and interval data.
5. Distinguish between nominal and ordinal scale.
6. Classify different types of measurement scales.
7. Distinguish between single-item scale and continuous rating scale.
8. Distinguish between single-item scale and multiple-item scale.
9. Describe each of the following:
   a. Paired comparison scale
   b. Multiple-choice scale
   c. Constant sum scale
   d. Q sort scale
   e. Rank order scale
   f. Likert scale

g. Semantic differential scale
h. Stapel scale
i. Thurstone scale

10. Indicate the type of measurement scale that should be used in each of the following attributes and explain the reason for choosing them. Prepare the question for each attribute.
    a. Customer satisfaction of mobile service
    b. Brand loyalty
    c. Battery longevity
    d. Purchase intension
    e. Post-sales service facility
    f. Occupation
    g. Income level
11. Indicate the type of measurement scale (nominal, ordinal, interval or ratio) that is being used in each of the following questions and explain the reason for choosing them.
    a. Students with which background prefer to pursue the MBA degree?
       i. Science
       ii. Arts
       iii. Commerce
    b. How do you rate the quality of education at B-schools in India?
       5 = Very good
       4 = Good
       3 = Neither good nor poor
       2 = Poor
       1 = Very poor
    c. Rank the order of your preference criteria for selecting a B-school.
       i. Fee structure
       ii. Rank
       iii. Placement
       iv. Infrastructure
       v. Quality education
       vi. Availability of qualified teachers

CHAPTER

6

Reliability and Validity

LEARNING OBJECTIVES

After studying this chapter, you should be able to

- Understand the concept of reliability and validity.
- Understand the importance and inevitable requirement of reliability and validity in research study.
- Know different types of reliability and validity measurement techniques.
- Learn how reliability and validity can be calculated with the help of SPSS (statistical software) and different formulas.

6.1. RELIABILITY AND VALIDITY

Reliability and validity are generally used for the evaluation of scale. These emphasize the criteria for good measurement.

6.2. RELIABILITY

Reliability testing focuses on the analysis of the properties of measurement scale and its items. Actually, it provides information about the interrelationships of items in the scale. In a questionnaire, at first researchers try to determine the relationship among the items and internal consistency of the scale as a whole. Also, they can easily spot unrelated items that should be excluded from the questionnaire.

6.2.1. Types of Reliability

There are five types of reliability estimates which evaluate reliability in different ways (Figure 6.1).

6.2.1.1. Test–Retest Reliability

Different time frames are used to measure the consistency of items of the same sample through the same questionnaire. Researchers administer the reliability measurement approach to the same sample assuming that there is no significant change in the items and constructs being estimated between two time frames (see Figure 6.2). A decision taken on the time gap allowed between two measurements is very critical for the researcher. Generally, the correlation between the two observations varies on the time gap between two time frames. The correlation between the two observations is high for a shorter time gap and low for a longer the time gap because a shorter time gap emphasizes more similar factors between two observations. The method is not practically viable because a biased answer may be introduced in the second time frame due to unwillingness of the respondents or inability to receive response in the second-time survey. Different internal consistency reliability models such as Cronbach's alpha and split-half model can remove these issues.

FIGURE 6.1
Classification of Reliability

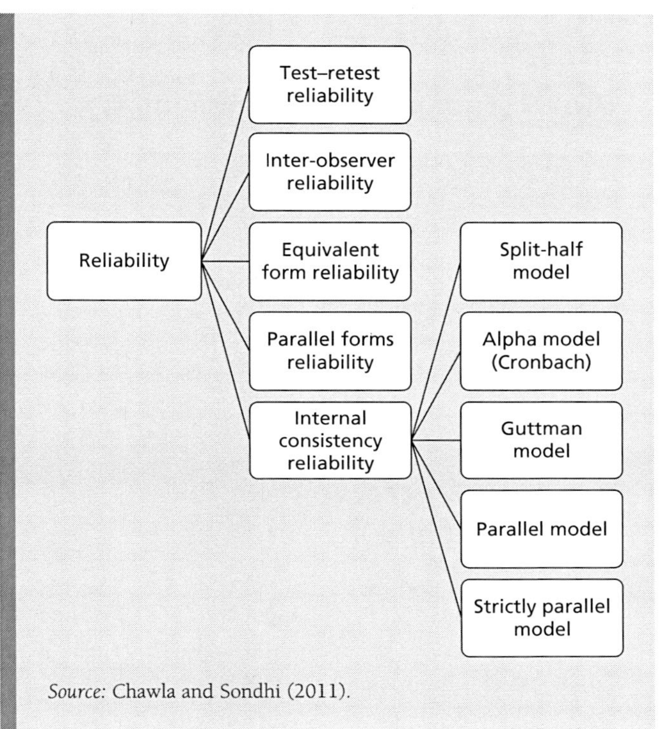

Source: Chawla and Sondhi (2011).

FIGURE 6.2
Test–Retest Reliability

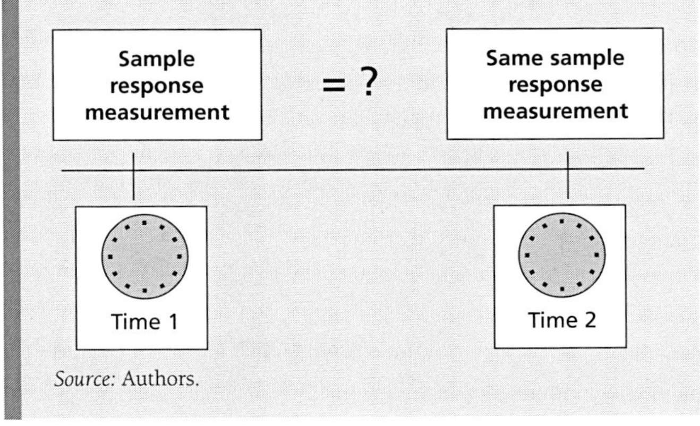

Source: Authors.

6.2.1.2. Inter-observer Reliability

Different observers are assigned to assess the consistency of the items of the same sample through the same questionnaire. In other words, researchers try to determine whether two observers are consistent in their observed estimate for the same sample (see Figure 6.3). The correlation between ratings of the two observers would provide the actual estimate of the reliability. Basically, this method is used in pilot studies. For long-time survey, the inter-observer reliability method should be executed time to time to establish the reliability of the study.

FIGURE 6.3
Inter-observer Reliability

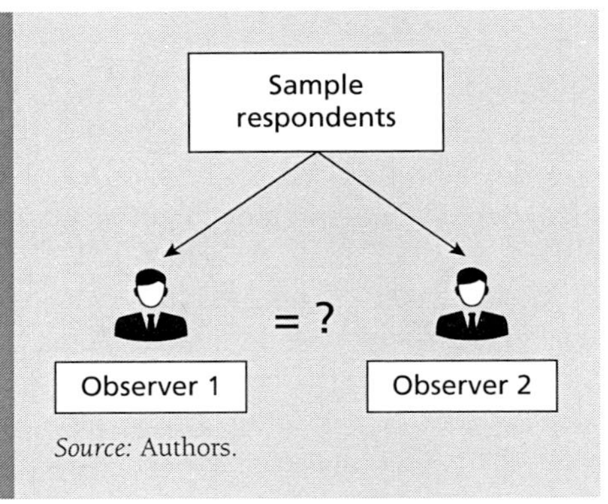

Source: Authors.

6.2.1.3. Equivalent Form Reliability

In equivalent form reliability, the researcher administers two equivalent survey-instrument forms at two different time frames. These survey-instrument forms contain different samples of items with the same type of questions and structure (see Figure 6.4). Selection of the time frame depends on the discretion of the researcher. Here, reliability is measured by evaluating the correlation coefficient between the two equivalent forms at two different times.

FIGURE 6.4
Equivalent Form Reliability

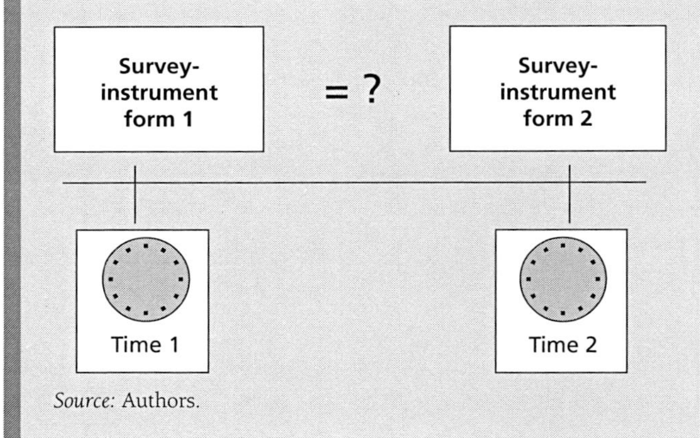

Source: Authors.

6.2.1.4. Parallel Forms Reliability

Different survey-instrument forms under the same domain at the same time frame are used to assess the consistency of the items. Two parallel questionnaire forms are created by the researcher from a large set of question banks that focuses on the same construct. Researcher should apply both survey-instrument forms to the same sample (see Figure 6.5). Here, reliability is calculated by measuring correlation between the two parallel survey-instrument forms. In this approach, large item generation for the same construct is a difficult task for the researchers. Also, randomly divided parallel halves are not always equivalent in all the cases. The split-half reliability test is the similar type of test like parallel forms reliability approach.

6.2.1.5. Internal Consistency Reliability

Internal consistency reliability indicates the internal consistency of a summated scale of items (construct). In other words, internal consistency is checked for different items for the same construct in the survey instrument. Different techniques can be used for internal consistency reliability measurement in a wide variety of social science research. These are (a) split-half model, (b) alpha model (Cronbach), (c) Guttman model and (d) parallel and strictly parallel model.

The models of reliability are described in the following:

1. Split-half model

This model randomly divides the items into two parts of a scale and examines the correlation between them. The main purpose of this model is to measure the reliability of the same construct in two sets. It shows Cronbach alpha for split (half), correlation between halves, Guttman split-half reliability and Spearman–Brown reliability. For Guttman split-half and Spearman–Brown reliability, 0.80 or higher value means the scale has very good reliability. If the range is 0.70–0.80, the scale has fair reliability and sometimes 0.06 is taken as a cut-off level for some exploratory research. After putting data and variables in the 'Data View' window and 'Variable View' window, click Analyze → Scale → Reliability Analysis in the SPSS window. One pop-up window will appear as 'Reliability Analysis'. Go to 'Model' and select 'Split-half' (Exhibit 6.1).

FIGURE 6.5
Parallel Forms Reliability

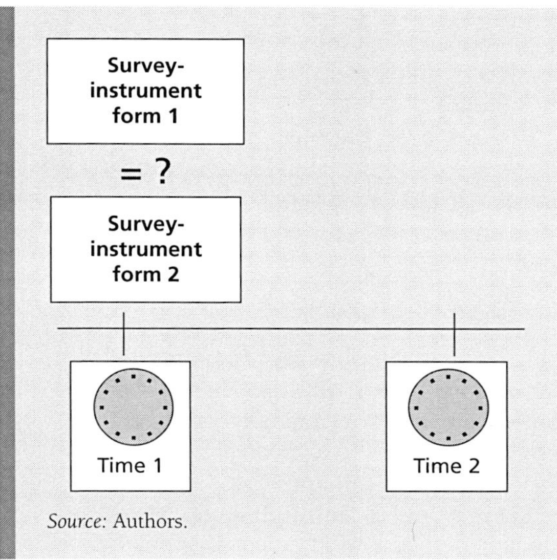

Source: Authors.

EXHIBIT 6.1
SPSS Window for Split-half (1)

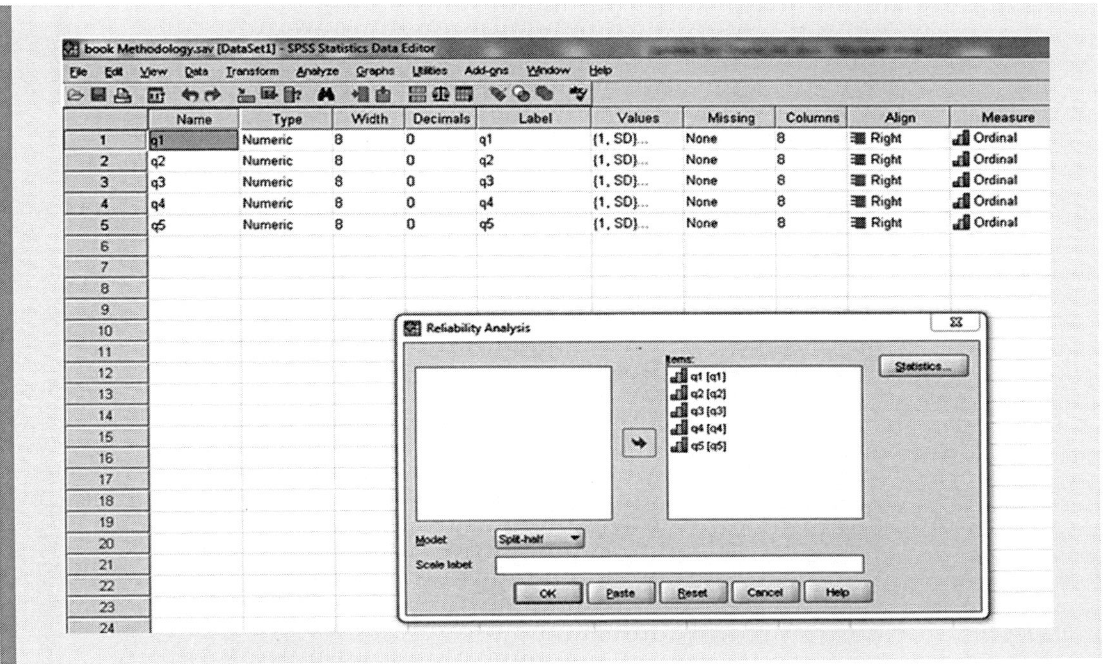

Then click 'Statistics' and another pop-up window will appear. Tick 'Scale' (Exhibit 6.2).

Then click 'Continue' → 'OK'. At last, an SPSS output box will appear as shown in Table 6.1.

The provided Guttman split-half and Spearman–Brown reliability values indicate that there is a very good reliability between different items of a multiple-item scale.

2. Alpha model (Cronbach)

This model emphasizes the internal consistency of a multiple-item scale depending on their internal correlation. Cronbach's alpha is calculated by taking the average of all possible split-half estimates for a multiple-item scale. Researchers evaluate all split-half estimates from the same sample. The range of alpha coefficient must be from 0 to 1. The value of alpha coefficient determines the acceptance level of reliability for a multiple-item scale (see Table 6.2).

EXHIBIT 6.2
SPSS Window for Split-half (2)

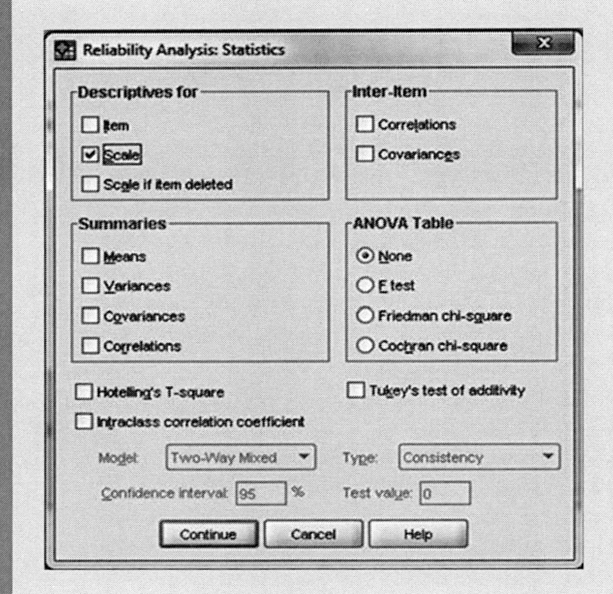

TABLE 6.1
Reliability Statistics (Cronbach's Alpha, Spearman–Brown and Guttman Split-Half)

Cronbach's alpha	Part 1	Value	0.882
		N of items	3[a]
	Part 2	Value	0.892
		N of items	2[b]
		Total *N* of items	5
		Correlation between forms	0.963
Spearman–Brown coefficient		Equal length	0.981
		Unequal length	0.982
		Guttman split-half coefficient	0.949

Source: Authors.
Notes: 1. [a]The items are q1, q2, q3.
2. [b]The items are q3, q4, q5.

TABLE 6.2
Interpretations of Different Cronbach's Alpha Values

Cronbach's Alpha Value (α)	Interpretation
α > 0.80	Excellent reliability between different items of a multiple-item scale.
0.70 ≤ α ≤ 0.80	Good reliability between different items of a multiple-item scale.
0.60 ≤ α ≤ 0.70	Fair reliability between different items of a multiple-item scale.
α < 0.60	Generally unaccepted and poor reliability between different items of a multiple-item scale.

Source: Chawla and Sondhi (2011).

EXHIBIT 6.3
SPSS Window for Alpha (1)

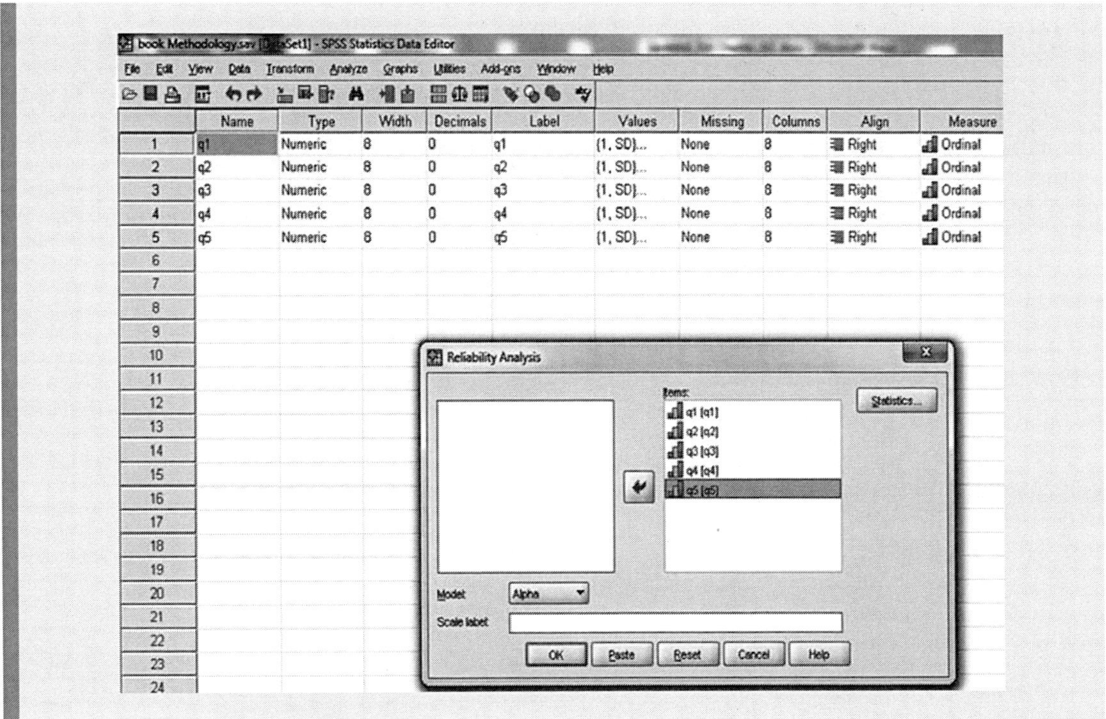

After putting data and variables in the 'Data View' window and 'Variable View' window, click Analyze → Scale → Reliability Analysis in the SPSS window. One pop-up window will appear as 'Reliability Analysis'. Go to 'Model' and select 'Alpha' (Exhibit 6.3).

Then click 'Statistics', another pop-up window will appear. Tick 'Item' and 'Correlations' (Exhibit 6.4).

Then click 'Continue' → 'OK'. At last, an SPSS output box will appear as shown in Table 6.3.

The mentioned Cronbach's alpha value indicates that there is an excellent reliability between different items of a multiple-item scale.

3. Guttman model

This model computes Guttman's lower bounds for true reliability. It shows different reliability coefficients from lambda 1 to lambda 6 including Cronbach alpha and Guttman split-half reliability (see Table 6.4).

After putting data and variables in the 'Data View' window and 'Variable View' window, click Analyze → Scale → Reliability Analysis in the SPSS window. One pop-up window will appear as 'Reliability Analysis'. Go to 'Model' and select 'Guttman' (Exhibit 6.5).

Then click 'OK'. At last, an SPSS output box will appear as shown in Table 6.5.

L_3 (Cronbach's alpha) and L_4 (Guttman split-half) reliability values are excellent. Guttman split-half is a lower bound for the true reliability for any split forms. Guttman stated that the best split maximizes L_4 and reliability can be measured by selecting the largest lower bound comparing with it.

4. Parallel and strictly parallel model

The parallel model emphasizes equal variance of all items and the strictly parallel model emphasizes equal means across items. It shows estimated common inter-item correlation, estimated reliability, common variance and test for goodness of fit of model. These models provide variance estimates which are actually unavailable in the previously discussed models.

After putting data and variables in the 'Data View' window and 'Variable View' window, click Analyze → Scale → Reliability Analysis in the SPSS window. One pop-up window will appear as 'Reliability Analysis'. Go to 'Model' and select 'Parallel' (Exhibit 6.6).

Then click 'OK'. At last, an SPSS output box will appear as shown in Table 6.6.

EXHIBIT 6.4
SPSS Window for Alpha (2)

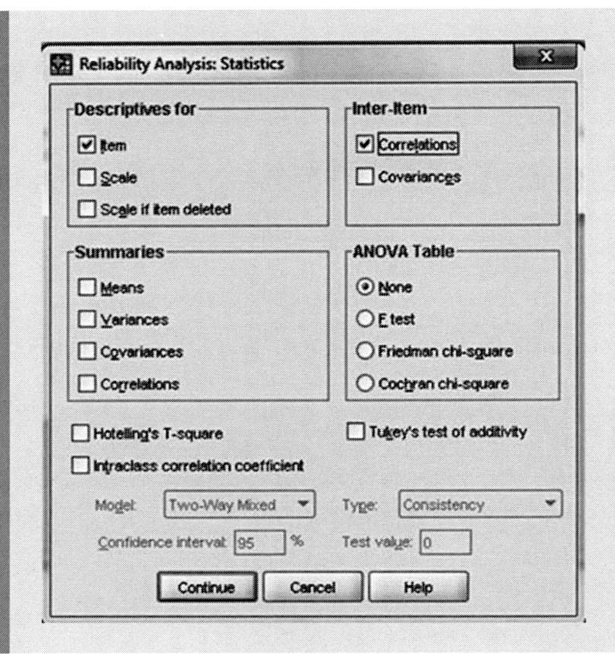

TABLE 6.3
Reliability Statistics (Cronbach's Alpha)

Cronbach's Alpha	Cronbach's Alpha Based on Standardized Items	N of Items
0.949	0.950	5

Source: Authors.

TABLE 6.4
Interpretation of Lamda

Lamda	Interpretation
L1	An intermediate coefficient used for other Lamdas
L2	More complicated reliability coefficient than Cronbach's alpha
L3	Cronbach's alpha
L4	Guttman split-half reliability
L5	Related to co-variances between items
L6	Related to squared multiple correlations

Source: IBM SPSS Tutorials.

EXHIBIT 6.5
SPSS Window for Guttman

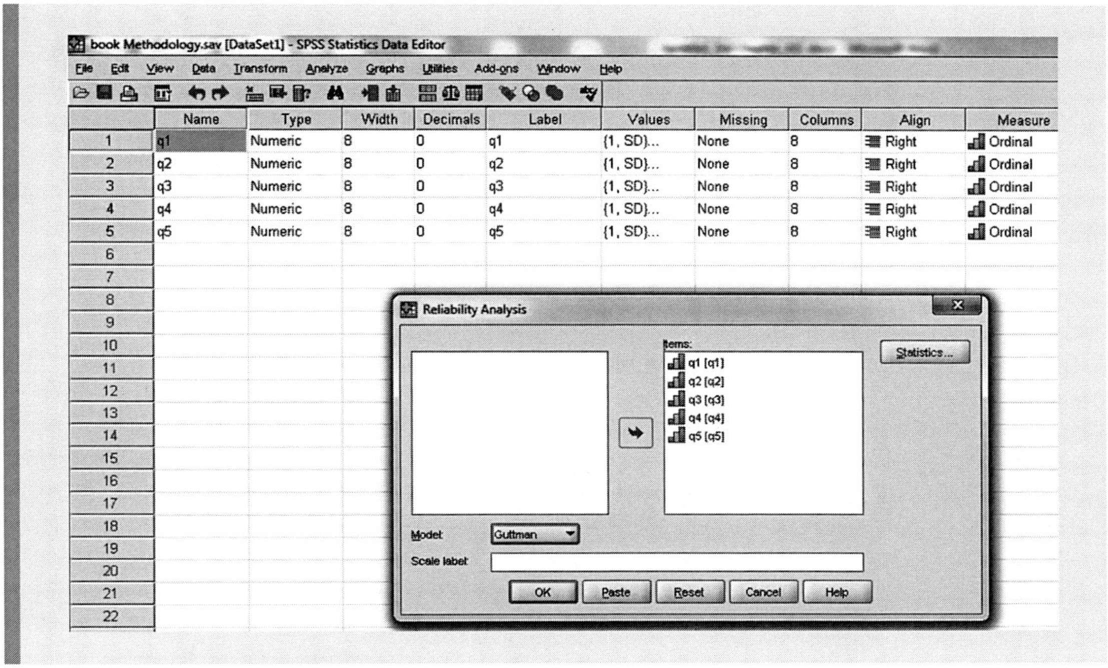

TABLE 6.5
Reliability Statistics (Lambda)

Lambda	1	0.759
	2	0.951
	3	0.949
	4	0.949
	5	0.919
	6	0.902
N of items		5

Source: Authors.

The hypothesis of the parallel model states that there is the same variance but not necessarily the same mean, and the hypothesis of the strictly parallel model states that there is the same mean and variance for true items. Then model goodness of fit should be checked. If the value of significance level is more than 0.05, this implies the acceptance the hypothesis. For less than cut-off significance value of 0.05, the hypothesis must be rejected for the parallel model.

Interestingly, the reliability estimates for the parallel model and strictly parallel model are equivalent to Cronbach's alpha. Here, the acceptance of parallel model implies that the strictly parallel model will be also accepted (Table 6.7).

EXHIBIT 6.6
SPSS Window for Parallel

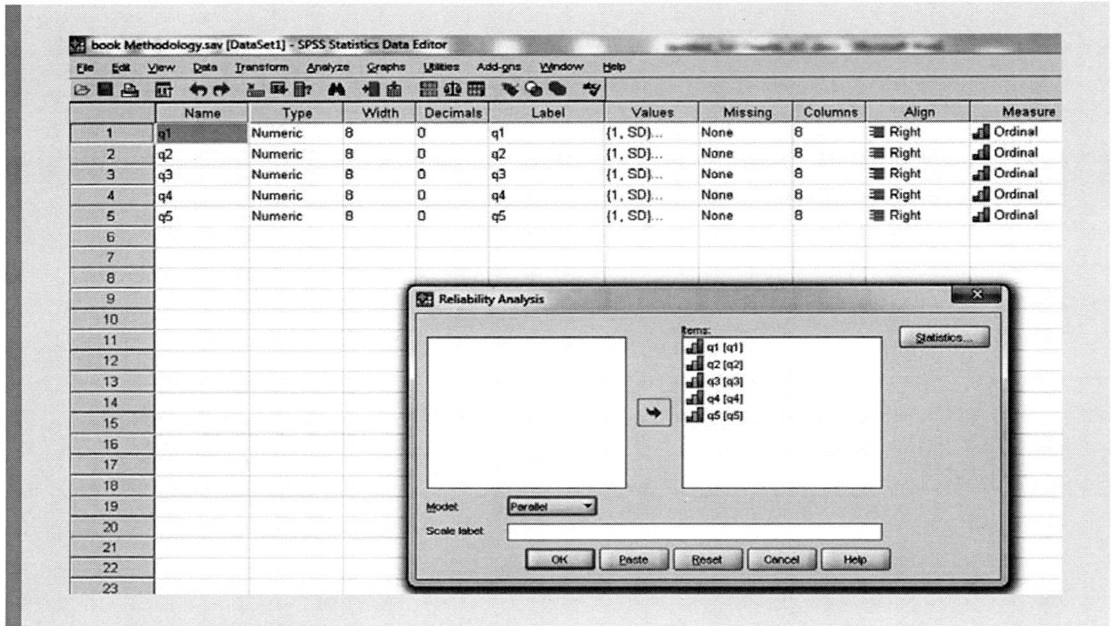

TABLE 6.6
Test for Model Goodness of Fit

Chi-square	Value	1,530.573
	df	13
	Sig.	1.000
Log of determinant of	Unconstrained matrix	0.000
	Constrained matrix	–7.770
Under the parallel model assumption		

Source: Authors.

TABLE 6.7
Reliability Statistics (Parallel and Strictly Parallel Model)

Common variance	0.549
True variance	0.432
Error variance	0.117
Common inter-item correlation	0.788
Reliability of scale	0.949
Reliability of scale (unbiased)	0.949

Source: Authors.

TABLE 6.8
Relationship Between Reliability and Validity

Diagram	Meaning	Explanation
	Valid, not reliable	Randomly spread values across the target (target means right value for all respondents) create inconsistent response. But the right answers for the group on average are received.
	Reliable, not valid	Consistent and systematic measurement of the wrong value for all respondents.
	Reliable and valid	Consistent and systematic measurement of the right values for all respondents.
	Neither reliable nor valid	Inconsistent and unsystematic measurement of the wrong value for all respondents.

Source: Authors.

6.3. RELATIONSHIP BETWEEN RELIABILITY AND VALIDITY THROUGH PICTORIAL DIAGRAM

Reliability and validity concepts are related to each other. Table 6.8 explains this idea clearly with pictorial diagrams.

6.4. VALIDITY

Validity focuses on the accuracy of instrument's measurement. Actually, it checks the systematic and random error in the measurement process. In practical scenario, it is a huge task for the researchers. There are different types of validity measurement processes listed as follows (Figure 6.6).

6.4.1. Face Validity

Face validity is probably the weakest way to find out the validity of the measurement instrument for a research. It may be a weak process but this validation method is not wrong. It mainly prioritizes the subjective judgement of an item or a construct. Here, researchers need to trust subjective judgement that may not be very convincing to other researchers and authors throughout the research process. The authentication of source evidence must be verified through proper reference and empirical proof for improving the quality of face validity assessment.

FIGURE 6.6
Classification of Validity

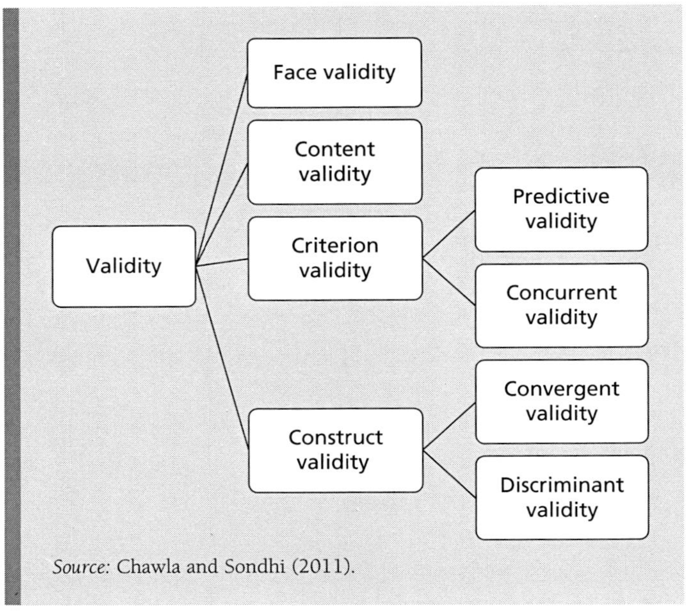

Source: Chawla and Sondhi (2011).

6.4.2. Content Validity

Content validity emphasizes the adequate coverage and appropriateness of all constructs in the research study and focuses on the relevant content domain for them. It is established by taking views/opinions from other investigators or experts in the same field of research study and the members of the population. At first, different hypotheses should be constructed from an extensive literature review to capture the overall intended measures. Then the scale, constructs and selected items in the research should be reviewed by experts in statistics and related fields.

6.4.3. Criterion Validity

Criterion validity deals with the appropriateness of the variables or criterion in a research study. It checks the performance of the scale with respect to variables or criteria which may include behavioural and attitudinal measures, demographic attributes and the likes, or scales obtained from other scales. In comparison with content validity, the criterion validity focuses on the variables or items related to scale but content validity talks about correctness of construct definition. There are two types of criterion validity: (a) Concurrent validity (b) Predictive validity.

1. Concurrent validity

At first, researchers evaluate the collected data from the research scale. At the same time, collected data on criterion variables are evaluated. If both are shown to be valid, it is called concurrent validity. It actually correlates new and established measuring techniques. It calculates the correlation coefficient of two measures under similar events and conditions.

2. Predictive validity

It is established when the measuring instrument enables to predict some future events theoretically. It actually tries to correlate present and future measurements. If the correlation coefficient is high, the present measurement has a high predictive capability.

6.4.4. Construct Validity

Construct validity is a validation process of construct by existing conceptual or theoretical bases through statistical analysis. There are two types of construct validity: (a) convergent validity and (b) discriminant validity. These two aspects of validity can be measured by confirmatory factor analysis (CFA) and structural equation modelling (SEM) through AMOS software. Convergent validity deals with sufficient convergence or internal consistency in between the items of underlying factors. On the other hand, discriminant validity deals with divergence or inconsistency in between factors constructed by different items (see Figure 6.7). So a construct must be associated within (convergent validity) but not with other factors, which is the supportive proof of discriminant validity.

FIGURE 6.7
Pictorial Representation of Convergent and Discriminant Validity

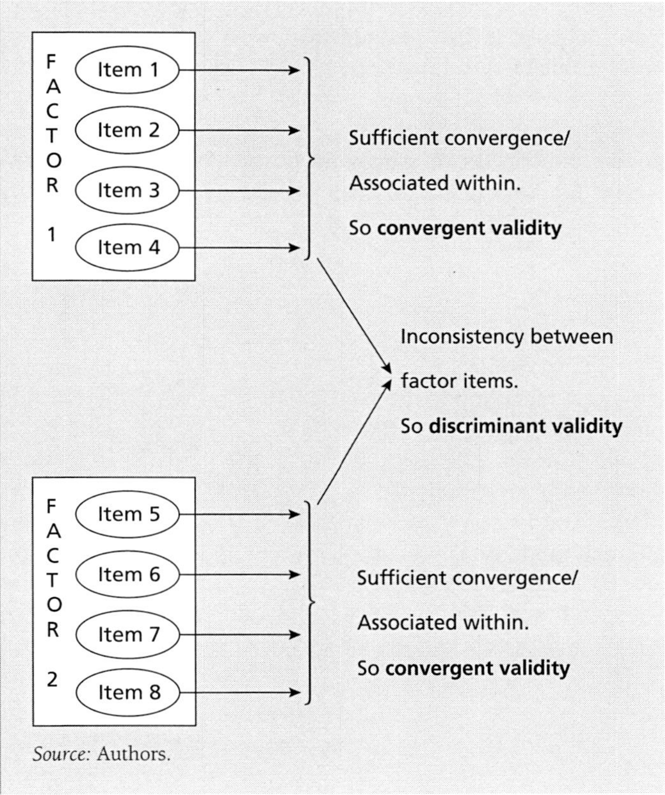

Source: Authors.

Also convergent and discriminant validity can be checked through composite reliability (CR), average variance extracted (AVE), maximum shared variance (MSV) and average shared variance (ASV). A CFA is executed with the help of AMOS software. As per Hair et al. (2010), threshold levels have been suggested for CR (> 0.7), convergent validity (CR > AVE and AVE > 0.5) and discriminant validity (MSV < AVE and ASV < AVE). These calculations cannot be measured by AMOS software. They have their individual formula as shown in Table 6.9.

TABLE 6.9
Important Formula for Validity Measurement

CR = (Σ Standardized loadings)^2 / [(Σ Standardized loadings)^2 + Σ (measurement error for each indicator)]
AVE = Σ (Standardized loadings^2) / [Σ (Standardized loadings^2) + Σ (measurement error for each indicator)]
MSV = (Maximum value of correlation estimate between a particular construct and other related factors)^2
ASV = Average value of [(correlation estimate between a particular construct and other related factors)^2]

Source: Fornell and Larcker (1981) and Hair et al. (1998).

SUMMARY

Reliability and validity are generally used for the evaluation of scale. These emphasize the criteria for good measurement. Reliability testing focuses on the analysis of the properties of measurement scale and its items. Actually, it provides information about the interrelationships of items in the scale. There are five types of reliability estimates (test–retest reliability, inter-observer reliability, equivalent form reliability, parallel forms reliability and internal consistency reliability) which evaluate reliability in different ways. Validity focuses on the accuracy of instrument's measurement. Actually, it checks the systematic and random error in the measurement process. There are different types of validity measurement processes, namely, (a) face validity (b) content validity (c) criterion validity and (d) construct validity.

KEY TERMS

reliability (60)
test–retest reliability (61)
inter-observer reliability (61)
equivalent form reliability (62)
parallel-forms reliability (62)
internal consistency reliability (62)
split-half model (63)
Cronbach alpha model (64)
Guttman model (66)
parallel and strictly parallel model (66)
validity (69)
face validity (69)
content validity (70)
criterion validity (70)
construct validity (71)
concurrent validity (70)
predictive validity (70)
convergent validity (71)
discriminant validity (71)

EXERCISES

1. Define reliability. Discuss different types of reliability measurement techniques.
2. Define validity. Discuss different types of validity measurement techniques.
3. Explain the relationship between reliability and validity.
4. Elaborate different types of internal consistency reliability.
6. Differentiate between concurrent validity and predictive validity.
7. Differentiate between convergent validity and discriminant validity.
8. Differentiate between test–retest reliability and inter-observer reliability.
9. Describe each of the following:
   a. Face validity
   b. Content validity
   c. Split-half model
   d. Alpha model (Cronbach)
   e. Guttman model
   f. Parallel and strictly parallel model

CHAPTER

7

Descriptive Statistics and Graphical Presentation of Data

LEARNING OBJECTIVES

After studying this chapter, you should be able to

- Understand classification of data.
- Understand classification of variable.
- Learn how to summarize the data numerically in a meaningful way through descriptive statistics.
- Interpret descriptive statistics from SPSS output.
- Learn representation of data through various types of graphs.

7.1. CLASSIFICATION OF DATA

In order to understand the descriptive statistics of data, first we have to understand the concept of data. Data is a collection of facts, such as numbers, words, measurements, observations or even just descriptions of things.

It can be classified into the following two different types:

1. Quantitative data: A variable differing in quantity is called quantitative variable, for example, the weight of a person and number of people in a car. There are two types of quantitative data—continuous and discrete. As a general rule, counts are discrete data and measurements are continuous data.

Discrete data is a count that cannot be made more precise. Typically, it involves integer numbers. For instance, the number of children in your family is discrete data, because we are counting whole, indivisible entities—one cannot have 2.5 kids. Therefore, we can say that discrete data cannot take any value.

On the other hand, continuous data may be of any value. It may be an integer or fractional number. For instance, height of a student, age of a person, rainfall or weight of a student may take any value within a specified range.

2. Qualitative data: A variable differing in quality is called a qualitative variable or attribute. When we classify or categorize something, we create qualitative or attribute data. There are three main kinds of qualitative data. These are as follows:
   a. *Binary data* place things in one of two mutually exclusive categories: right/wrong, true/false or accept/reject.
   b. *Nominal values* or observations can be assigned a code in the form of a number where the numbers are simply labels. We can only count but not order or measure nominal data. Examples are gender, eye colour, roll number of student and the likes.
   c. *Ordinal values* or observations can be ranked or ordered, for example you having a variable, economic status, with three categories (low, medium and high).

Another example is a survey question that asks us to rate an item on a 1–10 scale, with 10 being the best. This implies that 10 is better than 9, which is better than 8 and so on.

7.2. CLASSIFICATION OF VARIABLES

Depending on their intended use, variables may be classified as independent, dependent, moderating, mediating or control variables. Variables that explain other variables are called independent variables, those that are explained by other variables are dependent variables, those that are explained by independent variables while also explaining dependent variables are mediating variables (or intermediate variables) and those that influence the relationship between independent and dependent variables are called moderating variables. As an example, if we state that higher intelligence causes improved learning among students, then intelligence is an independent variable and learning is a dependent variable. There may be other extraneous variables that are not pertinent to explaining a given dependent variable, but may have some impact on the dependent variable. These variables must be controlled for in a scientific study, and are therefore called control variables.

To understand the differences between these different variable types, consider the example stated here. If we believe that intelligence influences (or explains) students' academic achievement, then a measure of intelligence such as an IQ score is an independent variable, while a measure of academic success such as grade point average (GPA) is a dependent variable. If we believe that the effect of intelligence on academic achievement also depends on the effort invested by the student in the learning process (i.e., between two equally intelligent students, the student who puts in more effort achieves higher academically than one who puts in less effort), then effort becomes a moderating variable. Incidentally, one may also view effort as an independent variable and intelligence as a moderating variable. If academic achievement is viewed as an independent variable to higher earning potential, then earning potential becomes the dependent variable for the independent variable academic achievement, and academic achievement becomes the mediating variable in the relationship between intelligence and earning potential. Hence, variables are defined as an independent, dependent, moderating or mediating variable based on their nature of association with each other. The overall network of relationships between a set of related constructs is called a nomological network.

7.3. DESCRIPTIVE STATISTICS

Descriptive statistics are numbers that are used to summarize and describe data. Descriptive statistics provide a concise summary of data. We can summarize data numerically or graphically. Descriptive statistics is the term given to the analysis of data that helps to describe, show or summarize data in a meaningful way. Descriptive statistics do not, however, allow us to make conclusions beyond the data we have analysed or reach conclusions regarding any hypotheses we might have made. They are simply a way to describe our data.

Descriptive statistics are very important because if we simply present our raw data, it would be hard to visualize what the data are showing, especially if there are a lot of it. Descriptive statistics therefore enable us to present the data in a more meaningful way, which allows simpler interpretation of the data. For example, if we had the results of 100 students, we may be interested in the overall performance of those students. We would also be interested in the distribution or spread of the marks. Descriptive statistics allow us to do this. Typically, there are two general types of statistics that are used to describe data. These are discussed as follows:

1. Measures of central tendency: These are ways of describing the central position of a frequency distribution for a group of data. We can describe this central position using a number of statistics, including the mode, median and mean. The measure of central tendency measures the average value of the sample. In descriptive statistics, there are two types of averages: The first is the mathematical average and the second is the positional average.

   Mathematical averages are of three types—arithmetic mean, geometric mean and harmonic mean. Arithmetic mean is the most widely used measure for central tendency. It can be obtained by adding all the items of the series and dividing this total by the number of items. The mean is sensitive to extremely large or small values. In descriptive statistics, the geometric mean is defined as the *n*th root of the products of all the *n* values of the variable. In descriptive statistics, the geometric mean is used when the items in the series are very large. Harmonic mean is defined as the reciprocal of the items. It is useful in finding the averages that involve speed, time, price and ratio.

   There are two types of positional averages—median and mode. Median is the average value of the series in which half the values are less than the median and half the values are greater than the median. Mode, the second positional average, shows a higher frequency in the series.
2. Measures of spread: These are ways of summarizing a group of data by describing how spread out the scores are. For example, the mean score of our 100 students may be 60 out of 100. However, not all students will have scored 60 marks. Rather, their scores will be spread out. Some will be lower and others higher. Measures of spread help us to summarize how spread out these scores are. To describe this spread, a number of statistics are available to us. These include range, interquartile range, standard deviation, variance and so on. In descriptive statistics, range is defined as the difference between the highest and the lowest value. The interquartile range is the difference between the upper and the lower quartiles. It measures the spread of a data set. It is robust to extreme observations. Standard deviation is also called the root mean square deviation. It measures the spread of a set of observations. The larger the standard deviation is,

the more spread out the observations are. Variance is also used to measure the dispersion, which can be simply derived from the square of the standard deviation. We do not generally use variance as an index of spread because it is in squared units. Instead, we use standard deviation.

7.4. DESCRIPTIVE STATISTICS IN SPSS

The screen in Exhibit 7.1 is the data editor. The first step here is to enter variable names into the 'Variable View' and feed the required data against these variables into the data editor. In the case of our example (Exhibit 7.1), we have taken into consideration three different variables and these are age, gender and religion of 10 respondents. Out of these variables, age is continuous in nature and the other two variables are grouping variables.

From the data that we have entered, we can calculate four types of descriptive statistics and the options are as follows:

1. Frequencies: It is used when the nature of the data is grouping or categorical, for example, religion, sex and caste.
2. Crosstabs: It is used when there are two grouping variables in the data set.
3. Descriptives: Descriptives command is used only when we deal with continuous variables.
4. Explore: The command is used when we want to compare one continuous variable against one categorical variable.

EXHIBIT 7.1

SPSS Window for Descriptive Statistics (1)

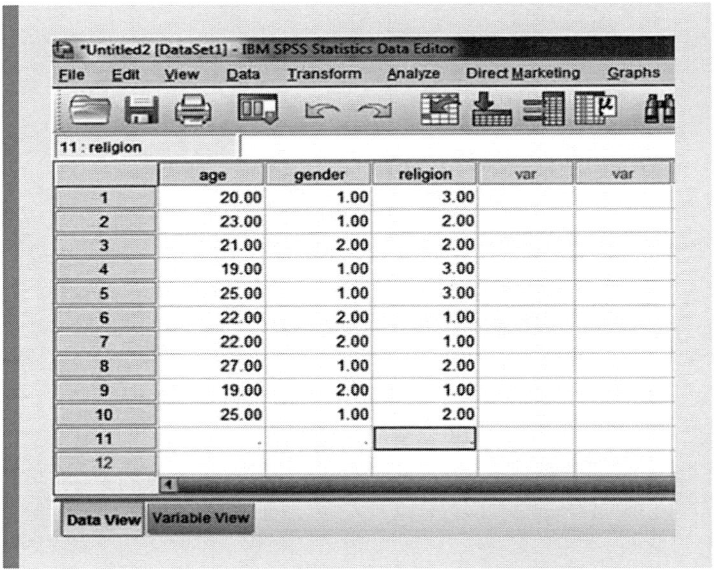

*Untitled2 [DataSet1] - IBM SPSS Statistics Data Editor

File Edit View Data Transform Analyze Direct Marketing Graphs

11 : religion

	age	gender	religion	var	var
1	20.00	1.00	3.00		
2	23.00	1.00	2.00		
3	21.00	2.00	2.00		
4	19.00	1.00	3.00		
5	25.00	1.00	3.00		
6	22.00	2.00	1.00		
7	22.00	2.00	1.00		
8	27.00	1.00	2.00		
9	19.00	2.00	1.00		
10	25.00	1.00	2.00		
11	.	.			
12					

Data View | Variable View

Let us discuss how to use the four types of descriptive statistics in SPSS.

7.4.1. FREQUENCY

First click on 'Analyze', which will produce a menu and then choose 'Descriptive Statistics', then click on the 'Frequencies' as shown in Exhibit 7.2. Then, the frequency dialog box will be opened which is shown in Exhibit 7.3.

Analyze → Descriptive Statistics → Frequency

EXHIBIT 7.2
SPSS Window for Descriptive Statistics (2)

Transfer 'gender' from the left-hand side into the 'Variable(s)' box by clicking the arrow. Here, we have to select or highlight the variable which we want to transfer and then just click on the arrow that is located between the two boxes. Once the variable is successfully transferred, then the analysis is possible.

Now, if we just click on 'OK', then SPSS will generate the results as shown in Table 7.1.

From Table 7.1, we can say how many male and female members have been considered in our data set and their percentage as well as cumulative percentage.

EXHIBIT 7.3
SPSS Window for Descriptive Statistics (3)

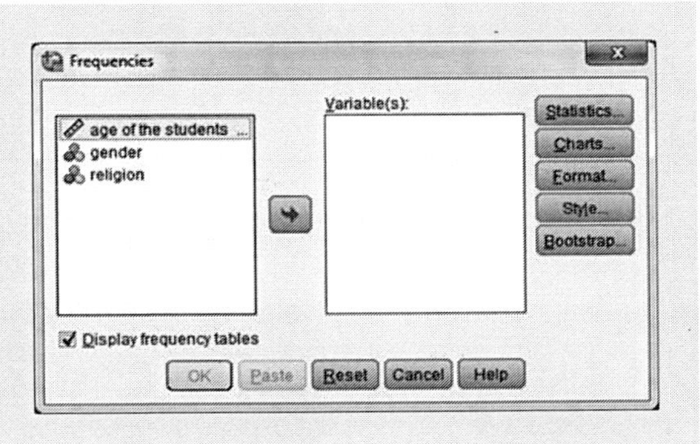

TABLE 7.1
SPSS Output of Descriptive Statistics (1)

Statistics		
Gender		
N	Valid	10
	Missing	0

Gender					
		Frequency	Percentage	Valid Percentage	Cumulative Percentage
Valid	Male	6	60.0	60.0	60.0
	Female	4	40.0	40.0	100.0
	Total	10	100.0	100.0	

Source: Authors.

But we want more specification in our analysis. Suppose, from the frequencies drop box, we will select chart and select bar chart option and click continue and then OK. Then, SPSS will generate a bar chart as shown in Figure 7.1.

FIGURE 7.1
SPSS Output of Descriptive Statistics (2)

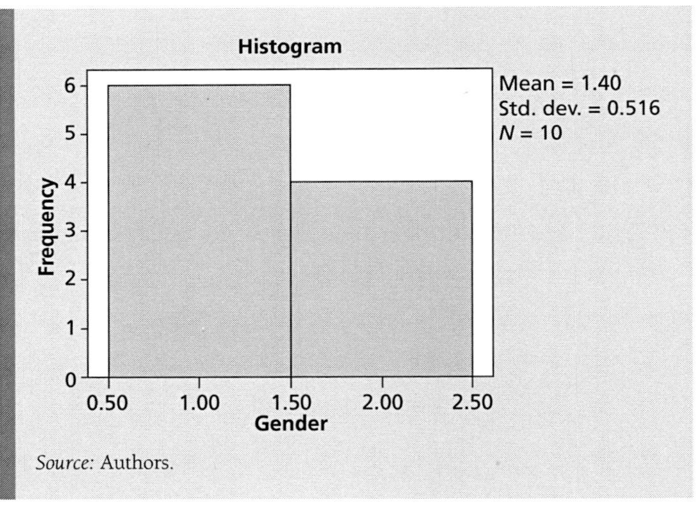

Source: Authors.

7.4.2. Crosstabs

The Crosstabs command is used when we want to work with two discrete/grouping/categorical variables, one in the column and another in the row.

The way to open Crosstabs Analyze → Descriptive Statics → Crosstabs, and then a dialog box will open up as shown in Exhibit 7.4. From this box, we will have to transfer the two grouping variables into the 'variable box', one will be put in 'Row(s)' and another in 'Column(s)'. In our example, we have transferred gender in 'Row(s)' and religion in 'Column(s)'.

Now, we will click on 'Cells' and one drop box will open, where we select the checkbox against 'Observed', 'Row', 'Column' and 'Total' and then click 'Continue'. This is shown in Exhibit 7.5. Finally, we will click on 'OK' to get the outcome of our analysis. The outcome is shown in Table 7.2.

From Table 7.2, it is clearly observed that in the case of males, three males belong to the Muslim community, three males to the Christian community and no male belongs to the Hindu community. This is also shown in percentage form. If we observe the percentage within gender, we observe that

EXHIBIT 7.4
SPSS Window for Descriptive Statistics (4)

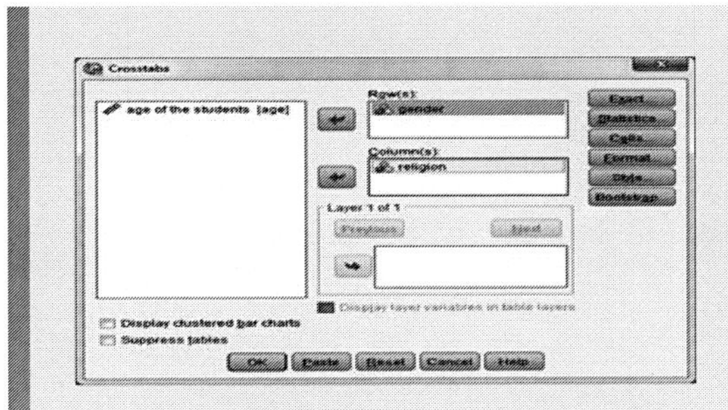

EXHIBIT 7.5
SPSS Window for Descriptive Statistics (5)

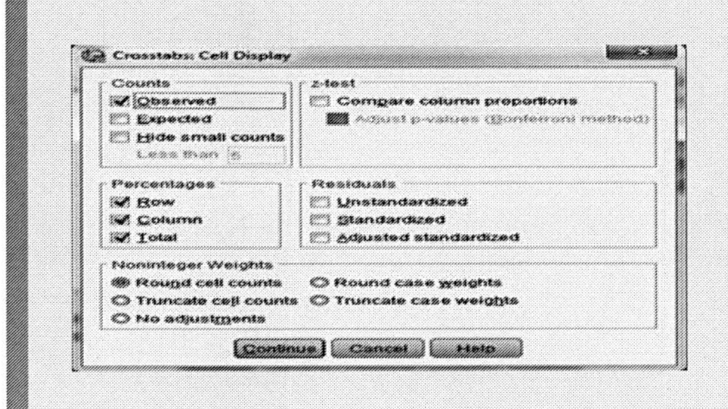

TABLE 7.2
SPSS Output of Descriptive Statistics (3)

Gender × Religion Cross Tabulation

			Religion			
			Hinduism	Islam	Christianity	Total
Gender	Male	Count	0	3	3	6
		Percentage within gender	0.0%	50.0%	50.0%	100%
		Percentage within religion	0.0%	75.0%	100%	60.0%
		Percentage of total	0.0%	30.0%	30.0%	60.0%
	Female	Count	3	1	0	4
		Percentage within gender	75.0%	25.0%	0.0%	100%
		Percentage within religion	100%	25.0%	0.0%	40.0%
		Percentage of total	30.0%	10.0%	0.0%	40.0%
Total		Count	3	4	3	10
		Percentage within gender	30.0%	40.0%	30.0%	100%
		Percentage within religion	100%	100%	100%	100%
		Percentage of total	30.0%	40.0%	30.0%	100%

Source: Authors.

50% males are Muslims, 50% males are Christians and 0% is Hindu. If we also observe the percentage within religion, then we see that out of four Muslims, three are males and one is female. Therefore, 75% males are Muslims and in the same way 100% males are Christians as in this community, no female has been observed. If we take the percentage of 'Total' in the case of male, then we observe that out of total 10 people, three males are Muslims which is exactly 30% and three males are Christians which is also 30%. In the same way, we can explain the other figures in the crosstab result.

7.4.3. Descriptives

Descriptives command is used only when we deal with continuous variables.

The way to open Descriptives is as follows:

Analyze → Descriptive Statistics → Descriptives, and then a dialog box will open up as shown in Exhibit 7.6. From that box, we will have to transfer the continuous variable 'age' into the 'Variable(s)' box to the right side and then click on the button labelled 'Option' at the top right-hand side of the dialog box. Clicking on this will produce the dialog box that is shown in Exhibit 7.7.

EXHIBIT 7.6
SPSS Window for Descriptive Statistics (6)

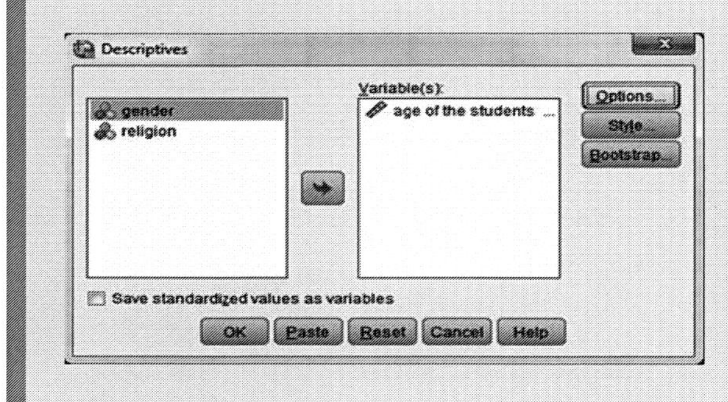

EXHIBIT 7.7
SPSS Window for Descriptive Statistics (7)

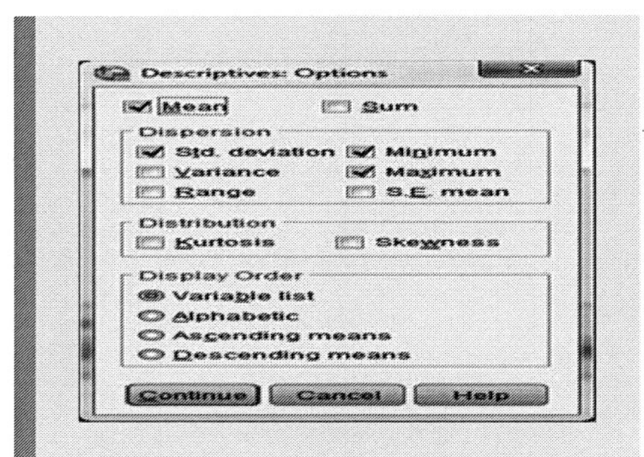

In the Descriptive's 'Options' dialog box, there are some default selections made about the statistics to be shown in the output. Here, we can select a particular statistic or deselect by clicking on the boxes against their names. In our example, we have selected only 'Mean', 'Std. deviation', 'Minimum' and 'Maximum', then click on the 'Continue' button to return to the previous dialog box and then click 'OK' to get the outcome shown in Table 7.3.

TABLE 7.3
SPSS Output of Descriptive Statistics (4)

	N	Minimum	Maximum	Mean	Std. Deviation
Age of the students valid *N* (list-wise)	10	19.00	27.00	22.3000	2.71006

Source: Authors.

7.4.4. Explore

The Explore command is used when we want to compare one continuous variable against one categorical variable. This command can be used to determine measures of central tendency (mean and median), measures of dispersion (range, interquartile range, standard deviation, variance, minimum and maximum), measures of kurtosis and skewness, and prepare histograms, stem-and-leaf plots, and Tukey box plots. The following command will generate the output: Analyze → Descriptive Statistics → Explore. A drop box will open where we can transfer one continuous variable into the 'Dependent List' and the categorical variable into the 'Factor List'. This is shown in Exhibit 7.8.

EXHIBIT 7.8
SPSS Window for Descriptive Statistics (8)

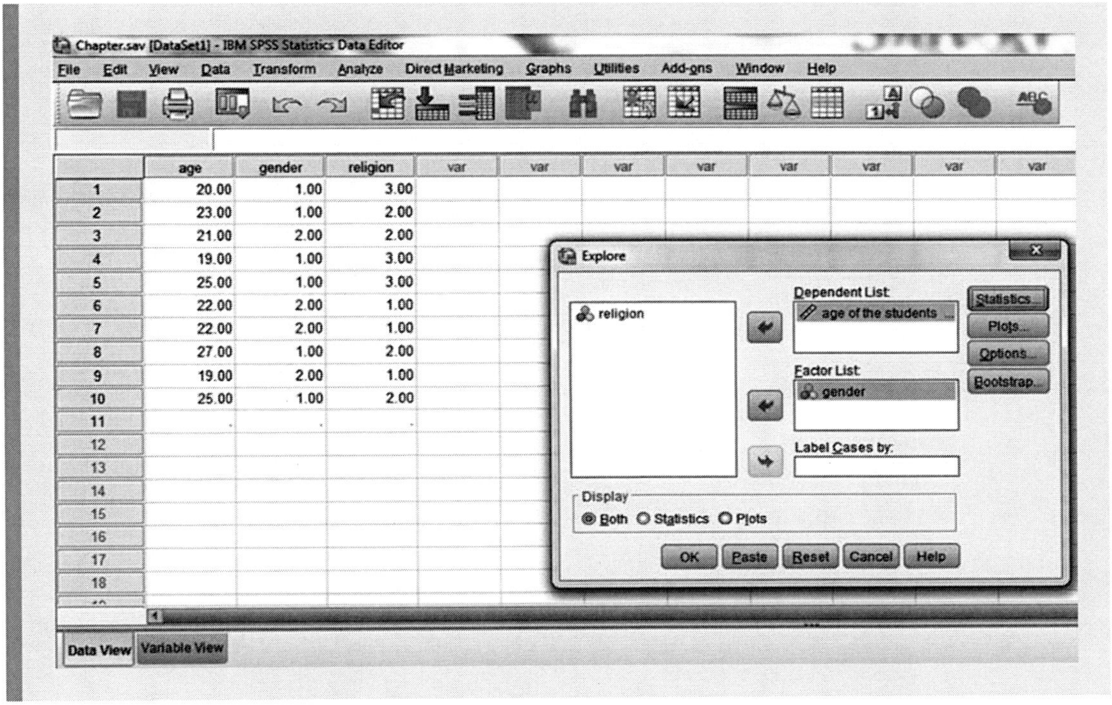

After that we will go into the plots and give the stem-and-leaf option. The 'plots' dialog box lets us select options for graphical display of the data including a stem-and-leaf plot. The Explore command also gives us descriptive statistics (Table 7.4, Figures 7.2 and 7.3) for each variable with more extensive results than the Descriptives command.

TABLE 7.4
SPSS Output of Descriptive Statistics (5)

Descriptives					
	Gender			Statistics	Std. Error
Age	Male	Mean		23.3333	1.33333
		95% confidence interval for mean	Lower bound	19.9059	
			Upper bound	26.7608	
		5% trimmed mean		23.3704	
		Median		24.0000	
		Variance		10.667	
		Std. deviation		3.26599	

(Table 7.4 Continued)

(Table 7.4 Continued)

Descriptives				
Gender			Statistics	Std. Error
	Minimum		19.00	
	Maximum		27.00	
	Range		8.00	
	Interquartile range		6.50	
	Skewness		–0.392	0.845
	Kurtosis		–1.850	1.741
Female	Mean		21.0000	0.70711
	95% confidence interval for mean	Lower bound	18.7497	
		Upper bound	23.2503	
	5% trimmed mean		21.0556	
	Median		21.5000	
	Variance		2.000	
	Std. deviation		1.41421	
	Minimum		19.00	
	Maximum		22.00	
	Range		3.00	
	Interquartile range		2.50	
	Skewness		–1.414	1.014
	Kurtosis		1.500	2.619

Source: Authors.

FIGURE 7.2
Stem-and-leaf Plots

Age Stem-and-leaf plot for Gender = Male	
Frequency	Stem and Leaf
1.00	1.9
2.00	2.03
3.00	2.567
Stem width	10.00
Each leaf	1 case(s)

Source: Authors.

FIGURE 7.3
Box Plot

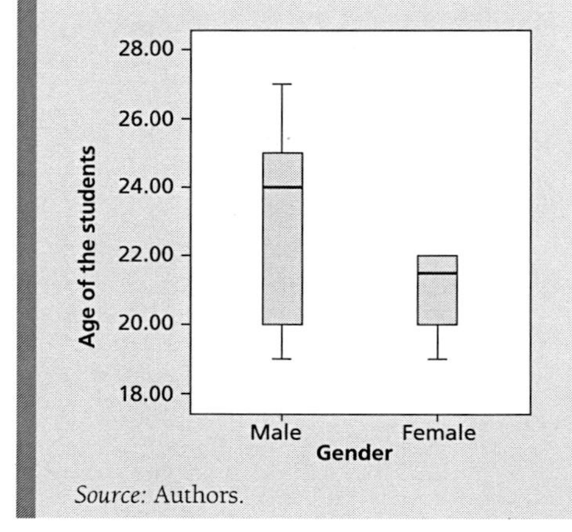

Source: Authors.

7.5. INTERPRETING STATISTICS

When we will do the descriptive statistics in SPSS, then we will get different results. The interpretations of different results in SPSS are mentioned as follows:

Valid: This refers to the non-missing cases. In this column, *N* is given, which is the number of non-missing cases; and per cent is given, which is the percentage of non-missing cases.

Missing: This refers to the missing cases. In this column, *N* is given, which is the number of missing cases; and per cent is given, which is the percentage of the missing cases.

Total: This refers to the total number cases, both non-missing and missing. In this column, *N* is given, which is the total number of cases in the data set; and per cent is given, which is the total percentage of cases in the data set.

Std. error: These are the standard errors for the descriptive statistics. Standard error gives some idea about the variability possible in the statistic.

95% confidence interval for mean lower bound: This is the lower (95%) confidence limit for the mean. If we repeatedly draw samples of 100 student's writing test scores and calculated the mean for each sample, we would expect that 95% of them would fall between the lower and the upper 95% confidence limits. This gives us some idea about the variability of the estimate of the true population mean.

95% confidence interval for mean upper bound: This is the upper (95%) confidence limit for the mean.

5% trimmed mean: This is the mean that would be obtained if the lower and upper 5% of values of the variable are deleted. If the value of the 5% trimmed mean is very different from the mean, this indicates that there are some outliers. However, we cannot assume that all outliers have been removed from the trimmed mean.

Tukey's hinges: These are the first, second and third quartiles. They are calculated the way that Tukey originally proposed when he came up with the idea of a 'box plot'.

25: This is the 25% percentile, also known as the first quartile.

50: This is the 50% percentile, also known as the median. It is a measure of central tendency. It is the middle number when the values are arranged in ascending (or descending) order. Sometimes, the median is a better measure of central tendency than the mean. It is less sensitive than the mean to extreme observations.

75: This is the 75% percentile, also known as the third quartile.

Histogram: It shows the frequency of values of a variable. It gives us an idea about the distribution of the variable.

Stem: It is the number in the 10's place of the value of the variable. For example, the value of the variable is 31. So the stem is 3 and leaf is 1. The digit 3 is in the 10s place, so it is the stem.

Leaf: It is the number in the first place of the value of the variable. The number of leaves tells us how many of these numbers are in the variable. For example, there is one 8 and five 9s (hence, the frequency is six), this means that there is one value of 38 and five values of 39 in the variable.

Minimum: This is the minimum or smallest value of a variable.

Maximum: This is the maximum or largest value of a variable.

Skewness: It measures the degree and direction of asymmetry. A symmetric distribution such as a normal distribution has a skewness of 0. This means that the right and the left of the distribution are perfect mirror images of one another. Not every distribution of data is symmetric. Sets of data that are not symmetric are said to be asymmetric. The measure of how asymmetric a distribution can be is called skewness.

Skewed to the right: Data that are skewed to the right have a long tail that extends to the right. An alternate way of talking about a data set skewed to the right is to say that it is positively skewed. In this situation, the mean and the median are both greater than the mode. As a general rule, most of the time, for data skewed to the right, the mean will be greater than the median. In summary, for a data set skewed to the right,

- Always: mean greater than mode
- Always: median greater than mode
- Most of the time: mean greater than median

Skewed to the left: The situation reverses itself when we deal with data skewed to the left. Data that are skewed to the left have a long tail that extends to the left. An alternate way of talking about a data set skewed to the left is to say that it is negatively skewed. In this situation, the mean and the median are both less than the mode. As a general rule, most of the time for data skewed to the left, the mean will be less than the median. In summary, for a data set skewed to the left,

- Always: mean less than mode
- Always: median less than mode
- Most of the time: mean less than median

Kurtosis: It is a measure of whether the data are heavy-tailed or light-tailed relative to a normal distribution. That is, data sets with high kurtosis tend to have heavy tails or outliers. Data sets with low kurtosis tend to have light tails or lack of outliers. A uniform distribution would be the extreme case.

Histogram is an effective graphical technique for showing both the skewness and kurtosis of a data set.

7.6. GRAPHICAL PRESENTATION OF DATA

In our thesis, dissertation and project work, we frequently present our data with the help of different types of graphs. This is the most suitable way to present the data in a very systematic way for understanding the facts and figures better at a glance. It has an effective impact on the viewers.

Graphical presentation of data helps the researcher understand the specific shape of the distribution of data. Nowadays, we are taking the help of different software to present the data graphically to the viewers.

Some of the commonly used methods of presenting data in graphs are stated further.

7.6.1. Bar Chart

A bar chart mainly depicts the frequency. Here, the class intervals are shown in the horizontal axis and the relative frequencies are specified along the vertical axis of the graph. Bar chart depicts data from left to right horizontally.

Let us take an example to comprehend the procedure of constructing a bar chart.

Example: Construct a bar chart for the following data of month-wise revenue:

Month	Revenue (Rev)
J	25,000
F	26,000
M	27,000
A	28,000
M	30,000
J	32,000

Solution: First, we will enter the data in Excel and follow the following command:

> Select the Data → Go to Insert Option → Select Bar Option → From the Drop-down Menu of Bar Option, Select Any Option of Your Choice → Right-click in the Middle of the Newly Created Graph → Select the Option Add Data Labels.

After giving this command, we will be presented with a graph as shown in Figure 7.4.

FIGURE 7.4
Bar Graph

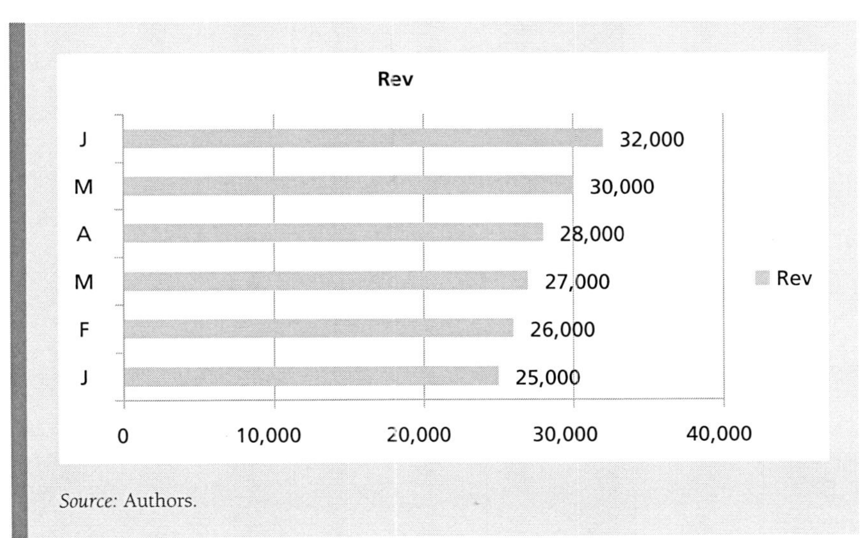

Source: Authors.

If we want to give a suitable title to the graph, then we will have to select the 'Design' option and then go to the 'Chart Layout' option and from its drop-down menu, select the first option. Then, we will get a space to write the title of the graph.

If we select the 'Design' option and then press the option 'Switch Row/column', then the entire chart will look as that shown in Figure 7.5.

FIGURE 7.5
Bar Graph (Switch Row/Column)

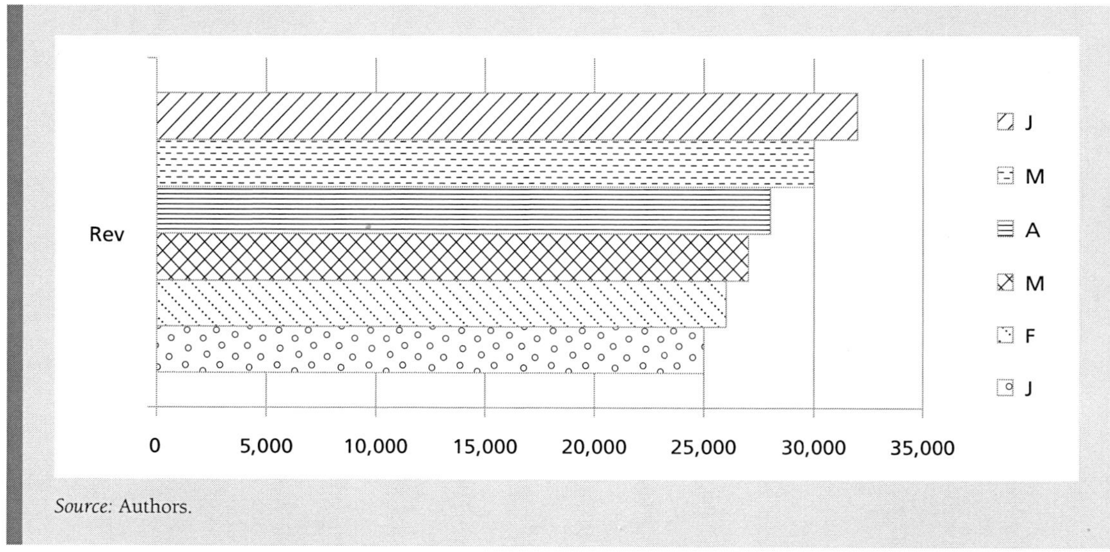

Source: Authors.

7.6.2. Column Chart

Column chart is one of the popular methods of presenting frequency distribution graphically. It can be defined as a set of rectangles, each proportional in width to the range of the values within a class and proportional in height to the class frequencies of the respective class interval.

Let us take the earlier example to comprehend the procedure of constructing a column chart.

First, we will enter the data in Excel and follow the following command:

> Select the Data → Go to Insert Option → Select Column Option → From Drop-down Menu of Column Option, Select Any Option of Your Choice.

After giving this command, we will be presented with a graph as shown in Figure 7.6.

Now, if we right-click in the middle of the newly created Graph and select the option 'Add Data Labels', then we will be presented with a graph as shown in Figure 7.7.

If we select the 'Design' option and then press the option 'Switch Row/column', then the entire chart will look as shown in Figure 7.8.

FIGURE 7.6
Column Graph

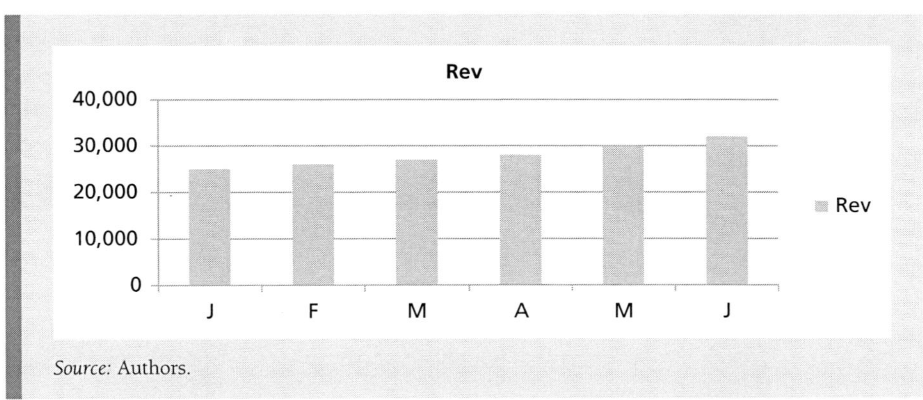

Source: Authors.

FIGURE 7.7
Column Graph (Add Data Labels)

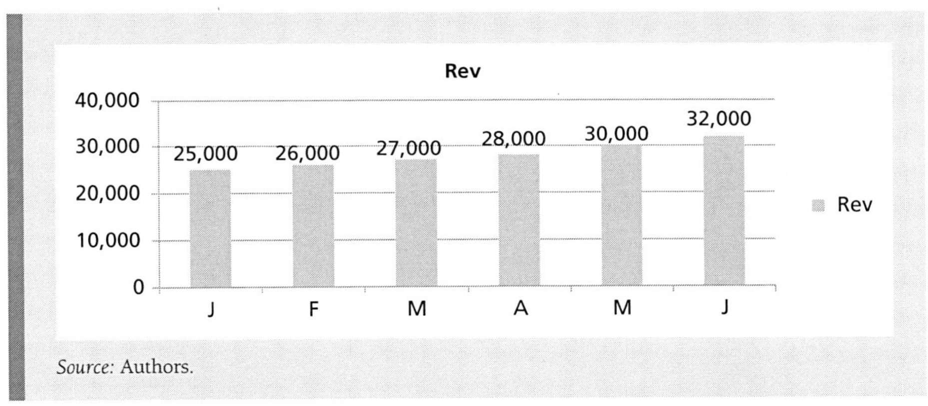

Source: Authors.

FIGURE 7.8
Column Graph (Switch Row/Column)

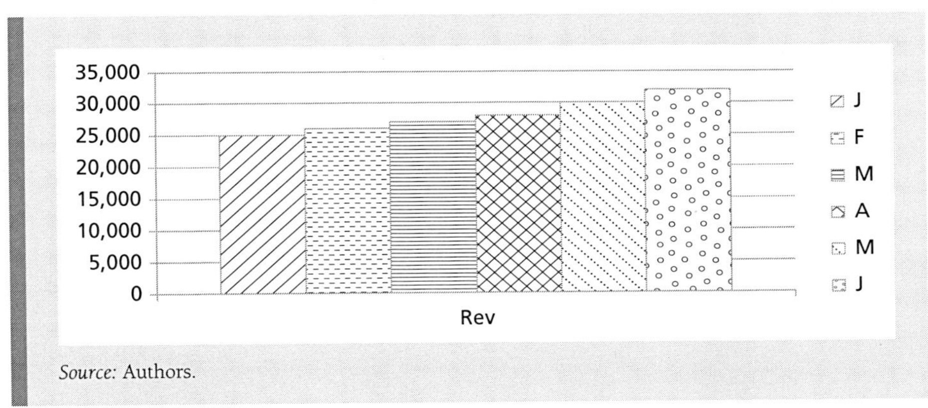

Source: Authors.

After getting the graph, if we want to add data labels, then we have to select every column separately and select the option 'Add Data Labels'. Thereafter, we will be presented with a graph as shown in Figure 7.9.

FIGURE 7.9
Column Graph (Add Data Labels)

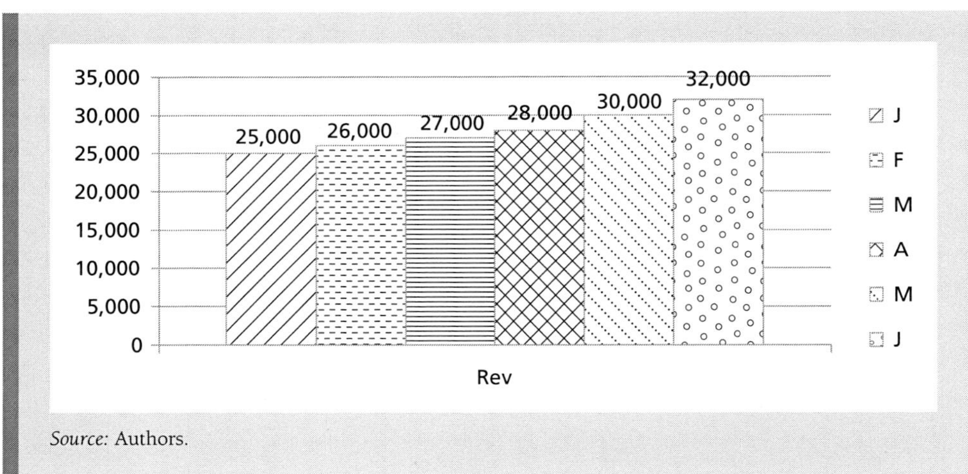

Source: Authors.

If we want to give a suitable title to the graph, then we will have to select the 'Design' option and go to the 'Chart Layout' option and from its drop-down menu, select the first option. Then, we will get a space to write the title of the graph. It will look as the graph shown in Figure 7.10.

FIGURE 7.10
Column Graph (Chart Layout)

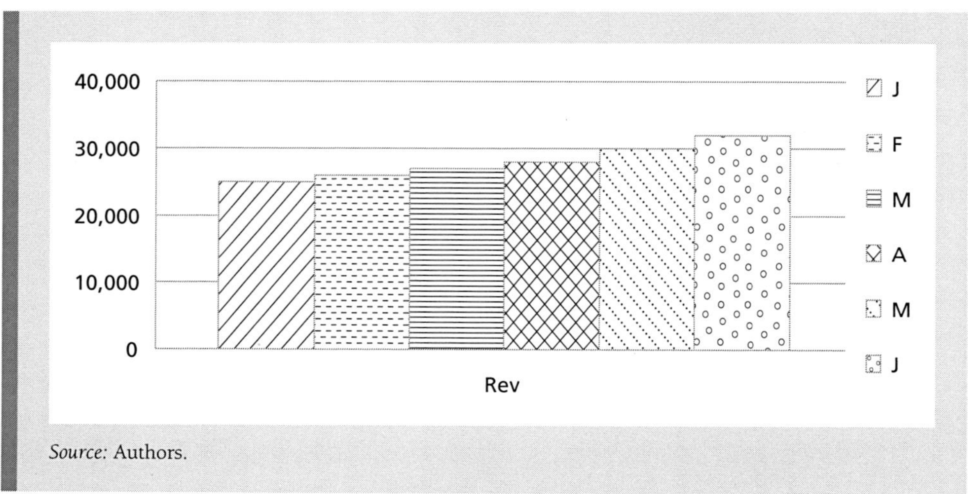

Source: Authors.

7.6.3. Pie Chart

A pie chart represents the data in which a circle is divided into sectors, with areas equal to the corresponding component. As it is a circular presentation, each component proportion is multiplied by 360 in order to get the respective degree of each component of the circle.

Let us take an example to comprehend the procedure of constructing a pie chart.

Example: Construct a pie chart for the following data:

Dogs	1,110
Cats	987
Rodents	312
Reptiles	97
Fish	398

Solution: First, we will enter the above data in Excel and follow the following command:

> Select the Data → Go to Insert Option → Select Pie Option → From the Drop-down Menu of Pie Option, Select Any Option of Your Choice.

After giving this command, we will be presented with a graph as shown in Figure 7.11.

Now, if we right-click in the middle of the newly created graph and select the option 'Add Data Labels', then we will be presented with a graph as shown in Figure 7.12.

FIGURE 7.11
Pie Chart

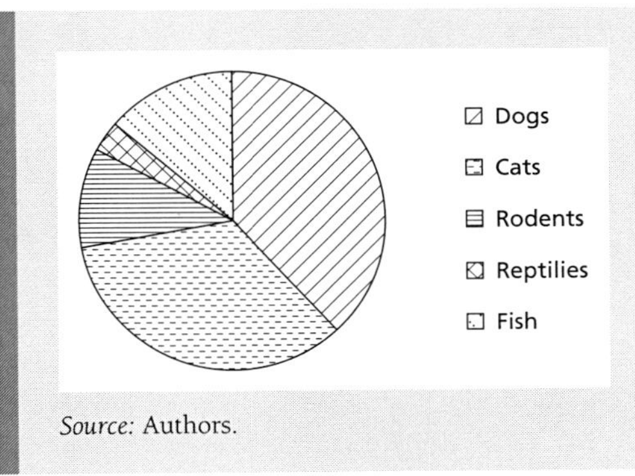

Source: Authors.

FIGURE 7.12
Pie Chart (Add Data Labels)

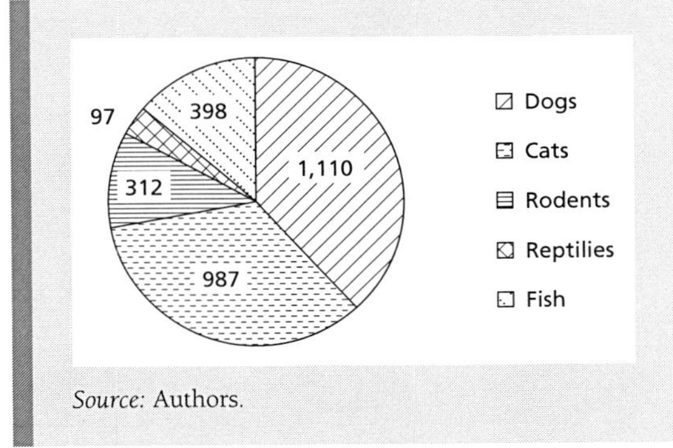

Source: Authors.

7.6.4. Scatter Plot

A scatter plot represents the graphical representation of bivariate data in order to express the nature of relationship between two variables. It is widely applied in correlation and regression. Let us take an example to comprehend the procedure of constructing a scatter plot.

Example: Construct a scatter plot for income and expenses

Income	Expenses
100	40
120	50
130	45
140	70
150	100
200	140
250	180
500	400

Solution: First, we will enter the data in Excel and follow the following command:

> Select the Data → Go to Insert Option → Select Scatter Option → From the Drop-down Menu of Scatter, Select Any Option of Your Choice.

After giving this command, we will be presented with a graph as shown in Figure 7.13.

FIGURE 7.13
Scatter Plot

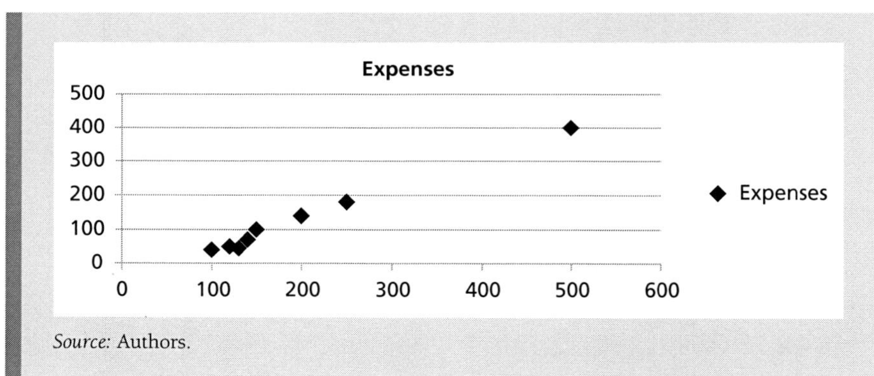

Source: Authors.

7.6.5. Line Chart

A line chart represents separate lines for separate variables.

Let us take an example to comprehend the procedure of constructing a line graph.

Example: Construct a line chart for the following data:

Salesman	January	February	March	April	May
A	200	300	300	100	300
B	100	400	200	200	800
C	400	600	600	100	600

Solution: First, we will enter the data in Excel and follow the following command:

> Select the Data → Go to Insert Option → Select Line Option → From the Drop-down Menu of Line Options, Select Any Option of Your Choice.

After giving this command, we will be presented with a line graph as shown in Figure 7.14.

FIGURE 7.14
Line Chart

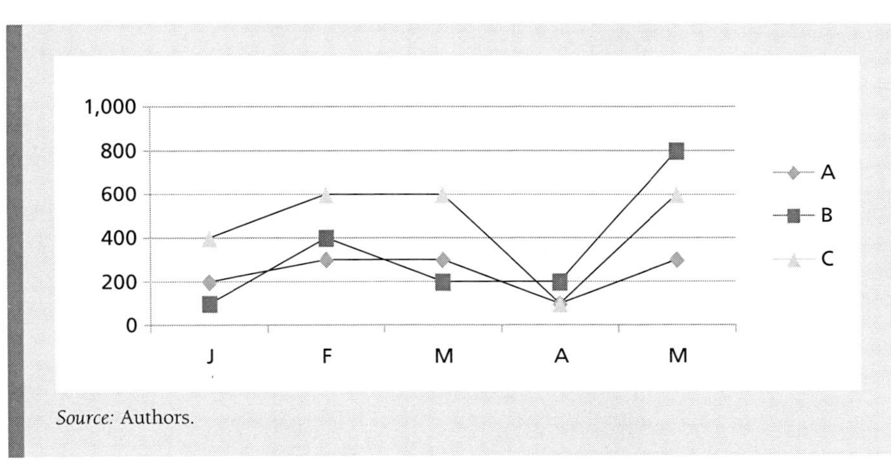

Source: Authors.

7.6.6. Two-variables Line Chart

Let us take an example to comprehend the procedure of constructing a two-variables line chart.

Example: Construct a two-variables line chart for the following data:

Year	Users	Percentage
2000	100	10
2001	200	20
2002	300	30
2003	400	40
2004	500	50
2005	600	60
2006	700	70
2007	800	80
2008	900	90
2009	1,000	100

Solution: First, we will enter the data in Excel and follow the following command:

> Select the Data → Go to Insert Option → Select Line Option → From the Drop-down Menu of Line Options, Select Any Option of Your Choice.

After giving this command, we will be presented with a two-variables line chart as shown in Figure 7.15.

FIGURE 7.15
Two-variables Line Chart

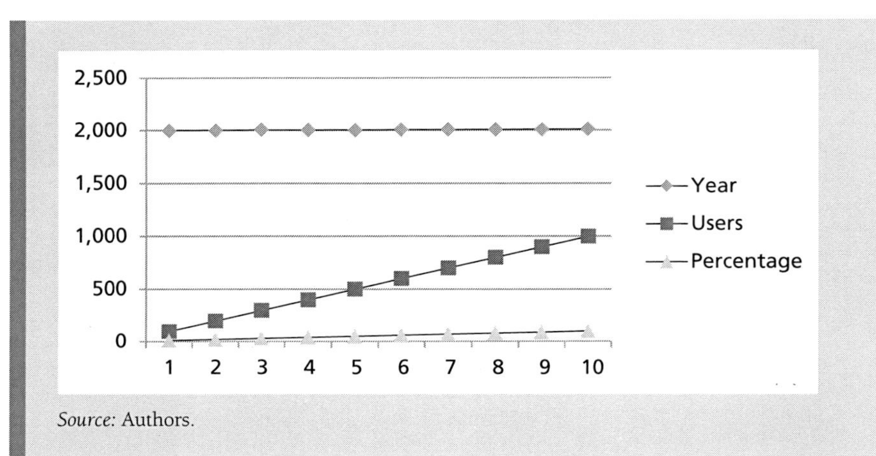

Source: Authors.

After getting the two-variables line graph, we will select the percentage line and right-click. Then, we will select the option 'format data series' and under the 'series' option, we will select 'secondary axis option' and then close the dialog box. Finally, we will get a graph as shown in Figure 7.16.

FIGURE 7.16
Two-variables Line Chart (Secondary Axis Option)

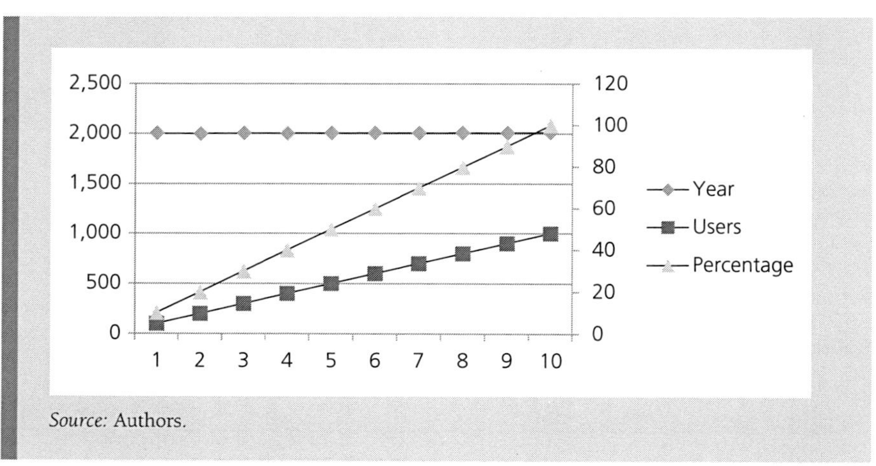

Source: Authors.

7.6.7. Multiple Data Sets on Line Chart

Let us take an example to comprehend the procedure of constructing multiple data sets on line chart.

Example: Construct multiple data sets on line chart using the following data:

Month	Rev	North	South	East	West
Jan	25,000	300	400	500	600
Feb	26,000	340	440	540	640
Mar	27,000	380	480	580	680
Apr	28,000	400	500	600	700
May	30,000	420	520	620	720
Jun	32,000	450	550	650	750

Solution: First, we will enter the data in Excel and follow the following command:

> Select the Data → Go to Insert Option → Select Line Option → From the Drop-down Menu of Line Options, Select Any Option of Your Choice.

After giving the command, we will be presented with a chart as shown in Figure 7.17.

FIGURE 7.17
Multiple Data Sets on Line Chart

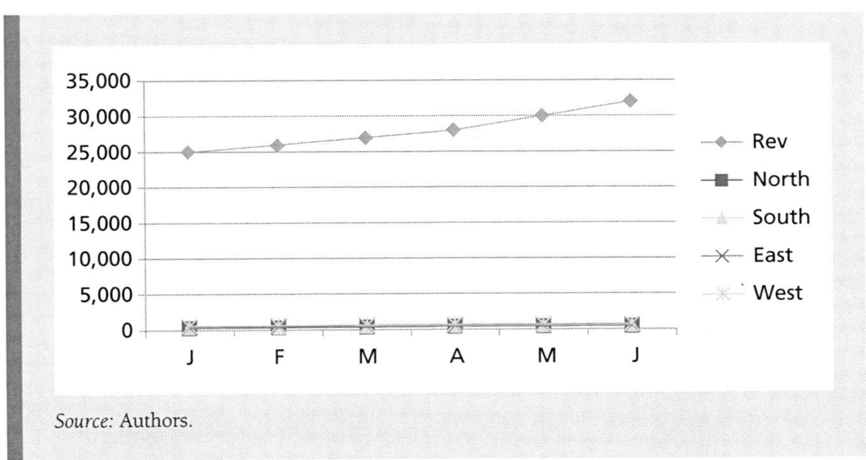

Source: Authors.

In this chart, we observe that four lines mingle with one another. In order to separate them from each other, we have to select any one of the four lines and right-click and select the option 'format data series'. After that, we will select 'secondary axis option' and then close the dialog box. We will repeat the procedure for other three lines also. Finally, we will get a graph as shown in Figure 7.18.

FIGURE 7.18
Multiple Data Sets on Line Chart (Secondary Axis Option)

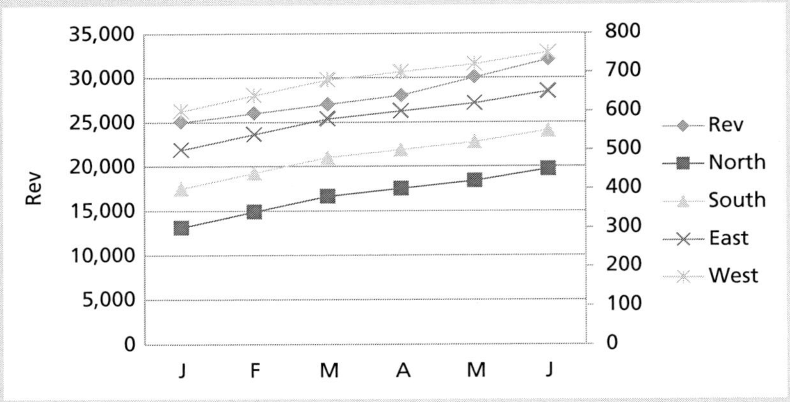

Source: Authors.

After getting the graph, we will select the right axis and right-click. Then, we will select the option 'format axis'. Now, we can select 'fixed' in 'Axis Options' and then close the dialog box.

7.6.8. Combination of Column and Line Chart

Let us take an example to comprehend the procedure of combining of column and line chart.

Example: Construct a combination of a column and line chart using the following data:

Month	Rev	North
J	25,000	300
F	26,000	340
M	27,000	380
A	28,000	400
M	30,000	420
J	32,000	450

Solution: First, we will enter the data in Excel and follow the following command:

> Select the Data → Go to Insert Option → Select Column Option → From the Drop-down Menu of Column Option Select the First Design from 2D Column.

After giving this command, we will be presented with a chart as shown in Figure 7.19.

FIGURE 7.19
Combination of Column and Line Chart

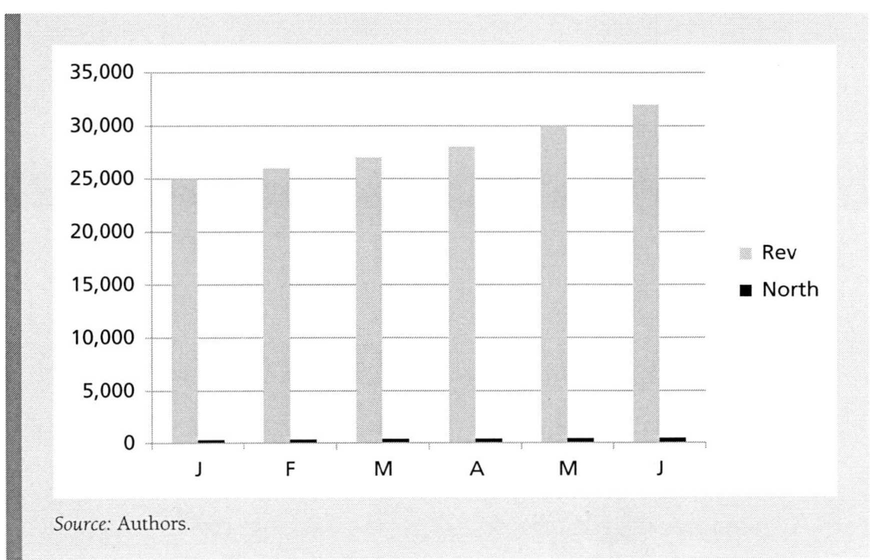

Source: Authors.

Now, we will select the revenue lines and by right-clicking we will select the option 'Change Series Chart Type' and select the fourth design of the line and click on the 'OK' option. This will give us a chart as shown in Figure 7.20.

FIGURE 7.20
Combination of Column and Line Chart (Change Series Chart Type)

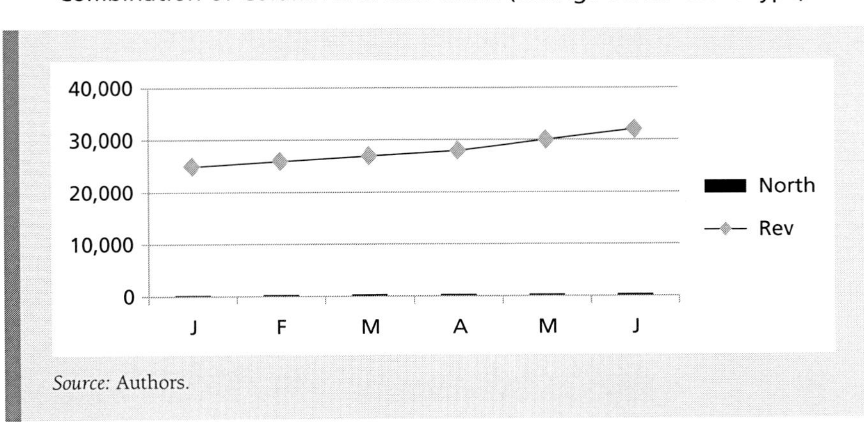

Source: Authors.

Again, we have to select the line and by right-clicking we will select the option 'Format Data Series' and from the series dialog box, we have to select the secondary axis and select the close option. Then, we will get a chart as shown in Figure 7.21.

FIGURE 7.21
Combination of Column and Line Chart (Format Data Series)

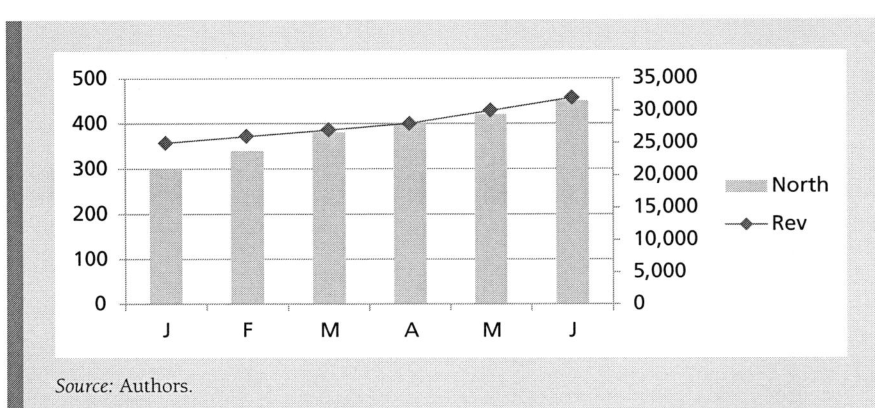

Source: Authors.

Now, we right-click within the box and select the 'move chart' option and select the New Sheet. Selecting any point of the green line, if we right-click and choose the option 'Add Trend Line' and tick the option 'Display Equation on Chart' and close it, then the trend equation will be clearly shown in the chart (Figure 7.22).

FIGURE 7.22
Combination of Column and Line Chart (Add Trend Line)

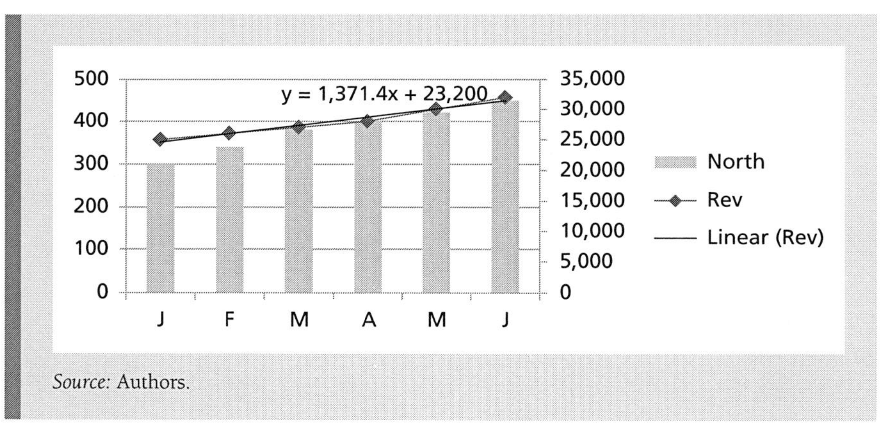

Source: Authors.

SUMMARY

Data is a collection of facts, such as numbers, words, measurements, observations or even just descriptions of things. It can be classified into two different types. These are quantitative data and qualitative data. A variable differing in quantity is called quantitative variable. There are two types of quantitative data—continuous and discrete. Depending on their intended use, variables may be classified as independent, dependent, moderating, mediating or control variables. Descriptive statistics are numbers that are used to summarize and describe data. Descriptive statistics provide a concise summary of data. We can summarize data numerically or graphically. Typically, there are two general types of statistic (measures of central tendency and measures of spread) that are used to describe data. With the help of SPSS, we can calculate four types of descriptive statistics such as Frequencies, Crosstabs, Descriptives and Explore. Graphical presentation of data helps the researcher to understand the specific shape of the distribution of data. Some of the commonly used methods of presenting data in graphs are bar chart, column chart, pie chart, scatter plot, line chart, two-variables line chart, multiple data sets on line chart and combination of column and line chart.

KEY TERMS

quantitative data (73)
continuous and discrete data (74)
qualitative data (74)
binary data (74)
nominal values (74)
ordinal values (74)
independent and dependent variable (74)
moderating and mediating variables (74)
control variables (74)
measures of central tendency (75)
measures of spread (75)
Frequencies (76)
Crosstabs (76)
Descriptives (76)
Explore (76)
valid and missing data (83)
stem-and-leaf plots (83)
box plot (83)
std. error (83)
95% confidence interval for mean upper and lower bound (83)
5% trimmed mean (83)
Tukey's hinges (83)
histogram (83)
skewness (84)
kurtosis (84)
bar chart (85)
column chart (86)
pie chart (89)
scatter plot (89)
line chart (90)
two-variables line chart (91)
multiple data sets on line chart (93)
combination of column and line chart (94)

EXERCISES

1. Classify different types of data.
2. Classify different types of variables.
3. Define descriptive statistics. How do you interpret descriptive statistics through SPSS?
4. Distinguish between quantitative data and qualitative data.
5. Distinguish between continuous and discrete data.
6. Distinguish between moderating and control variables.
7. Explain different types of graphs for representing data, with examples.
8. Describe each of the following:
   a. Measures of central tendency
   b. Measures of spread
   c. Histogram
   d. Skewness
   e. Kurtosis

9. Draw a pie chart using the following data:

Types	Monthly Family Expenses
Food	6,500
Rent	2,500
Clothes	1,000
Education	1,700
Savings	2,700
Miscellaneous	1,300

10. The number of male, female and child labours in two states (A and B) in a year is recorded in the following table. Represent the data by means of a suitable diagram.

State	Male	Female	Child
A	250,000	135,000	115,000
B	310,000	205,000	145,000

11. The following table lists the daily profits and losses of 14 days (2 weeks) of a business organization. Represent the data by means of a suitable diagram.

Days	1	2	3	4	5	6	7	8	9	10	11	12	13	14
Profit (₹)	945	815	–	470	–	–	350	–	560	610	–	350	300	125
Loss (₹)	–	–	250	–	600	280	–	275	–	–	150	–	–	–

CHAPTER

8

Online Analytical Processing

LEARNING OBJECTIVES

After studying this chapter, you should be able to

- Understand the concept of online analytical processing (OLAP).
- Learn the applied area of OLAP in research.

8.1. MEANING OF OLAP

The OLAP cubes procedure calculates totals, means and other univariate statistics for continuous summary variables within categories of one or more categorical grouping variables. A separate layer in the table is created for each category of each grouping variable.

It is used to compare the performance between grouping variables. Under this analysis, two types of variables are considered. One is called summary variable or continuous variable which is measured using ratio or interval scale. The other variable is grouping variable or categorical variable. Summary variables are quantitative while the values of categorical variables can be numeric or string.

Example

Total and average sales for different regions are available here. An example is the total and average sale for different regions, in which sale is a summary variable that is measured using the ratio scale and region is considered a categorical variable.

Data

The summary variables are quantitative (continuous variables measured on an interval or ratio scale) and the grouping variables are categorical. The values of categorical variables can be numeric or string.

8.2. TEST PROCEDURE IN SPSS STATISTICS

The following steps will demonstrate how to analyse data using OLAP in SPSS statistics. At the end of these steps, we will discuss how to interpret the results from this test. We have considered the data set shown in Table 8.1 for the OLAP procedure in SPSS.

We have taken two summary variables which are age and education in the data set that we have considered. On the other hand, we have also taken two grouping variables which are sex and region.

After entering the data, we will follow the following command to obtain OLAP cubes:

> Click Analyze → Reports → OLAP Cubes → Select and Transfer Summary as Well as Grouping Variables → OK.

We can select one or more continuous summary variable as well as one or more categorical grouping variable.

After giving the aforementioned command, we will get output Tables 8.2 and 8.3.

If we double click on OLAP cubes, then a top-down menu will appear. With the help of this menu, we can easily get gender- and region-wise age and education.

Suppose, by using the top-down menu, we have selected 'Male' from 'Sex' and 'North' region from the 'Region' option. Then we will get the result as shown in Table 8.4.

TABLE 8.1
Data Set for OLAP

Sex	Region	Age	Education
1	1	61	12
2	1	32	20
1	1	35	20
2	1	26	20
1	2	25	12
1	2	59	10
2	2	46	10
2	3	99	16
1	3	57	10
2	1	64	14
1	1	72	9
2	2	67	12
1	3	33	14
2	3	30	15
1	2	50	10

Source: Authors.

TABLE 8.2
Case Processing Summary

	Cases					
	Included		Excluded		Total	
	N	%	*N*	%	*N*	%
Education * Sex * Region	15	100.0	0	0.0	15	100.0
Age * Sex * Region	15	100.0	0	0.0	15	100.0

Source: Authors.

TABLE 8.3
OLAP Cubes (Step 1)

	Sum	*N*	Mean	Std. Deviation	Percentage of Total Sum	Percentage of Total *N*
Age	756.00	15	50.4000	20.82855	100%	100%
Education	204.00	15	13.6000	3.88771	100%	100%

Source: Authors.
Notes: Sex: 15 (Total number of candidates either male or female).
Region: 3 (Total number of regions).

TABLE 8.4
OLAP Cubes (Step 2)

	Sum	*N*	Mean	Std. Deviation	Percentage of Total Sum	Percentage of Total *N*
Age	168.00	3	56.0000	19.00000	22.2%	20.0%
Education	41.00	3	13.6667	5.68624	20.1%	20.0%

Source: Authors.
Notes: Sex: Male (Total number of male candidates).
Region: North (Total number of candidates from the North).

SUMMARY

OLAP is used to compare the performance between grouping variables. Under this analysis, two types of variables are considered. One is called summary variable which is measured using ratio or interval scale. The other variable is grouping variable or categorical variable.

KEY TERMS

OLAP (99)
summary variable (99)
grouping variable (99)

EXERCISES

1. What is the purpose of OLAP in research?
2. Apply the OLAP tool in SPSS with the following information:

Sex	Education
1	22
2	20
1	20
2	10
1	19
1	18
2	11
2	12
1	17
2	11
1	19
2	12
1	18
2	13
1	18

CHAPTER

9

Growth Rate

LEARNING OBJECTIVES

After studying this chapter, you should be able to

- Learn the computation procedure of average annual growth rate (AAGR).
- Understand the computation procedure of compound annual growth rate (CAGR).
- Understand the concept of profit percentage and the computation process.
- Know the concept of sales by value versus sales by volume.

9.1. AVERAGE ANNUAL GROWTH RATE

AAGR is the arithmetic mean of a series of growth rates, and it is easily calculated using a normal average formula. However, it totally ignores the compounding effects and, therefore, the growth of an investment can be overestimated.

9.2. COMPUTATION OF AAGR

From Table 9.1, we can calculate the AAGR of the number of bikes sold from 2011 to 2015.

Simple annual growth rate or AAGR of number of bikes sold from 2011 to 2015 = [(6000 – 2000)/2000] × 100 × 1/4 = 50%.

Here, no. of years = 5 years and the period is = 4 years.

How can we calculate the AAGR using Excel? Table 9.2 provides year-wise sales value of a company. From this information, we have calculated the annual growth rate by using the following formula. For example, annual growth rate in 2012 = [(12 – 10)/10] × 100 = 20%. In this way, we have computed the annual growth rate in 2013, 2014, 2015 and 2016.

Now, if we use the formula of '= Average (Position of 20: Position of 29.41)', then we will get the value of AAGR, that is, 18.154%.

TABLE 9.1
Information on Bikes Sold (Year-wise)

Year	2011	2012	2013	2014	2015
Bikes sold	2,000	5,000	1,000	7,000	6,000

Source: Authors.

TABLE 9.2
AAGR Calculation

Year	Sales	Annual Growth Rate
2011	10	–
2012	12	**20**
2013	11	–8.33
2014	15	36.36
2015	17	13.33
2016	22	**29.41**
	AAGR	**18.154**

Source: Authors.
Note: Bold values in the table indicate the different positions of the values.

9.3. COMPOUND ANNUAL GROWTH RATE

The CAGR measures the return on an investment over a certain period of time. It is the mean annual growth rate of an investment over a specified period of time longer than one year.

The concept of the CAGR is relatively straightforward and requires only three primary inputs—an investment's beginning value, ending value and the time period. The CAGR represents the growth rate of an initial investment assuming it is compounding by the period of time specified.

Most simply, the CAGR can be used to calculate the average growth of a single investment. Because of market volatility, the year-to-year growth of an investment may be difficult to interpret. For example, an investment may increase in value by 8% in one year, decrease in value by 2% the following year and increase in value by 5% in the next. With inconsistent annual growth, CAGR may be used to give a broader picture of an investment's progress.

9.4. COMPUTATION OF THE CAGR

9.4.1. FORMULA OF THE CAGR

Following is an overview of how to calculate the CAGR manually, and in Excel. The generic CAGR formula used in business, finance and investment analysis in Excel is as follows:

'= (EV/BV) ^ (1/n) – 1'

where BV is the beginning value of investment, EV is the ending value of investment and n is the number of periods (such as years, quarters, months and days).

9.4.2. A Brief Example of the CAGR Calculation

Assume that an investment's beginning value is 1,000 and it grows to 5,000 in 10 years. The CAGR calculation is as follows:

$$= ((5000/1000) \wedge (1/10)) - 1.$$

The CAGR is 17.4% and details that the investment grew at this annual rate for a decade.

Table 9.3 provides year-wise sales value of a company. From this information, we have calculated the CAGR.

At the time of calculation of the CAGR in Excel, we will use the following formula: '= (End Value/ Start Value) ^ (1/n) – 1' = (Position of 22/Position of 10) ^ (1/5) – 1. Then we will get the CAGR, that is, 0.170804913 = 17.08%. Here, n = number of periods = 4 years.

9.5. PROFIT PERCENTAGE

From Table 9.4, we will compute the profit percentage and percentage change in profit percentage.

TABLE 9.3
CAGR Calculation

Year	Sales
2011	10
2012	12
2013	11
2014	15
2015	17
2016	22
CAGR	0.170804913

Source: Authors.

TABLE 9.4
Information on Sales and Profit (Year-wise)

Years	2012	2013	2014	2015	2016
Sales	200	240	260	320	350
Profit	40	50	60	70	50

Source: Authors.

TABLE 9.5
Sales by Value Versus Sales by Volume

Year	2014	2015	2016
Sales by volume	500	700	800
Sales by value	15,000	21,000	64,000

Source: Authors.

Suppose that the question is what the profit percentage in 2012 is.

We know that Profit = Sales – Cost
Therefore, Cost = Sales – Profit = 200 – 40 = 160
Profit Percentage = (40 × 100)/160 = 25%

Now, the question is what is the percentage change in profit percentage in the year 2015 over that in 2014?

Again using Table 9.4, we calculate the following:

Profit percentage in the year 2015 = (70 × 100)/250 = 28%

Profit percentage in the year 2014 = (60 × 100)/200 = 30%

Therefore, percentage change in profit percentage in the year 2015 over that in 2014 = [(28 – 30)/30] × 100 = –6.66%.

9.6. SALES BY VALUE VERSUS SALES BY VOLUME

If we want to know the price per unit, then we will apply the following ratio, that is, sales by value/sales by volume. From Table 9.5, we have determined price per unit in 2015 and price per unit in 2016.

Price per unit in 2015 = 21,000/700 = 30
Price per unit in 2016 = 64,000/800 = 80

If we know the price per unit in two periods, then we can also determine the percentage increase in price of one unit between two periods. Here, percentage increase in price of one unit in 2016 over 2015 = [(80 – 30)/30] × 100 = 166.67%.

SUMMARY

AAGR is the arithmetic mean of a series of growth rates, and it is easily calculated using a normal average formula. On the other hand, the CAGR is the mean annual growth rate of an investment over a specified period of time longer than one year. If we want to know the price per unit, then we will apply the following ratio, that is, sales by value/sales by volume.

KEY TERMS

average annual growth rate (103)
compound annual growth rate (104)
profit percentage (105)
sales by value versus sales by volume (106)

EXERCISES

1. What is AAGR?
2. What do you mean by CAGR?
3. How is Profit Percentage calculated?
4. What are the implications of Sales by Value and Sales by Volume?
5. From the following table, calculate AAGR of number of cars sold from 2012 to 2016.

Year	2012	2013	2014	2015	2016
Bikes Sold	2,000	4,000	1,000	5,000	6,000

6. From the following table, calculate CAGR.

Year	Sales
2013	10
2014	12
2015	11
2016	15

7. From the following information, compute profit percentage and percentage change in profit percentage.

Years	2013	2014	2015	2016	2017
Sales	220	240	260	300	330
Profit	40	60	60	70	70

8. From the following information, determine price per unit in 2016 and price per unit in 2017.

Year	2015	2016	2017
Sales by Volume	500	700	800
Sales by Value	25,000	30,000	50,000

CHAPTER

10

Hypothesis Testing and Normality Test

LEARNING OBJECTIVES

After studying this chapter, you should be able to

- Understand the concept and formation of hypothesis in any research study.
- Know the attributes and different types of hypothesis.
- Learn the application of hypothesis in different scenario.
- Understand the concept and importance of normality testing in research study.
- Learn how normality of data sets can be evaluated with the help of SPSS statistical software.

10.1. CONCEPT OF HYPOTHESIS

Hypothesis is a predictive statement of assumption or supposition to be proved or disproved by statistical means. In social science research, where population parameter(s) is not available, hypothesis testing is used in that case for deciding whether a sample data support the problem statement. Hypothesis testing helps to prepare probability statements about population parameter(s). It helps to guide some investigation or highly probable established facts. Few examples of hypotheses are as follows:

Examples of Hypotheses:

'Overall performance of Student A is same as the overall performance of Student B'
'Efficiencies of the employees are same before and after the training programme'

Here, hypotheses are verified and tested to fulfil the objectives of the research as per the problem statement. So we can say that hypothesis testing is a proposition to check the validity of the problem statement of a research. A hypothesis can be 'descriptive' or 'relational' in nature. Descriptive hypothesis is a statement which indicates trends or behaviour of the population under a research study. On the other hand, relational hypothesis is a statement which indicates the relationship between two variables. 'One-tailed hypothesis' (directional hypothesis) indicates the direction of a research study by using the words increase, decrease, less than or more than. 'Two-tailed hypothesis' does not indicate any expected direction of relationship under a research study.

10.2. BASIC ATTRIBUTES OF HYPOTHESIS

The basic attributes of hypothesis have been listed as follows:

- A hypothesis must be clear and specific.
- It should be stated in a simple and understandable way for all concerned. On the other hand, simplicity does not have any impact on the significance of hypothesis.
- It should be consistent with known established facts from literature review.
- It must be agreeable to testing within a specific time frame.
- It should indicate the relationship between variables and be capable of being tested.

10.3. NULL AND ALTERNATIVE HYPOTHESIS

If we want to establish the assumption that two or more sample data from different population are equal, then this assumption is called as the null hypothesis. As against this, if we propose that they are not equal to each other ($\neq$ or $<$ or $>$), then the assumption is called the alternative hypothesis. When sample attributes do not support the null hypothesis, we can conclude that the alternative hypothesis is true and the null hypothesis is false. Here, the null hypothesis is denoted by H_0 and the alternative hypothesis is denoted by H_1.

10.4. TYPE-I AND TYPE-II ERRORS

There are mainly two types of errors in hypothesis testing. The first error is rejecting a null hypothesis when it is true (type-I error) and the second error is accepting a null hypothesis when it is false (type-II error). Type-I error is represented by α (alpha) called α error or testing level of significance. Type-II error is represented by β (beta) called β error (Table 10.1).

TABLE 10.1
Type-I and Type-II Errors

	Accept H_0	Reject H_0
H_0 (True)	Correct	Type-I error (α error)
H_0 (False)	Type-II error (β error)	Correct

Source: Levin and Rubin (2009).

10.5. ACCEPTANCE AND REJECTION REGION FOR ONE- AND TWO-TAILED TEST

The null hypothesis is rejected if the statistically calculated standardized value (Z) from a research study is greater than the standardized table value of Z (Z [calculated value] >Z [tabulated value]). Therefore, it falls in the 'rejection region'. The null hypothesis is accepted if the statistically calculated standardized value (Z) from a research study is less than the standardized table value of Z (Z [calculated value] <Z [tabulated value]). Therefore, it falls in the 'acceptance region'. For a one-tailed test, the rejection region is occupied only on one side (right or left) of the sampling distribution as shown in Figures 10.1 and 10.2.

FIGURE 10.1
Acceptance and Rejection Region for One-tailed Test (Right Tail) with α Significance Level

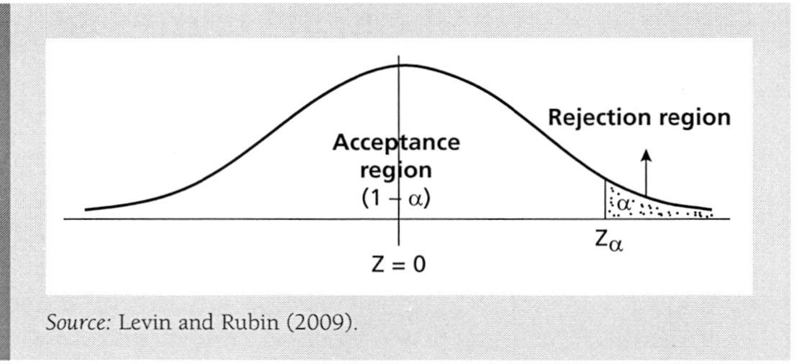

Source: Levin and Rubin (2009).

FIGURE 10.2
Acceptance and Rejection Region for One-tailed Test (Left Tail) with α Significance Level

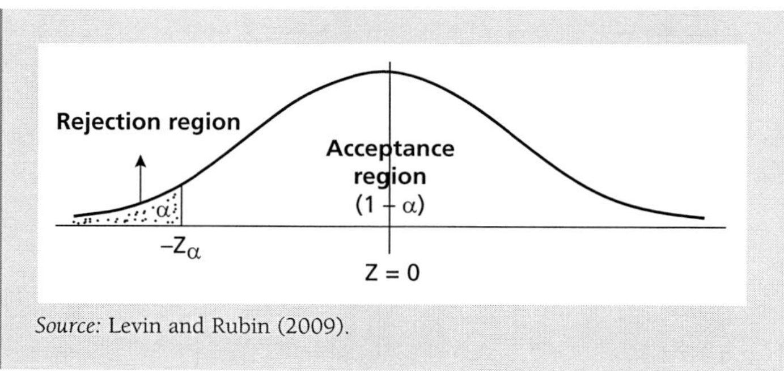

Source: Levin and Rubin (2009).

For a two-tailed test, the rejection region is occupied on both the sides of the sampling distribution as shown in Figure 10.3. Here, the null hypothesis is rejected, if the sample statistics (calculated value) is significantly higher than or lower than the hypothesized population parameter (tabulated value).

Some important 'table values' of Z at different significant levels for two-tailed and one-tailed tests are given in the Table 10.2.

10.6. CONCEPT OF NORMAL DISTRIBUTION CURVE AND NORMALITY TEST

Normal distribution which is used in normality test for data is the most important continuous probability distribution. It is also called the Gaussian distribution. One of the assumptions for most parametric tests to be reliable is that the data is approximately normally distributed. The normal distribution peaks in the middle and is symmetrical about the mean. In the case of a normal distribution curve, the value of mean, median and mode are the same. The two tails of the normal distribution extend indefinitely and do not touch the horizontal axis. Data do not need to be perfectly normally distributed for the tests to be reliable. Normal distribution comes close to fitting the actual frequency distributions of many cases such as characteristics and behaviour of human being. From Figure 10.4, we can understand that 99.7% (approximately) of all the data in normally distributed population lie within ± 3σ (σ = standard deviation) from μ (μ = mean).

FIGURE 10.3
Acceptance and Rejection Region for Two-tailed Test with α Significance Level

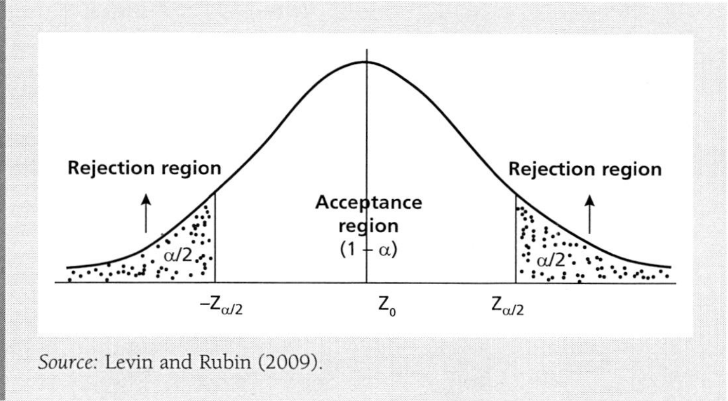

Source: Levin and Rubin (2009).

10.7. NORMALITY TEST WITH SPSS

Given a set of data, say examination scores and gender, we would like to check if the distribution is normal or not.

In this example, the null hypothesis is that the data is normally distributed and the alternative hypothesis is that the data is not normally distributed.

TABLE 10.2
Some Important 'Table Values' of Z at Different Significant Levels

Significant Levels	Two-sided Test	One-sided Test Right (R) and Left (L)
10%	–1.645 and +1.645	+1.282 (R) –1.282 (L)
5%	–1.96 and +1.96	+1.645 (R) –1.645 (L)
2%	–2.326 and +2.326	+2.054 (R) –2.054 (L)
1%	–2.575 and +2.575	+2.326 (R) –2.326 (L)

Source: Levin and Rubin (2009).

FIGURE 10.4
Normal Distribution Curve

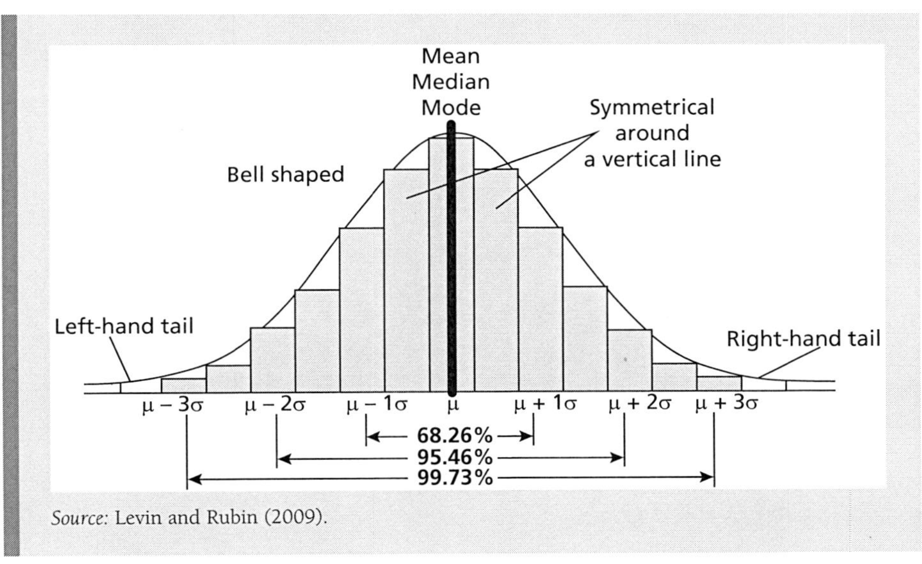

Source: Levin and Rubin (2009).

Click Analyze → Descriptive Statistics → Explore (see Exhibit 10.1).

EXHIBIT 10.1
SPSS Window for Normality Test (1)

Then, you will be presented with the 'Explore' dialog box, as shown in Exhibit 10.2.

If you want to establish whether your variable is normally distributed for each level of your independent variable, transfer the variables that need to be tested for normality into the 'Dependent List' and others in the 'Factor List' box by drag-and-drop. In this example, we transfer the 'Exam_scores' variable into the 'Dependent List' box and 'gender' in 'Factor List'. You will have to click on the 'Plots' option thereon and then you will be presented with a screen as shown in Exhibit 10.3.

EXHIBIT 10.2
SPSS Window for Normality Test (2)

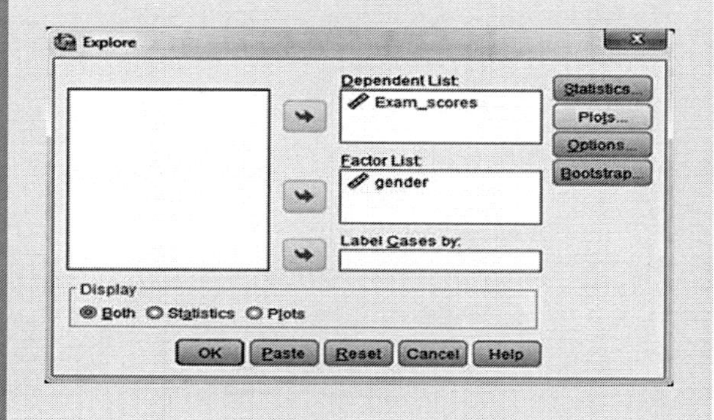

Here you have to mark against the 'Histogram' and 'Normality plots with tests' checkboxes, then click on the 'Continue' option and finally select 'OK' to get the outcome. The result will pop out in the output window.

EXHIBIT 10.3
SPSS Window for Normality Test (3)

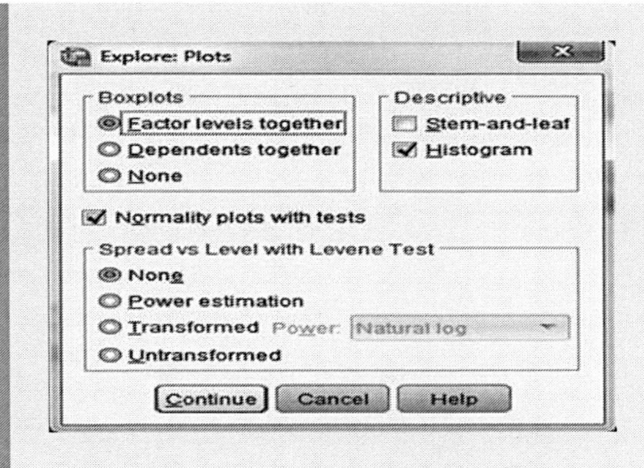

10.8. EXPLANATION OF SPSS OUTPUT FOR NORMALITY TEST

You will now see that the output has been split into separate sections based on the combination of groups of the two independent variables. In our example, we have considered the exam scores of 50 students consisting of males and females, where male students are 23 and females are 27. The case processing summary of the SPSS output has been presented in Table 10.3.

The skewness and kurtosis measures should be as close to zero as possible, in SPSS. In reality, however, data are often skewed and kurtotic. A small departure from 'zero' is therefore no problem, as long as the measures are not too large compared to their standard errors. As a consequence, you must divide the measure by its standard error; this will give you the Z-value, which should be somewhere between –1.96 and +1.96.

In the case of male, to calculate the skewness of the Z-value, divide the skewness measure by its standard error, that is, for males the value of skewness is –0.818/0.481 = –1.700 and the value of kurtosis is 0.110/0.935 = 0.117. In both the cases, the Z-value is neither below –1.96 nor above +1.96. Similarly, in the case of females, the skewness is 0.120 and the value of kurtosis –0.009. From the descriptives statistics (see Table 10.4), we can conclude that our data is normally distributed.

The test statistics are shown in Table 10.5. Here, two tests for normality are run. For data sets smaller than 2,000 elements, we use the Shapiro–Wilk test; otherwise, the Kolmogorov–Smirnov test is used. In our case, since we have only 50 elements, the Shapiro–Wilk test has to be taken into consideration.

The null hypothesis for this test of normality is that the data are normally distributed.

The null hypothesis is rejected if the *p*-value is below 0.05. In our example for males, the *p*-value is 0.034 and for females, it is 0.215. Therefore, we can say that data for females are approximately normally distributed. Results are shown in Table 10.5.

TABLE 10.3
Case Processing Summary

		Cases					
		Valid		Missing		Total	
	Gender	N	%	N	%	N	%
Exam_scores	Male	23	100.0	0	0.0	23	100.0
	Female	27	100.0	0	0.0	27	100.0

Source: Authors.

TABLE 10.4
Descriptives

		Gender					Statistic		Std. Error
Exam_scores		Male		Mean			76.3478		2.69798
				95% confidence interval for mean	Lower bound		70.7526		
					Upper bound		81.9431		
				5% trimmed mean			76.9130		
				Median			78.0000		
				Variance			167.419		
				Std. deviation			12.93905		
				Minimum			46.00		
				Maximum			96.00		
				Range			50.00		
				Interquartile range			20.00		
				Skewness			–0.818		0.481
				Kurtosis			0.110		0.935
		Female		Mean			77.1481		2.01328
				95% confidence interval for mean	Lower bound		73.0098		
					Upper bound		81.2865		
				5% trimmed mean			77.1091		
				Median			78.0000		
				Variance			109.439		
				Std. deviation			10.46130		
				Minimum			57.00		
				Maximum			98.00		
				Range			41.00		
				Interquartile range			18.00		
				Skewness			0.054		0.448
				Kurtosis			–0.008		0.872

Source: Authors.

TABLE 10.5
Tests of Normality

		Kolmogorov–Smirnov[a]			Shapiro–Wilk		
	Gender	Statistic	df	Sig.	Statistic	df	Sig.
Exam_scores	Male	0.228	23	0.003	0.906	23	**0.034**
	Female	0.134	27	0.200[b]	0.950	27	**0.215**

Source: Authors.
Notes: 1. [a]Lilliefors significance correction.
2. [b]This is a lower bound of the true significance.
3. Bold values signify the level of significance.

Next, let us look at the graphical figure for both male and female data, starting with the histogram (see Figures 10.5 and 10.6). The histogram should have the approximate shape of a normal curve in the case of females. Therefore, we can assert that 'Exam_scores' of females is approximately a normal shape. This is shown in Figure 10.6.

FIGURE 10.5
Histogram (for Gender = Male)

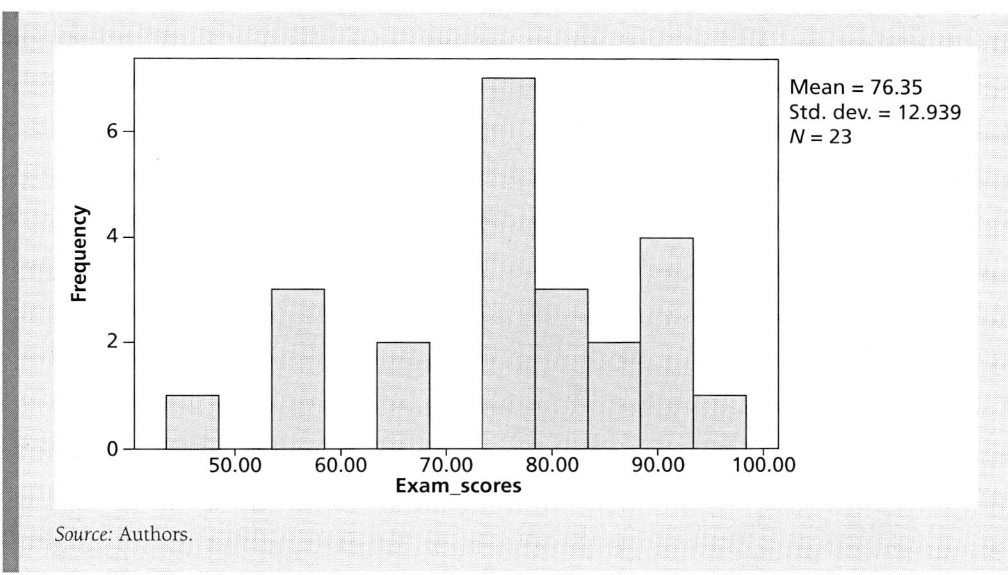

Source: Authors.

FIGURE 10.6
Histogram (for Gender = Female)

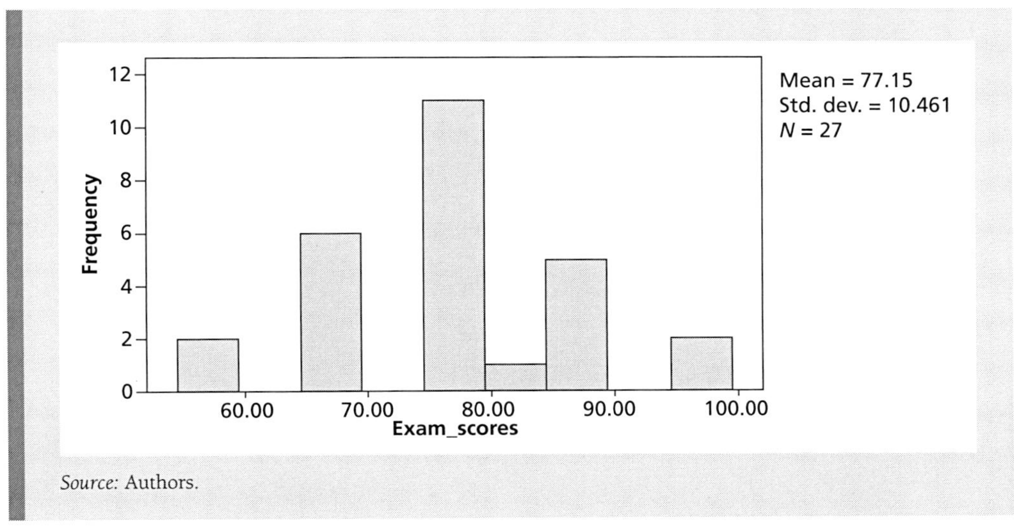

Source: Authors.

The same data from the same individuals are now also being analysed in the light of normal Q-Q plot which is depicted in Figure 10.7. From this graph, we can conclude that the male data do not appear to be normally distributed as data do not follow the diagonal line closely.

FIGURE 10.7
Normal Q-Q Plot of Exam_scores (for Gender = Male)

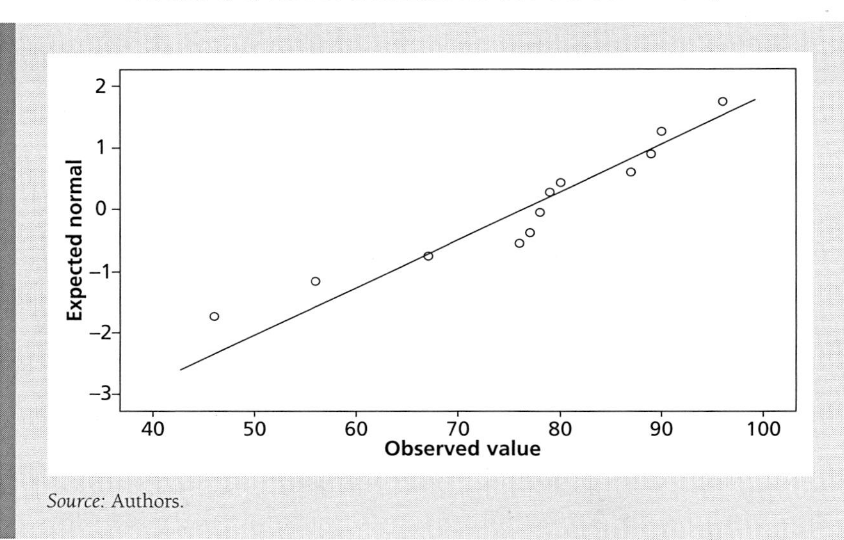

Source: Authors.

From Figure 10.8, we can conclude that the female data appear to be normally distributed as they follow the diagonal line closely.

FIGURE 10.8
Normal Q-Q Plot of Exam_scores (for Gender = Female)

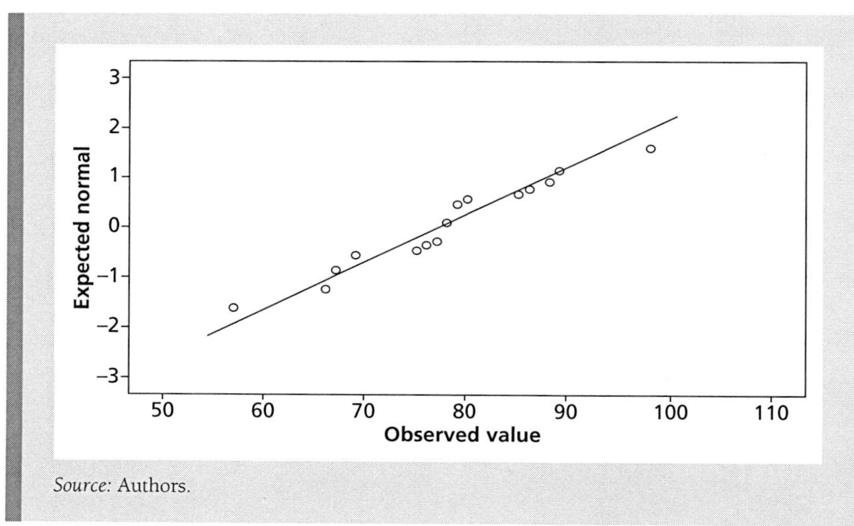

Source: Authors.

The last criterion in this test is box plots (Figure 10.9). The box plots should be as symmetrical as possible. In our example, it is clearly observed that the box for females is approximately symmetric. Finally, we can conclude that if our data set is normal, then we can use the data set for parametric test.

FIGURE 10.9
Box Plots

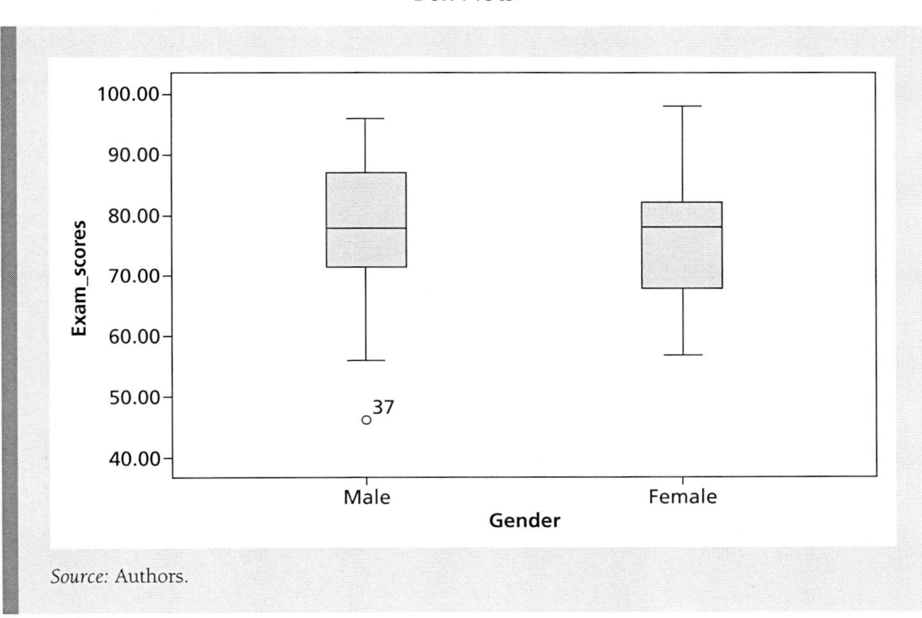

Source: Authors.

Key points to keep in mind for doing a normality test are as follows:

1. Skewness and kurtosis Z-values should be somewhere in the span of –1.96 to +1.96.
2. The Shapiro–Wilk test *p*-value should be above 0.05.
3. Histograms, normal Q-Q plots and box plots should be visually inspected in order to check the normality.

SUMMARY

Hypothesis is a predictive statement of assumption or supposition to be proved or disproved by statistical means. A hypothesis can be 'descriptive' or 'relational' in nature. The one-tailed hypothesis (directional hypothesis) indicates the directions of a research study by using the words increase, decrease, less than or more than. Two-tailed hypothesis does not indicate any expected direction of relationship under a research study. If Z (calculated value) > Z (tabulated value), the null hypothesis is rejected. The null hypothesis is accepted if Z (calculated value) < Z (tabulated value). Normal distribution (called Gaussian distribution) which is used in a normality test for data is the most important continuous probability distribution. One of the assumptions for most parametric tests to be reliable is that the data is approximately normally distributed. Two tests for normality are usually run. For data sets smaller than 2,000 elements, we use the Shapiro–Wilk test; otherwise, the Kolmogorov–Smirnov test is used.

KEY TERMS

hypothesis (108)
descriptive hypothesis (108)
relational hypothesis (109)
one-tailed test (110)
two-tailed test (111)
null hypothesis (109)
alternative hypothesis (109)
type-I error (109)
type-II error (109)
acceptance region (110)
rejection region (110)
normality test (110)
normal distribution curve (110)
Shapiro–Wilk test (113)
Kolmogorov–Smirnov test (113)
histogram (115)
normal Q-Q plot (116)
box plots (117)

EXERCISES

1. Define hypothesis. What attributes it must possess in order to be a good research hypothesis?
2. Distinguish between null and alternative hypothesis.
3. Distinguish between type-I and type-II errors.
4. Explain the acceptance and rejection region with a suitable diagram.
5. Distinguish between one-tailed test and two-tailed test.
6. What is normality testing?
7. Explain the importance of normality testing.
8. What tests should be adopted to check the normality of a data set?

CHAPTER

11

Correlation

LEARNING OBJECTIVES

After studying this chapter, you should be able to

- Visualize the meaning, characteristics and assumptions of correlation coefficient.
- Learn the procedure of different types of correlation coefficients using SPSS.

11.1. PEARSON'S PRODUCT-MOMENT CORRELATION

The Pearson product-moment correlation coefficient is a measure of the strength and direction of association that exists between two variables measured on at least an interval scale. A Pearson's correlation attempts to draw a line of best fit through the data of two variables, and the Pearson correlation coefficient, r, indicates how far away all these data points are from this line of best fit.

If one of the two variables is dichotomous, you can use a point-bi serial correlation instead, or if you have one or more control variables, you can run a Pearson's partial correlation.

For example, you could use a Pearson's correlation to understand whether there is an association between examination performance and time spent on education.

Karl Pearson's Coefficient of Correlation

Karl Pearson's coefficient of correlation is a quantitative measure of the degree of relationship between two variables. Correlation coefficient is universally denoted by 'r'. Suppose these variables are x and y, then Karl Pearson's coefficient of correlation is defined as

$$r = (\text{Co-variance of } x \text{ and } y)/(\text{standard deviation of } x \times \text{standard deviation of } y)$$

Mathematically,

$$r = \frac{\sum_{i=1}^{n}((x_i - \bar{x})(y_i - \bar{y}))}{\sqrt{\sum_{i=1}^{n}(x_i - \bar{x})^2 \sum_{i=1}^{n}(y_i - \bar{y})^2}}$$

Product-moment correlation coefficient can be also expressed in the following way:

$$r = (n\Sigma xy - \Sigma x \Sigma y) / \sqrt{(n\Sigma x2 - (\Sigma x)2)(n\Sigma y2 - (\Sigma y)2)}$$

11.1.1. Characteristics of Correlation Coefficient

Following are the characteristics of correlation coefficient:

1. Correlation coefficient can only be calculated for quantitative data.
2. Positive value of '*r*' indicates positive association between the variables, that is, the variables move in the same direction; negative value of '*r*' indicates negative association between the variables, that is, the variables move in the opposite direction.
3. The correlation coefficient (r) is always a number lying between –1 and +1.
4. The correlation coefficient (r) is a pure number without units. It is not affected by interchanging the two variables, that is, $r_{xy} = r_{yx}$.
5. As '*r*' uses the standardized values of the observations, '*r*' does not change when we change units of measurement (inches versus centimetres, pounds versus kilograms, miles versus metres). It is 'scale-invariant'.
6. The correlation coefficient measures clustering about a line, but only relative to the SDs.
7. The correlation can be misleading in the presence of outliers or non-linear association. It does not describe curved relationships. It is affected by outliers. Therefore, we have to check the scatter plot.
8. Correlation measures association but association does not necessarily show causation. Both variables may be influenced simultaneously by some third variable.
9. Correlation coefficient is independent of the change of origin and scale.

11.1.2. Assumptions of Correlation Coefficient

However, before we introduce you to this procedure, you need to understand the different assumptions that your data must meet in order for a Pearson's correlation to give you a valid result. The assumptions are as follows:

Assumption 1: Your two variables should be measured at the interval or ratio level (i.e., they are continuous). Examples of variables that meet this criterion include revision time (measured in hours), intelligence (measured using IQ score), exam performance (measured from 0 to 100), weight (measured in kg), age, height, rainfall and so forth.

Assumption 2: There must be a linear relationship between the two variables. There are a number of ways to check whether a linear relationship exists between the two variables or not. We suggest creating a scatter

FIGURE 11.1
Scatter Plot

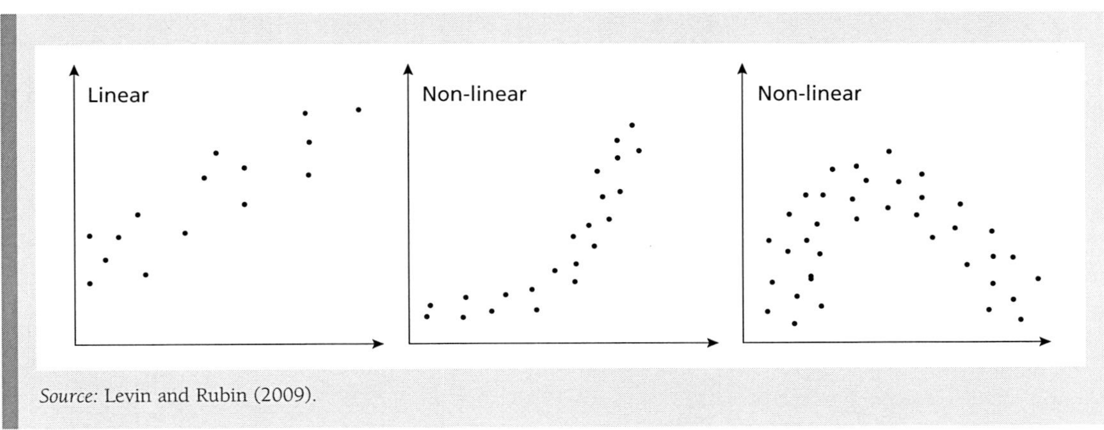

Source: Levin and Rubin (2009).

plot using SPSS statistics, where you can plot one variable against the other variable, and then visually inspect the scatter plot to check for linearity. Your scatter plot may look like the one shown in Figure 11.1.

If the relationship displayed in the scatter plot is not linear, you will have to either run a non-parametric equivalent to Pearson's correlation or transform your data, which you can do using SPSS statistics. We show you how to (a) create a scatter plot to check for linearity when carrying out Pearson's correlation using SPSS statistics; (b) interpret the results of different scatter plots; and (c) transform data using SPSS statistics if a linear relationship does not exist between the two variables.

Assumption 3: There should be no significant outliers. Outliers are simply single data points within the data that do not follow the usual pattern (e.g., in a study of 100 students' IQ scores, the mean score was 108 but one student had a score of 156, which is very unusual). It obviously enhances the value of mean. The scatter plots shown in Figure 11.2 highlight the potential impact of outliers.

FIGURE 11.2
Impact of Outliers in Scatter Plot

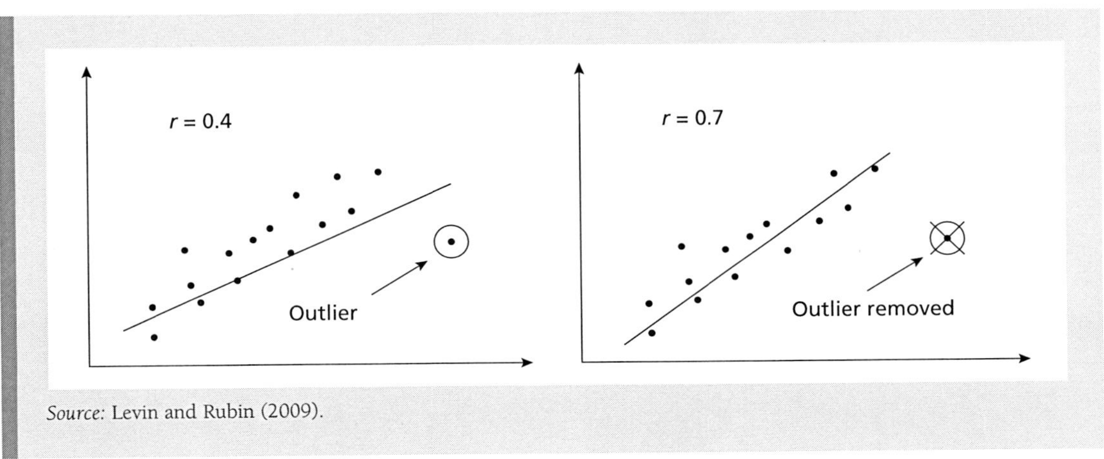

Source: Levin and Rubin (2009).

Pearson's correlation coefficient, r, is sensitive to outliers, which can have a very large effect on the line of best fit and the Pearson correlation coefficient. Therefore, in some cases, including outliers in analysis can lead to misleading results. Therefore, it is the best if there are no outliers or they are kept to a minimum. Fortunately, when using SPSS statistics to run Pearson's correlation on data, you can easily include procedures to screen for outliers. We will show you how to detect outliers using a scatter plot, which is a simple process when using SPSS statistics, and discuss some of the options available to you in order to deal with outliers.

Assumption 4: Variables should be approximately normally distributed. In order to assess the statistical significance of the Pearson correlation, you need to have bivariate normality, but this assumption is difficult to assess. Therefore, a simple method is more commonly used. This simple method involves determining the normality of each variable separately. To test for normality you can use the Shapiro–Wilk test of normality, which is easily tested for using SPSS statistics. We will also explain what you can do if your data fails this assumption.

Remember that if you do not test these assumptions correctly, the results you get when running a Pearson's correlation might not be valid.

11.2. THE PEARSON PRODUCT-MOMENT CORRELATION COEFFICIENT USING SPSS

We illustrate the SPSS statistics procedure to perform a Pearson's correlation assuming that no assumptions have been violated. First, we set out the example we use to explain the Pearson's correlation procedure in SPSS statistics.

Example: A researcher wants to know whether a person's height is related to how well they perform in a long jump. The researcher selected untrained individuals from the general population, measured their heights and their performance in a long jump. The researcher then investigated whether there was an association between height and long jump performance by running a Pearson's correlation.

Solution: In SPSS statistics, we will create two variables so that we could enter our data: Height (i.e., participants' height) and Jump_Dist (i.e., distance jumped in a long jump).

Respondents	Height	Jump_Dist
1	1.63	2.34
2	1.80	2.48
3	1.75	2.29
4	1.86	2.62
5	1.73	2.64
6	1.71	2.30
7	1.75	2.44
8	1.96	2.67
9	1.60	2.39
10	1.68	2.47

Respondents	Height	Jump_Dist
11	1.80	2.60
12	1.87	2.75
13	1.74	2.40
14	1.67	2.46

From this data, we can calculate the value of Σx, Σy, Σxy, Σx^2 and Σy^2 and put the information in the following formula in order to calculate the value of Pearson's correlation. Here, $n = 14$, $\Sigma x = 24.55$, $\Sigma y = 34.85$, $\Sigma xy = 61.2426$, $\Sigma x^2 = 43.1759$ and $\Sigma y^2 = 87.0237$.

$$r = (n\Sigma xy - \Sigma x\Sigma y) / \sqrt{(n\Sigma x^2 - (\Sigma x)^2)(n\Sigma y^2 - (\Sigma y)^2)} = +0.706$$

11.2.1. Test Procedure in SPSS Statistics

The following steps will show you how to analyse data using Pearson's correlation in SPSS statistics when none of the four assumptions have been violated. At the end of these steps, we will show you how to interpret the results from this test.

After entering the data, we will follow the following command (Exhibit 11.1):

Click Analyze → Correlate → Bivariate.

EXHIBIT 11.1

SPSS Window for Pearson's Correlation (1)

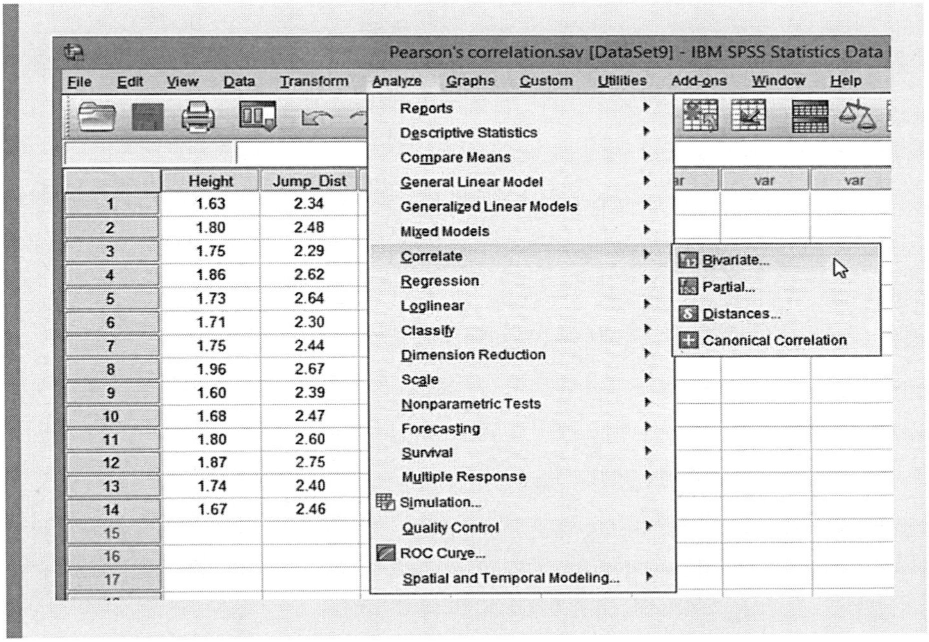

EXHIBIT 11.2

SPSS Window for Pearson's Correlation (2)

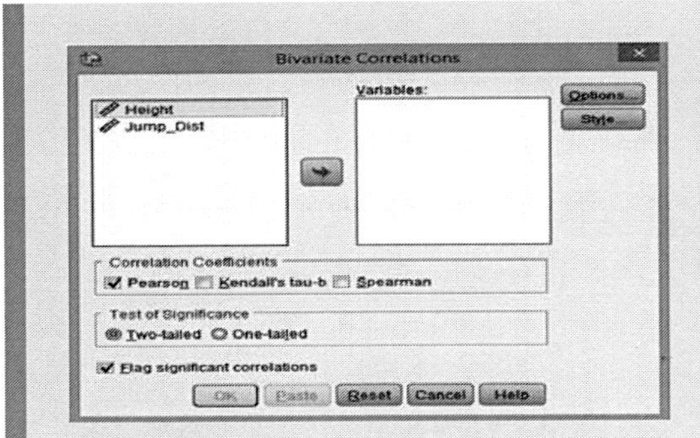

EXHIBIT 11.3

SPSS Window for Pearson's Correlation (3)

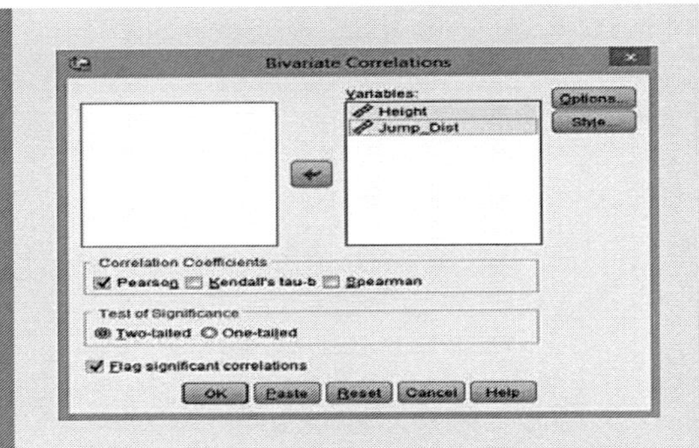

After giving the stated command, you will be presented with the bivariate correlations dialog box as shown in Exhibit 11.2.

Now, we will transfer the variables 'Height' and 'Jump_Dist' into the variables box using drag-and-drop. You will end up with a screen similar to the one shown in Exhibit 11.3.

Make sure that the 'Pearson' checkbox is selected under 'Correlation Coefficients' (although it is selected by default in SPSS statistics).

Click the SPSS 'Options' button and you will be presented with the 'Bivariate Correlations: Options' dialog box (Exhibit 11.4). If you wish to generate some descriptives, you can do it here by clicking on the relevant checkbox in the statistics area.

EXHIBIT 11.4

SPSS Window for Pearson's Correlation (4)

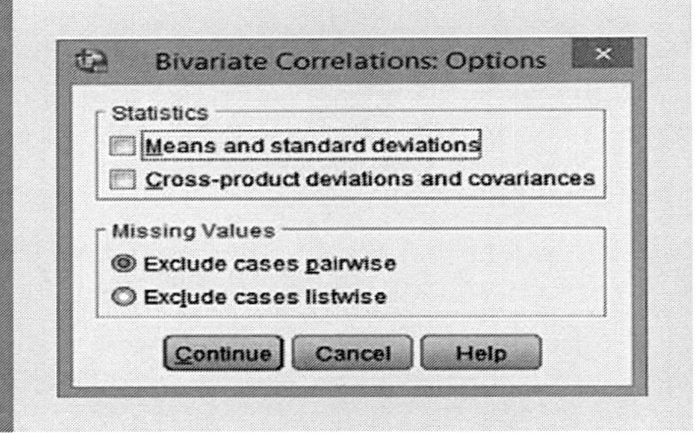

Click the continue button. You will be returned to the bivariate correlations dialog box. Then click the OK button. This will generate the results of Pearson's correlation.

11.2.2. Output for Pearson's Correlation

The Pearson's correlation result is highlighted in Table 11.1.

In this example, we can see that the Pearson correlation coefficient, r, is 0.706, and that it is statistically significant ($p = 0.005$).

11.2.3. Reporting the Output

In our example, you might report the results as follows:

A Pearson product-moment correlation was run to determine the relationship between height and distance jumped in a long jump. There was a strong, positive correlation between height and distance jumped, which was statistically significant ($r = 0.706$, $n = 14$, $p = 0.005$).

TABLE 11.1
SPSS Output for Pearson's Correlation

Correlations			
		Height	Jump_Dist
Height	Pearson Correlation	1	0.706*
	Sig. (two-tailed)		0.005
	N	14	14
Jump_Dist	Pearson Correlation	0.706*	1
	Sig. (two-tailed)	0.005	
	N	14	14

Source: Authors.
Note: *Correlation is significant at the 0.01.

11.3. OTHER TYPES OF CORRELATION COEFFICIENTS USING SPSS

Apart from Pearson correlation coefficient, we can compute other types of correlation coefficients depending upon the nature of variables in our research study. These are as follows.

11.3.1. Spearman's Rank Correlation Coefficient

If two variables are ordinal in nature or one variable is ordinal and the other one is ratio or interval, then we have to compute rho or Spearman's rank correlation coefficient.

After entering the data, we will follow the following command:

> Click Analyze → Correlate → Bivariate → Take one ordinal and one interval/ratio variable or two ordinal variables → Put a check mark on the option 'Spearman' → Ok.

Interpretation of the output will be the same as Pearson's correlation coefficient.

11.3.2. Phi Coefficient

If two variables are dichotomous in nature, then we have to compute the phi coefficient. Suppose that we want to establish the degree of relationship between gender and smoking status of students. In this case, gender is of two types and smoking status is also of two types.

After entering the data, we will follow the following command:

> Click Analyze → Descriptive statistics → Crosstabs → One variable will be taken under row and the other variable will be taken under column → Statistics → Put a check mark on the option 'Phi & Cramer's V' → Continue → Ok.

Interpretation of the output will be the same as Pearson's correlation coefficient.

11.3.3. Cramer's V

If the two variables are grouping, then we have to compute Cramer's V. It indicates the strength of relationship with the chi-square test. Suppose that we want to establish the degree of relationship between gender and educational status of students. In this case, gender is of two types and educational status is of more than two types.

After entering the data, we will follow the following command:

> Click Analyze → Descriptive statistics → Crosstabs → One variable will be taken under row and the other variable will be taken under column → Statistics → Put a check mark on the option 'Phi & Cramer's V and 'Chi square' → Continue → Ok.

The value of Cramer's V indicates the strength of relationship. If the value is greater than 0.15 then we can say that the effect size is large.

11.3.4. Eta

If one variable is ratio or interval and the other variable is nominal, then we calculate eta. Suppose that we want to establish the degree of relationship between gender and intelligent quotients of students. In this case, gender is a nominal variable and intelligent quotients are ratio data.

After entering the data, we will follow the following command:

> Click Analyze → Descriptive statistics → Crosstabs → One variable will be taken under row and the other variable will be taken under column → Statistics → Put a check mark on the option 'Eta' → Continue → Ok.

The value of eta square implies the effect size. The value closer to 1 implies the large effect size.

11.3.5. Partial Correlation

In the partial correlation, we compute the degree of association between two variables keeping the third variable as control variable. Suppose that we want to establish the degree of relationship between intelligent quotients and academic achievement where socio-economic status is taken as a control variable.

After entering the data, we will follow the following command:

> Click Analyze → Correlate → Partial → Intelligent Quotients and Academic Achievement will be taken into variable box and Socio-economic Status is taken into control box → Ok.

Interpretation of the output will be the same as Pearson's correlation coefficient.

SUMMARY

Karl Pearson's coefficient of correlation is a quantitative measure of the degree of relationship between two variables. If two variables are ordinal in nature or one variable is ordinal and the other one is ratio or interval, then we have to compute rho or spearman's rank correlation coefficient. If two variables are dichotomous in nature, then we have to compute the phi coefficient. If the two variables are grouping, then we have to compute Cramer's V. If one variable is ratio or interval and the other variable is nominal, then we calculate eta. In the partial correlation, we compute the degree of association between two variables keeping the third variable as control variable.

KEY TERMS

Pearson's product-moment correlation (119)
Spearman's rank correlation coefficient (125)
Phi coefficient (125)
Cramer's V (126)
eta (126)
partial correlation (126)

EXERCISES

1. What is the purpose of computation of the correlation coefficient?
2. Explain different types of correlation coefficients.
3. Mention the characteristics of a correlation coefficient.
4. State the assumptions of a correlation coefficient.
5. Describe the computational procedure of different types of correlation coefficients using SPSS.

CHAPTER

12

Linear Regression Analysis

LEARNING OBJECTIVES

After studying this chapter, you should be able to

- Visualize the meaning of linear regression.
- Learn the procedure for the formation of the linear regression equation.
- Understand the linear regression equation using SPSS.

12.1. LINEAR REGRESSION

Linear regression is the next step after correlation. It is used when we want to predict the value of a variable based on the value of another variable. The variable we want to predict is called the dependent variable. The variable we are using to predict the other variable's value is called the independent variable. For example, you could use linear regression to understand whether exam performance can be predicted based on revision time, whether cigarette consumption can be predicted based on smoking duration and so on. If you have two or more independent variables, rather than just one, you need to use multiple regression.

In regression analysis, one is called the dependent and the other is called the independent variable. Suppose, you want to forecast sales for your company and you have concluded that your company's sales go up and down depending on changes in GDP. In this case, you will consider sales to be the dependent variable and changes in GDP to be the independent variable.

You can develop a linear regression equation to predict sales of your company with respect to the change in GDP in the following way:

$$Y = a + b \times X,$$

where Y = dependent variable, a = Y intercept, that is, intercept along y-axis, b = regression coefficient of Y on X and X = independent variable.

The intercept, or 'a', is the value of y (dependent variable) if the value of x (independent variable) is zero. So, if there was no change in GDP, your company would still make some sales. This value, when the change in GDP is zero, is the intercept.

The value of 'b' indicates that if there is 1% increase in GDP, the sale is likely to go up (or down) by 'b' units. If the coefficient is positive, then it will go up or else go down.

However, before we introduce you to this procedure, you need to understand the different assumptions that your data must meet in order for linear regression to give you a valid result. When your data fails certain assumptions, there is often a solution to overcome this. First, let us take a look at these assumptions. We discuss these assumptions here.

Assumption 1: Your two variables should be measured at the continuous level (i.e., they are either interval or ratio variables). Examples of continuous variables include revision time (measured in hours), intelligence (measured using IQ score), exam performance (measured from 0 to 100), weight (measured in kg) and so on.

Assumption 2: There needs to be a linear relationship between the two variables. There are a number of ways to check whether a linear relationship exists between two variables. We suggest creating a scatter plot using SPSS statistics, where you can plot one variable against the other variable, and then visually inspect the scatter plot to check for linearity. Your scatter plot (Figure 12.1) may look like one of the following:

FIGURE 12.1
Scatter Plot

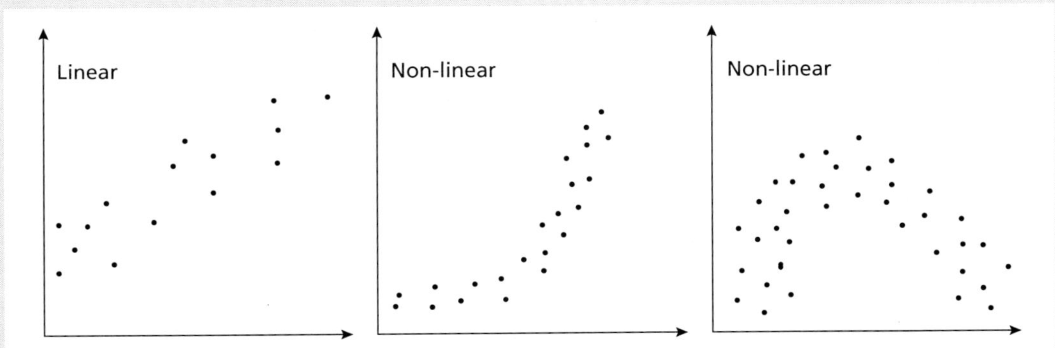

Linear

Non-linear

Non-linear

Source: Levin and Rubin (2009).

If the relationship displayed in your scatter plot is not linear, you will have to either run a non-parametric equivalent to Pearson's correlation or transform your data, which you can do using SPSS statistics. We show you how to (a) create a scatter plot to check for linearity when carrying out Pearson's correlation using SPSS statistics, (b) interpret the results of different scatter plots and (c) transform your data using SPSS statistics if no linear relationship exists between the two variables.

FIGURE 12.2
Outlier in Scatter Plot

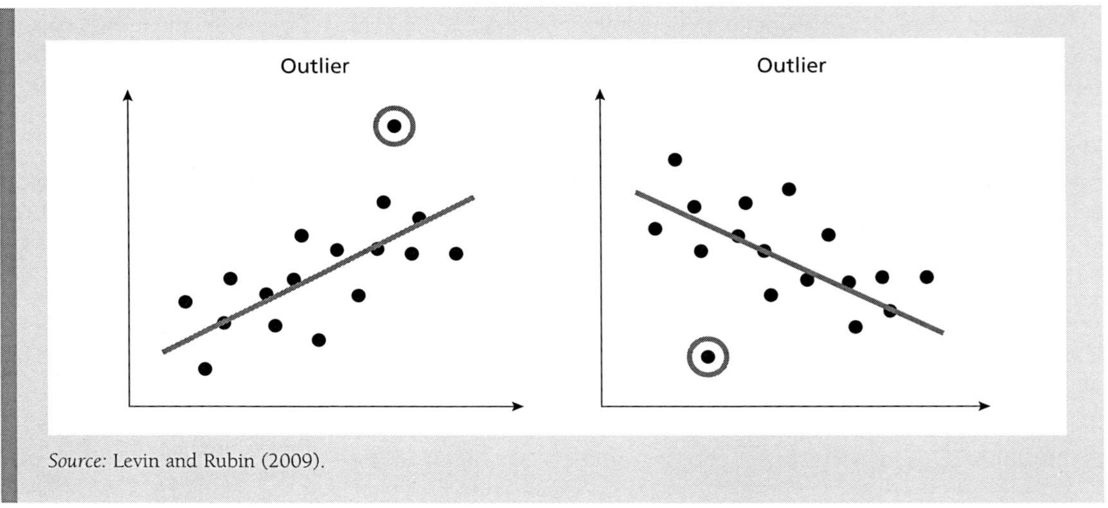

Source: Levin and Rubin (2009).

Assumption 3: There should be no significant outliers. An outlier is an observed data point that has a dependent variable value that is very different to the value predicted by the regression equation. As such, an outlier will be a point on a scatter plot that is (vertically) far away from the regression line indicating that it has a large residual, as highlighted in Figure 12.2.

The problem with outliers is that they can have a negative effect on the regression analysis (e.g., reduce the fit of the regression equation) that is used to predict the value of the dependent (outcome) variable based on the independent (predictor) variable. This will change the output that SPSS statistics produces and reduce the predictive accuracy of results. Fortunately, when using SPSS statistics to run a linear regression on your data, you can easily include criteria to help you detect possible outliers. We will show you how to detect outliers using a scatter plot, which is a simple process when using SPSS statistics and discuss some of the options available to you in order to deal with outliers.

Assumption 4: You should have independence of observations, which you can easily check using the Durbin–Watson statistic, which is a simple test to run using SPSS statistics. We explain how to interpret the result of the Durbin–Watson statistic.

Assumption 5: Your data needs to show homoscedasticity, which is where the variances along the line of best fit remain similar as you move along the line. Take a look at the three scatter plots shown in Figure 12.3, which provide three simple examples—two of data that fail the assumption (called heteroscedasticity) and one of data that meets this assumption (called homoscedasticity).

Assumption 6: Finally, you need to check that the residuals (errors) of the regression line are approximately normally distributed. Two common methods to check this assumption include using either a histogram (with a superimposed normal curve) or a normal P-P plot.

Remember that if you do not test these assumptions correctly, the results you get when running a regression equation might not be valid.

FIGURE 12.3
Scatter Plots on Heteroscedasticity and Homoscedasticity

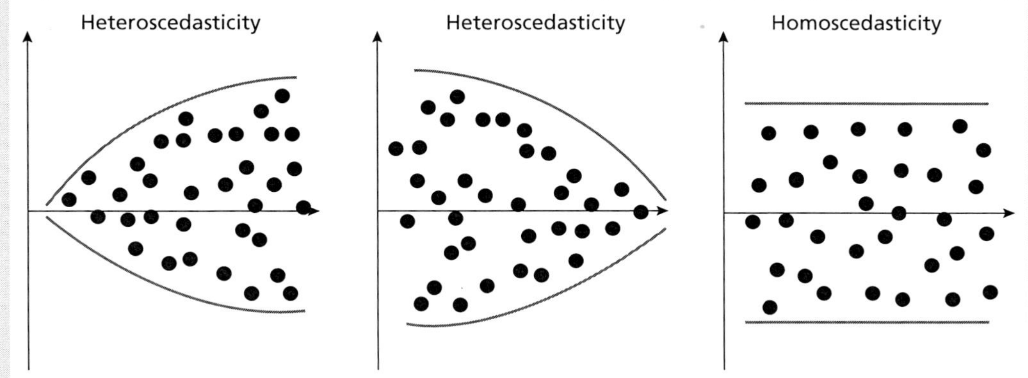

Source: Levin and Rubin (2009).

12.2. LINEAR REGRESSION USING SPSS

We illustrate the SPSS statistics procedure to perform a linear regression assuming that no assumptions have been violated. First, we set out the example we use to explain the linear regression procedure in SPSS statistics.

Example: A salesperson for a large car brand wants to determine whether there is a relationship between an individual's income and the price they pay for a car. As such, the individual's income is the independent variable and the price they pay for a car is the dependent variable. The salesperson wants to use this information to determine which cars to offer potential customers in new areas where the average income is known.

Find the regression equations from the following data (price is assumed as X and income is assumed as Y):

X (Fig. in lakh)	6	2	10	4	8
Y (Fig. in lakh)	9	11	5	8	7

Solution: Calculation for the regression equation is as follows:

S. No.	X	Y	X^2	Y^2	XY
1	6	9	36	81	54
2	2	11	4	121	22
3	10	5	100	25	50
4	4	8	16	64	32
5	8	7	64	49	56
Total	30	40	220	340	214

Here,

$$\text{Variance of } X(\sigma_X^2) = \left(\frac{1}{n}\sum_{i=1}^{n} X^2\right) - (\bar{X})^2$$

$$= \left(\frac{1}{5} \times 220\right) - (6)^2.$$

Therefore, standard deviation $(\sigma_X) = \sqrt{\sigma_X^2} = 2.8$

$$\text{Variance of } Y(\sigma_Y^2) = \left(\frac{1}{n}\sum_{i=1}^{n} Y^2\right) - (\bar{Y})^2$$

$$= \left(\frac{1}{5} \times 340\right) - (8)^2.$$

Therefore, standard deviation $(\sigma_Y) = \sqrt{\sigma_Y^2} = 2.$

Then, the correlation coefficient $(r_{XY}) = \dfrac{n\sum_{i=1}^{n} X_i \times Y_i - \sum_{i=1}^{n} X_i \sum_{i=1}^{n} Y_i}{n^2 \times \sigma_X \times \sigma_Y}$

$$= \frac{5 \times 214 - 30 \times 40}{25 \times 2.8 \times 2} = -0.9.$$

Now, the regression line of Y on X is

$(Y - \bar{Y}) = b_{YX}(X - \bar{X})$, where b_{YX} (regression coefficient of Y on X) $= r_{XY} \times \dfrac{\sigma_Y}{\sigma_X}$

$$(Y - 8) = \left(r_{XY} \times \frac{\sigma_Y}{\sigma_X}\right) \times (X - 6)$$

$$(Y - 8) = \left(-0.9 \times \frac{2}{2.8}\right) \times (X - 6)$$

Hence, the required regression line Y on X is $Y = 11.9 - 0.65X$.

Now, the regression line of X on Y is

$(X - \bar{X}) = b_{XY}(Y - \bar{Y})$, where b_{XY} (regression coefficient of X on Y) $= r_{XY} \times \dfrac{\sigma_X}{\sigma_Y}$

$$(X - 6) = \left(r_{XY} \times \frac{\sigma_X}{\sigma_Y}\right) \times (Y - 8)$$

$$(X - 6) = \left(-0.9 \times \frac{2.8}{2}\right) \times (Y - 8).$$

Hence, the required regression line X on Y is $X = 16.4 - 1.3Y$.

12.2.1. Alternative Way

Regression equation of Y on X is $Y = a + bX$ and the normal equations are:

$$\sum Y = na + b\sum X$$

$$\sum XY = a\sum X + b\sum X^2$$

Substituting the values, we get:

$$40 = 5a + 30b \quad (1)$$

$$214 = 30a + 220b \quad (2)$$

Multiplying Equation (1) by 6

$$240 = 30a + 180b \quad (3)$$

$$(2) - (3) - 26 = 40b$$

$$\text{Or} = -26/40 = -0.65.$$

Now, substituting the value of 'b' in Equation (1)

$$40 = 5a - 19.5$$

$$5a = 59.5$$

$$a = 59.5/5 = 11.9.$$

Hence, the required regression line Y on X is $Y = 11.9 - 0.65X$.

Again, the regression equation of X on Y is

$$X = a + bY$$

The normal equations are

$$\sum X = na + b\sum Y \text{ and}$$

$$\sum XY = a\sum Y + b\sum Y^2.$$

Now, substituting the corresponding values from the earlier table for calculation of the regression equation, we get

$$30 = 5a + 40b \quad (4)$$

$$214 = 40a + 340b. \quad (5)$$

Multiplying (4) by 8, we get

$$240 = 40a + 320b \quad (6)$$

$$(5) - (6) \text{ gives}$$

$$-26 = 20b$$

$$b = -26/20 = -1.3.$$

Substituting $b = -1.3$ in equation (4) gives

$$30 = 5a - 52$$

$$5a = 82$$

$$a = 82/5 = 16.4.$$

Hence, the required regression line of X on Y is

$$X = 16.4 - 1.3Y.$$

In our SPSS analysis, we will consider only X on Y.

12.2.2. Setup in SPSS Statistics

In SPSS statistics, we have created two variables so that we could enter our data—income (the independent variable) and price (the dependent variable).

12.3. TEST PROCEDURE IN SPSS STATISTICS

The following steps will show you how to analyse your data using linear regression in SPSS statistics when none of the six assumptions have been violated. At the end of these four steps, we show you how to interpret the results from your linear regression.

After entering the data, we will give the following command (Exhibit 12.1):

Click Analyze → Regression → Linear.

EXHIBIT 12.1

SPSS Window for Linear Regression (1)

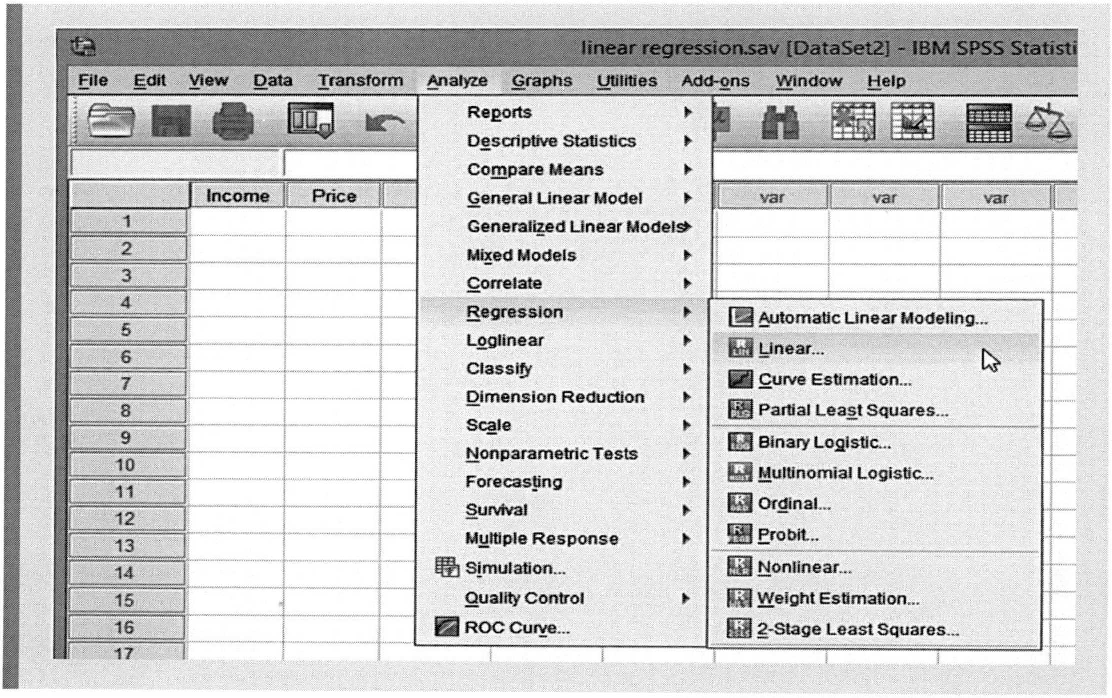

EXHIBIT 12.2
SPSS Window for Linear Regression (2)

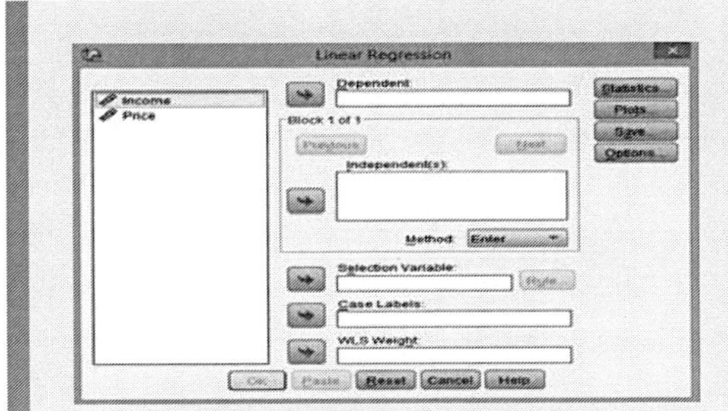

EXHIBIT 12.3
SPSS Window for Linear Regression (3)

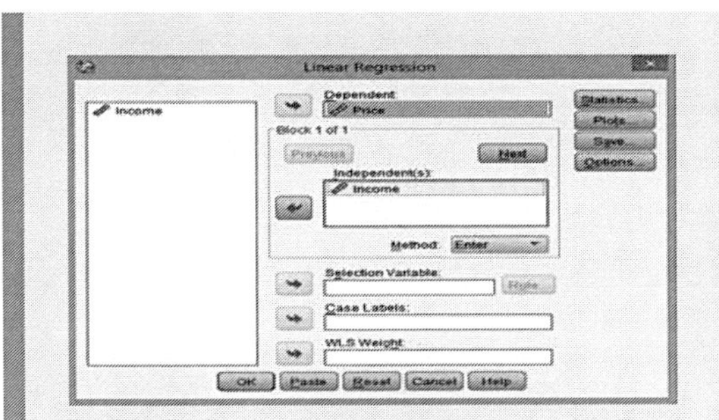

After giving the aforementioned command, you will be presented with the linear regression dialog box which is shown in Exhibit 12.2.

Transfer the independent variable, 'Income', to the 'Independent(s)' box and the dependent variable, 'Price', into the 'Dependent' box. You can drag-and-drop the variables. You will end up with a screen as shown in Exhibit 12.3.

Then click the OK button. This will generate the results of regression. The regression result is highlighted in the following section.

12.3.1. Output for Simple Regression

SPSS statistics will generate quite a few tables of output for a linear regression. In this section, we show you only the three main tables required to understand your results from the linear regression procedure, assuming that no assumptions have been violated.

The first table is the model summary table (Table 12.1). This table provides the R and R^2 values. The R value represents the simple correlation and it is 0.919, which indicates a high degree of positive correlation. The R^2 value indicates how much of the total variation in the dependent variable, price, can be explained by the independent variable, income. In this case, 84.5% variance of the dependent variable can be explained by the independent variable, which is very large.

$$\text{Here, } R^2 = \frac{\text{Regression sum of squares}}{\text{Total sum of square}} = \frac{33.8}{40} \text{ (where values are taken from Table 12.2)}$$

$$= 0.845.$$

TABLE 12.1
Model Summary for Simple Regression from SPSS Output

Model	R	R-square	Adjusted R-square	Std. Error of the Estimate
1	0.919[a]	0.845	0.793	1.43759

Source: Authors.
Note: [a]Predictors: (Constant), Income.

TABLE 12.2
ANOVA for Simple Regression from SPSS Output

ANOVA						
Model		Sum of Squares	df	Mean Square	F	Sig.
1	Regression	33.800	1	33.800	16.355	0.027[a]
	Residual	6.200	3	2.067		
	Total	40.000	4			

Source: Authors.
Notes: 1. [a]Predictors: (Constant), Income.
2. Dependent variable: Price.

TABLE 12.3
Coefficients for Simple Regression from SPSS Output

Coefficients						
		Unstandardized Coefficients		Standardized Coefficients		
Model		B	Std. Error	Beta	t	Sig.
1	(Constant)	16.400	2.651		6.187	0.009
	Income	–1.300	0.321	–0.919	–4.044	0.027

Source: Authors.
Note: Dependent variable: Price.

Also, standard error of the estimate $= \sqrt{\dfrac{\text{Residual}}{n-2}} = \sqrt{\dfrac{6.2}{5-2}}$ (where values are taken from Table 12.2)
$= 1.43759.$

The next table is the ANOVA table (Table 12.2), which reports how well the regression equation fits the data (i.e., predicts the dependent variable).

This table indicates that the regression model predicts the dependent variable significantly well. How do we know this from Table 12.2? Look at the 'Regression' row and go to the 'Sig.' column. This indicates the statistical significance of the regression model that was run. Here, $p = 0.027$, which is less than 0.05, and indicates that, overall, the regression model statistically significantly predicts the outcome variable (i.e., it is a good fit for the data).

Table 12.3 provides us with the necessary information to predict price from income, as well as determine whether income contributes statistically significantly to the model. Furthermore, we can use the values in the 'B' column under the 'Unstandardized Coefficients' column, as follows.

By taking the constant value and regression coefficient value from Table 12.3, we can establish the regression equation. The regression equation is as follows:

$$\text{Price} = 16.4 - 1.3\ (\text{Income}), \text{ that is, } X = 16.4 - 1.3Y.$$

12.3.2. T-TEST FOR REGRESSION LINE

For the t-test for regression line, the hypotheses will be as follows:

The null hypothesis (H_0) = There is no significant relationship between two variables ($B_0 = 0$)

Alternative hypothesis (H_1) = There is a significant relationship between two variables ($B_0 \neq 0$)

$$\text{T-statistics} = \frac{\text{Unstandardized coefficient} - B_0}{\text{Standard error}} = \frac{-1.3-0}{0.321} = -4.044.$$

As *p*-value is 0.027, the null hypothesis is rejected and alternative hypothesis is accepted at 5% significant level. Also, we can say that a negative relationship exists between variables as the value of unstandardized coefficient is negative (–1.3).

SUMMARY

Linear regression is the next step after correlation. It is used when we want to predict the value of a variable based on the value of another variable. The variable we want to predict is called the dependent variable. The variable we are using to predict the other variable's value is called the independent variable.

KEY TERMS

linear regression (128)
outlier (130)
heteroscedasticity (130)
homoscedasticity (130)
R^2 value (135)
adjusted R-square (135)
std. error of the estimate (135)
unstandardized coefficients (136)

EXERCISES

1. Distinguish between correlation coefficient and regression.
2. What is the implication of R^2 value?
3. What is the objective of regression equation?

CHAPTER

13

Multiple Regression Analysis and Structural Equation Modelling (SEM) by AMOS

LEARNING OBJECTIVES

After studying this chapter, you should be able to

- Visualize the meaning of multiple regression analysis.
- Learn the procedure of multiple regression analysis using SPSS.
- Develop SEM through AMOS.
- Understand the concept of multicollinearity.

13.1. MULTIPLE REGRESSION ANALYSIS

Multiple regression analysis deals with two or more independent variables (explanatory variables) and at least one dependent variable. So, it is used to assess the influence of independent variables on dependent variables. So we can write the multiple regression equation as follows:

$$Y = a + b_1X_1 + b_2X_2 + b_3X_3 + \cdots + b_mX_m$$

Here, Y is the dependent variable and 'a' is the regression constant estimation. $b_1, b_2, b_3, \ldots, b_m$ are the regression coefficient estimations of 'm' number of independent variables $X_1, X_2, X_3, \ldots, X_m$. The simple regression equation emphasizes few independent variables with highest power of '1'.

13.2. EXPLANATION OF MULTIPLE REGRESSION ANALYSIS

A researcher wants to assess the performance of postgraduate (PG) students and reputation of the institution. A survey was carried out and a sample of 100 respondents was collected for this purpose (part of this example has been discussed in Chapter 18 'Factor Analysis'). Different variables and constructs of the topic from literature review were included in the questionnaire (see Table 13.1) and model (see Figure 13.1).

TABLE 13.1

Questionnaire for Assessing Performance of the Student

[Please tick one box on each line according to your answer]

	Academic Life Related Concern	Strongly Agree	Agree	Neither Agree Nor Disagree	Disagree	Strongly Disagree
AL_1	Friendly classmates available					
AL_2	Friendly teachers available					
AL_3	Enjoyable classroom environment available					
AL_4	Marks assessment process comfortable					
AL_5	Availability of interesting syllabus and curriculum of the course					
	Personal & Family Life Related Concern	**Strongly Agree**	**Agree**	**Neither Agree Nor Disagree**	**Disagree**	**Strongly Disagree**
PFL_1	Mental support from the family members					
PFL_2	Sufficient availability of pocket money					
PFL_3	Availability of intimate guidance from the guardians					
PFL_4	Availability of good hostel environment					
	Career Related Concern	**Strongly Agree**	**Agree**	**Neither Agree Nor Disagree**	**Disagree**	**Strongly Disagree**
CR_1	Good job opportunity available					
CR_2	Availability of good exposure with industrial interaction					
CR_3	Supportive teachers available					
	Performance of the Student	**Strongly Agree**	**Agree**	**Neither Agree Nor Disagree**	**Disagree**	**Strongly Disagree**
PS_1	Enhances efficiencies and productive activities					
PS_2	Increases good marks-based results					
	Reputation of the Institution	**Strongly Agree**	**Agree**	**Neither Agree Nor Disagree**	**Disagree**	**Strongly Disagree**
RI_1	High achievement of the students in their working place					
RI_2	Increases the awareness of the institution's good performance					

Source: Authors.

FIGURE 13.1

Model for Regression Analysis (from Theoretical Observation)

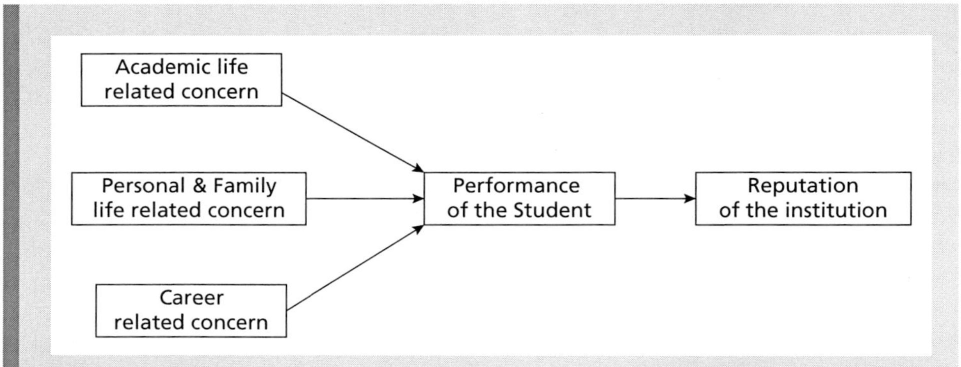

Source: Authors.

The collected data has been presented in Chapter 18, 'Factor Analysis' excluding 'Performance of the Student' and 'Reputation of the institution'. For this problem, the data related with these two constructs were collected. After factor analysis, each factor (consisting of different items) was converted into single variable as dependent or independent variable.

After putting data and variable in the 'Data View' window and 'Variable View' window, click Transform → Compute Variable. One pop-up window will appear as 'Compute Variable' (Exhibit 13.1).

Now go to 'Target variable' and put the name 'AL_Total' for 'Academic life related concern'. Now go to 'Numeric Expression' and put the expression '(AL_1 + AL_2 + AL_3 + AL_4 + AL_5)/5' and click 'OK'. Then we will get one single variable as expressed in Table 13.2. Other variables are constructed in a similar way.

EXHIBIT 13.1

SPSS Window for Compute Variables

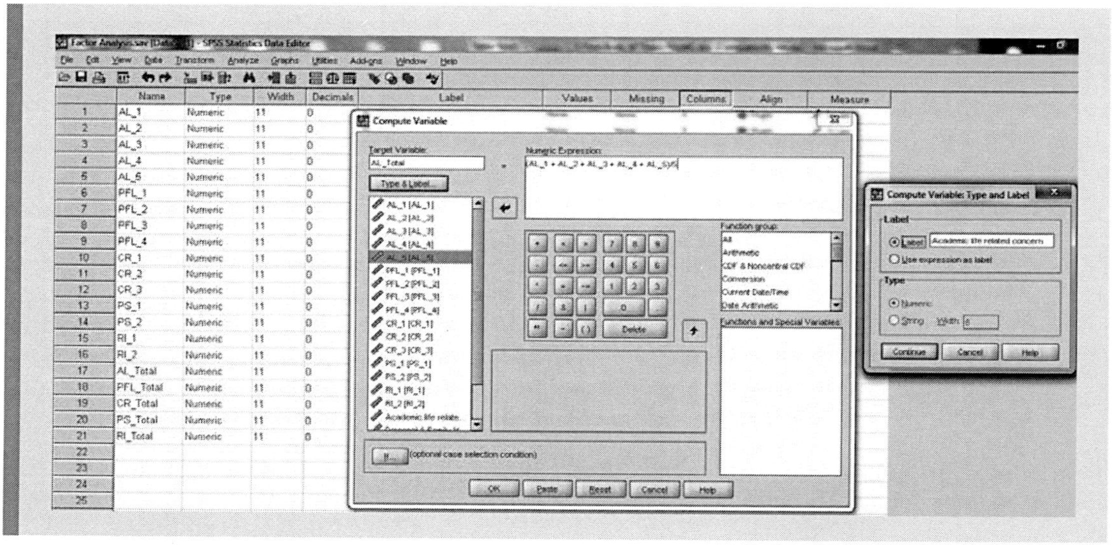

TABLE 13.2
Variables Construction for Multiple Regression Analysis

Respondent No.	Academic Life Related Concern (AL_Total)	Personal & Family Life Related Concern (PFL_Total)	Career Related Concern (CR_Total)	Performance of the Student (PS_Total)	Reputation of the Institution RI_Total)
1	5	4	5	5	5
2	4	4	5	4	4
3	5	4	5	5	5
4	4	4	4	4	4
5	5	4	5	5	5
6	4	4	4	4	4
7	5	4	5	5	5
8	4	4	5	4	4
9	4	4	5	4	4
10	4	4	5	4	5
11	4	4	5	4	4
12	4	4	5	5	4
13	4	5	5	4	5
14	4	4	3	5	4
15	4	4	5	3	4
16	4	5	4	5	5
17	4	4	4	3	4
18	5	4	4	4	5
19	4	4	4	2	5
20	4	4	4	2	4
21	3	5	5	4	5
22	4	4	4	5	4
23	4	5	4	4	4
24	4	4	5	5	5
25	5	4	4	4	4
26	5	5	4	5	4
27	4	4	5	4	5
28	5	5	5	5	5
29	4	4	4	4	4
30	5	4	5	4	5
31	4	4	5	4	5
32	4	4	5	4	5

(Table 13.2 Continued)

(Table 13.2 Continued)

Respondent No.	Academic Life Related Concern (AL_Total)	Personal & Family Life Related Concern (PFL_Total)	Career Related Concern (CR_Total)	Performance of the Student (PS_Total)	Reputation of the Institution RI_Total)
33	4	5	5	5	5
34	4	4	4	4	4
35	5	4	5	4	5
36	4	4	5	4	5
37	5	3	5	3	5
38	4	4	5	4	5
39	4	5	5	5	5
40	4	4	4	5	4
41	5	4	4	4	5
42	4	4	5	4	5
43	4	4	5	4	5
44	5	4	5	4	5
45	3	4	4	4	4
46	5	5	5	5	5
47	4	4	5	4	5
48	5	5	5	5	5
49	4	4	5	4	5
50	4	4	5	4	4
51	4	5	5	5	5
52	4	4	4	4	4
53	5	4	5	5	5
54	4	4	5	5	5
55	4	4	4	4	4
56	5	5	5	5	5
57	4	4	4	4	4
58	5	5	4	4	4
59	4	4	5	5	5
60	5	4	5	5	5
61	4	4	4	4	4
62	5	5	5	5	5
63	4	4	5	5	5
64	4	4	5	5	5
65	5	5	5	5	5
66	3	4	4	4	4

Respondent No.	Academic Life Related Concern (AL_Total)	Personal & Family Life Related Concern (PFL_Total)	Career Related Concern (CR_Total)	Performance of the Student (PS_Total)	Reputation of the Institution RI_Total)
67	5	5	5	5	5
68	4	4	5	5	5
69	5	5	5	5	5
70	4	4	5	5	5
71	4	5	5	5	5
72	4	4	4	4	4
73	3	5	5	5	5
74	4	4	5	5	5
75	3	4	5	5	5
76	5	4	5	5	5
77	4	4	5	5	5
78	3	5	4	4	4
79	5	4	5	5	5
80	4	4	5	5	5
81	5	4	5	5	4
82	4	4	4	4	5
83	5	4	5	5	4
84	4	4	4	4	4
85	5	5	5	5	5
86	4	4	5	5	5
87	3	5	4	4	4
88	5	4	5	5	5
89	4	4	5	5	5
90	5	5	5	5	5
91	4	4	5	5	5
92	5	5	5	5	5
93	4	4	4	4	4
94	4	5	5	4	4
95	4	4	5	4	4
96	5	4	5	5	5
97	4	4	3	4	4
98	5	4	5	5	5
99	4	4	4	4	4
100	5	4	4	5	5

Source: Authors.

13.3. MULTIPLE REGRESSION ANALYSIS WITH SPSS

At first, we will establish the regression equation, taking 'Performance of the Student' as dependent variable and 'Academic Life Related Concern', 'Personal & Family Life Related Concern' and 'Career Related Concern' as independent variables.

After putting data and variable in the 'Data View' window and 'Variable View' window, click Analyze → Regression → Linear in the SPSS window. One pop-up window will appear as 'Linear Regression'. Then send 'Performance of the Student [PS_Total]' to 'Dependent'. Then in 'Linear Regression' dialog box, send 'Academic Life Related Concern [AL_Total]', 'Personal & Family Life Related Concern [PFL_Total]' and 'Career Related Concern [CR_Total]' to 'Independent(s)'. In the same dialog box, select 'Method' and choose 'Enter' or 'Stepwise', 'Backward' or 'Forward'. The 'Enter' method is used where all independent variables are included in the regression model. The 'Stepwise' method is used for creating the best regression model where variables are added or eliminated from this model. The 'Backward' method is a type of 'Stepwise' method where the variable is dropped from the model if insignificant independent variables are found. The 'Forward' method is a type of 'Stepwise' method where the significant independent variable is selected for the model in the first step and next variable will be selected as per its significance. In this method, the significance of the independent variable is not checked once it is included in the model. For the earlier example, the 'Enter' method is used. Then in the 'Linear Regression' dialog box, click 'Statistics' and a pop-up window will appear as 'Linear Regression: Statistics'. Go to 'Residuals' and tick 'Durbin–Watson'. After that, click 'Continue' (Exhibit 13.2).

EXHIBIT 13.2

SPSS Window for Multiple Regression Analysis (1)

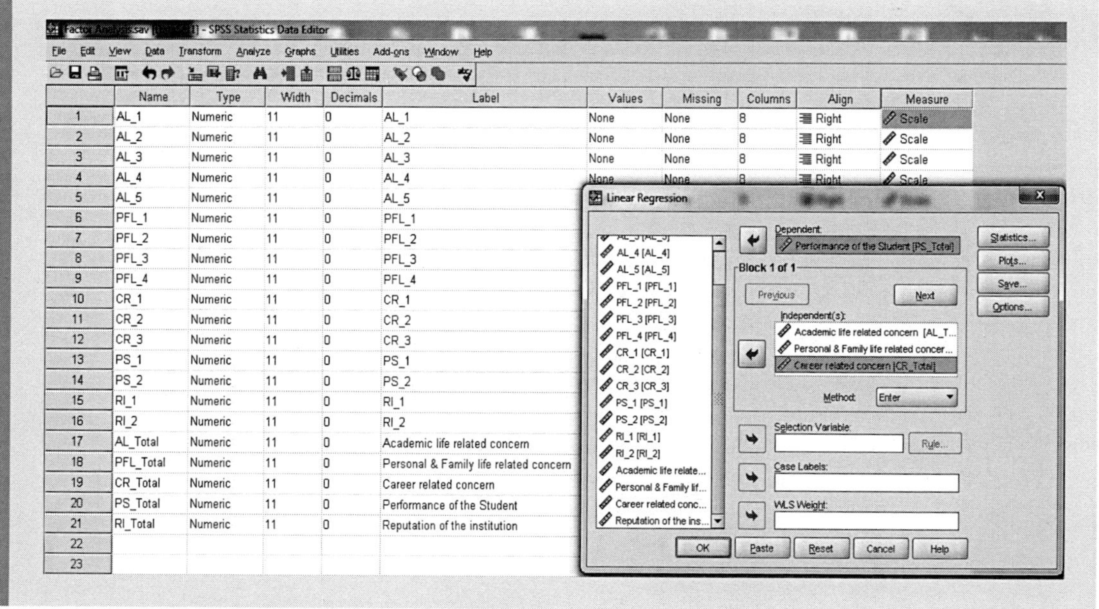

TABLE 13.3
Regression Model Summary

Model	*R*	*R*-square	Adjusted *R*-square	Std. Error of the Estimate	Durbin–Watson
1	0.519[a]	0.269	0.246	0.551	1.703

Source: Authors.
Notes: 1. [a]Predictors: (Constant), Career Related Concern, Personal & Family Life Related Concern, Academic Life Related Concern.
2. Dependent Variable: Performance of the Student.

TABLE 13.4
ANOVA for Regression Model

Model		Sum of Squares	df	Mean Square	F	Sig.
1	Regression	10.730	3	3.577	**11.768**	**0.000[a]**
	Residual	29.177	96	0.304		
	Total	39.907	99			

Source: Authors.
Notes: 1. Bold values indicate estimations with level of significance.
2. [a]Predictors: (Constant), Career Related Concern, Personal & Family Life Related Concern, Academic Life Related Concern.
3. Dependent Variable: Performance of the Student.

Now click 'OK'. Then an SPSS output box will appear as shown in Table 13.3.

Here, *R* value is 0.519, which indicates a medium degree of positive correlation. The R^2 value emphasizes how much of the total variation in the dependent variable, 'Performance of the Student', can be explained by the independent variables. In this case, 26.9% variance of the dependent variable can be explained by the independent variable, which is low. Also, adjusted *R*-square is used when two or more regression models are compared, having same dependent variable but different independent variables. The gap between *R*-square and adjusted *R*-square value widens when significant independent variables are incorporated in the model.

Durbin–Watson D statistic value is used to judge the autocorrelation between residuals and varies from 0 to 4. Generally, the desirable range of 'Durbin–Watson D statistic' value is $1 < D < 3$. Here, the value of the Durbin–Watson D statistic (1.703) for 'Multiple Regression' shows that residuals do not have any autocorrelation.

On the other hand, the ANOVA table (Table 13.4) depicts how well the regression equation fits the data (i.e., predicts the dependent variable).

Table 13.4 indicates that the regression model predicts the dependent variable significantly well. Here, *p* (Sig.) is less than 0.001, which is actually less than 0.05. It means that this regression model statistically and significantly predicts the outcome variable. So model is a suitable fit for the data.

Table 13.5 provides the values of 'Unstandardized Coefficients' and reflects if independent variables are significant or not for the regression model.

By taking regression coefficient values from this table, we can establish the regression equation. The regression equation is as follows:

Performance of the Student = 0.206 × (Academic Life Related Concern)
+ 0.370 × (Personal & Family Life Related Concern) + 0.387 × (Career Related Concern).

TABLE 13.5
Regression Coefficient and Significance of the Variables

Model		Unstandardized Coefficients		Standardized Coefficients		
		B	Std. Error	Beta	T	Sig.
1	(Constant)	**0.167**	0.715		0.234	**0.816**
	Academic Life Related Concern	**0.206**	0.098	0.190	2.106	**0.038**
	Personal & Family Life Related Concern	**0.370**	0.118	0.277	3.139	**0.002**
	Career Related Concern	**0.387**	0.115	0.307	3.367	**0.001**

Source: Authors.
Notes: 1. Bold values indicate estimations with level of significance.
2. Dependent Variable: Performance of the Student.

As *p*-values (Sig.) of three independent variables are less than 0.05 and the value of 'Unstandardized Coefficients' are positive, we can say that a positive relationship exists between dependent and independent variables at 5% level of significance.

Secondly, we will establish the regression equation, taking 'Reputation of the Institution' as a dependent variable and 'Performance of the Student' as an independent variable.

After putting data and variable in the 'Data View' window and 'Variable View' window, click Analyze → Regression → Linear in the SPSS window. One pop-up window will appear as 'Linear Regression'. Then send 'Reputation of the Institution [RI_Total]' to 'Dependent'. Then in the 'Linear Regression' dialog box, send 'Performance of the Student [PS_Total]', to 'Independent(s)'. In the same dialog box, select 'Method' and choose 'Enter'. Then in the 'Linear Regression' dialog box, click 'Statistics' and one pop-up window will appear as 'Linear Regression: Statistics'. Go to 'Residuals' and tick 'Durbin–Watson'. After that, click 'Continue' (Exhibit 13.3).

EXHIBIT 13.3
SPSS Window for Multiple Regression Analysis (2)

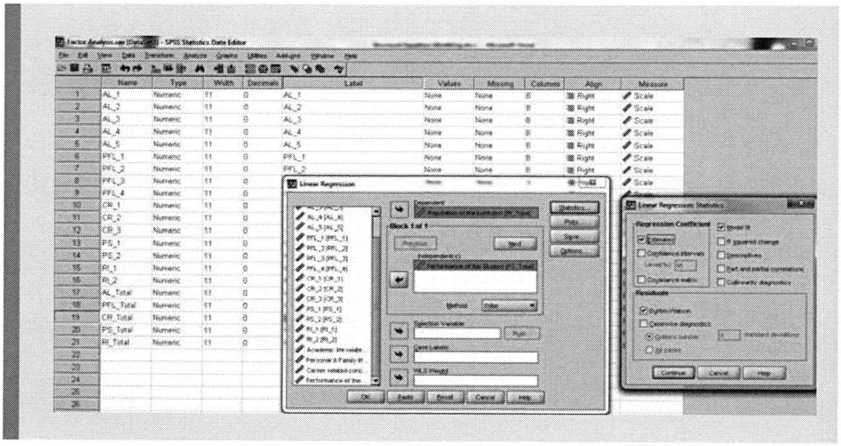

TABLE 13.6
Regression Model Summary

Model	*R*	*R*-square	Adjusted *R*-square	Std. Error of the Estimate	Durbin–Watson
1	0.471[a]	0.222	0.214	0.421	1.935

Source: Authors.
Notes: 1. [a]Predictors: (Constant), Performance of the Student.
2. Dependent Variable: Reputation of the Institution.

TABLE 13.7
ANOVA for Regression Model

Model		Sum of Squares	df	Mean Square	F	Sig.
1	Regression	4.963	1	4.963	**28.012**	**0.000[a]**
	Residual	17.364	98	0.177		
	Total	22.328	99			

Source: Authors.
Notes: 1. Bold values indicate estimations with level of significance.
2. [a]Predictors: (Constant), Performance of the Student.
3. Dependent Variable: Reputation of the Institution.

Now click 'OK'. Then an SPSS output box will appear as shown in Table 13.6.

Here, *R* value is 0.471, which indicates a low degree of positive correlation. Also, R^2 value says that 22.2% variance of the dependent variable can be explained by the independent variable, which is low. The value of Durbin–Watson D statistic (1.935) for 'Multiple Regression' shows that residuals do not have any autocorrelation.

Table 13.7 indicates that the regression model predicts the dependent variable significantly well. Here, *p* (Sig.) is less than 0.001, which is actually less than 0.05. It means that this regression model statistically and significantly predicts the outcome variable at 5% level of significance. So model is a suitable fit for the data.

By taking constant and regression coefficient value from Table 13.8, we can establish the following regression equation:

Reputation of the Institution = 3.016 + 0.353 × (Performance of the Student).

As *p*-value (Sig.) of independent variable is less than 0.05 and the value of 'Unstandardized Coefficient' is positive, we can say that a positive relationship exists between dependent and independent variable at 5% level of significance.

13.4. STRUCTURAL EQUATION MODELLING (SEM) THROUGH AMOS

SEM can easily explain the relationships among multiple variables. It verifies the interrelationship conditions, observing in a series of multiple regression equations. It consists of both dependence and

TABLE 13.8
Regression Coefficient and Significance of the Variables

Model		Unstandardized Coefficients		Standardized Coefficients		
		B	Std. Error	Beta	*t*	Sig.
1	(Constant)	**3.016**	0.296		10.199	**0.000**
	Performance of the Student	**0.353**	0.067	0.471	5.293	**0.000**

Source: Authors.
Notes: 1. Bold values indicate estimations with level of significance.
2. Dependent Variable: Reputation of the Institution.

interdependence techniques of the variables which is required when one dependent variable converts into an independent variable in the subsequent relationship. The proposed relationship of a model, depending on the literature review can be developed in terms of a series of equations through SEM. So the main attributes of SEM are (a) Estimation of multiple interrelated relationships of the variables, (b) Finding the latent independent variables which cannot be detected easily from regression equations and (c) Preparation of a model. Now, we will evaluate the variables of the model (from the earlier example) in terms of model fit measurement. There are generally two types of relationships among variables. In 'AMOS Graphics', the dependence relationship is drawn by a straight arrow which is used between independent and dependent variable and a two-headed arrow is used between independent variables.

A model's 'goodness of fit' is evaluated with the help of different indexes. The Relative χ^2 (χ^2/df), which varies depending on the sample size, should be less than 3. Normed fit index (NFI) assumes that all latent variables are not correlated and the value should be more than 0.90. The goodness-of-fit index (GFI) is equivalent to R^2 which can provide the best result if it is more than 0.90. Adjusted goodness-of-fit index (AGFI) which adjusts the GFI depending on the degrees of freedom and the value more than 0.09 provides the best result. The comparative fit index (CFI) compares the model fit improvement of the proposed model over a model which defines no relationships among variables and the value more than 0.09 provides the best model fit. The value of root mean square error of approximation (RMSEA) emphasizes that the sampling error must be less than 0.06.

Now, we will execute SEM through 'AMOS Graphics' for the model mentioned in the earlier example. First of all, go to the 'Start' button and click 'AMOS Graphics'. Now, one window will open (Exhibit 13.4). Go to 'File'. Then click 'Data Files'.

One pop-up window will appear as 'Data Files'.

Then in the 'Data Files' dialog box, click the 'File Name' and search the SPSS file where all variables are available. Then click 'OK'.

Now click 'List variables in data set'. A pop-up window will appear as 'Variables in Dataset'. After that, drag all the required variables to the new template (Exhibit 13.5).

For proper drawing of the model on template, it is required to shape and move the object. Then go to the individual variable box and right-click. Now click on 'Object Properties' and check 'Variable name' and 'Variable label' (Exhibit 13.6).

EXHIBIT 13.4
AMOS Window (Step 1)

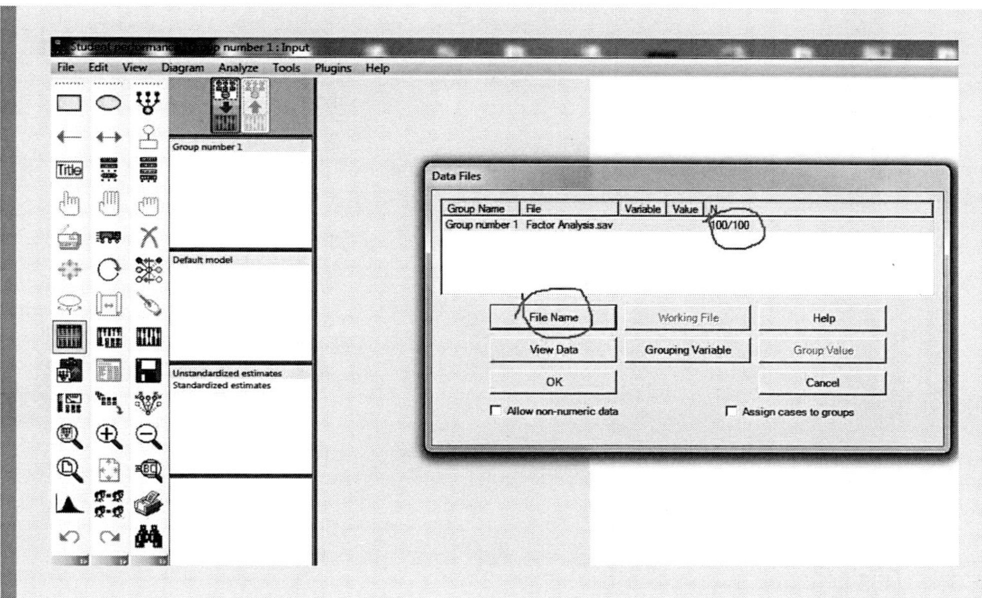

EXHIBIT 13.5
AMOS Window (Step 2)

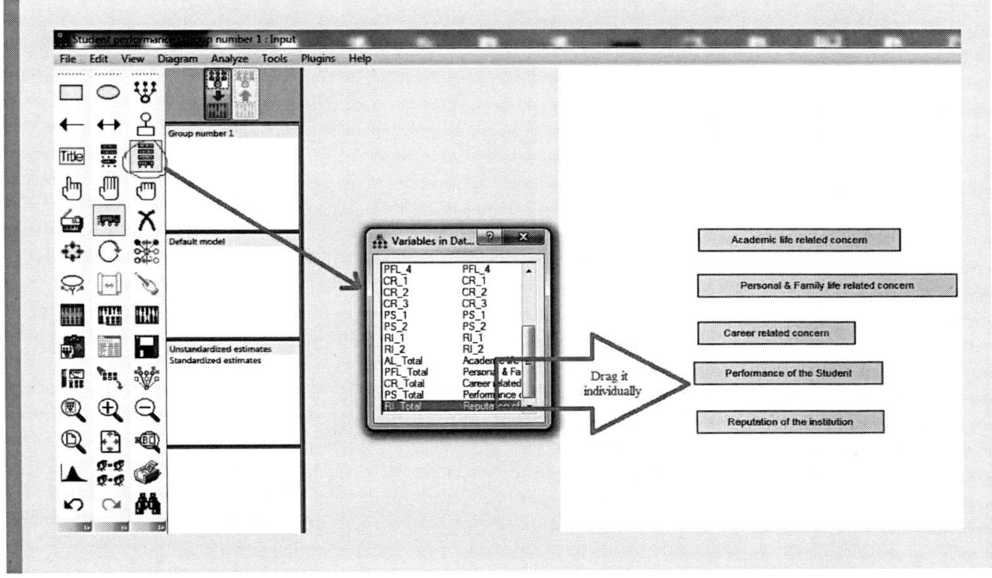

EXHIBIT 13.6
AMOS Window (Step 3)

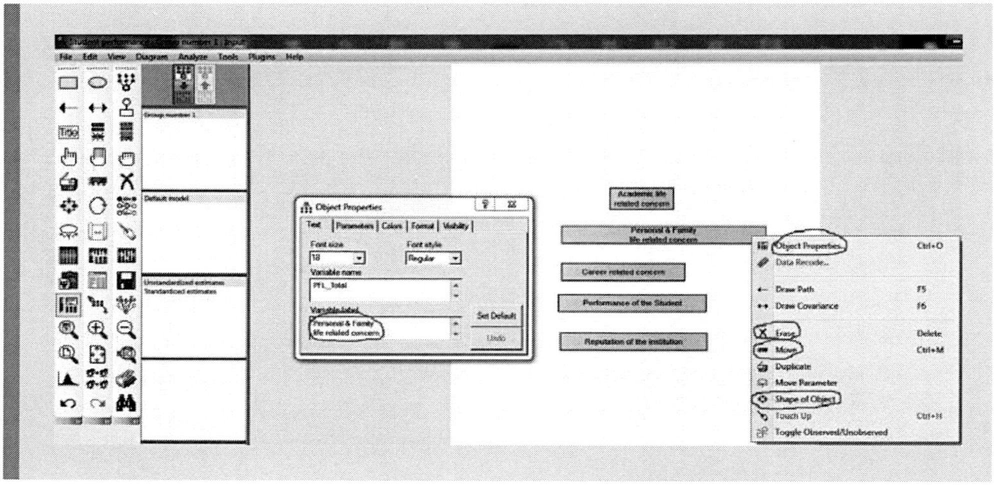

Now connect independent and dependent variables with a single-headed arrow and connect independent variables with a double headed arrow (Exhibit 13.7).

EXHIBIT 13.7
AMOS Window (Step 4)

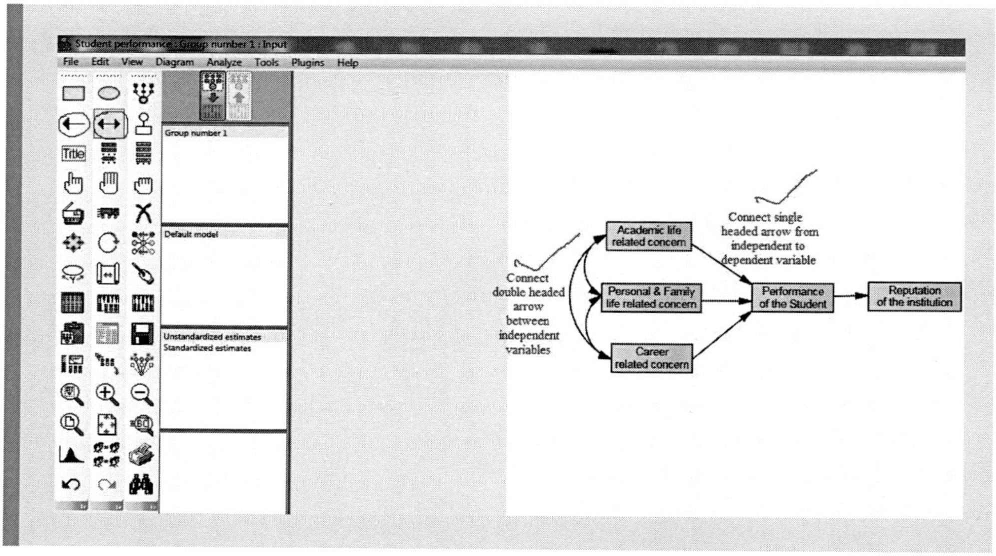

Then add the unique variable (error term) with dependent variables. After that right-click on the unique variable and go to 'Object Properties'. Then put 'Variable name' and 'Variable label' (Exhibit 13.8).

EXHIBIT 13.8
AMOS Window (Step 5)

Then go to 'View' and click 'Analysis Properties'. One pop-up window will appear as 'Analysis Properties'. Then in the 'Analysis Properties' dialog box, click the 'Output' and tick 'Minimization history', 'Standardized estimates', 'Squared multiple correlations' and 'Modification indices'. Then close the dialog box (Exhibit 13.9).

EXHIBIT 13.9
AMOS Window (Step 6)

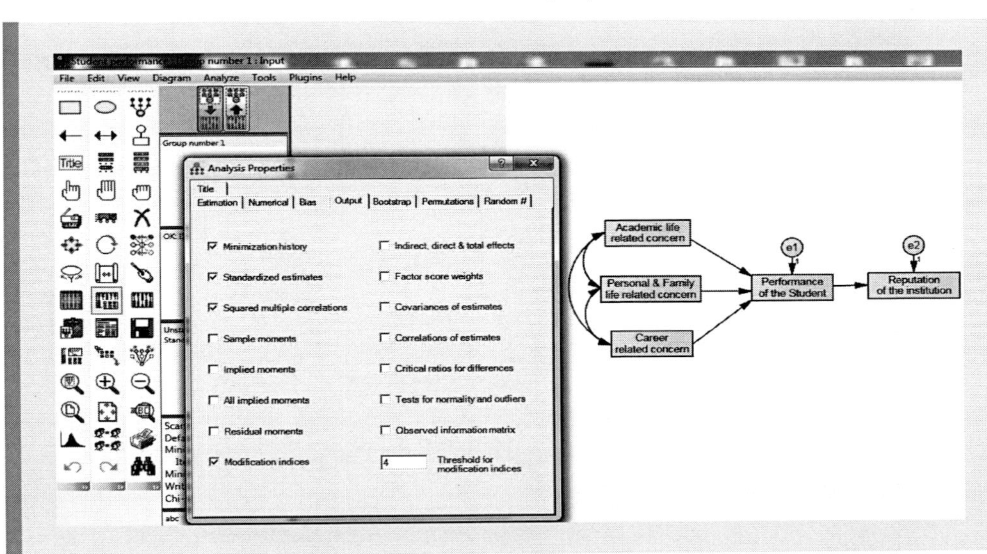

Then go to 'Analyze' and click 'Calculate Estimates'. After that, go to 'View' and click 'Text Output'. One pop-up window will appear as 'Amos Output'. Then in the 'Amos Output' dialog box, click the 'Modification Indices'. It indicates the minor change of the model as 'CR_Total → RI_Total' for maximum possible improvement. So connect it (Exhibit 13.10).

EXHIBIT 13.10
AMOS Window (Step 7)

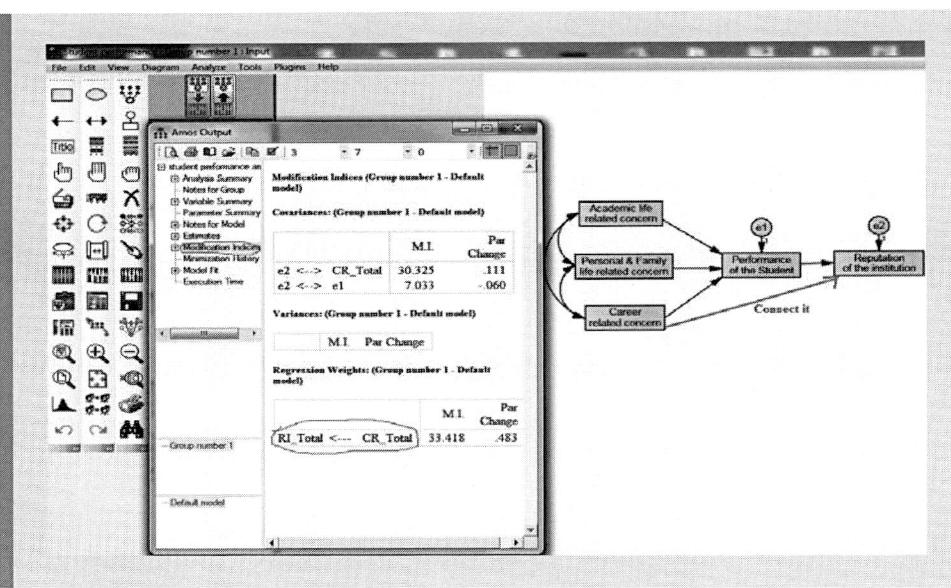

Then we get the final model with all regression estimates by clicking 'View the output path diagram' as shown in Figure 13.2.

FIGURE 13.2
Final Structure Equation Model

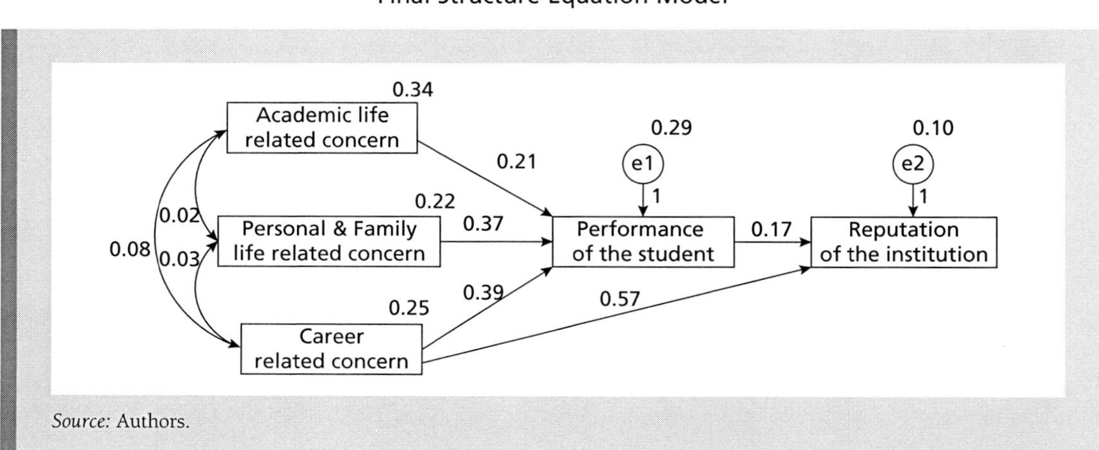

Source: Authors.

Then, go to 'View' and click 'Text Output'. One pop-up window will appear as 'Amos Output'. Then in the 'Amos Output' dialog box, click the 'Estimates' (Exhibit 13.11).

EXHIBIT 13.11

AMOS Window (Step 8)

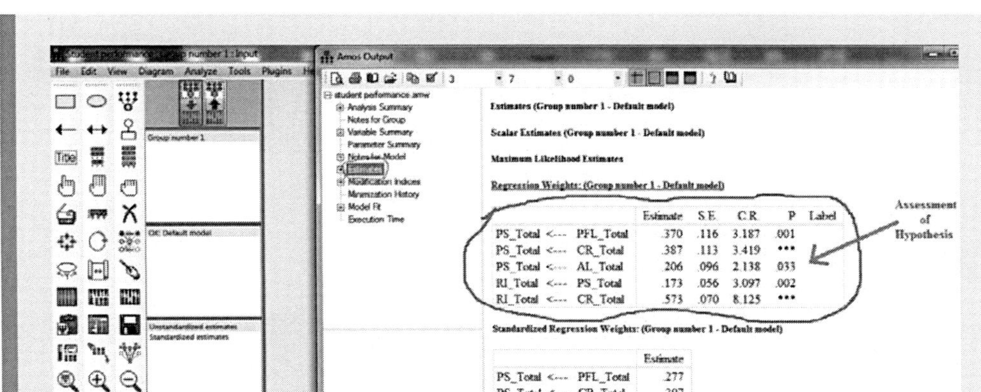

TABLE 13.9

Path Analysis with Regression Weights

Measurement Path			Estimate	S.E.	C.R.	p	Assessment
PS_Total	<---	AL_Total	**0.206**	0.096	2.138	**0.033**	**Supported**
PS_Total	<---	PFL_Total	**0.370**	0.116	3.187	**0.001**	**Supported**
PS_Total	<---	CR_Total	**0.387**	0.113	3.419	*	**Supported**
RI_Total	<---	PS_Total	**0.173**	0.056	3.097	**0.002**	**Supported**
RI_Total	<---	CR_Total	**0.573**	0.070	8.125	*	**Supported**

Source: Authors.

Notes: 1. Bold values indicate estimations with level of significance.

2. *Significant regression coefficient ($p < 0.01$ and 0.05).

Here, the p-values (Table 13.9) for path coefficient for each relationship between dependent and independent variable is significant where $p < 0.01$ and 0.05. Also, observing the positive regression estimates, it is concluded that 'Academic Life Related Concern', 'Personal & Family Life Related Concern' and 'Career Related Concern' have a positive relationship with 'Performance of the Student'. On the other hand, 'Career Related Concern' and 'Performance of the Student' have the positive relationship with 'Reputation of the Institution'.

At last, go to 'View' and click 'Text Output'. One pop-up window will appear as 'Amos Output'. Then in the 'Amos Output' dialog box, click 'Model Fit' (Exhibit 13.12).

EXHIBIT 13.12
AMOS Window (Step 9)

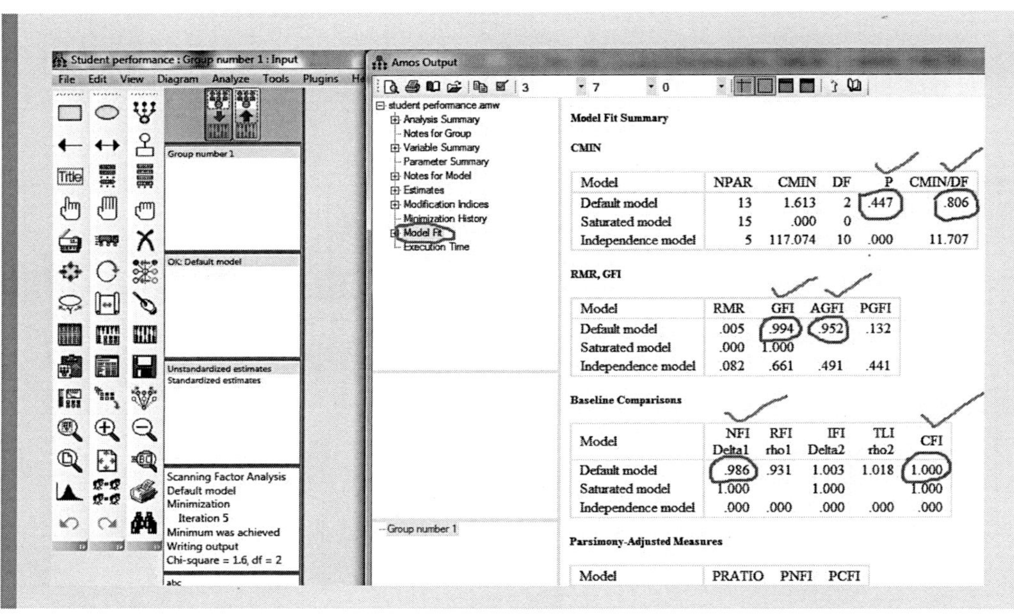

Generally, the indices shown in Table 13.10 are observed for checking the model fit.

TABLE 13.10
Fit Indices of the Model

Name of the Fit Indexes	Acceptable Threshold Levels	Model Fit Index Values
χ^2/df (chi-square/degree of freedom)	Values less than 3	0.806
RMSEA	Values less than 0.06	<0.001
GFI	Values greater than 0.90	0.994
AGFI	Values greater than 0.90	0.952
NFI	Values greater than 0.90	0.986
CFI	Values greater than 0.90	1.000

Source: Authors.
Note: Indices as suggested by Schumacker (1992), Hair et al. (1998) and Iacobucci (2010).

Here, all the fit indices for this model fulfil the acceptable threshold level. So these values indicate a good model fit.

13.5. MULTICOLLINEARITY

When two or more than two independent variables are highly correlated to each other among several independent variables, used in the model, this condition is called as multicollinearity. The value of variance inflation factor (VIF), which describes multicollinearity, must be less than 3 for acceptability range.

After putting data and variable in the 'Data View' window and 'Variable View' window, click Analyze → Regression → Linear in the SPSS window. One pop-up window will appear as 'Linear Regression'. Then send 'Performance of the Student [PS_Total]' to 'Dependent'. Then in the 'Linear Regression' dialog box, send 'Academic Life Related Concern [AL_Total]', 'Personal & Family Life Related Concern [PFL_Total]' and 'Career Related Concern [CR_Total]', to 'Independent(s)'. Then in the 'Linear Regression' dialog box, click 'Statistics' and one pop-up window will appear as 'Linear Regression: Statistics'. Tick 'Collinearity diagnostics'. After that, click 'Continue' (Exhibit 13.13).

EXHIBIT 13.13
SPSS Window for Collinearity Diagnostics

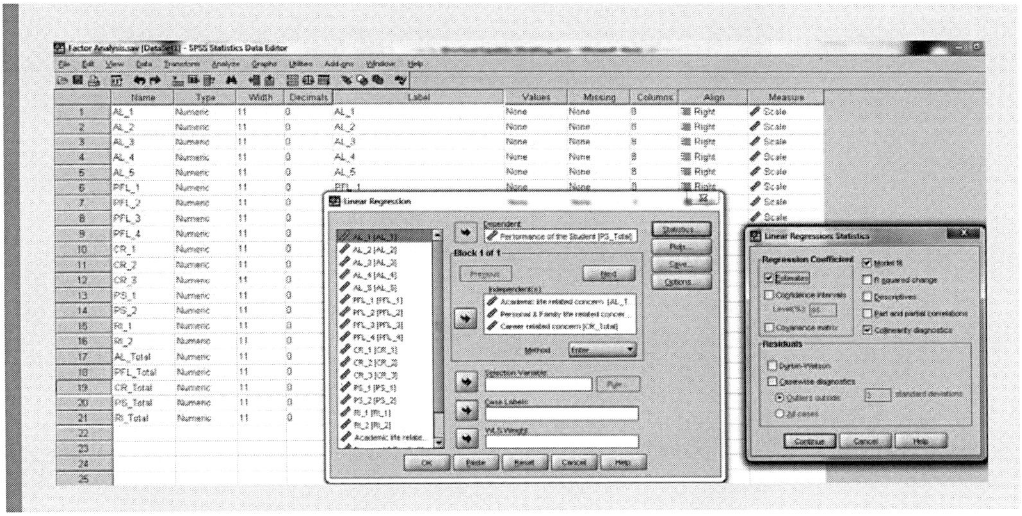

Now, click 'OK'. Then an SPSS output box will appear as shown in Table 13.11.

TABLE 13.11
Collinearity Statistics When 'Performance of the Student' Is Dependent Variable

	Collinearity Statistics	
	Tolerance	VIF
Academic Life Related Concern	0.932	1.073
Personal & Family Life Related Concern	0.978	1.022
Career Related Concern	0.918	1.089

Source: Authors.

Once again, click Analyze → Regression → Linear in the SPSS window. One pop-up window will appear as 'Linear Regression'. Then send 'Reputation of the Institution [RI_Total]' to 'Dependent'. Then in the 'Linear Regression' dialog box, send 'Performance of the Student [PS_Total]' and 'Career Related Concern [CR_Total]', to 'Independent(s)'. Then in the 'Linear Regression' dialog box, click 'Statistics' and one pop-up window will appear as 'Linear Regression: Statistics'. Tick 'Collinearity diagnostics'. After that, click 'Continue' (Exhibit 13.14).

EXHIBIT 13.14

SPSS Window for Collinearity Diagnostics

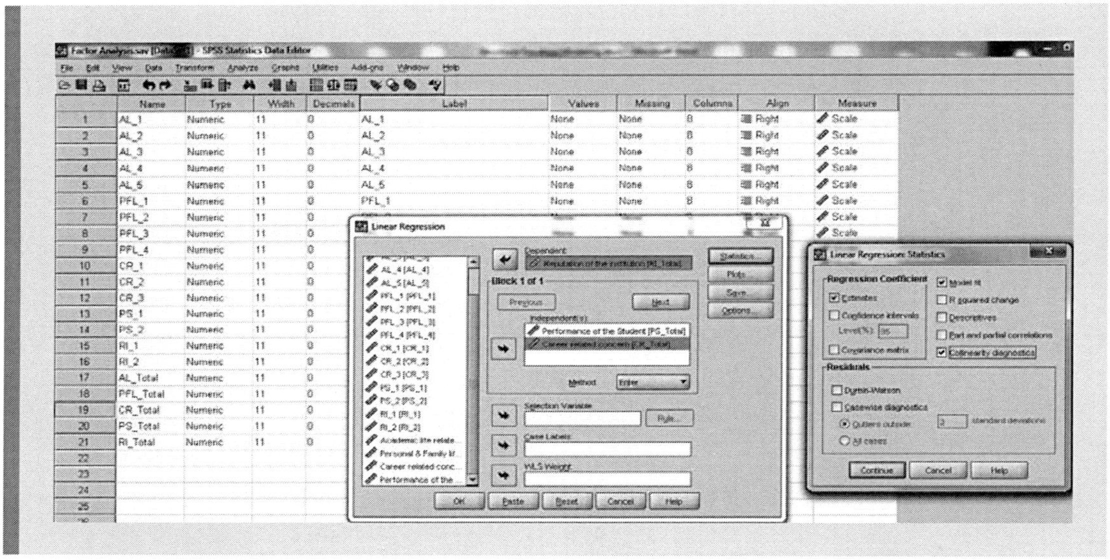

Now click 'OK'. Then an SPSS output box will appear as shown in Table 13.12.

TABLE 13.12

Collinearity Statistics When 'Reputation of the Institution' Is Dependent Variable

	Collinearity Statistics	
	Tolerance	VIF
Performance of the Student	0.844	1.185
Career Related Concern	0.844	1.185

Source: Authors.

In the earlier problem, it has been observed through Tables 13.11 and 13.12 (from SPSS output) that all values of VIF are in an acceptable range which says that all independent variables are free from multicollinearity.

SUMMARY

Multiple regression analysis deals with two or more independent variables (explanatory variables) and at least one dependent variable. Therefore, it is used to assess the influence of independent variables on dependent variables.

SEM can easily explain the relationships among multiple variables. It verifies the interrelationship conditions, observing in a series of multiple regression equations. It consists of both dependence and interdependence techniques of the variables which is required when one dependent variable converts into an independent variable in the subsequent relationship. The proposed relationship of a model, depending on the literature review, can be developed in terms of a series of equations through SEM.

When two or more than two independent variables are highly correlated to each other among several independent variables, used in the model, this condition is called multicollinearity. The value of VIF, which describes multicollinearity, must be less than 3 for acceptability range.

KEY TERMS

multiple regression analysis (138)
structural equation modelling (147)
goodness of fit (148)
RMSEA (148)
GFI (148)
AGFI (148)
NFI (148)
CFI (148)
multicollinearity (155)
VIF (155)

EXERCISES

1. What is the purpose of multiple regression?
2. What do you mean by the term 'multicollinearity'?
3. How would you develop SEM through AMOS?
4. What is the significance of VIF in multiple regression?

CHAPTER

14

T-tests

LEARNING OBJECTIVES

After studying this chapter, you should be able to

- Understand the meaning of t-test.
- Learn the procedure of different types of t-tests using SPSS.

14.1. T-TESTS

T-tests are used to compare two means to assess whether they are from the same population. T-tests presume that both groups are normally distributed and have relatively equal variances. The t-statistic is distributed on a curve that is based on the number of degrees of freedom (df). There are three kinds of t-tests and these have been discussed in the following sections.

14.2. ONE-SAMPLE T-TEST

Example: A random sample of 22 fifth-grade pupils have a GPA of 5.0 in mathematics with a standard deviation of 0.452, whereas marks range from 1 (worst) to 6 (excellent). The GPA of all fifth-grade pupils of the last five years is 4.7. Is the GPA of the 22 pupils different from the populations' GPA?

Solution: Information for one-sample T-test

Pupil	Grade Point
1	5
2	5.5
3	4.5
4	5
5	5
6	6

Pupil	Grade Point
7	5
8	5
9	4.5
10	5
11	5
12	4.5
13	4.5
14	5.5
15	4
16	5
17	5
18	5.5
19	4.5
20	5.5
21	5
22	5.5
Mean	**5.0**
Variance	**0.2045**

We estimate the standard deviation of the population:

$$\hat{\sigma}^2 = s^2 \times \frac{n}{n-1} = 0.2045 \times \frac{22}{21} = 0.214$$

and we get the standard deviation of the mean:

$$\hat{\sigma}_{\bar{x}} = \sqrt{\frac{\hat{\sigma}^2}{n}} = \sqrt{\frac{0.214}{22}} = 0.099$$

Now, we can compute the t-value:

$$t_{(n-1)} = \frac{\bar{x} - \mu}{\hat{\sigma}_{\bar{x}}} = \frac{5.0 - 4.7}{0.099} = 3.03$$

For the non-directed hypothesis, we have a critical t-value of t (df = 21, alpha = 0.05) = 2.080.

For the directed hypothesis, we have a critical t-value of t (df = 21, alpha = 0.05) = 1,721.

The obtained t-value is greater than the critical t-value. The GPA of the 22 pupils is different from the populations' GPA.

It is used to compare a sample mean to a population mean. Here, we do not know the population variance. If we know the population variance, then we use z-test.

Suppose sample mean of any sample is = 1.5. Is our sample different from the population or not?

Here, H_0: Sample mean = Population mean

Command

Analyze → Compare means → One-sample t-test → Variable drop into test variance box → Give the test value (i.e., population mean) → OK.

Output

From the output, we will get the t-value and its significance level in terms of *p*-value. If the *p*-value is less than 0.05, we will reject the H_0 and conclude that the sample mean is different from the population.

For example, an economist wants to know if the per capita income of a particular region is same as the national average. Here, one-sample t-test is used to draw the conclusion.

14.3. ONE-SAMPLE T-TEST IN SPSS

Example: A random sample of 22 fifth-grade pupils has a GPA of 5.0 in mathematics with a standard deviation of 0.452, whereas marks range from 1 (worst) to 6 (excellent). The GPA of all fifth-grade pupils of the last five years is 4.7. Is the GPA of the 22 pupils different from the populations' GPA?

Pupil	1	2	3	4	5	6	7	8	9	10	11	12	13	14	15	16	17	18	19	20	21	22
Grade Points	5	5.5	4.5	5	5	6	5	5	4.5	5	5	4.5	4.5	5.5	4	5	5	5.5	4.5	5.5	5	5.5

Solution:

H_0: There is no difference between the average grade point of pupil with the GPA of all fifth-grade pupils of the last five years.

The first step here is to enter variable names into the 'Variable View' and feed the required data against these variables into the data editor. In the case of our example (Exhibit 14.1), we have taken into consideration two different variables and these are pupil and grade points.

EXHIBIT 14.1

SPSS Window for One-sample T-test (1)

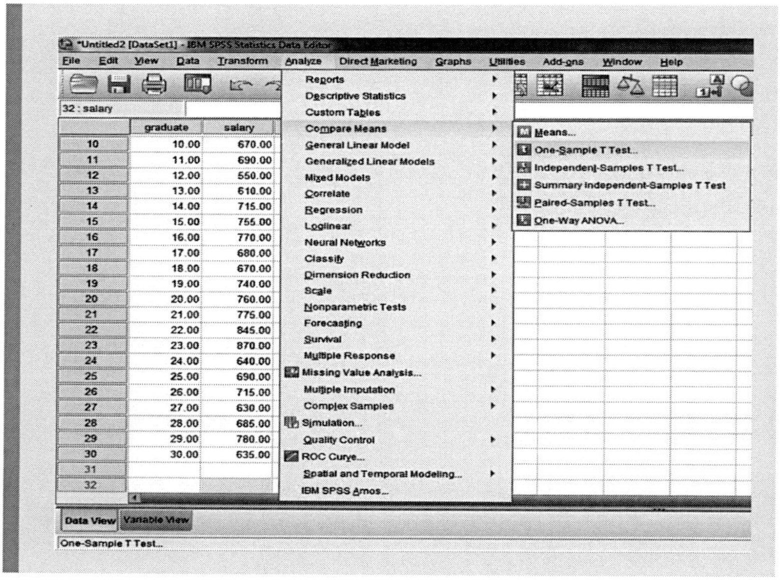

EXHIBIT 14.2

SPSS Window for One-sample T-test (2)

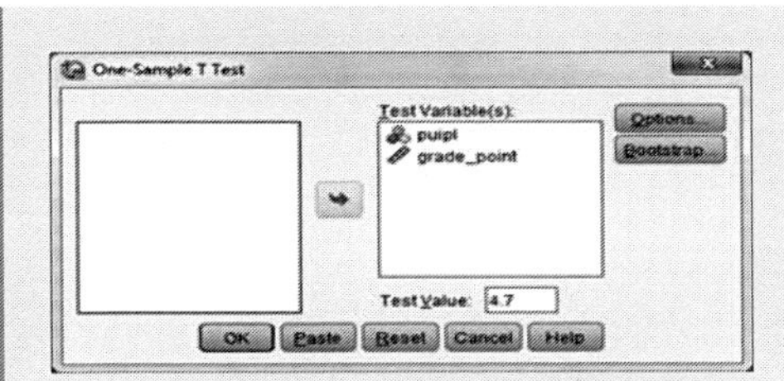

TABLE 14.1

One-sample Statistics from SPSS Output

	N	Mean	Std. Deviation	Std. Error Mean
Pupil	22	11.9545	7.07428	1.50824
Grade point	22	5.0000	0.46291	0.09869

Source: Authors.

TABLE 14.2

One-sample Test from SPSS Output

	Test Value = 4.7					
					95% Confidence Interval of the Difference	
	t	df	Sig. (Two-tailed)	Mean Difference	Lower	Upper
Pupil	**4.810**	**21**	**0.000**	**7.25455**	4.1180	10.3911
Grade point	**3.040**	**21**	**0.006**	**0.30000**	0.0948	0.5052

Source: Authors.
Note: Bold values indicate estimations with level of significance.

After feeding the data, we will drop these variables into test variable box and assign a test value. Here, we have test value of 4.7. This is shown in Exhibit 14.2.

If we run the analysis in SPSS, then we will get output as shown in Table 14.1.

As $p < 0.05$ (Table 14.2), we can reject H_0 at $\alpha = 0.05$, which means that the sample mean is significantly different from the hypothesized value, that is, assumed population mean.

14.4. INDEPENDENT SAMPLES T-TEST

We are interested in detecting differences between the means of two independent groups and this is called independent samples t-test.

Here, H_0: Sample mean of first group = Sample mean of the second group

Examples:

1. An economist wants to compare the per capita income of two different regions.
2. A labour union wants to compare the productivity levels of workers for two different groups.

Example: A study was conducted to compare the efficiency of the workers of two mines, one with private ownership and the other with government ownership. The researcher was of the view that there is no significant difference in their efficiency levels.

Four workers from the private sector mine and five from the government-owned mine were selected and their output was recorded.

Mine 1	5	8	7	8	7
Mine 2	3	5	2	3	

Solution:

H_0: Output of the workers from mine 1 equals to that of the workers from the mine 2. In this case, H_0: 1 = 2, and the H_1: 1 ≠ 2.

Mine 1	Mine 2
5	3
8	5
7	2
8	3
7	
Sum = 35	Sum = 13
$N = 5$	$N = 4$
Mean = 7	Mean = 3.5
$SS = 6$	$SS = 4.75$

Compute the value of t using the below-mentioned equation. All of the notation should be familiar at this point (mean, SS, N). The only difference in the notation is that the means, SSs and Ns are subscripted to show which group they represent:

$$t = \frac{(\bar{X}_1 - \bar{X}_2)}{\sqrt{\left[\frac{SS_1 + SS_2}{N_1 + N_2 - 2}\right]\left[\frac{1}{N_1} + \frac{1}{N_2}\right]}}$$

$$t = \frac{(7.00 - 3.25)}{\sqrt{\left[\frac{6.00 + 4.75}{5 + 4 - 2}\right]\left[\frac{1}{5} + \frac{1}{4}\right]}} = 4.52$$

To evaluate the results, you compare the computed t to the critical value of t. The critical value of t (obtained from the Student's t table) is 2.365 (alpha = 0.05 and df = $N_1 + N_2 - 2 = 7$). Because the computed value of t (4.52) exceeds the critical value (2.365), we reject the null hypothesis and conclude that the two populations from which the samples are drawn do have different means.

14.5. INDEPENDENT SAMPLES T-TEST USING SPSS

Command: Analyze → Compare means → Independent sample t-test → put out variable into test variable box → define groups (put 1 or 2) → Continue → OK.

EXHIBIT 14.3
SPSS Window for Independent Samples T-test

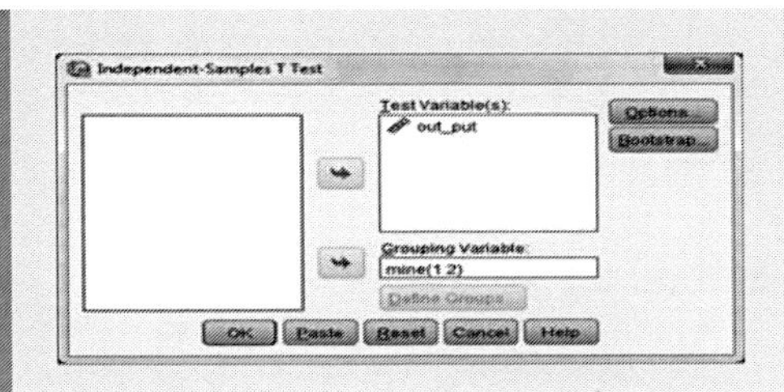

TABLE 14.3
Group Statistics

	Mine	N	Mean	Std. Deviation	Std. Error Mean
Output	1.00	5	7.0000	1.22474	0.54772
	2.00	4	3.2500	1.25831	0.62915

Source: Authors.

TABLE 14.4
Independent Samples Test

		Levene's Test for Equality of Variances		T-test for Equality of Means		
		F	Sig.	*t*	df	Sig. (two-tailed)
Output	Equal variances assumed	0.019	0.893	4.511	7	0.003
	Equal variances not assumed			4.496	6.479	0.003

Source: Authors.

The first step here is to enter variable names into the 'Variable View' and feed the required data against these variables into the data editor. In the case of our example (Exhibit 14.3), we have taken into consideration two different variables and these are mine and output. In our example, there are two types of mines denoted by mine 1 and mine 2, respectively.

After feeding the data, we will drop the output variable into test variable box and assign two grouping values. This is shown in Exhibit 14.3.

If we run the analysis in SPSS, then we will get output as shown in Table 14.3.

Here, from Table 14.4, we are observing that the value of F is not significant. It implies the rejection of H_0, that is, acceptance of H_1. Therefore, we will take the t-value of 4.496 corresponding to equal variances not assumed. Therefore, we can say that the average output of two groups is significantly different from each other at 5% level of significance as the *p*-value is less than 0.05. Therefore, we can reject H_0 at 5% level of significance.

However, if we were to test the assumption that the efficiency of workers of mine 1 is greater than that of the workers of mine 2, then the H_0 and H_1 would be different and we would need the *p*-value of one-tailed test. The new hypotheses would be

H_0: 01 ≤ 02
H_1: 01 > 02

We will get the corresponding *p*-value in one-tailed test if we divide the computed value of *p* in two-tailed test by 2. Therefore, *p*-value would be 0.003/2 = 0.0015 which is less than 0.01. Therefore, we reject the H_0 and conclude that the efficiency of the workers of mine 1 is greater than that of the workers of mine 2.

14.6. PAIRED SAMPLE T-TEST

When the observations are made on the same sample at two different times, it is called paired sample t-test.

Example: HR manager wants to know if a particular module of a training programme had impact in increasing the motivation level of the employees or not.

Solution:

H_0: Sample mean of pre-training score = Sample mean of post-training score

H_1: Sample mean of pre-training score ≠ Sample mean of post-training score

Employee	Pre-training Score	Post-training Score	Difference
1	18	22	+4
2	21	25	+4
3	16	17	+1
4	22	24	+2
5	19	16	–3
6	24	29	+5
7	17	20	+3
8	21	23	+2
9	23	19	–4
10	18	20	+2
11	14	15	+1
12	16	15	–1
13	16	18	+2
14	19	26	+7
15	18	18	0
16	20	24	+4
17	12	18	+6
18	22	25	+3
19	15	19	+4
20	17	16	–1

Using this example with n = 20 employees, the following results were obtained. Calculating the mean and standard deviation of the differences gives:

$$\bar{d} = 2.05 \text{ and } s_d = 2.837. \text{ Therefore, } SE(\bar{d}) = \frac{s_d}{\sqrt{n}} = \frac{2.837}{\sqrt{20}} = 0.634$$

So we have $t = \dfrac{2.05}{0.634} = 3.231$ on 19 df.

Here the calculated t value is 3.231 on 19 degree of freedom. On the other hand, the table value for the respective test is 2.093, which says that the calculated t-value is much higher. We can conclude that the null hypothesis is rejected and, therefore, we can say that results before and after training differ significantly.

14.7. PAIRED SAMPLE T-TEST USING SPSS

Command: Analyze → Compare means → Paired sample t-test → before score or value and after score or value → OK.

Example: HR manager wants to know if a particular module of a training programme had impact in increasing the motivation level of the employees or not (same dataset).

Solution:

H_0: Sample mean of pre-training score = Sample mean of post-training score.

H_1: Sample mean of pre-training score ≠ Sample mean of post-training score.

After feeding the data, we will assign the paired values in the appropriate box. This is shown in Exhibit 14.4.

EXHIBIT 14.4
SPSS Window for Paired Sample T-test

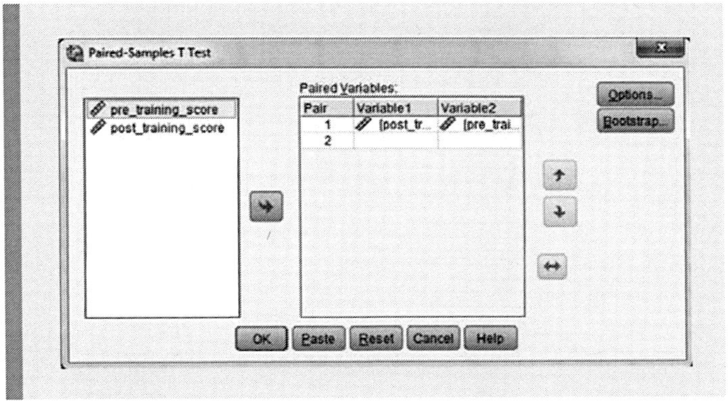

If we run the analysis in SPSS, then we will get output as shown in Table 14.5.

TABLE 14.5
Paired Samples Statistics

		Mean	N	Std. Deviation	Std. Error Mean
Pair 1	post_training_score	20.4500	20	4.05845	0.90750
	pre_training_score	18.4000	20	3.15228	0.70487

Source: Authors.

TABLE 14.6
Paired Samples Correlations

		N	Correlation	Sig.
Pair 1	post_training_score and pre_training_score	20	0.717	<0.01

TABLE 14.7
Paired Samples Test

		Paired Differences							
					95% Confidence Interval of the Difference				
		Mean	Std. Deviation	Std. Error Mean	Lower	Upper	*t*	df	Sig. (two-tailed)
Pair 1	post_training_score – pre_training_score	2.05000	2.83725	0.63443	0.72213	3.37787	**3.231**	19	**0.004**

Source: Authors.
Note: Bold values indicate the estimations of level of significance.

The test result shows that the t-value is 3.231 and *p*-value is 0.004 which is less than 0.05 (Table 14.7) which means that the average output of the employees has indeed changed after attending the training programme. If the t-value is significant, then we can say that results before and after the training differ significantly.

SUMMARY

T-tests are used to compare two means to assess whether they are from the same population. T-tests presume that both groups are normally distributed and have relatively equal variances. The t-statistic is distributed on a curve that is based on the number of degrees of freedom. There are three kinds of t-tests—(a) one-sample t-test, (b) independent sample t-test and (c) paired sample t-test. One-sample t-test is used to compare a sample mean to a population mean. Here, we do not know the population variance. If we know the population variance, then we use z-test. If we are interested in detecting differences between the means of two independent groups, then we will apply independent samples t-test. When the observations are made on the same sample at two different times, it is called paired sample t-test.

KEY TERMS

t-test (158)
one-sample t-test (158)
paired sample t-test (164)
independent samples t-test (161)

EXERCISES

1. When t-test is applied?
2. Distinguish between independent-samples t-test and paired-samples t-test.
3. How is one-sample t-test done using SPSS?
4. When can we apply paired sample t-test?

CHAPTER

15

Analysis of Variance (ANOVA)

LEARNING OBJECTIVES

After studying this chapter, you should be able to

- Visualize the meaning of analysis of variance (ANOVA).
- Learn the procedure of different types of ANOVA using SPSS.

15.1. ANALYSIS OF VARIANCE

In the case of more than two populations, if a researcher wants to test the equality of means of the samples which have been drawn from the different populations, ANOVA could be used. Application of ANOVA is important in the field of social science as well as business research. Basically, ANOVA can examine one or more number of variables which have an influence on a dependent variable. Also, it can examine the differences in various categories/groups under each variable. Scaling is important for different variables to execute ANOVA through SPSS. Dependent variables belong to interval or ratio scale and independent variables (categorical) belong to nominal scale. There are different experimental designs in ANOVA. These are (a) one-way ANOVA (completely randomized design), (b) two-way ANOVA (randomized block design) and (c) factorial design. An assumption for ANOVA is that samples must be drawn from the normal population with equal variance. For calculating ANOVA (F-value), two estimates of population variance—(a) between the samples and (b) within the samples—are used.

15.2. ONE-WAY ANOVA (COMPLETELY RANDOMIZED DESIGN)

Researchers use one-way ANOVA in the case of one dependent variable (interval or ratio scale) and one independent variable (nominal scale) with different categories/groups. It helps to test the equality of means of two or more categories/groups under independent variable. The sample size of each group could be same or not.

Example: A researcher wants to compare the satisfaction score of a product brand of five age groups with the help of the following data. A sample of three randomly taken product users was selected from each age group. They evaluated satisfaction score out of 100 marks.

Age Group			
20 years and below	34	54	25
21–30 years	39	56	31
31–40 years	41	51	29
41–50 years	44	49	45
Above 50 years	38	47	36

Basically, the researcher wants to test whether there is a significant difference between age groups with regards to the satisfaction score of a product brand at 5% level of significance.

Solution: First of all, the total variation in the data set (TSS: Total sum of squares) is calculated using the following formula:

$$\text{TSS} = \text{Total of squares} - \text{Correlation factor}$$

$$= \sum_{i=1}^{n} \sum_{j=1}^{m} x_{ij}^2 - \frac{T^2}{N}$$

x_{ij} = jth observation of ith (row/column) sample
T = Grand total of all data
m = Number of observations in each sample (in row/column)
n = Number of rows or columns in terms of treatments
N = Total number of observations ($m \times n$).

Then the sum of squares between treatments (SST) which refers to the variation between sample mean is calculated by

$$\text{SST} = \frac{1}{m} \sum_{i=1}^{n} T_i^2 - \frac{T^2}{N}$$

T_i = Total of observations for the ith (row/column) treatment.

If sample size of each treatment (category) is different, then

$$\text{SST} = \sum_{i=1}^{n} \frac{T_i^2}{m_i} - \frac{T^2}{N}$$

m_i = Number of observations in ith (row/column) treatment.

And the degree of freedom is ($N - n$) for the error sum.

Then the error sum of square (SSE) which refers to the variation within the sample is calculated by

$$\text{SSE} = \text{TSS} - \text{SST}.$$

TABLE 15.1
Format of One-way ANOVA Table

Sum of Squares	Degree of Freedom	Mean Square	F-value
SST: Sum of squares between treatments	$n - 1$	MST (Mean square for treatments) = $\frac{SST}{n-1}$	$\frac{MST}{MSE}$
SSE: Error sum of squares within samples	$n(m - 1)$	MSE (Mean square for error) = $\frac{SSE}{n(m-1)}$	
TSS: Total sum of squares	$N - 1$		

Source: Levin and Rubin (2009).

TABLE 15.2
Required Calculations for One-way ANOVA (1)

Age Group				Total (T_i)
20 years and below	34	54	25	113
21–30 years	39	56	31	126
31–40 years	41	51	29	121
41–50 years	44	49	45	138
Above 50 years	38	47	36	121
		Grand Total (T)		619

Source: Authors.

Null hypothesis (H_0): There is no significant difference between age group with regard to satisfaction score of a product brand.

So, H_0: $\mu_1 = \mu_2 = \mu_3 = \mu_4 = \mu_5$.

Alternative hypothesis (H_1): At least two means are not equal.

Now, for this example, the required calculations for one-way ANOVA are as shown in Table 15.2.

$$\text{So, TSS} = \sum_{i=1}^{5}\sum_{j=1}^{3} x_{ij}^2 - \frac{T^2}{N}$$

$$= 26749 - \frac{619^2}{15} = 1204.93.$$

$$\text{And, SST} = \frac{1}{m}\sum_{i=1}^{n} T_i^2 - \frac{T^2}{N}$$

$$= \left(\frac{113^2}{3} + \frac{126^2}{3} + \frac{121^2}{3} + \frac{138^2}{3} + \frac{121^2}{3}\right) - \frac{619^2}{15}$$

$$= 112.93.$$

$$\begin{aligned}\text{Now, SSE} &= \text{TSS} - \text{SST}\\ &= 1204.93 - 112.93\\ &= 1{,}092.\end{aligned}$$

TABLE 15.3
One-way ANOVA Table (1)

Sum of Squares	Degree of Freedom	Mean Square	F-value
SST: 112.93	$(n-1) = (5-1) = 4$	$MST = \frac{SST}{n-1} = 28.23$	$\frac{MST}{MSE} = 0.258$
SSE: 1,092	$n(m-1) = 5(3-1) = 10$	$MSE = \frac{SSE}{n(m-1)} = 109.20$	
TSS: 1,204.93	$(N-1) = (15-1) = 14$		

Source: Authors.

Here the calculated F-value is 0.258 (see Table 15.3) and the tabulated value with 4, 10 degree of freedom ($F_{4,10}$) is 3.48. As the tabulated value is greater than the corresponding calculated value at 5% level of significance, we accept the null hypothesis. So there is no significant difference between age group with regard to satisfaction score of a product brand.

15.3. THE ONE-WAY ANOVA PROBLEM WITH SPSS

At first, we need to identify dependent and independent variables. Here, satisfaction score is the dependent variable and age group is the independent variable. Age group, which belongs to nominal measure type in SPSS, is coded as 1 = 20 years and below, 2 = 21–30 years, 3 = 31–40 years, 4 = 41–50 years, 5 = above 50 years.

Data for solving the one-way ANOVA problem with SPSS are as follows:

Age Group	Satisfaction Score
1	34
1	54
1	25
2	39
2	56
2	31
3	41
3	51
3	29
4	44
4	49
4	45
5	38
5	47
5	36

Null hypothesis (H_0): $\mu_1 = \mu_2 = \mu_3 = \mu_4 = \mu_5$

EXHIBIT 15.1
SPSS Window for One-way ANOVA (1)

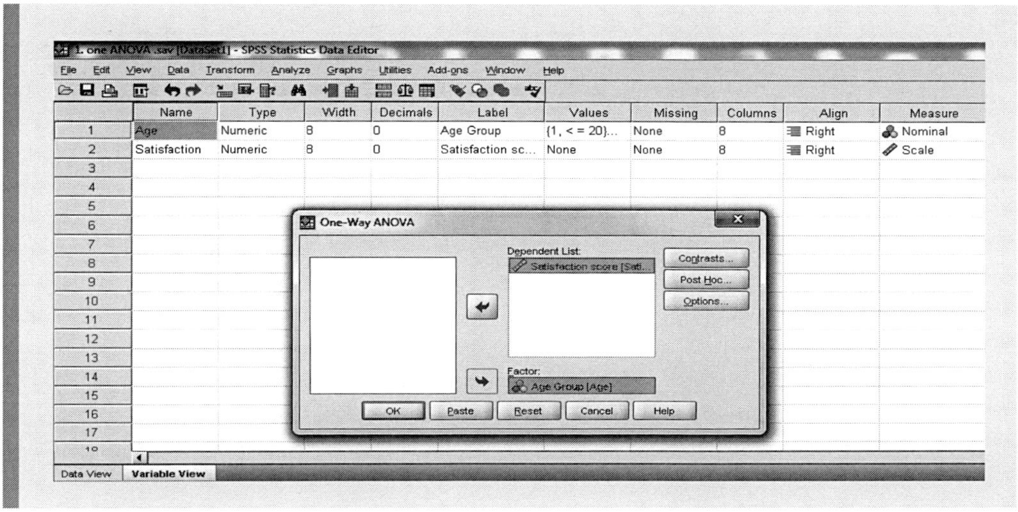

Alternative hypothesis (H_1): At least two means are not equal.

After putting data and variables in the 'Data View' window and 'Variable View' window, click Analyze → Compare Means → One-way ANOVA in the SPSS window. One pop-up window will appear as 'One-way ANOVA'. Then send 'Satisfaction Score' to 'Dependent List' as the dependent variable and send 'Age Group' to 'Factor' as the independent variable. Go to 'Options' and another pop-up window will appear. Tick 'Descriptive'. Then click 'Post Hoc' and another pop-up window will appear. Tick 'Duncan' (Exhibit 15.1).

Then click 'Continue' → 'OK'. At last, an SPSS output box will appear as shown in Table 15.4.

TABLE 15.4
Descriptive Statistics from SPSS Output (1)

Satisfaction Score								
					95% Confidence Interval for Mean			
Age Group	N	Mean	Std. Deviation	Std. Error	Lower Bound	Upper Bound	Minimum	Maximum
<= 20	3	37.67	14.844	8.570	0.79	74.54	25	54
21–30	3	42.00	12.767	7.371	10.28	73.72	31	56
31–40	3	40.33	11.015	6.360	12.97	67.70	29	51
41–50	3	46.00	2.646	1.528	39.43	52.57	44	49
>50	3	40.33	5.859	3.383	25.78	54.89	36	47
Total	15	41.27	9.277	2.395	36.13	46.40	25	56

Source: Authors.

TABLE 15.5
One-way ANOVA Table from SPSS Output (2)

Satisfaction Score					
	Sum of Squares	df	Mean Square	F	Sig.
Between groups	112.933	4	28.233	**0.259**	**0.898**
Within groups	1,092.000	10	109.200		
Total	1,204.933	14			

Source: Authors.
Note: Bold values indicate estimation with significance level.

TABLE 15.6
Post Hoc Tests from SPSS Output

Satisfaction Score		
Duncan[a]		
		Subset for alpha = 0.05
Age Group	N	1
<= 20	3	37.67
31–40	3	40.33
>50	3	40.33
21–30	3	42.00
41–50	3	46.00
Sig.		0.388
Means for groups in homogeneous subsets are displayed.		

Source: Authors.
Note: [a]Uses harmonic mean sample size = 3.000.

Here, the *p*-value (Sig.) of the problem is 0.898 (see Table 15.5) which is greater than 0.05 (5% level of significance). So we accept the null hypothesis.

Based on Duncan test (see Table 15.6), we can understand that all age groups are homogeneous subsets. It means that age groups do not differ with each other with regard to the satisfaction score of a product brand.

Example: A researcher wants to compare knowledge of the social structure of two genders (male and female respondents) with the help of following data. Different sample sizes were chosen for male and female. Knowledge was evaluated out of 50 marks for the respondents.

Gender							
Male	22	24	26	28	25	29	32
Female	18	15	19	21	14		

Test whether there is any significant difference between the two genders with regard to knowledge of the social structure at 5% level of significance.

Null hypothesis (H_0): There is no significant difference between two genders with regard to knowledge of social structure.

TABLE 15.7
Required Calculations for One-way ANOVA (2)

Gender								Total (T_i)
Male	22	24	26	28	25	29	32	186
Female	18	15	19	21	14			87
				Grand total (T)				273

Source: Authors.

So, H_0: $\mu_1 = \mu_2$

Alternative hypothesis (H_1): $\mu_1 \neq \mu_2$

Now, for this example, the required calculations for one-way ANOVA are as shown in the Table 15.7.

$$\text{So, TSS} = \sum_{i=1}^{2}\sum_{j=1}^{m_i} x_{ij}^2 - \frac{T^2}{N}$$

$$= 6557 - \frac{273^2}{12} = 346.25.$$

$$\text{And, SST} = \sum_{i=1}^{n} \frac{T_i^2}{m_i} - \frac{T^2}{N}$$

$$= \left(\frac{186^2}{7} + \frac{87^2}{5}\right) - \frac{273^2}{12}$$

$$= 245.34.$$

Now, SSE = TSS – SST
= 346.25 – 245.34
= 100.91.

Here the calculated F-value is 24.32 (see Table 15.8) and the tabulated value with 1, 10 degree of freedom ($F_{1,10}$) is 4.96. As the calculated value is greater than corresponding tabulated value at 5% level of significance, we reject the null hypothesis. So there is significant difference between two genders with regard to knowledge of the social structure.

TABLE 15.8
One-way ANOVA Table (2)

Sum of Squares	Degree of Freedom	Mean Square	F-value
SST: 245.34	$(n - 1) = (2 - 1) = 1$	$\text{MST} = \frac{\text{SST}}{n-1} = 245.34$	$\frac{\text{MST}}{\text{MSE}} = 24.32$
SSE: 100.91	$(N - n) = (12 - 2) = 10$	$\text{MSE} = \frac{\text{SSE}}{(N-n)} = 10.09$	
TSS: 346.25	$(N - 1) = (12 - 1) = 11$		

Source: Authors.

15.4. THE SECOND ONE-WAY PROBLEM WITH SPSS

Here, knowledge of the social structure is the dependent variable and gender is the independent variable. Gender, which belongs to nominal measure type in SPSS, is coded as 1 = Male, 2 = Female.

Data for solving the second one-way ANOVA problem with SPSS are as follows:

Gender	Knowledge of Social Structure
1	22
1	24
1	26
1	28
1	25
1	29
1	32
2	18
2	15
2	19
2	21
2	14

Null hypothesis (H_0): $\mu_1 = \mu_2$

Alternative hypothesis (H_1): $\mu_1 \neq \mu_2$

Click Analyze → Compare Means → One-way ANOVA in the SPSS window. One pop-up window will appear as 'One-way ANOVA'. Then send 'Knowledge' to 'Dependent List' as the dependent variable and send 'Gender' to 'Factor' as the independent variable. Go to 'Options' and another pop-up window will appear. Tick 'Descriptive' (Exhibit 15.2).

EXHIBIT 15.2

SPSS Window for One-way ANOVA (2)

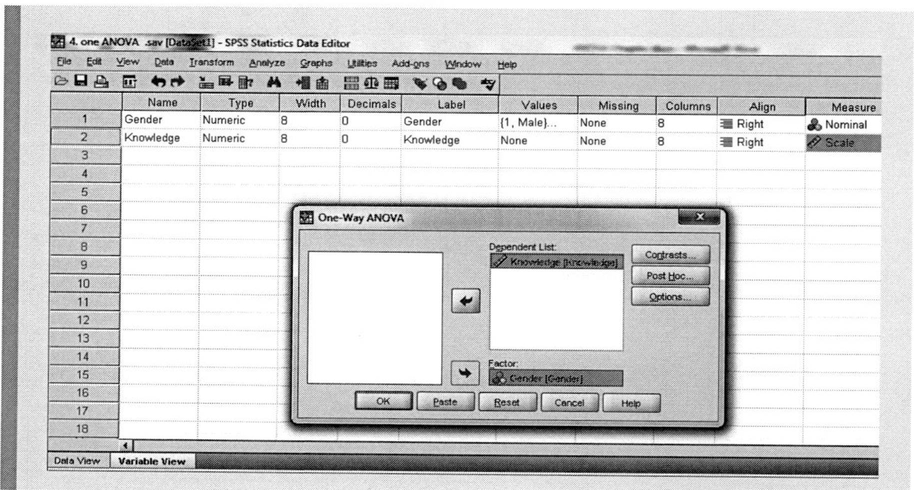

TABLE 15.9
Descriptive Statistics from SPSS Output (2)

Knowledge								
					95% Confidence Interval for Mean			
Gender	*N*	Mean	Std. Deviation	Std. Error	Lower Bound	Upper Bound	Minimum	Maximum
Male	7	26.57	3.359	1.270	23.46	29.68	22	32
Female	5	17.40	2.881	1.288	13.82	20.98	14	21
Total	12	22.75	5.610	1.620	19.19	26.31	14	32

Source: Authors.

TABLE 15.10
One-way ANOVA Table from SPSS Output (2)

Knowledge					
	Sum of Squares	df	Mean Square	*F*	Sig.
Between groups	245.336	1	245.336	**24.311**	**0.001**
Within groups	100.914	10	10.091		
Total	346.250	11			

Source: Authors.
Note: Bold values indicate estimation with significance level.

Then click 'Continue' → 'OK'. At last, an SPSS output box will appear as shown in Table 15.9.

Here, *p*-value (Sig.) of the problem is 0.001 (see Table 15.10) which is less than 0.05 (5% level of significance). So we reject the null hypothesis.

15.5. TWO-WAY ANOVA (RANDOMIZED BLOCK DESIGN)

For one dependent variable (interval or ratio scale) and two independent variables (nominal scale) with different categories/groups, two-way ANOVA is used. The important feature of a randomized block design is that each block contains equal number of treatments.

Example: In the first example, if we have additional information that the first value of each sample is included under respondents with below 5 years usage experiences. The second value of each sample is included under 6–10 years usage experiences and the third value of each sample is included under more than 10 years usage experiences. Here, the researcher wants to test whether there is a significant difference between age groups as well as experiences with regard to satisfaction score of a product brand.

Solution: For rows:

Null hypothesis (H_0): There is no significant difference between age groups with regard to satisfaction score of a product brand.

So, H_0: $\mu_1 = \mu_2 = \mu_3 = \mu_4 = \mu_5$

Alternative hypothesis (H_1): At least two means are not equal.

For columns:

H_0: There is no significant difference between experiences with regard to satisfaction score of a product brand.

So, H_0: $\mu_I = \mu_{II} = \mu_{III}$

Alternative hypothesis (H_1): At least two means are not equal.

Now, total sum of squares (TSS) = $\sum_{i=1}^{n}\sum_{j=1}^{m} x_{ij}^2 - \frac{T^2}{N}$

$= \sum_{i=1}^{5}\sum_{j=1}^{3} x_{ij}^2 - \frac{T^2}{N}$

$= 26749 - \frac{619^2}{15} = 1204.93$ (see Table 15.11).

Then, sum of square between rows (SSR) = $\frac{1}{m}\sum_{i=1}^{n} T_i^2 - \frac{T^2}{N}$

$= \left(\frac{113^2}{3} + \frac{126^2}{3} + \frac{121^2}{3} + \frac{138^2}{3} + \frac{121^2}{3}\right) - \frac{619^2}{15}$

= 112.93. (As shown in Table 15.11.)

And, sum of square between column (SSC) = $\frac{1}{n}\sum_{i=1}^{m} T_j^2 - \frac{T^2}{N}$

$= \left(\frac{196^2}{5} + \frac{257^2}{5} + \frac{166^2}{5}\right) - \frac{619^2}{15}$

= 860.13. (As shown Table 15.11.)

Then, error sum of square (SSE) = TSS – SSR – SSC
= 1204.93 – 112.93 – 860.13
= 231.87.

TABLE 15.11
Required Calculations for Two-way ANOVA (1)

Age Groups	Experiences			Total (T_i)
	Below 5 Years	6–10 Years	More Than 10 Years	
20 years and below	34	54	25	113
21–30 years	39	56	31	126
31–40 years	41	51	29	121
41–50 years	44	49	45	138
Above 50 years	38	47	36	121
Total (T_j)	196	257	166	T = 619

Source: Authors.

TABLE 15.12
Format of Two-way ANOVA Table

Sum of Squares	Degree of Freedom	Mean Square	F-value
SSR: Sum of squares between rows	$n - 1$	MSR (Mean square for rows) = $\frac{SSR}{n-1}$	$\frac{MSR}{MSE}$
SSC: Sum of squares between columns	$M - 1$	MSC (Mean square for columns) = $\frac{SSC}{m-1}$	$\frac{MSC}{MSE}$
SSE: Error sum of squares	$(n - 1)(m - 1)$	MSE (Mean square for error) = $\frac{SSE}{(n-1)(m-1)}$	
TSS: Total sum of squares	$N - 1$		

Source: Levin and Rubin (2009).

TABLE 15.13
Two-way ANOVA Table (1)

Sum of Squares	Degree of Freedom	Mean Square	F-value
SSR: 112.93	$(n - 1) = (5 - 1) = 4$	$MSR = \frac{SSR}{n-1} = 28.23$	$\frac{MSR}{MSE} = 0.97$
SSC: 860.13	$(m - 1) = (3 - 1) = 2$	$MSC = \frac{SSC}{m-1} = 430.07$	$\frac{MSC}{MSE} = 14.84$
SSE: 231.87	$(n - 1) \times (m - 1) = 4 \times 2 = 8$	$MSE = \frac{SSE}{(n-1)(m-1)} = 28.98$	
TSS: 1,204.93	$(N - 1) = (15 - 1) = 14$		

Source: Authors.

Here, the calculated F-value for the age group is 0.97 (see Table 15.13) and the tabulated value with 4, 8 degree of freedom ($F_{4,8}$) is 3.84. As the tabulated value is greater than the corresponding calculated value at 5% level of significance, we accept the null hypothesis. So there is no significant difference between age group with regard to satisfaction score of a product brand. On the other hand, the calculated F-value for experiences is 14.84 (Table 15.13) and the tabulated value with 2, 8 degree of freedom ($F_{2,8}$) is 4.46. As the tabulated value is less than the corresponding calculated value at 5% level of significance, we reject the null hypothesis. So there is significant difference between experiences with regard to the satisfaction score of a product brand.

15.6. TWO-WAY ANOVA PROBLEM WITH SPSS

At first we need to identify dependent and independent variables. Here, satisfaction score is the dependent variable. On the other hand, age group and experience are the independent variables. Age group and experiences belong to nominal measure type in SPSS. Age group is coded as 1 = 20 years and below, 2 = 21–30 years, 3 = 31–40 years, 4 = 41–50 years, 5 = above 50 years. Experience is coded as 1 = below 5 years, 2 = 6–10 years, 3 = more than 10 years.

Data for solving the two-way ANOVA problem with SPSS are as follows:

Age Group	Experiences	Satisfaction Score
1	1	34
1	2	54
1	3	25
2	1	39
2	2	56
2	3	31
3	1	41
3	2	51
3	3	29
4	1	44
4	2	49
4	3	45
5	1	38
5	2	47
5	3	36

For rows:
So, null hypothesis (H_0): $\mu_1 = \mu_2 = \mu_3 = \mu_4 = \mu_5$
Alternative hypothesis (H_1): At least two means are not equal.

For columns:
So, null hypothesis (H_0): $\mu_I = \mu_{II} = \mu_{III}$
Alternative hypothesis (H_1): At least two means are not equal.

After putting data and variables in the 'Data View' window and 'Variable View' window, click Analyze → General Linear Model → Univariate in the SPSS window. One pop-up window will appear as univariate. Then send 'Satisfaction Score' to 'Dependent List' as the dependent variable and send 'Age Group' and 'Experience' to 'Fixed Factor' as the independent variables.

Then click 'Model' → tick 'Custom'. Then transfer 'Factors & Covariates' to 'Model' (Exhibit 15.3).

Then click 'Continue' → 'OK'. At last, an SPSS output box will appear as shown in Table 15.14.

Here, *p*-value (Sig.) for age group is 0.472 which is greater than 0.05 (5% level of significance). So we accept the null hypothesis. On the other hand, *p*-value (Sig.) for experiences is 0.002 which is less than 0.05 (5% level of significance). So we reject the null hypothesis.

Example: A researcher wants to compare family health consciousness of five occupational groups as well as three different educational groups with the help of following data. Health consciousness is rated on a 10-point scale.

EXHIBIT 15.3

SPSS Window for Two-way ANOVA (1)

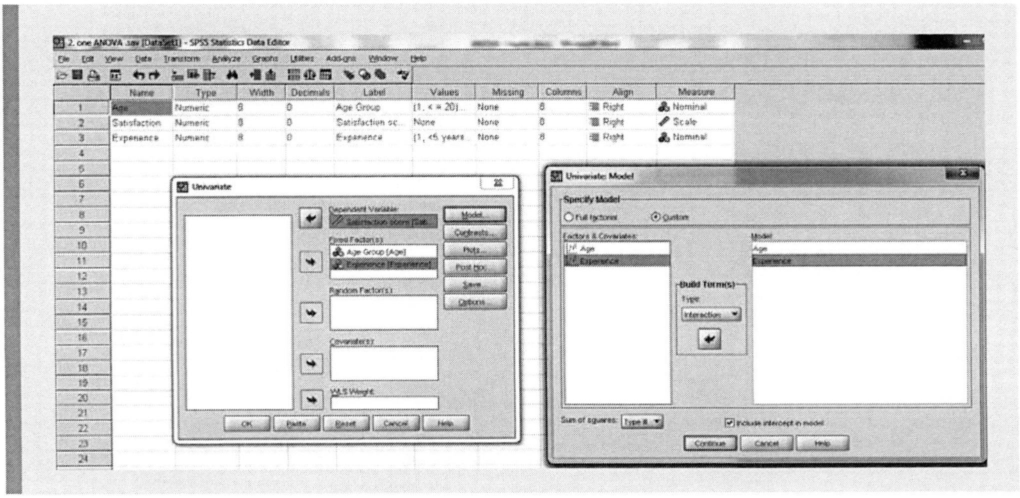

TABLE 15.14

Two-way ANOVA: Tests of Between-subjects Effects (from SPSS Output) (1)

Dependent Variable: Satisfaction Score					
Source	Type III Sum of Squares	df	Mean Square	F	Sig.
Corrected model	973.067[a]	6	162.178	5.596	0.015
Intercept	25,544.067	1	25,544.067	881.336	0.000
Age	112.933	4	**28.233**	**0.974**	**0.472**
Experience	860.133	**2**	**430.067**	**14.838**	**0.002**
Error	231.867	8	28.983		
Total	26,749.000	15			
Corrected total	1,204.933	14			

Source: Authors.

Notes: 1. Bold values indicate estimation with significance level.

2. [a]R-squared = 0.808 (Adjusted R-squared = 0.663).

	Education		
Occupation	Undergraduate	Graduate	Postgraduate
Student	2	5	4
Service holder (Man)	4	4	5
Service holder (Woman)	8	7	6
Housewife	9	7	8
Self-employed	4	5	3

Test whether there is significant difference between occupational groups as well as different educational groups with regard to family health consciousness at 5% level of significance.

Solution: For rows:

Null hypothesis (H_0): There is no significant difference between occupational groups with regard to family health consciousness.

So, H_0: $\mu_1 = \mu_2 = \mu_3 = \mu_4 = \mu_5$

Alternative hypothesis (H_1): At least two means are not equal.

For columns:

Null hypothesis (H_0): There is no significant difference between different educational groups with regard to family health consciousness.

So, H_0: $\mu_I = \mu_{II} = \mu_{III}$

Alternative hypothesis (H_1): At least two means are not equal.

Now, total sum of squares (TSS) = $\sum_{i=1}^{n}\sum_{j=1}^{m} x_{ij}^2 - \frac{T^2}{N}$

$$= \sum_{i=1}^{5}\sum_{j=1}^{3} x_{ij}^2 - \frac{T^2}{N}$$

$$= 495 - \frac{81^2}{15} = 57.6 \text{ (see Table 15.15).}$$

Then, sum of square between rows (SSR) = $\frac{1}{m}\sum_{i=1}^{n} T_i^2 - \frac{T^2}{N}$

$$= \left(\frac{11^2}{3} + \frac{13^2}{3} + \frac{21^2}{3} + \frac{24^2}{3} + \frac{12^2}{3}\right) - \frac{81^2}{15}$$

= 46.27. (As shown in Table 15.15.)

TABLE 15.15
Required Calculations for Two-way ANOVA (2)

	Education			
Occupation	Undergraduate	Graduate	Postgraduate	Total (T_i)
Student	2	5	4	11
Service holder (Man)	4	4	5	13
Service holder (Woman)	8	7	6	21
Housewife	9	7	8	24
Self-employed	4	5	3	12
Total (T_j)	27	28	26	$T = 81$

Source: Authors.

TABLE 15.16
Two-way ANOVA Table (2)

Sum of Squares	Degree of Freedom	Mean Square	F-value
SSR: 46.27	$(n - 1) = (5 - 1) = 4$	$MSR = \frac{SSR}{n-1} = 11.57$	$\frac{MSR}{MSE} = 8.46$
SSC: 0.4	$(m - 1) = (3 - 1) = 2$	$MSC = \frac{SSC}{m-1} = 0.2$	$\frac{MSC}{MSE} = 0.15$
SSE: 10.93	$(n - 1) \times (m - 1) = 4 \times 2 = 8$	$MSE = \frac{SSE}{(n-1)(m-1)} = 1.37$	
TSS: 57.6	$(N - 1) = (15 - 1) = 14$		

Source: Authors.

And, sum of square between column (SSC) $= \frac{1}{n}\sum_{i=1}^{m} T_j^2 - \frac{T^2}{N}$

$$= \left(\frac{27^2}{5} + \frac{28^2}{5} + \frac{26^2}{5}\right) - \frac{81^2}{15}$$

= 0.4. (As shown in Table 15.15.)

Then, error sum of square (SSE) = TSS – SSR – SSC
= 57.6 – 46.27 – 0.4
= 10.93.

Here, the calculated F-value for occupation is 8.46 (see Table 15.16) and the tabulated value with 4, 8 degree of freedom ($F_{4,8}$) is 3.84. As the tabulated value is less than the corresponding calculated value at 5% level of significance, we reject the null hypothesis. So, there is significant difference between occupational groups with regard to family health consciousness. On the other hand, the calculated F-value for education is 0.15 (Table 15.16) and the tabulated value with 2, 8 degree of freedom ($F_{2,8}$) is 4.46. As the tabulated value is greater than the corresponding calculated value at 5% level of significance, we accept the null hypothesis. So, there is no significant difference between different educational groups with regard to family health consciousness.

The second two-way ANOVA problem with SPSS

At first, we need to identify dependent and independent variables. Here, 'Family health consciousness' is the dependent variable. On the other hand, occupations and different educational levels are the independent variables. Occupations and different educational levels belong to nominal measure type in SPSS. Occupations are coded as 1 = Student, 2 = Service Holder (Man), 3 = Service Holder (Woman), 4 = Housewife, 5 = Self-employed. Educational levels are coded as 1 = Undergraduate, 2 = Graduate, 3 = Postgraduate.

Data for solving this two-way ANOVA problem with SPSS are as follows:

Occupation	Education	Health Consciousness
1	1	2
1	2	5
1	3	4

Occupation	Education	Health Consciousness
2	1	4
2	2	4
2	3	5
3	1	8
3	2	7
3	3	6
4	1	9
4	2	7
4	3	8
5	1	4
5	2	5
5	3	3

For rows:
So, null hypothesis (H_0): $\mu_1 = \mu_2 = \mu_3 = \mu_4 = \mu_5$
Alternative hypothesis (H_1): At least two means are not equal.

For columns:
So, null hypothesis (H_0): $\mu_I = \mu_{II} = \mu_{III}$
Alternative hypothesis (H_1): At least two means are not equal.

After putting data and variables in the 'Data View' window and 'Variable View' window, click Analyze → General Linear Model → Univariate in the SPSS window. One pop-up window will appear as 'Univariate'. Then send 'Health Consciousness' to 'Dependent List' as the dependent variable and send 'Occupation' and 'Education' to 'Fixed Factor' as the independent variables.

Then click 'Model' → tick 'Custom'. Then transfer 'Factors & Covariates' to 'Model' (Exhibit 15.4).

EXHIBIT 15.4

SPSS Window for Two-way ANOVA (2)

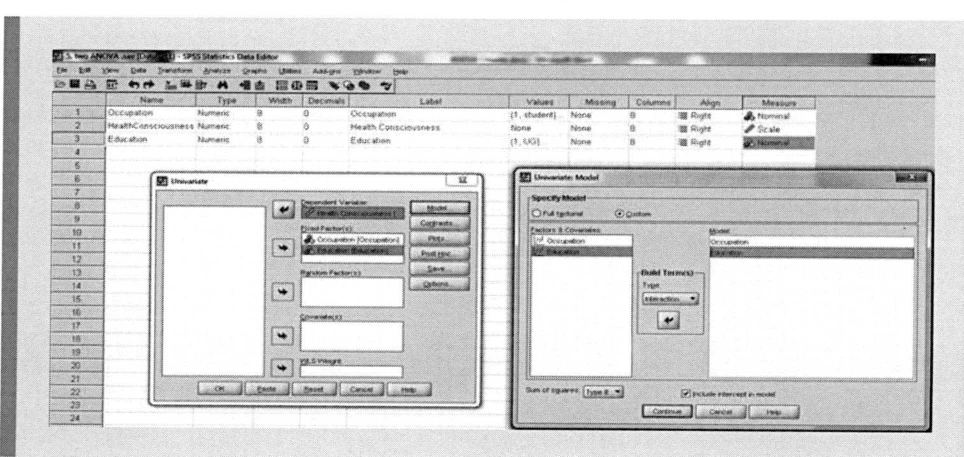

TABLE 15.17
Two-way ANOVA: Tests of Between-subjects Effects (from SPSS Output) (2)

Dependent Variable: Health Consciousness					
Source	Type-III Sum of Squares	df	Mean Square	F	Sig.
Corrected model	46.667[a]	6	7.778	5.691	0.014
Intercept	437.400	1	437.400	320.049	0.000
Occupation	46.267	4	**11.567**	**8.463**	**0.006**
Education	0.400	2	**0.200**	**0.146**	**0.866**
Error	10.933	8	1.367		
Total	495.000	15			
Corrected total	57.600	14			

Source: Authors.
Notes: 1. Bold values indicate estimation with significance level.
2. [a]*R*-squared = 0.810 (Adjusted *R*-squared = 0.668).

Then click 'Continue' → 'OK'. At last, an SPSS output box will appear as shown in Table 15.17.

Here *p*-value (Sig.) for occupational group is 0.006 which is less than 0.05 (5% level of significance). So we reject the null hypothesis. On the other hand, *p*-value (Sig.) for education is 0.866 which is greater than 0.05 (5% level of significance). So we accept the null hypothesis.

15.7. FACTORIAL DESIGN

Factorial design is used for one dependent variable (interval or ratio scale) and two or more independent variables (nominal scale). In this design, researchers can test the interaction between different variables. Number of interactions can be calculated by multiplying the number of categories of different independent variables. If two independent variables have three and four categories, then the total number of interactions would be 12. For more statistical accuracy, *the principle of replication* is used. It indicates that each treatment should be repeated more than once for each interaction.

Example: The following data represents the service quality of Big Bazaar, collected from the respondents with different income levels as well as genders in the local adjacent area. Here, three respondents are taken for each interaction between income levels and genders. The service quality of Big Bazaar is rated on a 10-point scale.

	Income Levels (₹)				
Gender	<15,000	15,001–30,000	30,001–45,000	45,001–60,000	>60,001
	4	8	9	7	5
Male	6	6	7	10	6
	5	5	6	9	7
	7	7	10	8	6
Female	6	6	7	9	5
	7	9	8	7	8

Conduct factorial design to test at 5% level of significance, whether there is any significant difference between (a) Genders, (b) Income levels and (c) all 10 interactions with regard to the service quality evaluation of Big Bazaar.

Solution: The following hypotheses are required to be checked:

For rows:
Null hypothesis (H_0): There is no significant difference between genders with regard to the service quality evaluation of Big Bazaar.
So, H_0: $\mu_1 = \mu_2$
Alternative hypothesis (H_1): $\mu_1 \neq \mu_2$

For columns:
Null hypothesis (H_0): There is no significant difference between different income levels with regard to the service quality evaluation of Big Bazaar.
So, H_0: $\mu_I = \mu_{II} = \mu_{III} = \mu_{IV} = \mu_V$
Alternative hypothesis (H_1): At least two means are not equal.

On all 10 interactions:
Null hypothesis (H_0): There is no significant difference between all 10 interactions with regard to the service quality evaluation of Big Bazaar.
So, H_0: $\mu_i = \mu_{ii} = \mu_{iii} = \mu_{iv} = \mu_v = \mu_{vi} = \mu_{vii} = \mu_{viii} = \mu_{ix} = \mu_x$
Alternative hypothesis (H_1): At least two means are not equal.

The first two hypotheses can be examined through two-way ANOVA. But factorial design is used for evaluating the significant difference of the average service quality evaluation score for all 10 interactions. See Table 15.18.

Now, Total sum of squares (TSS) = Total of squares – Correlation factor

$$= 1{,}540 - \frac{210^2}{30} = 70.$$

Then, sum of square between rows (SSR)

$$= \left(\frac{100^2}{15} + \frac{110^2}{15}\right) - \frac{210^2}{30}$$

$$= 3.33.$$

TABLE 15.18
Required Calculations for Factorial Design (1)

	Income Levels (₹)					
Gender	<15,000	15,001–30,000	30,001–45,000	45,001–60,000	>60,001	Total (T_i)
	4	8	9	7	5	
Male	6	6	7	10	6	100
	5	5	6	9	7	
	7	7	10	8	6	
Female	6	6	7	9	5	110
	7	9	8	7	8	
Total (T_j)	35	41	47	50	37	T = 210

Source: Authors.

And, sum of square between columns (SSC)

$$= \left(\frac{35^2}{6} + \frac{41^2}{6} + \frac{47^2}{6} + \frac{50^2}{6} + \frac{37^2}{6}\right) - \frac{210^2}{30}$$

$= 27.33.$

Now, we need to calculate the sum of squares between interactions (SSI)

$$= p\sum(\bar{x}_{ij} - \bar{x}_i - \bar{x}_j + \bar{\bar{x}})^2.$$

Here,

p = Number of observations for each interaction
$\bar{x}_{ij}$ = Average of observations of ith row and jth column
$\bar{x}_i$ = Average of observations of ith row
$\bar{x}_j$ = Average of observations of jth column
$\bar{\bar{x}}$ = Grand average of all observations

SSI can be calculated with the help of Table 15.19. First of all, it is required to calculate the averages of all the interactions and the averages of corresponding rows and columns.

$$\text{So, SSI} = p\sum\left(\bar{x}_{ij} - \bar{x}_i - \bar{x}_j + \bar{\bar{x}}\right)^2$$

$$= 3\{(5 - 6.67 - 5.84 + 7)^2 + (6.33 - 6.67 - 6.83 + 7)^2 + (6.33 - 7.33 - 6.17 + 7)^2\}$$

$= 3 \times 1.56 = 4.68.$

Then, error sum of square (SSE) = TSS – SSR – SSC – SSI

= 70 – 3.33 – 27.33 – 4.68

= 34.66.

Here, the calculated F-value for gender is 1.92 (see Table 15.20) and the tabulated value with 1, 20 degree of freedom ($F_{1,20}$) is 4.35. As the tabulated value is greater than the corresponding calculated value at 5% level of significance, we accept the null hypothesis. So there is no significant difference between genders with regard to the service quality evaluation of Big Bazaar. On the other hand, the calculated F-value for income levels is 3.95 (Table 15.20) and the tabulated value with 4, 20 degree of freedom ($F_{4,20}$) is 2.87. As the tabulated value is less than the corresponding calculated value at 5% level

TABLE 15.19
Required Calculations for SSI

	Income Levels (₹)					
Gender	<15,000	15,001–30,000	30,001–45,000	45,001–60,000	>60,001	$\bar{x}_i$
Male	5	6.33	7.33	8.67	6	6.67
Female	6.67	7.33	8.33	8	6.33	7.33
$\bar{x}_j$	5.84	6.83	7.83	8.34	6.17	$\bar{\bar{x}} = 7$

Source: Authors.

TABLE 15.20
Factorial Design Table (1)

Sum of Squares	Degree of Freedom	Mean Square	F-value
SSR: 3.33	$(n - 1) = (2 - 1) = 1$	MSR (Mean square for rows) = $\frac{SSR}{n-1} = 3.33$	$\frac{MSR}{MSE} = 1.92$
SSC: 27.33	$(m - 1) = (5 - 1) = 4$	MSC (Mean square for columns) = $\frac{SSC}{m-1} = 6.83$	$\frac{MSC}{MSE} = 3.95$
SSI: 4.68	$(n - 1) \times (m - 1)$ $= 1 \times 4 = 4$	MSI (Mean square for interactions) = $\frac{SSI}{(n-1)(m-1)} = 1.17$	$\frac{MSI}{MSE} = 0.68$
SSE: 34.66	$(29 - 1 - 4 - 4) = 20$	MSE (Mean square for error) = $\frac{SSE}{20} = 1.73$	
TSS: 70	$(N - 1) = (30 - 1) = 29$		

Source: Authors.

of significance, we reject the null hypothesis. So there is significant difference between different income levels with regard to the service quality evaluation of Big Bazaar. Lastly, the calculated F-value for interactions is 0.68 (Table 15.20) and the tabulated value with 4, 20 degree of freedom ($F_{4,20}$) is 2.87. As the tabulated value is greater than the corresponding calculated value at 5% level of significance, we accept the null hypothesis. So there is no significant difference between all 10 interactions with regard to the service quality evaluation of Big Bazaar.

15.8. FACTORIAL DESIGN PROBLEM WITH SPSS

At first, we need to identify dependent and independent variables. Here, 'Service quality' is the dependent variable. On the other hand, gender and different income levels are independent variable. Gender and different income levels belong to nominal measure type in SPSS. Gender is coded as 1 = Male, 2 = Female. Income levels are coded as 1 =< 15,000, 2 = 15,001–30,000, 3 = 30,001–45,000, 4 = 45,001–60,000, 5 => 60,001.

Data for solving the factorial design problem with SPSS are as follows:

Gender	Income Level	Service Quality
1	1	4
1	2	8
1	3	9
1	4	7
1	5	5
1	1	6
1	2	6

Gender	Income Level	Service Quality
1	3	7
1	4	10
1	5	6
1	1	5
1	2	5
1	3	6
1	4	9
1	5	7
2	1	7
2	2	7
2	3	10
2	4	8
2	5	6
2	1	6
2	2	6
2	3	7
2	4	9
2	5	5
2	1	7
2	2	9
2	3	8
2	4	7
2	5	8

For rows:
Null hypothesis (H_0): $\mu_1 = \mu_2$
Alternative hypothesis (H_1): $\mu_1 \neq \mu_2$

For columns:
Null hypothesis (H_0): $\mu_I = \mu_{II} = \mu_{III} = \mu_{IV} = \mu_V$
Alternative hypothesis (H_1): At least two means are not equal.

For all 10 interactions:
Null hypothesis (H_0): $\mu_i = \mu_{ii} = \mu_{iii} = \mu_{iv} = \mu_v = \mu_{vi} = \mu_{vii} = \mu_{viii} = \mu_{ix} = \mu_x$
Alternative hypothesis (H_1): At least two means are not equal.

After putting data and variables in the 'Data View' window and 'Variable View' window, click Analyze → General Linear Model → Univariate in the SPSS window. One pop-up window will appear as 'Univariate'. Then send 'Service quality' to 'Dependent List' as the dependent variable and send 'Gender' and 'Income Level' to 'Fixed Factor' as the independent variables.

Then click 'Model' → tick 'Full factorial' (Exhibit 15.5).

EXHIBIT 15.5

SPSS Window for Factorial Design (1)

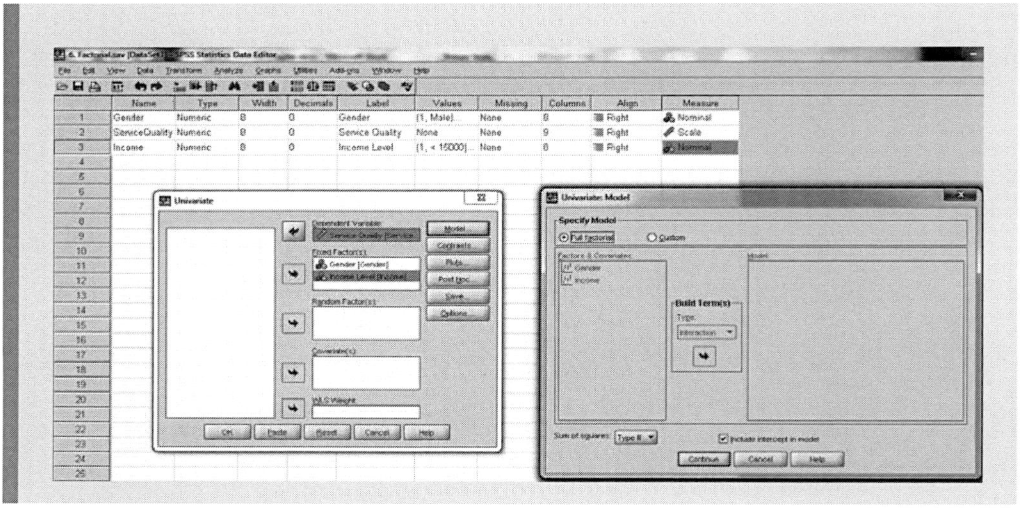

TABLE 15.21

Factorial Design: Tests of Between-subjects Effects (from SPSS Output) (1)

Dependent Variable: Service Quality					
Source	Type-III Sum of Squares	df	Mean Square	F	Sig.
Corrected model	35.333[a]	9	3.926	2.265	0.061
Intercept	1,470.000	1	1,470.000	848.077	0.000
Gender	3.333	**1**	**3.333**	**1.923**	**0.181**
Income	27.333	**4**	**6.833**	**3.942**	**0.016**
Gender × income	4.667	**4**	**1.167**	**0.673**	**0.618**
Error	34.667	20	1.733		
Total	1,540.000	30			
Corrected total	70.000	29			

Source: Authors.

Notes: 1. Bold values indicate estimation with significance level.
2. [a]*R*-squared = 0.505 (Adjusted *R*-squared = 0.282).

Then click 'Continue' → 'OK'. At last, an SPSS output box will appear as shown in Table 15.21.

Here *p*-value (Sig.) for gender is 0.181 which is greater than 0.05 (5% level of significance). So we accept the null hypothesis. On the other hand, *p*-value (Sig.) for income levels is 0.016 which is less than 0.05 (5% level of significance). So we reject the null hypothesis. Lastly, *p*-value (Sig.) for interactions is 0.618 which is greater than 0.05 (5% level of significance). So we accept the null hypothesis.

Example: The following data represents the 'Sex Awareness Score' of the people who are more than 18 years old. This data is collected from the respondents with different educational levels as well as different areas. Here, two respondents are taken for each interaction between educational levels and different areas. The 'Sex Awareness Score' is rated on a 5-point scale.

	Educational Levels			
Areas	Illiterate	Undergraduate	Graduate	Postgraduate
Urban	3	3	4	4
	1	2	5	4
Semi-urban	2	4	3	5
	1	2	4	3
Rural	1	1	4	3
	2	3	2	3

Conduct factorial design to test at 5% level of significance, whether any significant difference exists between (a) areas, (b) educational levels and (c) all 12 interactions with regard to 'Sex Awareness' of people.

Solution: The following hypotheses are required to be checked:

For rows:
Null hypothesis (H_0): There is no significant difference between areas with regard to 'Sex Awareness' of people.
So, H_0: $\mu_1 = \mu_2 = \mu_3$
Alternative hypothesis (H_1): At least two means are not equal.

For columns:
Null hypothesis (H_0): There is no significant difference between different educational levels with regard to 'Sex Awareness' of people.
So, H_0: $\mu_I = \mu_{II} = \mu_{III} = \mu_{IV}$
Alternative hypothesis (H_1): At least two means are not equal.

For all 12 interactions:
Null hypothesis (H_0): There is no significant difference between all 12 interactions with regard to 'Sex Awareness of people'.
So, H_0: $\mu_i = \mu_{ii} = \mu_{iii} = \mu_{iv} = \mu_v = \mu_{vi} = \mu_{vii} = \mu_{viii} = \mu_{ix} = \mu_x = \mu_{xi} = \mu_{xii}$
Alternative hypothesis (H_1): At least two means are not equal.

Now, total sum of squares (TSS) = Total of squares – Correlation factor

$$= 233 - \frac{69^2}{24} = 34.63 \text{ (see Table 15.22).}$$

Then, sum of square between rows (SSR)

$$= \left(\frac{26^2}{8} + \frac{24^2}{8} + \frac{19^2}{8}\right) - \frac{69^2}{24}$$

= 3.25. (As shown in Table 15.22.)

TABLE 15.22
Required Calculations for Factorial Design (2)

Areas	Educational Levels				Total (T_i)
	Illiterate	Undergraduate	Graduate	Postgraduate	
Urban	3	3	4	4	14
	1	2	5	4	12
Semi-urban	2	4	3	5	14
	1	2	4	3	10
Rural	1	1	4	3	9
	2	3	2	3	10
Total (T_j)	10	15	22	22	T = 69

Source: Authors.

TABLE 15.23
Required Calculations for SSI (2)

Areas	Educational Levels				$\bar{x}_i$
	Illiterate	Undergraduate	Graduate	Postgraduate	
Urban	2	2.5	4.5	4	3.25
Semi-urban	1.5	3	3.5	4	3.00
Rural	1.5	2	3	3	2.38
$\bar{x}_j$	1.67	2.50	3.67	3.67	$\bar{\bar{x}}$ = 2.88

Source: Authors.

And, sum of square between columns (SSC)

$$= \left(\frac{10^2}{6} + \frac{15^2}{6} + \frac{22^2}{6} + \frac{22^2}{6}\right) - \frac{69^2}{24}$$

= 17.13. (As shown in Table 15.22.)

SSI can be calculated with the help of Table 15.23. First of all, it is required to calculate the averages of all the interactions and the averages of corresponding rows and columns.

So, SSI = $p\sum(\bar{x}_{ij} - \bar{x}_i - \bar{x}_j + \bar{\bar{x}})^2$

$$= 2\{(2-3.25-1.67+2.88)^2 + (2.5-3.25-2.50+2.88)^2 + (3-2.38-3.67+2.88)^2\}$$

= 2 × 0.88 = 1.76.

Then, error sum of square (SSE) = TSS – SSR – SSC – SSI
= 34.63 – 3.25 – 17.13 – 1.76
= 12.49.

TABLE 15.24
Factorial Design Table (2)

Sum of Squares	Degree of Freedom	Mean Square	F-value
SSR: 3.25	$(n-1) = (3-1) = 2$	$MSR = \frac{SSR}{n-1} = 1.63$	$\frac{MSR}{MSE} = 1.57$
SSC: 17.13	$(m-1) = (4-1) = 3$	$MSC = \frac{SSC}{m-1} = 5.71$	$\frac{MSC}{MSE} = 5.49$
SSI: 1.76	$(n-1) \times (m-1) = 2 \times 3 = 6$	$MSI = \frac{SSI}{(n-1)(m-1)} = 0.29$	$\frac{MSI}{MSE} = 0.28$
SSE: 12.49	$(23-2-3-6) = 12$	$MSE = \frac{SSE}{12} = 1.04$	
TSS: 34.63	$(N-1) = (24-1) = 23$		

Source: Authors.

Here, the calculated F-value for areas is 1.57 (see Table 15.24) and the tabulated value with 2, 12 degree of freedom ($F_{2,12}$) is 3.89. As the tabulated value is greater than the corresponding calculated value at 5% level of significance, we accept the null hypothesis. So there is no significant difference between areas with regard to 'Sex Awareness' of people. On the other hand, the calculated F-value for educational levels is 5.49 (Table 15.24) and the tabulated value with 3, 12 degree of freedom ($F_{3,12}$) is 3.49. As the tabulated value is less than the corresponding calculated value at 5% level of significance, we reject the null hypothesis. So there is a significant difference between different educational levels with regard to 'Sex Awareness' of people. Lastly, the calculated F-value for interactions is 0.28 (Table 15.24) and the tabulated value with 6, 12 degree of freedom ($F_{6,12}$) is 3. As the tabulated value is greater than the corresponding calculated value at 5% level of significance, we accept the null hypothesis. So there is no significant difference between all 12 Interactions with regard to 'Sex Awareness of people'.

The second factorial design problem with SPSS

At first we need to identify dependent and independent variables. Here, 'Sex Awareness' is the dependent variable. On the other hand, areas and different educational levels are the independent variable. Areas and different educational levels belong to nominal measure type in SPSS. Areas are coded as 1 = Urban, 2 = Semi-urban and 3 = Rural. Educational levels are coded as 1 = Illiterate, 2 = Undergraduate, 3 = Graduate and 4 = Postgraduate.

Data for solving this factorial design problem with SPSS are as follows:

Area	Education	Sex Awareness
1	1	3
1	2	3
1	3	4
1	4	4
1	1	1
1	2	2

Area	Education	Sex Awareness
1	3	5
1	4	4
2	1	2
2	2	4
2	3	3
2	4	5
2	1	1
2	2	2
2	3	4
2	4	3
3	1	1
3	2	1
3	3	4
3	4	3
3	1	2
3	2	3
3	3	2
3	4	3

For rows:
Null hypothesis (H_0): $\mu_1 = \mu_2 = \mu_3$
Alternative hypothesis (H_1): At least two means are not equal.

For columns:
Null hypothesis (H_0): $\mu_I = \mu_{II} = \mu_{III} = \mu_{IV}$
Alternative hypothesis (H_1): At least two means are not equal.

For all 12 interactions:
Null hypothesis (H_0): $\mu_i = \mu_{ii} = \mu_{iii} = \mu_{iv} = \mu_v = \mu_{vi} = \mu_{vii} = \mu_{viii} = \mu_{ix} = \mu_x = \mu_{xi} = \mu_{xii}$
Alternative hypothesis (H_1): At least two means are not equal.

After putting data and variables in the 'Data View' window and 'Variable View' window, click Analyze → General Linear Model → Univariate in the SPSS window. One pop-up window will appear as 'Univariate'. Then send 'Sex Awareness' to 'Dependent List' as the dependent variable and send 'Area' and 'Education' to 'Fixed Factor' as the independent variables.

Then click 'Model' → tick 'Full factorial' (Exhibit 15.6).

Then click 'Continue' → 'OK'. At last, an SPSS output box will appear as shown in Table 15.25.

Here, *p*-value (Sig.) for area is 0.250 which is greater than 0.05 (5% level of significance). So we accept the null hypothesis. On the other hand, *p*-value (Sig.) for educational levels is 0.013 which is less than 0.05 (5% level of significance). So we reject the null hypothesis. Lastly, *p*-value (Sig.) for interactions is 0.936 which is greater than 0.05 (5% level of significance). So we accept the null hypothesis.

EXHIBIT 15.6

SPSS Window for Factorial Design (2)

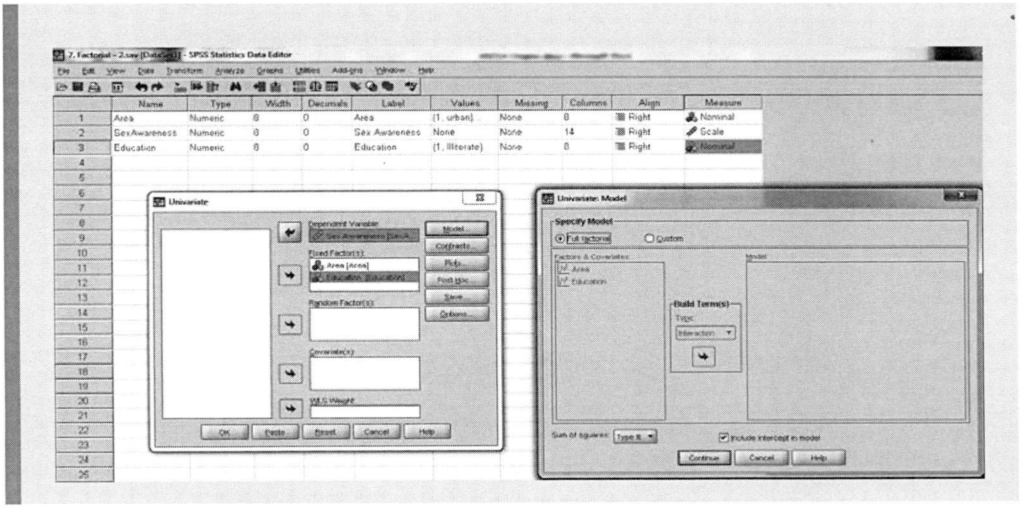

TABLE 15.25

Factorial Design: Tests of Between-subjects Effects (from SPSS Output) (2)

Dependent Variable: Sex Awareness					
Source	Type-III Sum of Squares	df	Mean Square	F	Sig.
Corrected model	22.125[a]	11	2.011	1.931	0.137
Intercept	198.375	1	198.375	190.440	0.000
Area	3.250	2	**1.625**	**1.560**	**0.250**
Education	17.125	3	**5.708**	**5.480**	**0.013**
Area × Education	1.750	6	**0.292**	**0.280**	**0.936**
Error	12.500	12	1.042		
Total	233.000	24			
Corrected total	34.625	23			

Source: Authors.

Notes: 1. Bold values indicate estimation with significance level.

2. [a]R-squared = 0.639 (Adjusted R-squared = 0.308).

SUMMARY

Application of ANOVA is important in the field of social science as well as business research. Basically, ANOVA can examine one or more number of variables which have an influence on the dependent variable. Also, it can examine the differences in various categories/groups under each variable. Scaling is important for different variables to execute ANOVA through SPSS. The dependent variable belongs to interval or ratio scale and independent variables (categorical) belong to nominal scale. There are different experimental designs in ANOVA. These are (a) One-way ANOVA (completely randomized design), (b) Two-way ANOVA (randomized block design) and (c) Factorial design.

KEY TERMS

analysis of variance (167)
completely randomized design (167)
one-way ANOVA (167)
randomized block design (175)
two-way ANOVA (175)
factorial design (183)

EXERCISES

1. What do you mean by the term ANOVA?
2. Distinguish between one-way ANOVA and two-way ANOVA with suitable examples.
3. Distinguish between randomized block design and factorial design.

CHAPTER

16

Chi-square Test

LEARNING OBJECTIVES

After studying this chapter, you should be able to

- Understand the concept and use of chi-square test in research study.
- Learn the theoretical calculations and explanation of chi-square test for a research study.
- Understand different types of chi-square test for different research perspectives.
- Know the use of SPSS software in chi-square test.
- Interpret chi-square test results from SPSS output.

16.1. CHI-SQUARE TEST FOR CATEGORICAL DATA

Types of distributions under a chi-square test depend on its degree of freedom. The distribution tends to normal distribution as the degree of freedom increases. So a chi-square test can be treated as a non-parametric test (detailed in Chapter 17) where a researcher does not need any prior knowledge about the shape of population distribution. Data in terms of proportion or percentage regarding a chi-square test is required in the form of frequencies (nominal scale). Both discrete and continuous types of data can be used in this test. In the case of continuous data, it must be converted to certain categorical data prior to using a chi-square test. The symbol of chi-square is χ^2 which is always greater than or equal to zero. Three important applications of a chi-square test have been discussed in this chapter.

16.2. χ^2 GOODNESS-OF-FIT TEST

The χ^2 goodness-of-fit test ascertains the validity of the observed data by examining whether the theoretical data is similar to the observed data or not. Chi-square value is calculated by the following formula:

$$\chi^2 = \sum_{i=1}^{k} \frac{(f_o - f_e)^2}{f_e}, \text{ where } f_o = \text{Observed frequency of the } i\text{th cell}$$

f_e = Expected frequency of the ith cell
K = Total number of cells

Here, degree of freedom can be calculated by (Total number of cells – 1) = (K – 1).

Example: A marketing research company conducted a survey to determine the liking pattern of a particular TV programme, among viewers with different occupations. The following results were found:

Occupation	Number of Viewers (Who Like that TV Programme)
Service person	9
Businessman	7
Student	10
Housewife	11
Retired person	8

Test with 5% level of significance that the liking pattern does not depend on profession.

Solution: Here, the hypothesis to be tested is as follows:

H_0 = The liking pattern does not depend on profession. It can be presented in the following form:

H_0: $p_1 = p_2 = p_3 = p_4 = p_5 = 1/5$,

Here, p_1, p_2, p_3, p_4 and p_5 are the proportions of viewers of service person, business man, student, housewife and retired person, respectively.

H_1 = The liking pattern depends on the profession.

Total number of viewers is 200. So expected frequencies for each occupation is (210 ÷ 5 =) 42

$$\text{Now, } \chi^2 = \sum_{i=1}^{k} \frac{(f_o - f_e)^2}{f_e}.$$

So the calculated value of χ^2 is 1.11, at (K – 1) or (5 – 1) or 4 degree of freedom.

At 5% level of significance and 4 degree of freedom, the tabulated value of χ^2 is 9.49. In this case, the calculated value (Table 16.1) is less than the tabulated value. So the null hypothesis is accepted and we can conclude that the liking pattern does not depend on the profession.

16.3. SOLVE χ^2 GOODNESS-OF-FIT TEST PROBLEM WITH SPSS

The null hypothesis (H_0) of the example problem discussed in the previous section is as follows:

H_0 = The liking pattern does not depend on the profession.

Alternative hypothesis (H_1). The liking pattern depends on the profession.

TABLE 16.1
Calculation of Chi-square Value

Occupation	Observed Frequency (f_o)	Expected Frequency (f_e)	$(f_o - f_e)$	$(f_o - f_e)^2$	$\frac{(f_o - f_e)^2}{f_e}$
Service person	9	9	0	0	0
Businessman	7	9	–2	4	0.444
Student	10	9	1	1	0.111
Housewife	11	9	2	4	0.444
Retired person	8	9	–1	1	0.111
Total					1.11

Source: Authors.

EXHIBIT 16.1
SPSS Window for a Chi-square Test

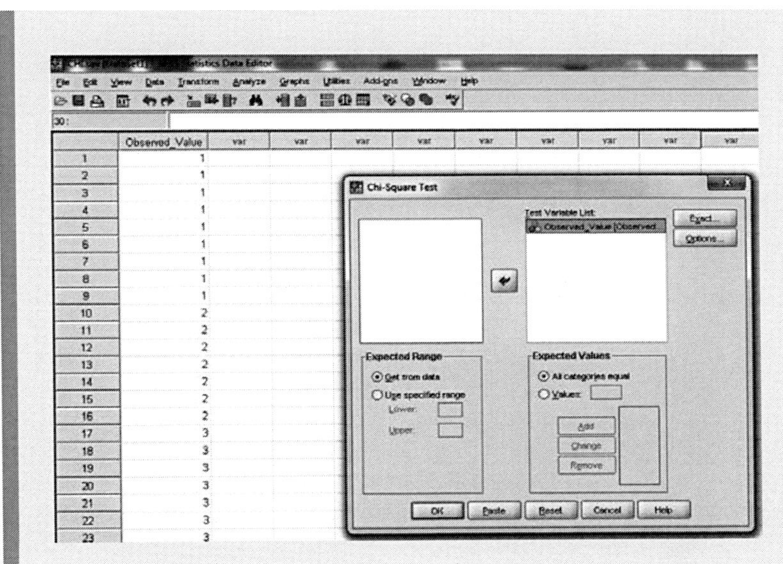

After putting nominal data and variable in the 'Data View' window and 'Variable View' window, click Analyze → Nonparametric Tests → Chi-square in the SPSS window. A pop-up window will appear as 'chi-square Test'. Now, send 'Observed Value' to 'Test Variables List'. Then in the 'Chi-square Test' dialog box, go to 'Expected Values' and tick 'All categories equal' (Exhibit 16.1).

Then click 'OK'. At last, an SPSS output box will appear as shown in Table 16.2.

Here, the chi-square value (Sig.) of the problem is 0.893 which is greater than 0.05 (5% level of significance). So we accept the null hypothesis.

TABLE 16.2
Chi-square Test Table from SPSS Output

	Observed_Value		
	Observed N	Expected N	Residual
Service person	9	9	0.0
Businessman	7	9	–2.0
Student	10	9	1.0
Housewife	11	9	2.0
Retired person	8	9	–1.0
Total	45	45	

Test Statistics	
	Observed_Value
Chi-Square	1.111[a]
df	4
Asymp. Sig.	0.893

Note: [a]0 cells (0.0%) have expected frequencies less than 5. The minimum expected cell frequency is 9.0.

Source: Authors.

16.4. χ^2 TEST OF INDEPENDENCE (TWO-WAY CONTINGENCY ANALYSIS)

χ^2 test of independence is used to examine the dependence of two variables arranged in a table (called the contingency table). These variables must contain minimum two categories.

Here, the expected frequency for any cell can be calculated by the following formula:

$$f_e = \frac{\text{Row total} \times \text{Column total}}{\text{Total number of frequencies}}$$

In this case, the degree of freedom can be calculated by (Number of rows – 1) × (Number of columns – 1).

Example: The following survey results depict the gender-wise educational attainment among 50 persons which were randomly selected from a locality.

Gender	Below 10th Std.	10th Std.	12th Std.	Graduate	Postgraduate	Total
Male	1	3	5	7	9	25
Female	5	6	6	4	4	25
Total	6	9	11	11	13	50

Test at 5% level of significance that education does not depend on gender.

Solution: Here, the hypothesis to be tested is as follows:

H_0 = Education does not depend on gender.

H_1 = Education depends on gender.

Total number of frequencies is 50.

So expected frequencies for each cell are presented in Table 16.3.

TABLE 16.3
Expected Frequencies Calculation

Gender	Below 10th Std.	10th Std.	12th Std.	Graduate	Postgraduate	Total
Male	(6 × 25)/50 = 3	(9 × 25)/50 = 4.5	(11 × 25)/50 = 5.5	(11 × 25)/50 = 5.5	(13 × 25)/50 = 6.5	25
Female	(6 × 25)/50 = 3	(9 × 25)/50 = 4.5	(11 × 25)/50 = 5.5	(11 × 25)/50 = 5.5	(13 × 25)/50 = 6.5	25
Total	6	9	11	11	13	50

Source: Authors.

TABLE 16.4
Calculation of Chi-square Value

Gender	Education	Observed Frequency (f_o)	Expected Frequency (f_e)	$(f_o - f_e)$	$(f_o - f_e)^2$	$\frac{(f_o - f_e)^2}{f_e}$
Male	Below 10th std.	1	3	−2	4	1.333
	10th std.	3	4.5	−1.5	2.25	0.500
	12th std.	5	5.5	−0.5	0.25	0.045
	Graduate	7	5.5	1.5	2.25	0.409
	Postgraduate	9	6.5	2.5	6.25	0.962
Female	Below 10th std.	5	3	2	4	1.333
	10th std.	6	4.5	1.5	2.25	0.500
	12th std.	6	5.5	0.5	0.25	0.045
	Graduate	4	5.5	−1.5	2.25	0.409
	Postgraduate	4	6.5	−2.5	6.25	0.962
Total						6.499

Source: Authors.

$$\text{Now, } \chi^2 = \sum_{i=1}^{k} \frac{(f_o - f_e)^2}{f_e}.$$

So the calculated value of χ^2 is 6.499, at {(2 – 1) × (5 – 1)} or 4 degree of freedom.

At 5% level of significance and 4 degree of freedom, the tabulated value of χ^2 is 9.49. In this case, the calculated value (Table 16.4) is less than the tabulated value. So the null hypothesis is accepted and we can conclude that education does not depend on gender.

16.5. SOLVE χ^2 TEST OF INDEPENDENCE PROBLEM WITH SPSS

The null hypothesis (H_0) of the example problem discussed in the preceding section is as follows:

H_0 = Education does not depend on gender.

Alternative hypothesis (H_1): Education depends on gender.

After putting nominal data and variables in the 'Data View' window and 'Variable View' window, click Analyze → Descriptive Statistics → Crosstabs in the SPSS window. One pop-up window will appear as 'Crosstabs'. Then send 'Gender' to 'Row' and 'Education' to 'Column'. Then in the 'Crosstabs' dialog box, go to 'Statistics'.

One pop-up window will appear as 'Crosstabs: Statistics'. Then tick 'Chi-square'. Then in the 'Crosstabs: Statistics' dialog box, go to 'Nominal' and tick 'Contingency Coefficient', and 'Phi and Cramer's V'. Then click 'Continue' (Exhibit 16.2).

Then in the 'Crosstabs' dialog box, go to 'Cells'.

One pop-up window will appear as 'Crosstabs: Cell Display'. Then go to 'Percentages', and tick 'Row' and 'Column'. Then click 'Continue' (Exhibit 16.3).

EXHIBIT 16.2

SPSS Window for the χ^2 Test of Independence (Step 1)

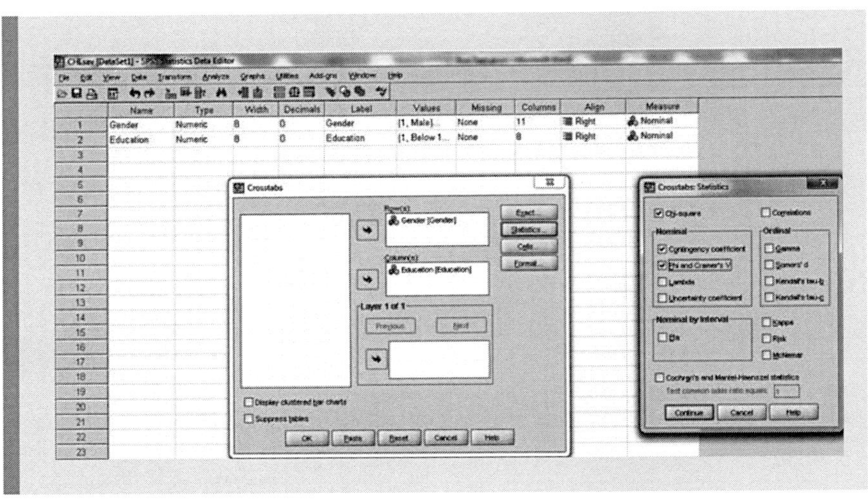

EXHIBIT 16.3

SPSS Window for the χ^2 Test of Independence (Step 2)

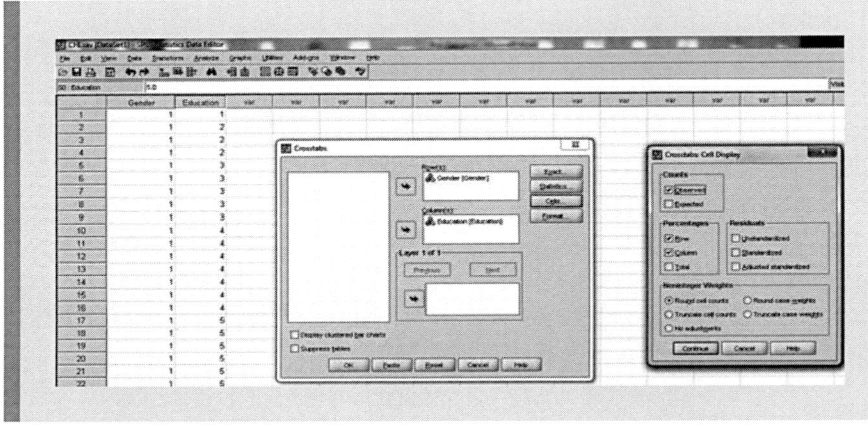

TABLE 16.5
'χ^2 Test of Independence' Table from SPSS Output

Chi-square Tests			
	Value	df	Asymp. Sig. (two-sided)
Pearson chi-square	6.499[a]	4	0.165
Likelihood ratio	6.824	4	0.146
Linear-by-linear association	6.211	1	0.013
N of valid cases	50		

Source: Authors.
Note: [a]Four cells (40.0%) have expected count less than 5. The minimum expected count is 3.00.

TABLE 16.6
Symmetric Measures from SPSS Output

Symmetric Measures			
		Value	Approx. Sig.
Nominal by Nominal	Phi	0.361	0.165
	Cramer's V	0.361	0.165
	Contingency coefficient	0.339	0.165
N of valid cases		50	

Source: Authors.

Then click 'OK'. At last, an SPSS output box will appear as shown in Table 16.5.

Here, the chi-square value (Sig.) of the problem is 0.165 which is greater than 0.05 (5% level of significance). So we accept the null hypothesis.

These symmetric measures (Table 16.6) describe the strength of relationship between variables.

Contingency coefficient is used when rows and columns in the contingency table become equal. The lower limit of the contingency coefficient is 0 and upper limit of the contingency coefficient is $\sqrt{\frac{r-1}{r}}$, where r = number of rows. Thus, 0 < Contingency coefficient < $\sqrt{\frac{r-1}{r}}$.

Phi coefficient is used in the case of a 2 × 2 contingency table. The lower limit of the Phi coefficient is –1 and the upper limit of the Phi coefficient is +1. Thus, –1 < Phi coefficient < +1. Generally, coefficient value more than 0.80 implies a strong relationship between the variables. On the other hand, coefficient value less than 0.40 implies a weak relationship between the variables.

Cramer's V is used when rows and columns in the contingency table are not equal. The lower limit of the Cramer's V is 0 and the upper limit of the Phi coefficient is +1. Thus, 0 < Cramer's V < +1. In this problem, the value of Cramer's V is 0.361 which implies that there is a weak association between the variables.

16.6. χ^2 TEST OF HOMOGENEITY

χ^2 test of homogeneity is used to determine whether the proportion of a particular attribute is the same across several populations. On the other hand, we can say that it helps to test whether two or more independent sample variables are selected from the same population or different populations.

Example: A brand manager of an organization is worried that the brand name may be unevenly distributed throughout India. At first, India was divided into four geographical regions (East, West, North and South). Then, 50 customers from each region were randomly selected for survey research. The following table shows the customer's purchase intention of the brand:

Customer's Purchase Intention	East India	West India	North India	South India	Total
Intention to purchase the brand	28	20	15	25	88
Intention not to purchase the brand	22	30	35	25	112
Total	50	50	50	50	200

Test whether the brand name of the product is the same across the four regions in India at 5% level of significance.

Here, the hypothesis to be tested is as follows:

H_0 = Brand name of the product is the same across the four regions in India.

H_1 = Brand name of the product is not the same across the four regions in India.

The total number of frequencies is 200.

The expected frequencies for each cell are presented in Table 16.7.

$$\text{Now, } \chi^2 = \sum_{i=1}^{k} \frac{(f_o - f_e)^2}{f_e}.$$

Thus, the calculated value of χ^2 is 7.955, at $\{(2-1) \times (4-1)\}$ or 3 degree of freedom.

At 5% level of significance and 3 degree of freedom, the tabulated value of χ^2 is 7.81. In this case, the calculated value (Table 16.8) is more than the tabulated value. So, the null hypothesis is rejected and we can conclude that the brand name of the product is not the same across the four regions in India.

TABLE 16.7

Expected Frequencies Calculation

Customer's Purchase Intention	East India	West India	North India	South India	Total
Intention to purchase the brand	(88 × 50)/200 = 22	(88 × 50)/200 = 22	(88 × 50)/200 = 22	(88 × 50)/200 = 22	88
Intention not to purchase the brand	(112 × 50)/200 = 28	(112 × 50)/200 = 28	(112 × 50)/200 = 28	(112 × 50)/200 = 28	112
Total	50	50	50	50	200

Source: Authors.

TABLE 16.8
Calculation of Chi-square Value

Customer's Purchase Intention	Area	Observed Frequency (f_o)	Expected Frequency (f_e)	$(f_o - f_e)$	$(f_o - f_e)^2$	$\frac{(f_o - f_e)^2}{f_e}$
Intention to purchase the brand	East India	28	22	6	36	1.636
	West India	20	22	–2	4	0.182
	North India	15	22	–7	49	2.227
	South India	25	22	3	9	0.409
Intention not to purchase the brand	East India	22	28	–6	36	1.286
	West India	30	28	2	4	0.143
	North India	35	28	7	49	1.750
	South India	25	28	–3	9	0.321
Total						7.955

Source: Authors.

16.7. SOLVE χ^2 TEST OF HOMOGENEITY PROBLEM WITH SPSS

The null hypothesis (H_0) of the example problem discussed in the preceding section is as follows:

H_0 = Brand name of the product is the same across the four regions in India.

Alternative hypothesis (H_1): Brand name of the product is not the same across the four regions in India.

After putting nominal data and variables in the 'Data View' window and 'Variable View' window, click Analyze → Descriptive Statistics → Crosstabs in the SPSS window. One pop-up window will appear as 'Crosstabs'. Then send 'Purchase Intention' to 'Row' and 'Area' to 'Column'. In the 'Crosstabs' dialog box, go to 'Statistics'.

One pop-up window will appear as 'Crosstabs: Statistics'. Tick 'Chi-square'. Then click 'Continue' (Exhibit 16.4).

EXHIBIT 16.4
SPSS Window for the χ^2 Test of Homogeneity

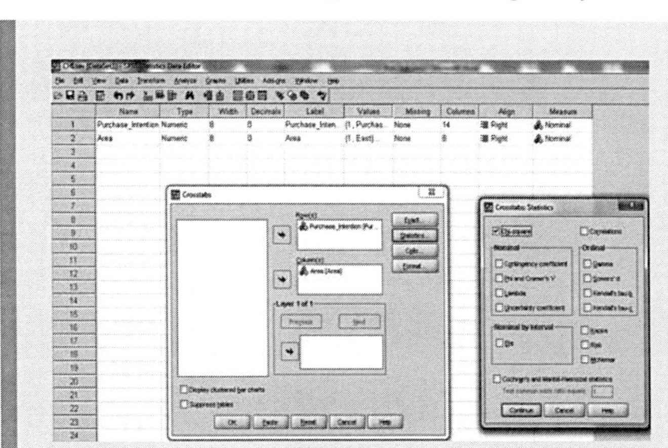

TABLE 16.9
'χ^2 Test of Homogeneity' Table from SPSS Output

Chi-square Tests			
	Value	df	Asymp. Sig. (two-sided)
Pearson chi-square	7.955[a]	3	0.047
Likelihood ratio	8.077	3	0.044
Linear-by-linear association	0.791	1	0.374
N of valid cases	200		

Source: Authors.
Note: [a]0 cells (0.0%) have expected count less than 5. The minimum expected count is 22.00.

Then click 'OK'. At last, an SPSS output box will appear as shown in Table 16.9.

Here, the chi-square value (Sig.) of the problem is 0.047 which is less than 0.05 (5% level of significance). So we reject the null hypothesis.

SUMMARY

Data in terms of proportion or percentage regarding a chi-square test is required in the form of frequencies. Discrete and continuous both types of data can be used in this test. In the case of continuous data, it must be converted to certain categorical data prior to using a chi-square test. The symbol of chi-square is χ^2 which is always greater than or equal to zero. Three important applications of a chi-square test (χ^2 goodness-of-fit test, χ^2 test of independence and χ^2 test of homogeneity) have been discussed in this chapter. χ^2 goodness-of-fit test ascertains the validity of the observed data by examining whether the theoretical data is similar with the observed data or not. χ^2 test of independence is used to examine the dependence of two variables arranged in a table (called the contingency table). These variables must contain minimum two categories. χ^2 test of homogeneity is used to determine whether the proportion of a particular attribute is the same across several populations.

KEY TERMS

chi-square test (195)
observed frequency (196)
expected frequency (196)
χ^2 goodness-of-fit test (195)
χ^2 test of independence (198)
χ^2 test of homogeneity (202)
contingency coefficient (201)
Phi coefficient (201)
Cramer's V (201)

EXERCISES

1. What is chi-square test? Describe the applications of chi-square test with suitable examples.
2. Differentiate χ^2 goodness-of-fit test and χ^2 test of independence.
3. Differentiate χ^2 test of homogeneity and χ^2 test of independence.

4. Describe each of the following:
   a. Contingency coefficient
   b. Cramer's V
   c. Phi coefficient
5. The results of a survey to know the educational ability among 130 persons randomly selected in an area are given as follows:

Gender	Middle	High School	College	Total
Male	15	20	30	65
Female	30	15	20	65
Total	45	35	50	130

   Can you say education depends on sex at 5% level of significance? (Given the chi-square value = 5.99 at df = 2 and 5% level of significance.)
6. The manager of a retail store obtained the data of random samples of credit customers and recorded the data given in the following table. The credit collection period is divided into three categories—below 20 days, 20–40 days and above 40 days. The sampling is done in three regions—urban, semi-urban and rural. Perform a chi-square test at 5% level of significance and prove the hypothesis that the credit payment period is independent of different regions. (The chi-square value at 5% significance level and four degrees of freedom is 9.488.)

	Regions		
Credit Collection Period (days)	Urban	Sub-urban	Rural
Below 20	40	70	40
Between 20 and 40	80	95	50
Above 40	35	40	25

CHAPTER

17

Non-parametric Test

LEARNING OBJECTIVES

After studying this chapter, you should be able to

- Understand the concept and use of different non-parametric tests in research study.
- Learn the theoretical calculations and explanation of different non-parametric tests.
- Understand the classifications of different non-parametric tests for different research demand.
- Know the use of SPSS software in different non-parametric tests.
- Interpret different non-parametric tests results from SPSS output.

17.1. CONCEPT OF NON-PARAMETRIC TEST

Non-parametric test is basically a distribution-free test. For executing a non-parametric test, it is not required to maintain any particular shape of population distribution from where the sample is chosen. It emphasizes nominal as well as ordinal scale data, that is, it deals with categorical data. In the case of a small sample size, execution of non-parametric tests are better than the parametric tests. In the case of a large sample size, non-parametric tests are difficult to compute. One important note is that the researcher must remember that non-parametric tests should be avoided where all the assumptions of parametric tests are fulfilled.

In this chapter, we will discuss important non-parametric tests used in social science research such as sign test, Mann–Whitney U test, Wilcoxon matched pair rank test, Kruskal–Wallis test, run test, Kolmogorov–Smirnov one-sample test and Spearman's rank correlation test.

17.2. ONE-SAMPLE SIGN TEST

It is a non-parametric test which handles basically non-metric ordinal and nominal data. In the case of one-sample test, we deal with the elements of only one sample. This test is based on basically binomial distribution (discrete and non-continuous data) which estimates the proportion of occurrences in a population. Now, we have to test the null hypothesis H_0: p = 1/2 (hypothesized proportion of getting success in the population) against the suitable alternative hypothesis. Here, p = Probability of success (+ sign); $q = (1 - p)$ = Probability of failure (– sign). For conducting the sign test, each sample element is replaced by either a '+ sign' or '– sign'. If any sample element is greater than the desired value of getting success, it is replaced by a '+ sign'. If any sample element is less than the desired value of getting success, it is replaced by a '– sign'. If any sample element is equal to the desired value, it is removed from the sample elements, and sample size (n) is reduced subsequently. Using binomial distribution is appropriate for sample proportions with a small sample. As sample size increases (when $n \times p$ and $n \times q$ are at least 5), the binomial distribution approaches to the normal distribution. In that case, Z-value can be calculated by the following formula:

$$|\text{Z-value}| = \left|\frac{S - n \times p}{\sqrt{n \times p \times q}}\right|,$$

where S = Total number of positive signs, $n \times p$ = Mean of the distribution and $\sqrt{n \times p \times q}$ = Standard deviation of the distribution.

In the case of $S > n \times p$, S is deducted by 0.5, and when $S < n \times p$, S is added by 0.5.

Example: A survey research was conducted to understand the acceptance level of a shopping mall in a semi-urban area. A random sample of 30 persons was selected and feedback was taken from each person as follows. More than 35 points out of 50 points (total points in the feedback form) indicate higher acceptance level by the population. Test the hypothesis that the average expectation level of the population is at least 35 points, using 5% level of significance.

Feedback Points of 30 Persons									
26	37	43	45	48	28	36	45	44	40
41	38	27	46	31	47	45	33	36	42
49	12	38	39	44	23	46	24	48	34

Solution: Here, the hypothesis to be tested is as follows:

H_0 (: p = 1/2) = Average expectation level of the population is at least 35 points.

H_1 (: p > 1/2) = Average expectation level of the population is more than 35 points.

Table 17.1 has been constructed by replacing each element more than 35 by a plus sign and those with less than 35 by a minus sign.

TABLE 17.1
Sign Conversion

Feedback Points of 30 Persons									
–	+	+	+	+	–	+	+	+	+
+	+	–	+	–	+	+	–	+	+
+	–	+	+	+	–	+	–	+	–

Source: Authors.

There are 21 plus and 9 minus signs. Here, $n \times p$ and $n \times q$ are both 15 and greater than 5, so z-test can be used as the approximation of the normal distribution.

So, $|\text{Z-value}| = \left|\dfrac{S - n \times p}{\sqrt{n \times p \times q}}\right| = \left|\dfrac{(21 - 0.5) - 30 \times 0.5}{\sqrt{30 \times 0.5 \times 0.5}}\right|$ (here, $S > n \times p$, S is deducted by 0.5)

= 2.008.

At 5% level of significance, the tabulated value of Z is 1.645. Here, the calculated value of Z is greater than the tabulated value. So the null hypothesis is rejected, that is, the average expectation level of the population is more than 35 points.

17.2.1. Solve the One-sample Sign Test Problem with SPSS

Null hypothesis (H_0): Average expectation level of the population is at least 35 points.

Alternative hypothesis (H_1): Average expectation level of the population is more than 35 points.

After putting data and variables in the 'Data View' window and 'Variable View' window, click Analyze → Nonparametric Tests → 'Two-Related-Samples' in the SPSS window. One pop-up window will appear as 'Two-Related-Samples Tests'. Then send 'Observed Value' and 'Desired Value' to 'Test Pairs'. Go to 'Test Type' and tick 'Sign' (Exhibit 17.1).

Then click 'OK'. At last, an SPSS output box will appear as shown in Table 17.2.

Here, Z-value (Sig.) of the problem is 0.045 which is less than 0.05 (5% level of significance). So we reject the null hypothesis.

EXHIBIT 17.1

SPSS Window for One-sample Sign Test

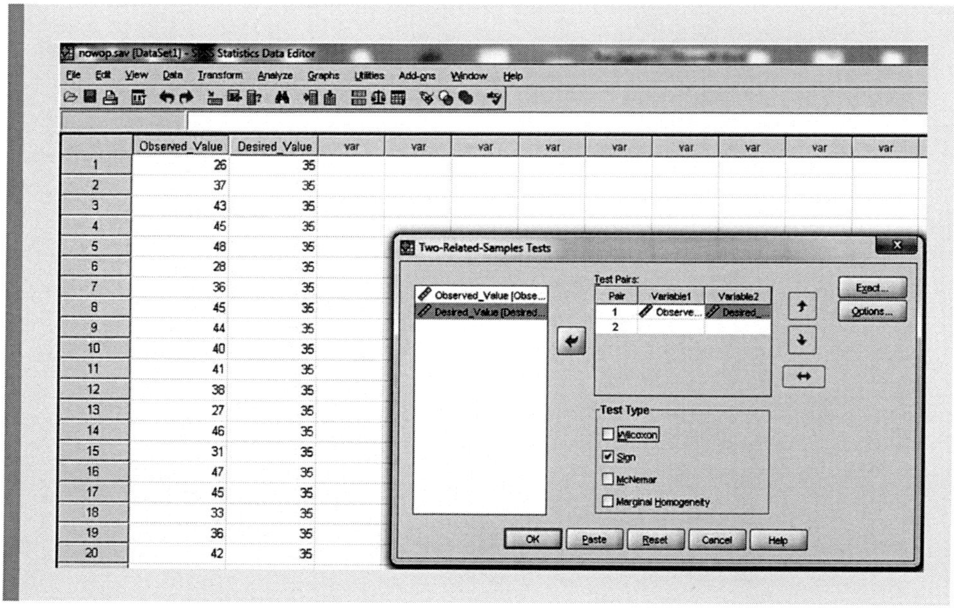

	Observed_Value	Desired_Value	var	var	var	var	var	var	var	var	var
1	26	35									
2	37	35									
3	43	35									
4	45	35									
5	48	35									
6	28	35									
7	36	35									
8	45	35									
9	44	35									
10	40	35									
11	41	35									
12	38	35									
13	27	35									
14	46	35									
15	31	35									
16	47	35									
17	45	35									
18	33	35									
19	36	35									
20	42	35									

TABLE 17.2
One-sample Sign Test Tables from SPSS Output

Frequencies		
		N
Observed_Value – Desired_Value	Negative Differences[a]	9
	Positive Differences[b]	**21**
	Ties[c]	0
	Total	**30**

Source: Authors.
Notes: 1. Bold values indicate estimations with significance level.
2. [a]Observed_Value < Desired_Value.
3. [b]Observed_Value > Desired_Value.
4. [c]Observed_Value = Desired_Value.

Test Statistics[a]	
	Observed_Value – Desired_Value
Z	–2.008
Asymp. Sig. (two-tailed)	**0.045**

Source: Authors.
Notes: 1. Bold values indicate estimations with significance level.
2. [a]Sign test.

17.3. TWO-SAMPLE SIGN TEST

It is also a non-parametric test based on two sample observations. The process of execution is similar to the one-sample sign test. Only '+ sign' and '– sign' are determined by comparing the pair of sample observations. It resembles with the 'paired sample t-test' which is a parametric test.

Example: A college wants to test the effectiveness of the teaching aids implemented in the class room. Before implementing the teachings aids, one test of 50 marks was conducted for a sample of 27 students and after implementing the teachings aids, another test of 50 marks is conducted for the same sample. Test the claim that there is any significant difference between the performance of the students before and after implementing the teaching aids at 5% level of significance. All results are presented in the following table:

S. No. of Students	Test Scores (Before Implementing the Teachings Aids)	Test Scores (After Implementing the Teachings Aids)	Sign
1	26	32	+
2	28	24	–
3	27	38	+
4	32	41	+
5	36	49	+
6	34	29	–
7	31	28	–
8	35	35	0
9	20	37	+
10	22	33	+
11	14	26	+

S. No. of Students	Test Scores (Before Implementing the Teachings Aids)	Test Scores (After Implementing the Teachings Aids)	Sign
12	30	45	+
13	25	36	+
14	37	43	+
15	39	46	+
16	14	26	+
17	27	30	+
18	33	24	–
19	43	41	–
20	37	46	+
21	30	40	+
22	32	36	+
23	38	46	+
24	23	27	+
25	25	30	+
26	34	33	–
27	35	29	–

Solution: Here, the hypothesis to be tested is as follows:

H_0 = There is no significant difference between the performance of the students before and after implementing the teaching aids.

H_1 = There is a significant difference between the performance of the students before and after implementing the teaching aids.

There are 19 plus signs, 7 minus signs and 1 zero (no upgradation). Thus, n will be 26 (27 – 1) in this case. Here, $n \times p$ and $n \times q$ are both 13 and greater than 5, so z-test can be used as the approximation of the normal distribution.

$$\text{Thus, } |\text{Z-value}| = \left|\frac{S - n\times p}{\sqrt{n\times p\times q}}\right| = \left|\frac{(19-0.5)-26\times 0.5}{\sqrt{26\times 0.5\times 0.5}}\right| \text{ (here, } S > n \times p, S \text{ is deducted by 0.5)}$$

= 2.157.

At 5% level of significance, the tabulated value of Z is 1.645. Here the calculated value of Z is greater than the tabulated value. So the null hypothesis is rejected, that is, there is a significant difference between the performance of the students before and after implementing the teaching aids.

17.3.1. Solve the Two-sample Sign Test Problem with SPSS

Null hypothesis (H_0): There is no significant difference between the performance of the students before and after implementing the teaching aids.

Alternative hypothesis (H_1): There is a significant difference between the performance of the students before and after implementing the teaching aids.

EXHIBIT 17.2

SPSS Window for Two-sample Sign Test

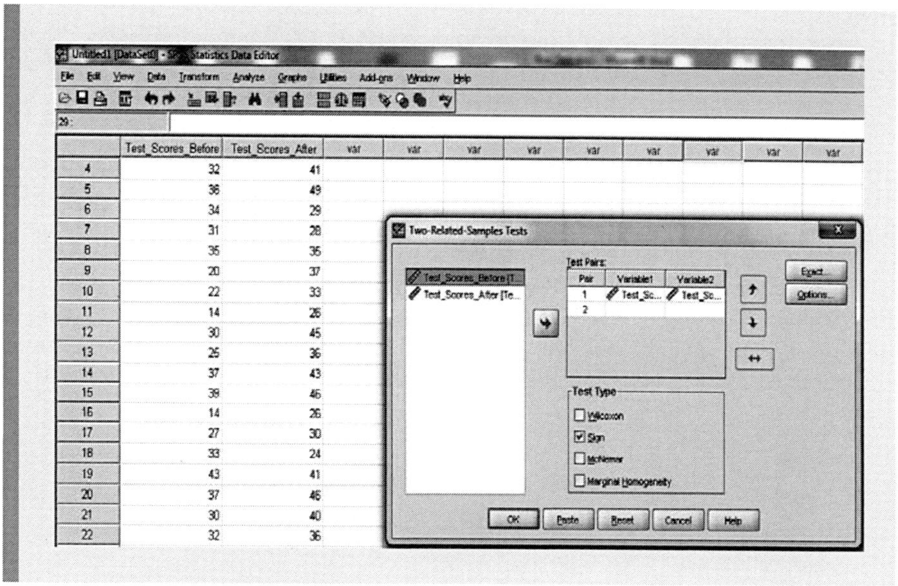

After putting data and variables in the 'Data View' window and 'Variable View' window, click Analyze → Nonparametric Tests → 'Two-Related-Samples' in the SPSS window. One pop-up window will appear as 'Two-Related-Samples Tests'. Then send 'Test_Scores_After' and 'Test_Scores_Before' to 'Test Pairs'. Go to 'Test Type' and tick 'Sign' (Exhibit 17.2).

Then click 'OK'. At last, an SPSS output box will appear as shown in Table 17.3.

Here, Z-value (Sig.) of the problem is 0.031 which is less than 0.05 (5% level of significance). So we reject the null hypothesis.

TABLE 17.3

Two-sample Sign Test Tables from SPSS Output

Frequencies		
		N
Test_Scores_After – Test_Scores_Before	Negative Differences[a]	7
	Positive Differences[b]	19
	Ties[c]	1
	Total	27

Source: Authors.

Notes: 1. Bold values indicate estimations with significance level.
2. [a]Test_Scores_After < Test_Scores_Before.
3. [b]Test_Scores_After > Test_Scores_Before.
4. [c]Test_Scores_After = Test_Scores_Before.

Test Statistics[a]	
	Test_Scores_After – Test_Scores_Before
Z	–2.157
Asymp. Sig. (two-tailed)	**0.031**

Source: Authors.

Notes: 1. Bold values indicate estimations with significance level.
2. [a]Sign test.

17.4. WILCOXON MATCHED PAIRS SIGNED RANK TEST

It also resembles with the 'paired sample t-test' which is a parametric test. In this case, a small sample is considered when the number of pairs is less than or equal to 15. When the number of pairs is more than 15, it is considered as a large sample.

17.5. WILCOXON SIGNED RANK TEST FOR SMALL SAMPLES

The execution process of this test is elaborately discussed in the following example:

Example: For evaluating the efficiencies of implementing a new traffic signal system, 10 locations (important intersections) were selected. Then, the number of accidents was counted during one month before and one month after installing a new traffic signal system as follows. Test the claim that there is no significant difference between the efficiencies of the new traffic signal system and previous system at 5% level of significance.

Accidents (before new traffic signal installation	9	9	5	10	8	7	4	11	6	10
Accidents (after new traffic signal installation)	4	6	7	2	5	3	5	4	8	4

Solution: Here the hypothesis to be tested is as follows:
H_0 = There is no significant difference between the efficiencies of the new traffic signal system and the previous system.
H_1 = There is a significant difference between the efficiencies of the new traffic signal system and the previous system.

So the calculated Wilcoxon T-statistics = Minimum (T+,T–) = Minimum (49, 6) = 6 (see Table 17.4).

At 5% level of significance, the tabulated value of Wilcoxon T-statistics is 8. Here, the calculated value of T is less than the tabulated value. So the null hypothesis is rejected, that is, there is a significant difference between the efficiencies of the new traffic signal system and previous system.

17.5.1. Solve Wilcoxon Signed Rank Test (for Small Samples) Problem with SPSS

Null hypothesis (H_0): There is no significant difference between the efficiencies of a new traffic signal system and the previous system.

Alternative hypothesis (H_1): There is a significant difference between the efficiencies of a new traffic signal system and the previous system.

After putting data and variables in the 'Data View' window and 'Variable View' window, click Analyze → Nonparametric Tests → 'Two-Related Samples' in the SPSS window. One pop-up window will appear as 'Two-Related-Samples Tests'. Then, send 'Accidents_Before' and 'Accidents_After' to 'Test Pairs'. Go to 'Test Type' and tick 'Wilcoxon' (Exhibit 17.3).

TABLE 17.4

Wilcoxon T-statistics Calculation (1)

Accidents (Before New Traffic Signal Installation)	Accidents (After New Traffic Signal Installation)	Difference	Rank	Rank with '+ Sign' T+	Rank with '– Sign' T–
9	4	+5	+7	+7	
9	6	+3	+4.5	+4.5	
5	7	–2	–2.5		–2.5
10	2	+8	+10	+10	
8	5	+3	+4.5	+4.5	
7	3	+4	+6	+6	
4	5	–1	–1		–1
11	4	+7	+9	+9	
6	8	–2	–2.5		–2.5
10	4	+6	+8	+8	
	Total			49	6

Source: Authors.

EXHIBIT 17.3

SPSS Window for Wilcoxon Signed Rank Test (Example for Small Sample)

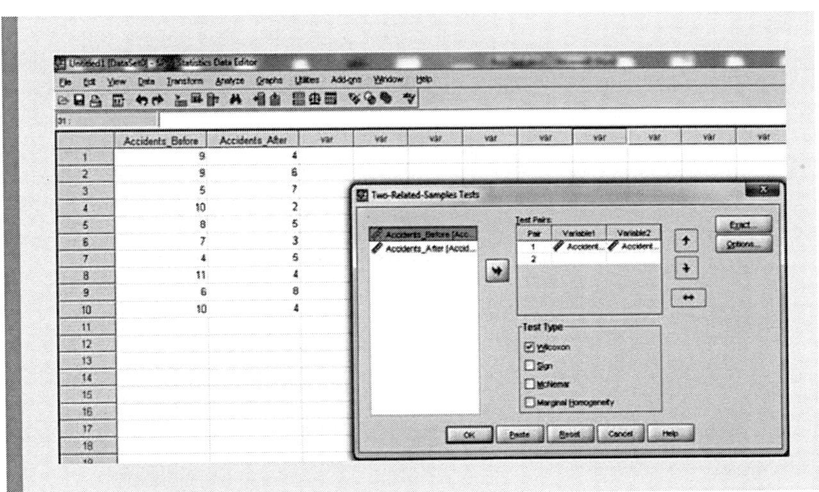

Then click 'OK'. At last, an SPSS output box will appear as shown in Table 17.5.

Here, Z-value (Sig.) of the problem is 0.028 which is less than 0.05 (5% level of significance). So we reject the null hypothesis.

TABLE 17.5
Wilcoxon Signed Rank Test Tables from SPSS Output

Ranks				
		N	Mean Rank	Sum of Ranks
Accidents_After – Accidents_Before	Negative Ranks	7[a]	7.00	**49.00**
	Positive Ranks	3[b]	2.00	**6.00**
	Ties	0[c]		
	Total	**10**		

Source: Authors.
Notes: 1. Bold values indicate estimations with significance level.
2. [a]Accidents_After < Accidents_Before.
3. [b]Accidents_After > Accidents_Before.
4. [c]Accidents_After = Accidents_Before.

Test Statistics[b]	
	Accidents_After – Accidents_Before
Z	**–2.194**[a]
Asymp. Sig. (two-tailed)	**0.028**

Source: Authors.
Notes: 1. Bold values indicate estimations with significance level.
2. [a]Based on positive ranks.
3. [b]Wilcoxon Signed Ranks Test.

17.6. WILCOXON SIGNED RANK TEST FOR LARGE SAMPLES

The execution process of this test is elaborately discussed in the following example.

Example: An organization collected the feedback scores (out of 100) through a structure questionnaire for evaluating the effectiveness of the training on skill improvements of their employees. Feedbacks were collected before and after the training programme by the HR department as follows. Questionnaires were distributed to 20 randomly selected employees in the organization. Test the claim that there is no significant difference between the effect before the training and that after the training on skill improvements of the employees at 5% level of significance.

S. No.	Before Training	After Training
1	62	85
2	55	80
3	72	64
4	61	77
5	64	61
6	45	75
7	78	90
8	66	52
9	70	82
10	73	92
11	83	96
12	67	87
13	77	70

S. No.	Before Training	After Training
14	59	51
15	81	86
16	56	76
17	50	66
18	57	83
19	74	91
20	80	76

Solution: Here, the hypothesis to be tested is as follows:
H_0 = The training has not significantly improved the skills of the employees in the organization.
H_1 = The training has significantly improved the skills of the employees in the organization.
So calculated Wilcoxon T-statistics = Minimum (T+, T–) = Minimum (28, 182) = 28 (see Table 17.6).

TABLE 17.6
Wilcoxon T-statistics Calculation (2)

Before Training	After Training	Difference	Rank	Rank with '+ Sign' T+	Rank with '– Sign' T–
62	85	–23	–17		–17
55	80	–25	–18		–18
72	64	+8	+5.5	+5.5	
61	77	–16	–11.5		–11.5
64	61	+3	+1	+1	
45	75	–30	–20		–20
78	90	–12	–7.5		–7.5
66	52	+14	+10	+10	
70	82	–12	–7.5		–7.5
73	92	–19	–14		–14
83	96	–13	–9		–9
67	87	–20	–15		–15
77	70	+7	+4	+4	
59	51	+8	+5.5	+5.5	
81	86	–5	–3		–3
56.	76	–20	–16		–16
50	66	–16	–11.5		–11.5
57	83	–26	–19		–19
74	91	–17	–13		–13
80	76	+4	+2	+2	
Total				+28	–182

Source: Authors.

Here, |Z|-statistics is calculated only for the large sample size.

And |Z|-statistics = $\frac{|T-\mu_T|}{\sigma_T}$, where μ_T = Mean and σ_T = Standard deviation.

$$\text{Now, } \mu_T = \frac{n\times(n+1)}{4} = \frac{20\times(20+1)}{4} = 105.$$

$$\text{And } \sigma_T = \sqrt{\frac{n\times(n+1)\times(2n+1)}{24}} = \sqrt{\frac{20\times(20+1)\times(2\times 20+1)}{24}} = 26.786.$$

$$\text{So, } |Z|\text{-statistics} = \frac{|T-\mu_T|}{\sigma_T} = \frac{|28-105|}{26.786} = 2.875.$$

At 5% level of significance, the tabulated value of |Z|-statistics is 1.96. Here, the calculated value of |Z| is greater than the tabulated value. So the null hypothesis is rejected, that is, training has significantly improved the skills of the employees in the organization.

17.6.1. Solve the Wilcoxon Signed Rank Test (for Large Samples) Problem with SPSS

Null hypothesis (H_0): The training has not significantly improved the skills of the employees in the organization.

Alternative hypothesis (H_1): The training has significantly improved the skills of the employees in the organization.

After putting data and variables in the 'Data View' window and 'Variable View' window, click Analyze → Nonparametric Tests → 'Two-Related-Samples' in the SPSS window. One pop-up window will appear as 'Two-Related-Samples Tests'. Then send 'Before_Training' and 'After_Training' to 'Test Pairs'. Go to 'Test Type' and tick 'Wilcoxon' (Exhibit 17.4).

Then click 'OK'. At last, an SPSS output box will appear as shown in Table 17.7.

Here, Z-value (Sig.) of the problem is 0.004 which is less than 0.05 (5% level of significance). So we reject the null hypothesis.

17.7. MANN–WHITNEY U TEST

This non-parametric test resembles the 't-test' which compares two independent population means. In the case of an ordinal scale and doubt about the normality of the distribution direct the researcher to execute the Mann–Whitney U test. It is based on the assumptions of independent samples.

17.8. MANN–WHITNEY U TEST (FOR SMALL SAMPLE)

Here, n_1 and n_2 (where two samples have n_1 and n_2 number of observations/items) should be less than or equal to 10 in the case of small sample consideration under Mann–Whitney U test. So U statistics are calculated in terms of U_1 and U_2 by the following formula:

$$U_1 = n_1\times n_2 + \frac{n_1\times(n_1+1)}{2} - R_1$$

EXHIBIT 17.4

SPSS Window for Wilcoxon Signed Rank Test (Example for Large Sample)

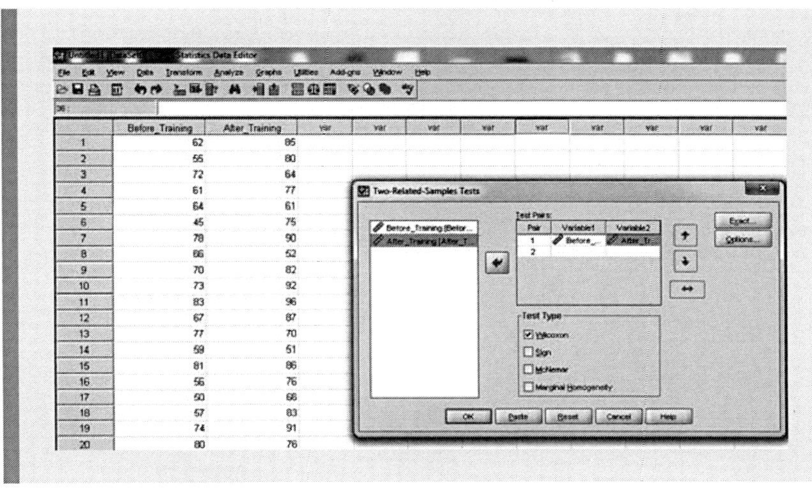

TABLE 17.7

Wilcoxon Signed Rank Test Tables from SPSS Output

Ranks				
		N	Mean Rank	Sum of Ranks
After_Training – Before_Training	Negative Ranks	6[a]	4.67	28.00
	Positive Ranks	**14[b]**	13.00	**182.00**
	Ties	0[c]		
	Total	20		

Source: Authors.

Notes: 1. Bold values indicate estimations with significance level.
2. [a]After_Training < Before_Training.
3. [b]After_Training > Before_Training.
4. [c]After_Training = Before_Training.

Test Statistics[b]	
	After_Training – Before_Training
Z	–2.876[a]
Asymp. Sig. (two-tailed)	**0.004**

Source: Authors.

Notes: 1. Bold values indicate estimations with significance level.
2. [a]Based on negative ranks.
3. [b]Wilcoxon Signed Ranks Test.

$$U_2 = n_1 \times n_2 + \frac{n_2 \times (n_2 + 1)}{2} - R_2$$

Here, R_1 = The sum of the ranks of the values of the first sample and R_2 = The sum of the ranks of the values of the second sample.

Basically, U statistics = Smallest value (U_1, U_2).

On the other hand, if any one value of U_1 and U_2 is calculated, the other value can be easily calculated by the following formula without using the aforementioned formula, that is, $U_1 = n_1 \times n_2 - U_2$.

Example: The following table represents netsurfing times (in hours) of the students from two departments (HR and Marketing) in a college. Seven and nine students were selected randomly from the HR and Marketing department, respectively. Use the Mann–Whitney U test to examine at a 5% level of significance whether the two samples come from identical populations.

HR Netsurfing Times (in Hours)	Marketing Netsurfing Times (in Hours)
5	2
3.5	3
5	5.5
3	4
4	6
4	3.5
6	4
	4.5
	6

Solution: Here, the hypothesis to be tested is as follows:
H_0 = Two samples come from identical populations.
H_1 = Two samples come from different populations.
Here, $n_1 = 7$ and $n_2 = 9$.

Now, $U_1 = n_1 \times n_2 + \frac{n_1 \times (n_1 + 1)}{2} - R_1 = 7 \times 9 + \frac{7 \times (7+1)}{2} - 60 = 31$ (see Table 17.8).

$U_2 = n_1 \times n_2 + \frac{n_2 \times (n_2 + 1)}{2} - R_2 = 7 \times 9 + \frac{9 \times (9+1)}{2} - 76 = 32$ (see Table 17.8).

U statistics = Smallest value (U_1, U_2) = Smallest value (31, 32) = 31.

At 5% level of significance, for $n_1 = 7$ and $n_2 = 9$, the tabulated value of U statistics = 12. Here, the calculated value is more than the tabulated value. Therefore, the null hypothesis is accepted, that is, the two samples come from identical populations.

17.8.1. Solve the Mann–Whitney U Test Problem with SPSS

Null hypothesis (H_0): Two samples come from identical populations.

Alternative hypothesis (H_1): Two samples come from different populations.

After putting data and variables in the Data View' window and 'Variable View' window, click Analyze → Nonparametric Tests → Two-Independent-Samples in the SPSS window. One pop-up window will appear as 'Two-Independent-Samples Tests'. Then, send 'Net_Surfing_Time' to 'Test Variable List' and 'Departments' to 'Grouping Variable'. Then, click 'Define Range' and another pop-up window will appear as 'Two Independent Samples: Define Range'. In this box, input 1 against Group 1

TABLE 17.8
Calculation of Sum of the Ranks in Each Sample (1)

HR Netsurfing Times (in Hours)	Rank	Marketing Netsurfing Times (in Hours)	Rank
5	11.5	2	1
3.5	4.5	3	2.5
5	11.5	5.5	13
3	2.5	4	7.5
4	7.5	6	15
4	7.5	3.5	4.5
6	15	4	7.5
		4.5	10
		6	15
R_1	60	R_2	76

Source: Authors.

EXHIBIT 17.5
SPSS Window for Mann–Whitney U Test (Example for Small Sample)

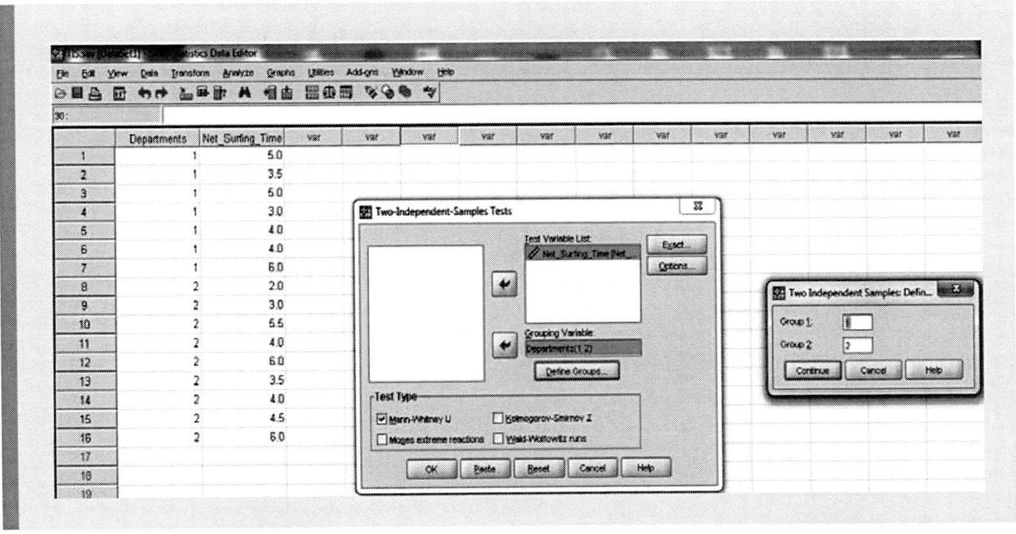

and 2 against Group 2 and click continue. Then in the 'Two-Independent-Samples Tests' dialog box, go to 'Test Type' and tick 'Mann-Whitney U' (Exhibit 17.5).

Then click 'OK'. At last, an SPSS output box will appear as shown in Table 17.9.

TABLE 17.9
Mann–Whitney U Test Tables from SPSS Output (1)

Ranks				
	Departments	N	Mean Rank	Sum of Ranks
Net_Surfing_Time	HR Dept	7	8.57	**60.00**
	Marketing Dept	9	8.44	**76.00**
	Total	**16**		

Source: Authors.
Note: Bold values indicate estimations with significance level.

Test Statistics[b]	
	Net_Surfing_Time
Mann–Whitney U	**31.000**
Wilcoxon W	**76.000**
Z	**–0.054**
Asymp. Sig. (two-tailed)	**0.957**
Exact Sig. [2*(one-tailed Sig.)]	1.000[a]

Source: Authors.
Notes: 1. Bold values indicate estimations with significance level.
2. [a]Not corrected for ties.
3. [b]Grouping Variable: Departments.

Here, Z-value (Sig.) of the problem is 0.957 which is greater than 0.05 (5% level of significance). So we accept the null hypothesis.

17.9. MANN–WHITNEY U TEST (FOR LARGE SAMPLE)

Here, n_1 and n_2 (where two samples have n_1 and n_2 number of observations/items) should be more than 10 in the case of large sample consideration under the Mann–Whitney U test. For a large sample, U statistic distribution resembles approximately to normal distribution. In this scenario, Z-statistics is calculated to test the hypothesis.

So, $\left|\text{Z-statistics}\right| = \dfrac{U - \mu}{\sigma}$.

Here, μ = Mean = $\dfrac{n_1 n_2}{2}$ and σ = Standard deviation = $\sqrt{\dfrac{n_1 n_2 (n_1 + n_2 + 1)}{12}}$.

Example: The following table represents marks obtained by two samples of students in an entrance examination. The number of students randomly selected for two samples were 17 and 14. Use the Mann–Whitney U test to examine at a 5% level of significance whether two samples belong to the same population.

Sample_1	Sample_2
85	83
87	40
75	61

Sample_1	Sample_2
90	42
77	49
81	66
85	85
96	57
46	89
97	82
53	71
98	58
80	55
65	76
99	
84	
95	

Solution: Here, the hypothesis to be tested is as follows:
H_0 = Two samples belong to the same population.
H_1 = Two samples belong to the different population.

Here, n_1 = 17 and n_2 = 14.

Now, $U_1 = n_1 \times n_2 + \dfrac{n_1 \times (n_1 + 1)}{2} - R_1 = 17 \times 14 + \dfrac{17 \times (17+1)}{2} - 338 = 53$ (see Table 17.10).

$U_2 = n_1 \times n_2 + \dfrac{n_2 \times (n_2 + 1)}{2} - R_2 = 17 \times 14 + \dfrac{14 \times (14+1)}{2} - 158 = 185$ (Table 17.10).

U statistics = Smallest value (U_1, U_2) = Smallest value (53, 185) = 53.

Now, μ = Mean = $\dfrac{n_1 n_2}{2} = \dfrac{17 \times 14}{2} = 119.$

Σ = Standard deviation = $\sqrt{\dfrac{n_1 n_2 (n_1 + n_2 + 1)}{12}} = \sqrt{\dfrac{17 \times 14 \times (17 + 14 + 1)}{12}} = 25.193.$

So, $|Z\text{-statistics}| = \left|\dfrac{U - \mu}{\sigma}\right| = \left|\dfrac{53 - 119}{25.193}\right| = 2.619.$

At 5% level of significance, the tabulated value of |Z|-statistics is 1.96. As the calculated value of |Z|-statistics is greater than the tabulated value, the null hypothesis is rejected. Thus, two samples belong to the different population.

TABLE 17.10
Calculation of Sum of the Ranks in Each Sample (2)

Sample_1	Rank	Sample_2	Rank
85	22	83	19
87	24	40	1
75	13	61	9
90	26	42	2
77	15	49	4
81	17	66	11
85	22	85	22
96	27	57	7
46	3	89	25
97	28	82	18
53	5	71	12
98	29	58	8
80	16	55	6
65	10	76	14
99	30.5		
84	20		
99	30.5		
R_1	338	R_2	158

Source: Authors.

17.9.1. Solve the Mann–Whitney U Test Problem with SPSS

Null hypothesis (H_0): Two samples belong to the same population.

Alternative hypothesis (H_1): Two samples belong to the different populations.

After putting data and variables in the 'Data View' window and 'Variable View' window, click Analyze → Nonparametric Tests → Two-Independent-Samples in the SPSS window. One pop-up window will appear as 'Two-Independent-Samples Tests'. Then send 'Marks_Obtained' to 'Test Variable List' and 'Samples' to 'Grouping Variable'. Then click 'Define Range' and another pop-up window will appear as 'Two Independent Samples: Define Range'. In this box, input 1 against Group 1 and 2 against Group 2 and click continue. Then in the 'Two-Independent-Samples Tests' dialog box, go to 'Test Type' and tick 'Mann-Whitney U' (Exhibit 17.6).

Then click 'OK'. At last, an SPSS output box will appear as shown in Table 17.11.

Here, Z-value (Sig.) of the problem is 0.009 which is less than 0.05 (5% level of significance). So we reject the null hypothesis.

EXHIBIT 17.6
SPSS Window for Mann–Whitney U Test (Example for Large Sample)

TABLE 17.11
Mann–Whitney U Test Tables from SPSS Output (2)

Ranks				
	Samples	N	Mean Rank	Sum of Ranks
Marks_ Obtained	Sample_1	**17**	19.88	**338.00**
	Sample_2	**14**	11.29	**158.00**
	Total	**31**		

Source: Authors.
Note: Bold values indicate estimations with significance level.

Test Statistics[b]	
	Marks_Obtained
Mann–Whitney U	53.000
Wilcoxon W	**158.000**
Z	–2.621
Asymp. Sig. (two-tailed)	**0.009**
Exact Sig. [2*(one-tailed Sig.)]	**0.008**[a]

Source: Authors.
Notes: 1. Bold values indicate estimations with significance level.
2. [a]Not corrected for ties.
3. [b]Grouping Variable: Samples.

17.10. KRUSKAL–WALLIS TEST

This non-parametric test resembles the 'one-way ANOVA' which is a parametric test. It can be performed in interval scales as well as ordinal scale. It is based on the assumptions of independent groups. Basically, it is used instead of 'one-way ANOVA' where the researchers have the confusion about the normality of the distribution. The Kruskal–Wallis statistics (K) is calculated by the following formula:

$$K = \frac{12}{n(n+1)} \sum_{i=1}^{g} \frac{T_i^2}{n_i} - 3 \times (n+1),$$

where n = total number of observations, g = number of groups, T_i = sum of the ranks in a particular group and n_i = number of observations in a particular group.

If the number of observations of each individual group is more than 5, then it is an approximation of χ^2 distribution with degree of freedom $(g - 1)$.

Example: Thirty students were selected randomly from four B-schools to understand if the category of students are equal in each B-schools or not. A 100-marks performance evaluating examination was conducted to evaluate 30 students and the obtained marks are presented in the following table. At 5% level of significance, test whether the categories of students of all B-schools are the same.

B-school_1	B-school_2	B-school_3	B-school_4
84	74	66	56
53	45	50	62
95	78	68	47
85	61	54	60
90	79	70	59
87	82	72	49
88	43	44	92
94			88

Solution: Here, the hypothesis to be tested is as follows:

H_0 = The categories of students of all B-schools are the same.

H_1 = At least one of the B-schools has a different category of students.

Here, $$\sum_{i=1}^{g} \frac{T_1^2}{n_1} = \frac{T_i^2}{n_i} + \frac{T_i^2}{n_i} + \frac{T_2^2}{n_2} + \frac{T_3^2}{n_3} + \frac{T_4^2}{n_4} = \frac{(187.5)^2}{8} + \frac{(94)^2}{7} + \frac{(78)^2}{7} + \frac{(105.5)^2}{8}$$

$$= 7{,}917.241. \text{ (As shown in Table 17.12.)}$$

TABLE 17.12

Calculation of Sum of the Ranks in Each Group (3)

B-school_1	Rank	B-school_2	Rank	B-school_3	Rank	B-school_4	Rank
84	22	74	18	66	14	56	9
53	7	45	3	50	6	62	13
95	30	78	19	68	15	47	4
85	23	61	12	54	8	60	11
90	27	79	20	70	16	59	10
87	24	82	21	72	17	49	5
88	25.5	43	1	44	2	92	28
94	29					88	25.5
T_1	**187.5**	T_2	**94**	T_3	**78**	T_4	**105.5**

Source: Authors.

Then, Kruskal–Wallis statistics (K) $= \dfrac{12}{n(n+1)}\sum_{i=1}^{g}\dfrac{T_i^2}{n_i} - 3\times(n+1)$

$$= \frac{12}{30\times(30+1)}\times(7917.241) - 3\times(30+1)$$

$$= 9.158.$$

At 5% level of significance with 3 degree of freedom (g – 1 = 3), the tabulated value of $\chi^2_{0.05,3} = 7.8147$. Here, the calculated value is more than the tabulated value. Therefore, the null hypothesis is rejected, that is, B-schools have different categories of students.

17.10.1. Solve the Kruskal–Wallis Test Problem with SPSS

Null hypothesis (H_0): The categories of students of all B-schools are the same.

Alternative hypothesis (H_1): At least one of the B-schools has a different category of students.

After putting data and variables in the 'Data View' window and 'Variable View' window, click Analyze → Nonparametric Tests → K Independent Samples in the SPSS window. One pop-up window will appear as 'Tests for Several Independent Samples'. Then send 'Marks_Obtained' to 'Test Variable List' and B_Schools to 'Grouping Variable' (Exhibit 17.7). Then click 'Define Range' and another pop-up window will appear as 'Several Independent Samples: Define Range'. In this box, input 1 against

EXHIBIT 17.7

SPSS Window for Kruskal–Wallis Test (Step 1)

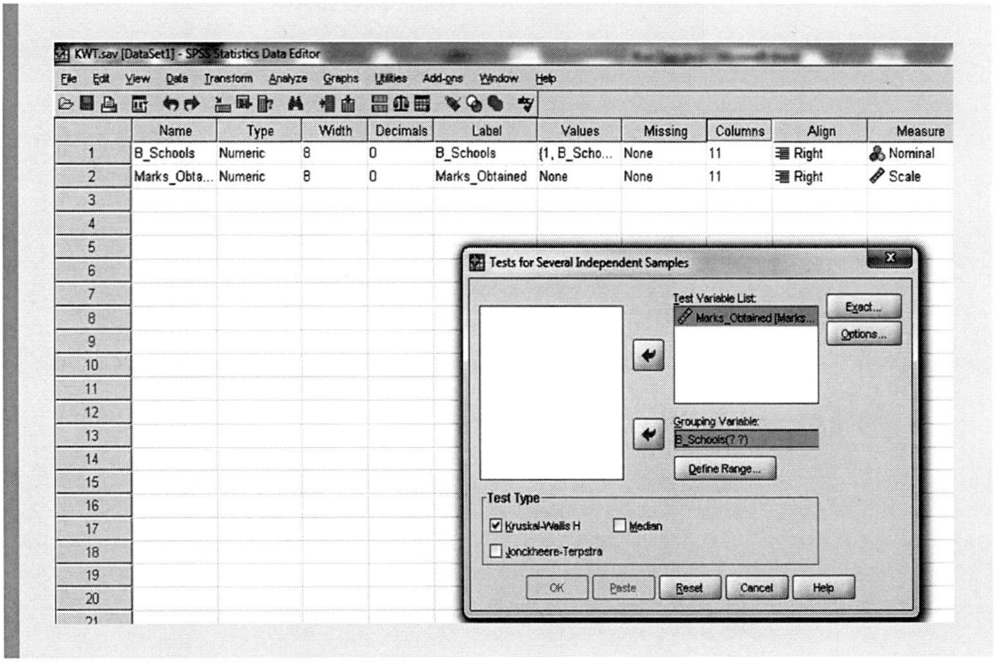

EXHIBIT 17.8

SPSS Window for Kruskal–Wallis Test (Step 2)

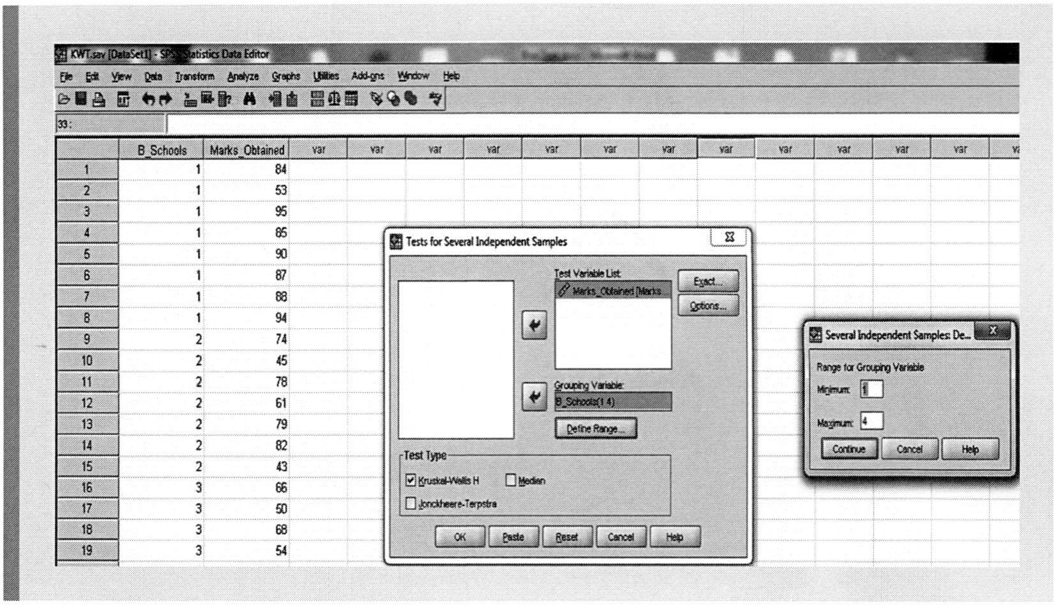

TABLE 17.13

Kruskal–Wallis Test Tables from SPSS Output

Ranks			
	B_Schools	*N*	Mean Rank
Marks_Obtained	B_School_1	8	23.44
	B_School_2	7	13.43
	B_School_3	7	11.14
	B_School_4	8	13.19
	Total	30	

Source: Authors.
Note: Bold values indicate estimations with significance level.

Test Statistics[a,b]	
	Marks_Obtained
Chi-Square	**9.160**
df	3
Asymp. Sig.	**0.027**

Source: Authors.
Notes: 1. Bold values indicate estimations with significance level.
2. [a]Kruskal—Wallis Test.
3. [b]Grouping Variable: B_Schools.

'Minimum' and 4 against 'Maximum' and click 'Continue'. Then in the 'Tests for Several Independent Samples' dialog box, go to 'Test Type' and tick 'Kruskal-Wallis H' (Exhibit 17.8).

Then click 'OK'. At last, the SPSS output box will appear as shown in Table 17.13.

Here, chi-square value (Sig.) of the problem is 0.027 which is less than 0.05 (5% level of significance). So we reject the null hypothesis. From the 'Mean Rank', we can easily understand good and bad category students available in four different B_Schools. Therefore, B_School_1 (23.44) has the best quality students and B_School_3 (11.14) has the worst quality students.

17.11. FRIEDMAN TEST

It is a very useful non-parametric test which is quite similar to a randomized block design, containing ranked data (approximately χ^2 distribution). It is applicable when all blocks will be independent and there will be no interaction effect between blocks and treatments. Friedman test statistics (χ_r^2) is calculated by the following formula:

$$\chi_r^2 = \frac{12}{b \times t \times (t+1)} \sum_{i=1}^{t} R_i^2 = -3b \times (t+1), \text{ with degree of freedom } (t-1).$$

Here, b = Number of blocks (rows), t = Number of treatments (columns), i = Particular treatment level and R_i^2 = Square of total rank for a particular treatment.

Example: A researcher wants to compare of four leading brands of soap available in the Indian market in terms of the acceptance level of the customers. Fifteen customers were randomly selected and asked to rank soaps with the help of a scale from 1 to 4 as per their acceptance level. Collected data are available in the following table. Test whether the acceptance level of all the brands are the same at 5% level of significance.

Customer No.	Brand_W	Brand_X	Brand_Y	Brand_Z
1	1	3	4	2
2	2	4	3	1
3	2	4	3	1
4	1	4	3	2
5	1	3	4	2
6	1	2	4	3
7	2	3	4	1
8	2	3	4	1
9	2	4	3	1
10	2	3	1	4
11	3	4	2	1
12	2	3	4	1
13	1	3	4	2
14	1	2	4	3
15	3	2	4	1

Solution: Here, the hypothesis to be tested is as follows:
H_0 = The acceptance levels of all the brands are the same.
H_1 = The acceptance levels of all the brands are not the same.

Here, b = Number of rows = 15 and t = Number of columns = 4.

$\sum_{i=1}^{t} R_i^2$ = Grand Total of all the squares = 6,134.

TABLE 17.14
Calculation of Square of Total Rank for a Particular Treatment

Customer No.	Brand_W	Brand_X	Brand_Y	Brand_Z
1	1	3	4	2
2	2	4	3	1
3	2	4	3	1
4	1	4	3	2
5	1	3	4	2
6	1	2	4	3
7	2	3	4	1
8	2	3	4	1
9	2	4	3	1
10	2	3	1	4
11	1	3	2	4
12	2	3	4	1
13	1	3	4	2
14	1	2	4	3
15	3	2	4	1
Sum of ranks (R_i)	$R_1 = 24$	$R_2 = 46$	$R_3 = 51$	$R_4 = 29$
Square of sum of ranks (R_i^2)	$R_1^2 = 576$	$R_2^2 = 2{,}116$	$R_3^2 = 2{,}601$	$R_4^2 = 841$
Grand total of all the squares $(R_1^2 + R_2^2 + R_3^2 + R_4^2) = 6{,}134$				

Source: Authors.

$$\text{Now, Friedman test statistics } (\chi_r^2) = \frac{12}{b \times t \times (t+1)} \sum_{i=1}^{t} R_i^2 - 3b \times (t+1)$$

$$= \frac{12}{15 \times 4 \times (4+1)} \times 6{,}134 - 3 \times 15 \times (4+1)$$

$$= 20.36.$$

At 5% level of significance with 3 degree of freedom ($t - 1 = 3$), the tabulated value of $\chi^2_{0.05,3} = 7.8147$. Here, the calculated value is more than the tabulated value. Therefore, the null hypothesis is rejected, that is, the acceptance levels of all the brands are not the same (Table 17.14).

17.11.1. Solve Friedman Test Problem with SPSS

Null hypothesis (H_0): The acceptance levels of all the brands are the same.

Alternative hypothesis (H_1): The acceptance levels of all the brands are not the same.

After putting data and variables in the 'Data View' window and 'Variable View' window, click Analyze → Nonparametric Tests → K Related Samples in the SPSS window. One pop-up window

EXHIBIT 17.9
SPSS Window for Friedman Test

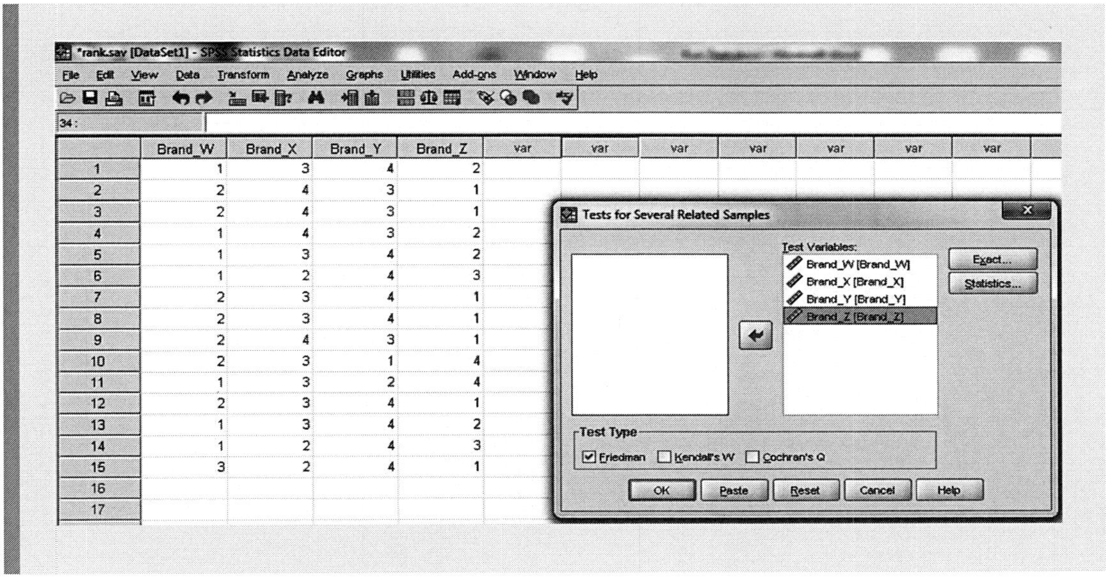

	Brand_W	Brand_X	Brand_Y	Brand_Z
1	1	3	4	2
2	2	4	3	1
3	2	4	3	1
4	1	4	3	2
5	1	3	4	2
6	1	2	4	3
7	2	3	4	1
8	2	3	4	1
9	2	4	3	1
10	2	3	1	4
11	1	3	2	4
12	2	3	4	1
13	1	3	4	2
14	1	2	4	3
15	3	2	4	1

TABLE 17.15
Friedman Test Tables from SPSS Output

Ranks	
	Mean Rank
Brand_W	**1.60**
Brand_X	**3.07**
Brand_Y	**3.40**
Brand_Z	**1.93**

Source: Authors.
Note: Bold values indicate estimations with significance level.

Test Statistics[a]	
N	15
Chi-Square	20.360
df	3
Asymp. Sig.	**<0.001**

Source: Authors.
Notes: 1. Bold values indicate estimations with significance level.
2. [a]Friedman Test.

will appear as 'Tests for Several Related Samples'. Then send all variables (including 'Brand_W', 'Brand_X', 'Brand_Y' and 'Brand_z') to 'Test Variables'. Go to 'Test Type' and tick 'Friedman' (Exhibit 17.9).

Then click 'OK'. At last, an SPSS output box will appear as shown in Table 17.15.

Here chi-square value (Sig.) of the problem is less than 0.001 which is again less than 0.05 (5% level of significance). So we reject the null hypothesis. From the 'Mean Rank', we can easily understand the most and least preferable brands among the four brands. Therefore, Brand_W (1.60) is the most preferable brand and Brand_Y (3.40) is the least preferable brand.

17.12. RUN TEST

It is a non-parametric test to examine the randomness of the sample which is drawn from a population. Run test is based on the sequence in which the order of observations is really found. The run depicts the sequence of identical elements that are followed and preceded by different types of elements or no element on any side. Generally, very small or large number of runs point towards the lack of randomness.

Example: Consider gender-wise (M—Male, F—Female) arrival pattern in a shopping mall as the following sequence. Test the randomness of the arrival pattern of the people at 5% level of significance.

At first, the number of runs is defined as follows:

MMMMM 1st Run	FFFF 2nd Run	MMM 3rd Run	FFFFF 4th Run	MMMM 5th Run	FFFFFF 6th Run	MMMM 7th Run	FF 8th Run
MMMM 9th Run	FFF 10th Run	MM 11th Run	FFFF 12th Run	MMMMM 13th Run	FFFFF 14th Run	MMM 15th Run	

And n_1 and n_2 are the number of occurrences of category 1 and category 2, respectively.

So, r (Number of runs) = 15

n_1 (Number of males in the sample) = 30

n_2 (Number of females in the sample) = 29

n (Total sample size) = 59.

Solution: Here, the hypothesis to be tested is as follows:

H_0 = Gender-wise arrival pattern of the people is random.

H_1 = Gender-wise arrival pattern of the people is not random.

For a large sample (when n_1 and/or n_2 are/is greater than 20)

$$\mu_r \text{(Mean)} = 1 + \frac{2n_1 n_2}{n_1 + n_2}$$

$$= 1 + \frac{2 \times 30 \times 29}{30 + 29}$$

$$= 30.49$$

$$\sigma_r \text{ (Standard deviation)} = \sqrt{\frac{2n_1 n_2 (2n_1 n_2 - n_1 - n_2)}{(n_1 + n_2)^2 (n_1 + n_2 - 1)}}$$

$$= \sqrt{\frac{2 \times 30 \times 29(2 \times 30 \times 29 - 30 - 29)}{(30 + 29)^2 (30 + 29 - 1)}}$$

$$= 3.81.$$

And, $|Z|$-statistics $= \dfrac{|r - \mu_r|}{\sigma_r}$

$$= \frac{|15 - 30.49|}{3.81}$$

$$= 4.07.$$

At 5% level of significance, the tabulated value of |Z|-statistics is 1.96. As the calculated value of |Z|-statistics is greater than the tabulated value, the null hypothesis is rejected. Thus, gender-wise arrival pattern of the people is not random.

17.12.1. Solve the First Run Test Problem with SPSS

Here, gender-wise (M—Male and F—Female) arrival pattern which belongs to nominal measure type in SPSS is coded as 1 = Male and 2 = Female.

Null hypothesis (H_0): Gender-wise arrival pattern of the people is random.

Alternative hypothesis (H_1): Gender-wise arrival pattern of the people is not random.

After putting data and variables in the 'Data View' window and 'Variable View' window, click Analyze → Nonparametric Tests → 'Runs' in the SPSS window. One pop-up window will appear as 'Runs Test'. Then send 'Gender-wise arrival pattern' to 'Test Variable List'. Go to 'Cut Point' and tick 'Mean' and 'Custom'. Then input the 'Custom value'. This value is generally calculated as the average of two nominal measurement value. In this case, 'Custom value' is $\frac{1+2}{2}$ = 1.5 (as 1 = Male, 2 = Female; Exhibit 17.10).

EXHIBIT 17.10

SPSS Window for Run Test (1)

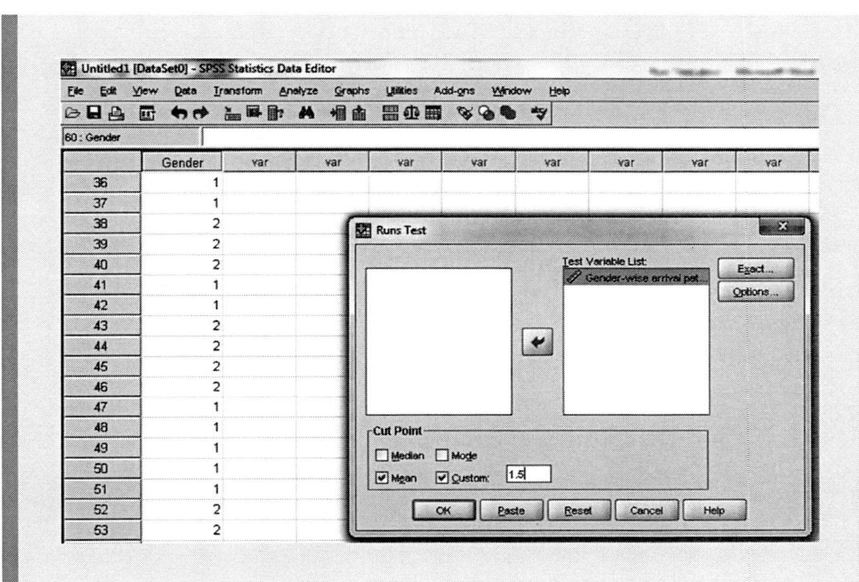

TABLE 17.16
Run Test Tables from SPSS Output

Runs Test 1	
	Gender-wise arrival pattern
Test Value[a]	1.49
Cases < Test Value	30
Cases >= Test Value	29
Total Cases	59
Number of Runs	15
Z	**–4.070**
Asymp. Sig. (two-tailed)	**<0.001**

Source: Authors.
Notes: 1. Bold values indicate estimations with significance level.
2. [a]Mean.

Runs Test 2	
	Gender-wise arrival pattern
Test Value[a]	1.50
Total Cases	59
Number of Runs	15
Z	**–4.070**
Asymp. Sig. (two-tailed)	**<0.001**

Source: Authors.
Notes: 1. Bold values indicate estimations with significance level.
2. [a]User-specified.

Then click 'OK'. At last, an SPSS output box will appear as shown in Table 17.16.

Here, Z-value (Sig.) of the problem is less than 0.001 which is less than 0.05 (5% level of significance). So we reject the null hypothesis.

Example: A researcher conducts a survey to understand whether Indian rural population is in favour of digital India (D) or against it (N). The following figure shows the sequence of responses of the respondents. Use 5% level of significance to determine whether the researcher has selected the sample randomly.

DDD NN DDDD NNN DD NN D NNNN DDD NNN DDDD NNNNN DDD NN
DDDDDD NNNN DDDDD NNNN DDDDDD NNNNN DD NNNN

Now, r (Number of runs) = 22

n_1 (Number of respondents in favour of digital India) = 39

n_2 (Number of respondents against digital India) = 38

n (Total sample size) = 77.

Solution: Here, the hypothesis to be tested is as follows:
H_0 = Sample of respondents are randomly generated.
H_1 = Sample of respondents are not randomly generated.

$$\text{Then, } \mu_r \text{ (Mean)} = 1 + \frac{2n_1n_2}{n_1 + n_2}$$

$$= 1 + \frac{2 \times 39 \times 38}{39 + 38}$$

$$= 39.49.$$

$$\sigma_r \text{ (Standard deviation)} = \sqrt{\frac{2n_1n_2(2n_1n_2 - n_1 - n_2)}{(n_1+n_2)^2(n_1+n_2-1)}}$$

$$= \sqrt{\frac{2 \times 39 \times 38(2 \times 39 \times 38 - 39 - 38)}{(39+38)^2(39+38-1)}}$$

$$= 4.36.$$

$$\text{And, } |Z|\text{-statistics} = \frac{|r - \mu_r|}{\sigma_r}$$

$$= \frac{|22 - 39.49|}{4.36}$$

$$= 4.01.$$

At 5% level of significance, the tabulated value of |Z|-statistics is 1.96. As the calculated value of |Z|-statistics is greater than the tabulated value, the null hypothesis is rejected. Thus, sample of respondents are not randomly generated.

17.12.2. Solve the Second Run Test Problem with SPSS

Here, favourable and non-favourable (D—Favour digital India and N—Against digital India) response patterns which belong to the nominal measure type in SPSS are coded as 1 = D and 2 = N.

Null hypothesis (H_0): Sample of respondents are randomly generated.

Alternative hypothesis (H_1): Sample of respondents are not randomly generated.

After putting data and variables in the 'Data View' window and 'Variable View' window, click Analyze → Nonparametric Tests → 'Runs' in the SPSS window. One pop-up window will appear as 'Runs Test'. Then send 'Response pattern' to 'Test Variable List'. Go to 'Cut Point' and tick 'Mean' and 'Custom'. Then input the 'Custom value' (Exhibit 17.11).

Then click 'OK'. At last, an SPSS output box will appear as shown in Table 17.17.

Here, Z-value (Sig.) of the problem is less than 0.001 which is less than 0.05 (5% level of significance). So we reject the null hypothesis.

When both n_1 and n_2 are less than 20, it is considered a small sample.

Example: Few students are selected for teacher's feedback from the Engineering (E) and Management (M) departments in a college as follows. Use 5% level of significance to determine whether the sample is randomly selected.

<u>EEEE</u> <u>MMM</u> <u>EEEEEE</u> <u>MMMMMM</u> <u>EEE</u>

Now, r (Number of runs) = 5
n_1 (Number of respondents from the Engineering department) = 13
n_2 (Number of respondents from the Management department) = 9
n (Total sample size) = 22.

EXHIBIT 17.11

SPSS Window for Run Test (2)

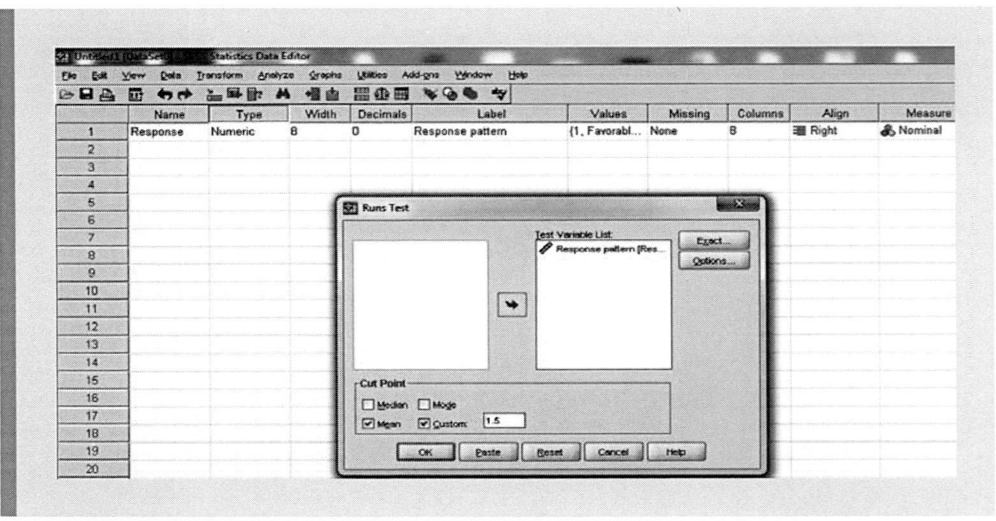

TABLE 17.17

Run Test Tables from SPSS Output

Runs Test 1	
	Response Pattern
Test Value[a]	1.49
Cases < Test Value	39
Cases >= Test Value	38
Total Cases	71
Number of Runs	22
Z	**–4.014**
Asymp. Sig. (two-tailed)	**<0.001**

Source: Authors.

Notes: 1. Bold values indicate estimations with significance level.

2. [a]Mean.

Runs Test 2	
	Response Pattern
Test Value[a]	1.50
Total Cases	77
Number of Runs	22
Z	**–4.014**
Asymp. Sig. (two-tailed)	**<0.001**

Source: Authors.

Notes: 1. Bold values indicate estimations with significance level.

2. [a]User-specified.

Solution: Here, the hypothesis to be tested is as follows:

H_0 = Sample elements are randomly selected.

H_1 = Sample elements are not randomly selected.

From the run table, for $n_1 = 13$ and $n_2 = 9$, the tabulated value of '*r*' for the lower tail is 6 and the tabulated value of '*r*' for the upper tail is 17. For the condition '$r < 6$' and '$r > 17$', the null hypothesis will be rejected.

Here, r (Number of runs) is 5 which is less than 6 (the tabulated value of 'r' for the lower tail). So the null hypothesis is rejected. That means, sample elements are not randomly selected.

17.12.3. Solve the Third Run Test Problem with SPSS

Here, engineering and management (E—Engineering and M—Management) students selection pattern which belongs to nominal measure type in SPSS is coded as 1 = E and 2 = M.

Null hypothesis (H_0): Sample elements are randomly selected.

Alternative hypothesis (H_1): Sample elements are not randomly selected.

After putting data and variables in the 'Data View' window and 'Variable View' window, click Analyze → Nonparametric Tests → 'Runs' in the SPSS window. One pop-up window will appear as 'Runs Test'. Then send 'Response pattern' to 'Test Variable List'. Go to 'Cut Point' and tick 'Mean' and 'Custom'. Then input the 'Custom value' (Exhibit 17.12).

Then click 'OK'. At last, the SPSS output box will appear as shown in Table 17.18.

Here Z-value (Sig.) of the problem is 0.005 which is less than 0.05 (5% level of significance). So we reject the null hypothesis.

17.13. KOLMOGOROV–SMIRNOV ONE-SAMPLE TEST

Kolmogorov–Smirnov one-sample test is a non-parametric test which finds out whether there is any significant difference between an observed and theoretical frequency distribution (normal/uniform/Poisson/exponential). It is used for comparing the observed and theoretical frequency distribution on

EXHIBIT 17.12

SPSS Window for Run Test (3)

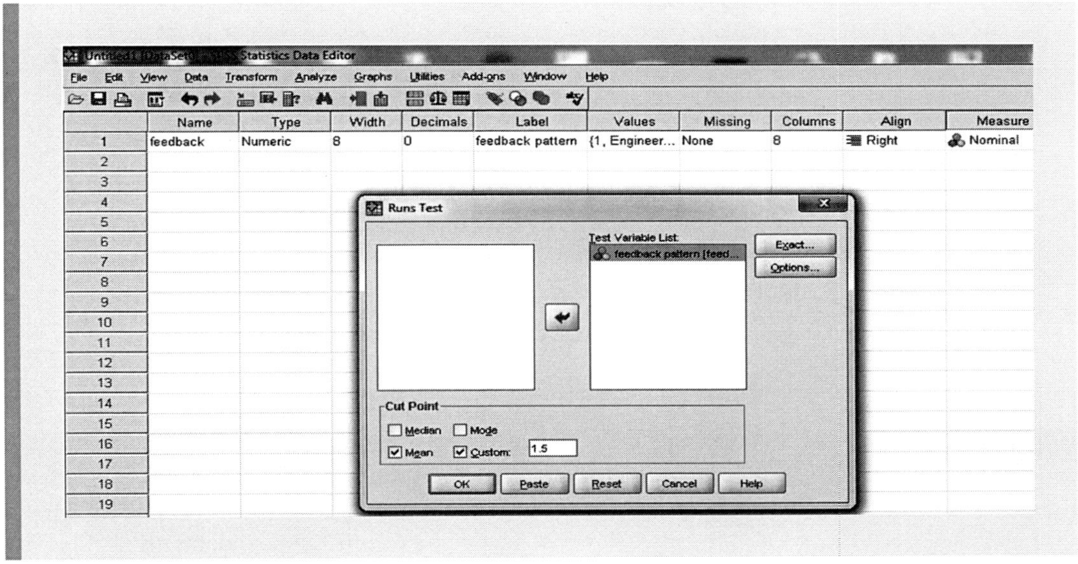

TABLE 17.18
Run Test Tables from SPSS Output

Runs Test 1	
	Feedback Pattern
Test Value[a]	1.41
Cases < Test Value	13
Cases >= Test Value	9
Total Cases	22
Number of Runs	5
Z	–2.778
Asymp. Sig. (two-tailed)	**0.005**

Source: Author.
Notes: 1. Bold values indicate estimations with significance level.
2. [a]Mean.

Runs Test 2	
	Feedback Pattern
Test Value[a]	1.50
Total Cases	22
Number of Runs	5
Z	–2.778
Asymp. Sig. (two-tailed)	**0.005**

Source: Authors.
Notes: 1. Bold values indicate estimations with significance level.
2. [a]User-specified.

an ordinal scale. Basically, it determines whether the chosen sample from the population is having the expected theoretical distribution. In this test, 'D' statistics is used to evaluate how close the observed frequency distribution is to the theoretical distribution.

Example: A researcher collected the following sample of 'total weekly time' (in hours) spent by 20 college students in a mobile phone. Use Kolmogorov–Smirnov one-sample test at 5% level of significance to check the null hypothesis that the sampled population is normally distributed.

21	17	23	27	18	25	19	13	15	24	24	16	20	26	19	23	22	14	17	25

Solution: Here, the hypothesis to be tested is as follows:
H_0 = Sampled population is normally distributed.
H_1 = Sampled population is not normally distributed.

'D' statistics is calculated by 'D' = maximum $|F_o - F_e|$.

In this case, 'D' statistics = 0.0211 (see Table 17.19). At 5% level of significance, the tabulated value of 'D' statistics is 0.294. As the calculated value of 'D' statistics is less than the tabulated value, the null hypothesis is accepted. So we can say that sampled population is normally distributed.

17.13.1. Solve the Kolmogorov–Smirnov One-sample Test Problem with SPSS

Null hypothesis (H_0): Sampled population is normally distributed.

Alternative hypothesis (H_1): Sampled population is not normally distributed.

After putting data and variables in the 'Data View' window and 'Variable View' window, click Analyze → Nonparametric Tests → 'One-Sample K-S Test' in the SPSS window. One pop-up window will appear as 'One-Sample Kolmogorov–Smirnov Test'. Then send 'Observed Frequency' to 'Test Variable List'. Go to 'Test Distribution' and tick 'Normal' (Exhibit 17.13).

TABLE 17.19
'D' Statistics Calculation for Kolmogorov–Smirnov One-sample Test

Sample Element No.	1	2	3	4	5	6	7	8	9	10
Observed Frequency	**21**	**17**	**23**	**27**	**18**	**25**	**19**	**13**	**15**	**24**
Observed Relative Cumulative Frequency (F_o)	0.0515	0.0931	0.1495	0.2157	0.2598	0.3211	0.3676	0.3995	0.4363	0.4951
Expected Relative Cumulative Frequency (F_e)	0.05	0.1	0.15	0.2	0.25	0.3	0.35	0.4	0.45	0.5
Absolute Deviation $\|F_o - F_e\|$	0.0015	–0.0069	–0.0005	0.0157	0.0098	***0.0211***	0.0176	–0.0005	–0.0137	–0.0049

Sample Element No.	11	12	13	14	15	16	17	18	19	20
Observed Frequency	**24**	**16**	**20**	**26**	**19**	**23**	**22**	**14**	**17**	**25**
Observed Relative Cumulative Frequency (F_o)	0.5539	0.5931	0.6422	0.7059	0.7525	0.8088	0.8627	0.8971	0.9387	1
Expected Relative Cumulative Frequency (F_e)	0.55	0.6	0.65	0.7	0.75	0.8	0.85	0.9	0.95	1
Absolute Deviation $\|F_o - F_e\|$	0.0039	–0.0069	–0.0078	0.0059	0.0025	0.0088	0.0127	–0.0029	–0.0113	0

Source: Authors.
Note: Bold values indicate estimations with significance level.

EXHIBIT 17.13
SPSS Window for One-sample Kolmogorov–Smirnov Test

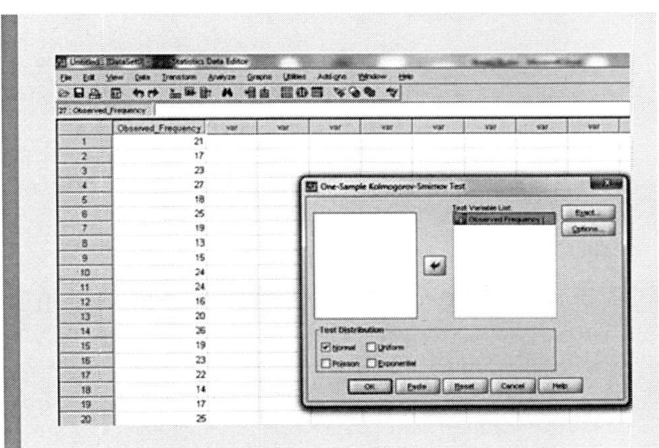

TABLE 17.20
One-sample Kolmogorov–Smirnov Test Table from SPSS Output

One-Sample Kolmogorov–Smirnov Test		
		Observed Frequency
N		20
Normal parameters[a,b]	Mean	20.40
	Std. deviation	4.210
Most extreme differences	Absolute	0.132
	Positive	0.090
	Negative	–0.132
Kolmogorov–Smirnov Z		0.588
Asymp. sig. (two-tailed)		**0.879**

Source: Authors.
Notes: 1. Bold values indicate estimations with significance level.
2. [a]Test distribution is normal.
3. [b]Calculated from data.

Then click 'OK'. At last, the SPSS output box will appear as shown in Table 17.20.

Here, Z-value (Sig.) of the problem is 0.879 which is greater than 0.05 (5% level of significance). So we accept the null hypothesis.

17.14. SPEARMAN'S RANK CORRELATION

Spearman's rank correlation is used to determine the correlation between two series of ranks (ordinal data). The association between two ranked variable data cannot be determined by the Pearson correlation coefficient. The formula of Spearman's rank correlation (r_s) is mentioned as follows:

$$\text{Spearman's rank correlation } (r_s) = 1 - \frac{6\left\{\sum d^2 + \sum \frac{t^3 - t}{12}\right\}}{n \times (n^2 - 1)}.$$

Here, d = Difference between pair of ranks of two variables, n = Total number of paired observations and t = Number of repetitions of an item weather in the first or second series.

Spearman's rank correlation (r_s) must be in the range of $-1 < r_s < +1$. If the correlation is close to +1, it indicates high degree of positive association between two variables. If correlation is close to –1, it indicates high degree of negative association between two variables. If it is 0 (zero), then there is no association between two variables.

Example: In a research survey, 15 students were randomly selected from a school to understand the degree of association between the study and sports performance. For evaluating the study and sports performance of selected students, 100-marks examinations were conducted separately for study and sports. The results are presented as follows. Find the Spearman's rank correlation from the following data and test the claim that there is no rank correlation between two variables at 5% level of significance.

Student's S. No.	Marks in Study	Marks in Sports
1	46	73
2	84	62
3	43	83
4	32	48
5	88	43
6	82	64
7	63	48
8	47	59
9	48	78
10	51	72
11	92	36
12	87	53
13	77	33
14	30	78
15	44	84

Solution: Here, the hypothesis to be tested is as follows:
H_0 (: $r = 0$) = There is no rank correlation between two variables.
H_1 (: $r \neq 0$) = There is a rank correlation between two variables.
Here, the total number of paired observations (n) is 15.

Here, t (Number of repetitions of an item in second series R2) = 2.

So, $\sum \frac{t^3 - t}{12} = \frac{2^3 - 2}{12} = 0.5.$

Now, Spearman's rank correlation (r_s) = $1 - \frac{6\left\{\sum d^2 + \sum \frac{t^3 - t}{12}\right\}}{n \times (n^2 - 1)}$

$$= 1 - \frac{6\{918.5 + 0.5\}}{15 \times (15^2 - 1)} \text{ (Table 17.21)}$$

$$= -\,0.641$$

For proving our hypothesis, |Z-value| needs to be calculated.

So, |Z-value| = $\left|\frac{r_s - r}{\sigma_s}\right|$, where r = Hypothesized value and σ_s = Standard error.

TABLE 17.21
Calculation of Spearman's Rank Correlation

Student's S. No.	Marks in Study	Marks in Sports	Rank for Marks in Study (R1)	Rank for Marks in Sports (R2)	Difference (d = R1 – R2)	d^2
1	46	73	5	11	–6	36
2	84	62	12	8	+4	16
3	43	83	3	14	–11	121
4	32	48	2	4.5	–2.5	6.25
5	88	43	14	3	+11	121
6	82	64	11	9	+2	4
7	63	48	9	4.5	+4.5	20.25
8	47	59	6	7	–1	1
9	48	78	7	12	–5	25
10	51	72	8	10	–2	4
11	92	36	15	2	+13	169
12	87	53	13	6	+7	49
13	77	33	10	1	+9	81
14	30	79	1	13	–12	144
15	44	84	4	15	–11	121
						$\Sigma d^2 = 918.5$

Source: Authors.

Also, $\sigma_s = \dfrac{1}{\sqrt{n-1}} = \dfrac{1}{\sqrt{15-1}} = 0.267.$

Then, $|\text{Z-value}| = \left|\dfrac{r_s - r}{\sigma_s}\right| = \left|\dfrac{0.641 - 0}{0.267}\right| = 2.4.$

Therefore, we reject the null hypothesis (as the calculated value is more than the tabulated value 1.96, at 5% level of significance) and conclude that there is a rank correlation between two variables. Observing Spearman's rank correlation (r_s) value –0.641, we can say that there is a medium negative correlation between them.

17.14.1. Solve Spearman's Rank Correlation Problem with SPSS

Null hypothesis (H_0): There is no rank correlation between two variables.

Alternative hypothesis (H_1): There is a rank correlation between two variables.

After putting data and variables in 'Data View' window and 'Variable View' window, click Analyze → Correlate → Bivariate in the SPSS window. One pop-up window will appear as 'Bivariate Correlations'.

EXHIBIT 17.14
SPSS Window for Spearman's Rank Correlation

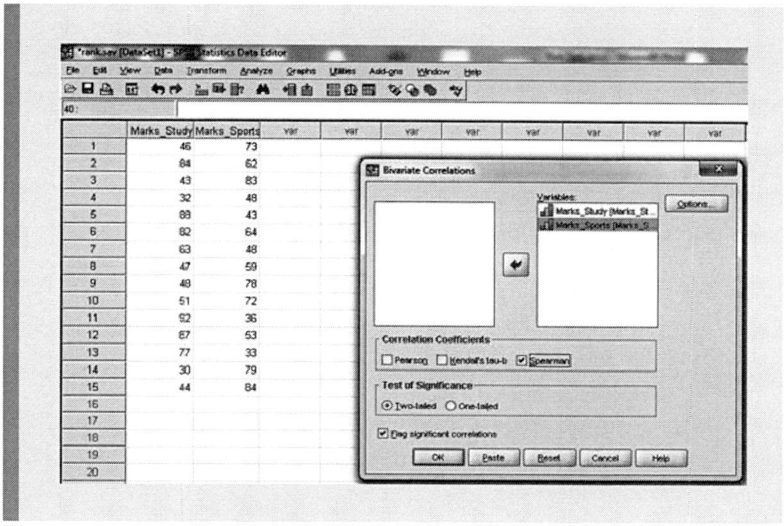

TABLE 17.22
Spearman's Rank Correlation Table from SPSS Output

Correlations				
			Marks_Study	Marks_Sports
Spearman's rho	Marks_Study	Correlation coefficient	1.000	**–0.642[a]**
		Sig. (two-tailed)	–	**0.010**
		N	15	15
	Marks_Sports	Correlation coefficient	**–0.642[a]**	1.000
		Sig. (two-tailed)	**0.010**	–
		N	15	15

Source: Authors.
Notes: 1. Bold values indicate estimations with significance level.
2. [a]Correlation is significant at the 0.01 level (two-tailed).

Then send 'Marks_Study' and 'Marks_Sports' to 'Variables'. Go to 'Correlation Coefficients' and tick 'Spearman' (Exhibit 17.14).

Then click 'OK'. At last, the SPSS output box will appear as shown in Table 17.22.

Here, Z-value (Sig.) of the problem is 0.01 which is less than 0.05 (5% level of significance). So we reject the null hypothesis.

TABLE 17.23
Tricks for Non-parametric Tests Through SPSS

Name of the Non-parametric Test	Resembles with Parametric Test	Number of Variables	Measurement Scale of 1st Variable	Measurement Scale of 2nd Variable
Chi-square test for goodness of fit	–	One	Nominal	–
Chi-square test for independence	–	Two	Nominal	Nominal
Wilcoxon sign rank test	Paired t test (dependent sample)	Two	Ordinal or scale	Ordinal or scale
Mann–Whitney U test	Independent sample t test	Two	Nominal—Two groups	Ordinal or scale
Kruskal–Wallis test	F Test (one-way between groups ANOVA)	Two	Nominal—More than two groups	Ordinal or scale
Friedman test	F Test (one-way repeated measures ANOVA)	More than Two	Ordinal or scale	–
Run test	Not available	One	Nominal	–
Kolmogorov–Smirnov one-sample test	–	One	Ordinal	–
Rank correlation	–	Two	Ordinal	Ordinal

Source: Authors.

17.15. IMPORTANT TRICKS

Table 17.23 summarizes the tricks that one should remember in non-parametric tests for SPSS.

SUMMARY

Non-parametric test is basically a distribution-free test. For executing a non-parametric test, it is not required to maintain any particular shape of population distribution from where the sample is chosen. It emphasizes nominal as well as ordinal scale data, that is, it deals with categorical data. In the case of one-sample sign test, we deal with the elements of only one sample. This test is based on basically binomial distribution. 'Two-sample sign test' is based on two sample observations. Wilcoxon matched pairs signed rank test resembles the 'paired sample t-test'. Here, a small sample is considered when a number of pairs is less than or equal to 15. When a number of pairs is more than 15, it is considered as a large sample. Mann–Whitney U test resembles 't-test' which compares two independent population means. The Kruskal–Wallis test resembles the 'one-way ANOVA'. It can be performed in interval scales as well as ordinal scale. It is based on the assumptions of independent groups. Friedman test is quite similar to a randomized block design, containing ranked data (approximately χ^2 distribution). The run test examines the randomness of the sample which is drawn from a population. The Kolmogorov–Smirnov one-sample test finds out whether there is any significant difference between an observed and theoretical frequency distribution (normal/uniform/Poisson/exponential). Spearman's rank correlation is used to determine the correlation between two series of ranks (ordinal data).

KEY TERMS

non-parametric test (206)
one-sample sign test (206)
two-sample sign test (209)
Wilcoxon signed rank test for small samples (212)
Wilcoxon signed rank test for large samples (214)
Mann–Whitney U test for small samples (216)
Mann–Whitney U test for large samples (220)
Kruskal–Wallis test (223)
Friedman test (227)
run test (230)
Kolmogorov–Smirnov one-sample test (235)
Spearman's rank correlation (238)

EXERCISES

1. Define non-parametric test. Explain the advantages and disadvantages of a non-parametric test.
2. Differentiate between a parametric test and a non-parametric test with examples.
3. Make a sign test for the following paired sample data and comment on the effectiveness of a new traffic control system. The number of accidents occurred in 10 places during one months before and after implementing the new traffic control system as follows. Test the hypothesis that the new system is effective or not at 5% level of significance.

Places	1	2	3	4	5	6	7	8	9	10
Before Implementation	11	9	10	7	4	3	5	15	13	5
After Implementation	6	5	8	3	4	5	2	11	4	5

4. Students in a digital marketing course were given a written final examination as well as a project to complete as part of their final grade. For a random sample of 10 students, the scores of both the exam and the project are as follows:

Exam	79	62	76	78	95	68	72	84	90	96
Project	75	70	69	74	83	62	81	76	93	78

   Find the Spearman rank correlation coefficient and also test for association. Given critical value is 0.648 (for n = 10 and 2.5% level of significance).
5. Consider the following sequence as the gender-wise (M—Male and F—Female) arrival pattern in a doctor's chamber. Test the randomness of the arrival pattern of the patients at 5% level of significance.

   MMMFFFFFMMFFFMMMMMMMFFFFMMFFFFFMMMMFFFMMFFFFMMFFF
6. Forty students were selected randomly from four engineering colleges to understand if the categories of students are equal in each college or not. A 100-marks performance evaluating examination was conducted to evaluate 40 students, and the obtained marks are presented in the

following table. At 5% level of significance, test whether the categories of students of all engineering colleges are the same.

B-school_1	B-school_2	B-school_3	B-school_4
74	66	81	47
45	50	56	51
89	78	68	66
86	67	80	70
90	79	70	59
87	82	72	49
88	43	44	92
94	62	55	88
84	81	78	56
53			62
95			47

7. The following table represents study hours of the students from a general college and B-school. From a general college and B-school, 10 and 12 students were randomly selected, respectively. Use the Mann–Whitney U test to examine at a 5% level of significance whether two samples come from identical populations.

General College (Study Hours)	B-school (Study Hours)
5	6
6	4
4.5	3
4	4
7	6
3	5.5
5.5	4
8	3.5
7	2
8	4.5
	3
	2

8. A researcher collected the following sample of road accidents in a city that occurred in the last 15 days of the last month. Use Kolmogorov–Smirnov one-sample test at 5% level of significance to check the null hypothesis that the sampled population is normally distributed.

13	15	23	24	18	25	19	21	15	17	26	16	22	25	19

9. A researcher wants to compare four leading brands of toothpaste available in the Indian market in terms of the acceptance level of the customers. Twelve customers were randomly selected and asked to rank the brands with the help of a scale from 1 to 4 as per their acceptance level. Collected data are available in the following table. Test whether the acceptance level of all the brands are the same at 5% level of significance.

Customer No.	Brand_W	Brand_X	Brand_Y	Brand_Z
1	3	4	2	1
2	2	3	4	1
3	1	4	3	2
4	1	2	3	4
5	3	2	4	1
6	1	4	2	3
7	2	3	4	1
8	3	2	4	1
9	2	3	4	1
10	2	3	1	4
11	3	2	1	4
12	2	1	4	3

CHAPTER

18

Factor Analysis

LEARNING OBJECTIVES

After studying this chapter, you should be able to

- Understand the concept and importance of factor analysis in a research study.
- Learn the theoretical calculations and explanation of factor analysis.
- Understand different types of factor analysis for different research demands.
- Know the use of SPSS software in factor analysis.
- Interpret factor analysis results from SPSS output.

18.1. CONCEPT OF FACTOR ANALYSIS

In a research study, researcher might have collected the data on huge amount of items or variables to fulfil the research objectives. This large number of variables may create some complication in data analysis. In this scenario, factor analysis, a multivariate method, is used to reduce a large number of variables to few controllable factors. These factors describe a major part of the variations of collected data. Factor analysis does not classify the variables as dependent or independent variables. On the other hand, 'Construct' is defined from theory through literature review. Researchers must have the objective to prove empirically by factor analysis that the constructs with underling variables are equivalent to factors with the same combination of variables. Here, all the interrelated variables are grouped to create independent factors. We have already discussed in detail the influences of independent factors on dependent factors in Chapter 13 'Multiple Regression Analysis and Structural Equation Modelling (SEM) by AMOS'. In any case, if independent factors are correlated, then it is difficult for the researchers to understand the separate influence of an independent variable on the dependent variable. It creates the problem of multicollinearity. Factor analysis always uses metric data which includes either interval or ratio scale data. For collecting data through survey research, generally a 5- or 7-point Likert scale is used.

18.2. TYPES OF FACTOR ANALYSIS

There are two types of factor analysis: (a) exploratory factor analysis (EFA) and (b) confirmatory factor analysis (CFA). The basic objective of EFA is to identify the underlying structure among the items/variables and summarize the data by converting a large number of items/variables to a smaller number of factors. EFA is executed on the basis of SEM along with the multiple regression analysis. Factors have been extracted according to their contributions by explaining the total variance of the scale from SPSS output. EFA helps to identify the relevant factors involved in the analysis. On the other hand, CFA follows the stages of SEM through AMOS for the hypothesized measurement model. It emphasizes on testing how well-defined variables represent factors. CFA statistic can determine how well factor specifications match with the actual data from the research study which also help the researchers to accept or reject the research model. CFA also estimates the intra-factor relationships (link factors to variables) and inter-factor relationships.

18.3. COMPONENTS IN FACTOR ANALYSIS

Communality: It describes the variance in each variable, shared with the other variables in a research study. Communality values show whether the variables/items are fit or unfit for this analysis. If the value is below 0.5, the variable should be removed from the analysis.

Kaiser–Meyer–Olkin (KMO) and Bartlett's tests: KMO test, the measuring tool of sampling adequacy, can indicate the proportion of variations of variables for different factors. The high values of the KMO test (from 0.5 to 1.0) indicate that factor analysis is appropriate with the data; otherwise, values less than 0.5 do not support the factor analysis. Bartlett's test of sphericity tests the hypothesis that variables are significantly related with each other. If the significance level is less than 0.05, it means that variables for factor analysis are significantly related to each other.

Factor loading: It implies the correlation coefficient between the variables under a factor. The high values of factor loading (from 0.5 to 1) indicate good correlation between variables.

Percentage of variance explained: It describes the percentage of variance of each factor relative to the total variance, taking all factors.

Eigen value: It explains the proportion of variance described by an individual factor. It should always be greater than 1. A factor can be removed from a research study if the eigen value is less than 1.

Scree plot: This plot shows the optimal number of factors retained after factor analysis. Actually, it is a plot between eigen value and factor number, as per its order of extraction.

Principal component method: It is a commonly used method in factor analysis for reducing a larger set of variables to fewer factors. It emphasizes on the transformation of interrelated variables to uncorrelated factors containing linear combination of those variables. This method extracts the minimum number of factors (principal components) that can explain the maximum percentage of variance in the total data set.

Rotation of factors: Rotation creates a simple structure where one factor includes high factor loading and all other factors hold low factor loading. Basically, it helps in understanding the association of factor loadings with a particular factor. Statistical software provides different rotation methods such as varimax, quartimax, equamax and pro-max. Generally, the varimax method is used for creating independent factors through factor analysis. In this method, each factor maximizes its own variance of factor loadings. The variance of the factor increases as its largest loading factor approaches towards '1'. Actually, it defines the factor containing highly correlated variables and segregates uncorrelated variables from that factor.

18.4. EXPLANATION OF FACTOR ANALYSIS THROUGH AN EXAMPLE

Example: A researcher wants to assess the stress under few factors for PG (postgraduate) students in colleges. A survey was carried out and a sample of 100 respondents was collected for this purpose. Responses were coded by assigning the following weights as 5-point scales depending upon the respondents' level of agreement towards their viewpoint (Strongly Agree—5, Agree—4, Neither Agree nor Disagree—3, Disagree—2, Strongly Disagree—1). Different variables/items of the topic were included in the questionnaire as follows:

[Please tick one box on each line according to your answer]

		Strongly Agree	Agree	Neither Agree Nor Disagree	Disagree	Strongly Disagree
Q_1	Friendly classmates available					
Q_2	Friendly teachers available					
Q_3	Enjoyable classroom environment available					
Q_4	Marks assessment process comfortable					
Q_5	Availability of interesting syllabus and curriculum of the course					
Q_6	Mental support from the family members					
Q_7	Sufficient availability of pocket money					
Q_8	Availability of intimate guidance from the guardians					
Q_9	Availability of a good hostel environment					
Q_10	Good job opportunity available					
Q_11	Availability of good exposure with industrial interaction					
Q_12	Supportive teachers available					

The collected data is presented in the following table:

Respondent No.	Q 1	Q 2	Q 3	Q 4	Q 5	Q 6	Q 7	Q 8	Q 9	Q 10	Q 11	Q 12
1	5	5	5	5	5	4	4	4	3	5	5	5
2	4	4	4	4	4	4	4	4	4	5	5	4
3	5	5	5	5	5	4	4	4	3	5	5	5

Respondent No.	Q 1	Q 2	Q 3	Q 4	Q 5	Q 6	Q 7	Q 8	Q 9	Q 10	Q 11	Q 12
4	4	4	4	4	4	4	4	4	2	4	4	4
5	5	5	5	5	5	4	4	4	4	5	5	5
6	4	4	4	4	4	4	4	4	4	4	4	4
7	5	5	5	5	5	5	5	5	2	5	5	5
8	4	4	4	4	4	4	4	4	4	5	5	5
9	4	4	4	4	4	4	4	4	3	5	5	5
10	4	5	5	4	3	4	3	4	4	5	5	5
11	4	4	3	4	4	4	4	4	4	5	5	5
12	4	4	4	4	3	4	4	4	4	5	5	5
13	4	4	3	4	4	5	5	5	5	5	5	5
14	4	4	3	4	3	4	4	4	4	3	3	3
15	4	4	3	4	4	4	4	4	4	5	5	5
16	5	5	5	5	2	5	5	5	5	5	3	5
17	4	4	4	4	4	4	4	4	4	4	4	4
18	5	5	5	5	5	4	4	4	4	5	2	5
19	4	4	4	4	4	4	4	4	4	5	2	5
20	4	4	4	4	4	4	4	4	2	4	4	4
21	3	3	3	3	3	5	5	5	5	5	5	5
22	4	4	4	4	4	4	4	4	4	4	4	4
23	4	5	5	4	4	5	5	5	5	5	5	3
24	4	4	4	4	4	4	4	4	4	5	5	5
25	5	5	5	5	5	4	4	4	4	5	5	2
26	5	5	5	5	5	4	5	4	5	5	5	3
27	4	4	4	4	4	4	4	4	4	5	5	4
28	5	5	5	5	5	5	5	5	5	5	5	5
29	4	4	4	4	4	4	4	4	4	4	4	4
30	5	5	5	5	5	4	4	4	4	5	5	5
31	4	4	4	4	2	4	4	4	4	5	5	5
32	4	4	4	4	2	4	4	4	4	5	5	5
33	4	5	5	4	2	5	5	5	4	5	5	5
34	4	4	4	4	4	4	4	4	4	4	4	4
35	5	5	5	5	5	4	4	4	4	5	5	5
36	4	4	4	4	4	4	4	4	4	5	5	5
37	5	5	5	5	5	3	3	3	3	5	5	5
38	4	4	4	4	4	4	4	4	4	5	5	5

Respondent No.	Q 1	Q 2	Q 3	Q 4	Q 5	Q 6	Q 7	Q 8	Q 9	Q 10	Q 11	Q 12
39	4	5	5	4	2	5	5	5	5	5	5	5
40	4	4	4	4	4	4	4	4	4	4	4	4
41	5	5	5	5	5	4	4	4	4	5	2	5
42	4	4	4	4	4	4	4	4	4	5	5	5
43	4	4	4	4	4	4	4	4	3	5	5	5
44	5	5	5	5	5	4	4	4	4	5	5	5
45	4	4	4	2	2	4	4	4	4	4	4	4
46	5	5	5	5	5	5	5	5	5	5	5	5
47	4	4	4	4	4	4	4	4	4	5	5	5
48	5	5	4	5	5	5	5	5	5	5	5	5
49	4	4	4	4	4	4	4	4	4	5	5	5
50	4	4	4	4	4	4	4	4	4	5	5	5
51	4	5	4	4	4	5	5	5	5	5	5	5
52	4	4	4	4	4	4	4	4	4	4	4	4
53	5	5	5	5	5	4	4	3	4	5	5	5
54	4	4	4	4	4	4	4	4	4	5	5	5
55	4	4	4	4	4	4	4	4	4	4	4	4
56	5	5	5	5	5	5	5	5	5	5	5	5
57	4	4	4	2	4	4	4	4	4	5	5	2
58	5	5	5	5	5	5	5	5	5	5	5	2
59	4	4	4	4	4	4	4	4	4	5	5	5
60	5	5	5	5	5	4	4	3	4	5	5	5
61	4	4	4	4	4	4	4	3	4	4	4	4
62	5	4	4	5	5	5	5	5	5	5	5	5
63	4	4	4	4	4	4	4	4	4	5	5	5
64	4	4	4	4	4	4	4	3	4	5	5	5
65	5	5	4	5	5	5	5	5	5	5	5	5
66	3	3	3	3	3	4	4	4	4	4	4	4
67	5	5	5	5	5	5	5	5	5	5	5	5
68	4	4	4	4	4	4	4	4	4	5	5	5
69	5	5	5	5	5	5	5	5	5	5	5	5
70	4	4	4	4	4	4	4	4	4	5	5	5
71	5	5	5	2	5	5	5	5	5	5	5	5
72	4	4	4	2	4	4	4	3	4	4	4	4
73	3	3	3	2	3	5	5	5	5	5	5	5

Respondent No.	Q 1	Q 2	Q 3	Q 4	Q 5	Q 6	Q 7	Q 8	Q 9	Q 10	Q 11	Q 12
74	4	4	4	4	4	4	4	4	4	5	5	5
75	3	3	3	3	3	4	4	4	4	5	5	5
76	5	5	5	5	5	4	4	4	4	5	5	5
77	4	4	4	4	4	4	4	4	4	5	5	5
78	3	3	3	3	3	5	5	5	5	4	4	4
79	5	5	5	5	5	4	4	4	4	5	5	5
80	4	4	4	4	4	4	4	3	4	5	5	4
81	5	5	5	5	5	4	4	3	4	5	5	5
82	4	4	4	4	4	4	4	4	5	4	4	4
83	5	5	5	5	3	4	4	3	4	5	5	5
84	4	4	4	4	4	4	4	4	4	4	4	4
85	5	5	5	5	5	5	5	5	5	5	5	5
86	4	4	4	4	4	4	4	4	4	5	5	5
87	3	3	3	3	3	5	5	5	5	4	4	4
88	5	5	5	5	5	4	4	4	4	5	5	5
89	4	4	4	4	4	4	4	4	4	5	5	5
90	5	5	5	5	5	5	5	5	5	5	5	5
91	4	4	4	4	4	4	4	4	4	5	5	5
92	5	5	5	5	5	5	5	5	5	5	5	5
93	4	4	4	5	4	4	4	4	4	4	4	4
94	4	4	4	4	4	5	5	5	5	5	5	5
95	4	4	4	4	4	4	4	4	4	5	5	5
96	5	5	5	5	5	4	4	4	4	5	5	5
97	4	4	4	4	4	4	4	4	4	3	3	3
98	5	5	5	5	5	5	5	2	5	5	5	5
99	4	4	4	4	4	4	4	4	4	4	4	4
100	5	5	5	4	5	4	4	4	4	4	4	4

18.4.1. Factor Analysis with SPSS

After putting data and variable in the 'Data View' window and 'Variable View' window, click Analyze → Dimension Reduction → Factor in the SPSS window. One pop-up window will appear as 'Factor Analysis'. Then send 'Q_1' to 'Q_12' to 'Variables'. Then in the 'Factor Analysis' dialog box, go to 'Descriptive' and another pop-up window will appear as 'Factor Analysis: Descriptives'. In this dialog box, go to 'Correlation Matrix' and tick 'KMO and Bartlett's test of sphericity' (Exhibit 18.1).

EXHIBIT 18.1
SPSS Window for Factor Analysis (Step 1)

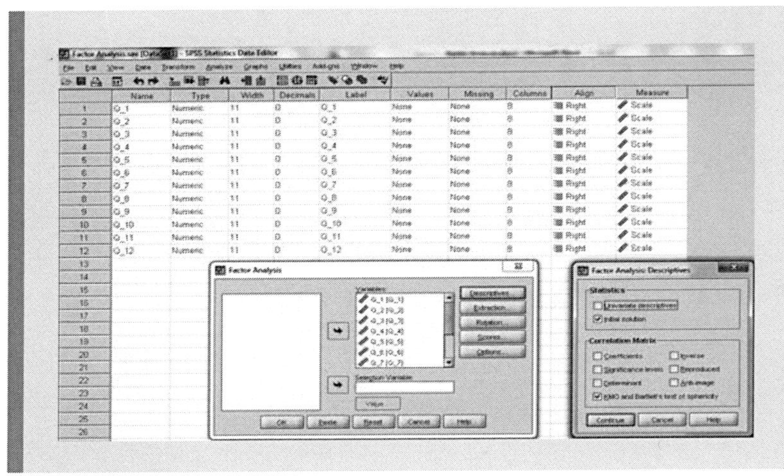

EXHIBIT 18.2
SPSS Window for Factor Analysis (Step 2)

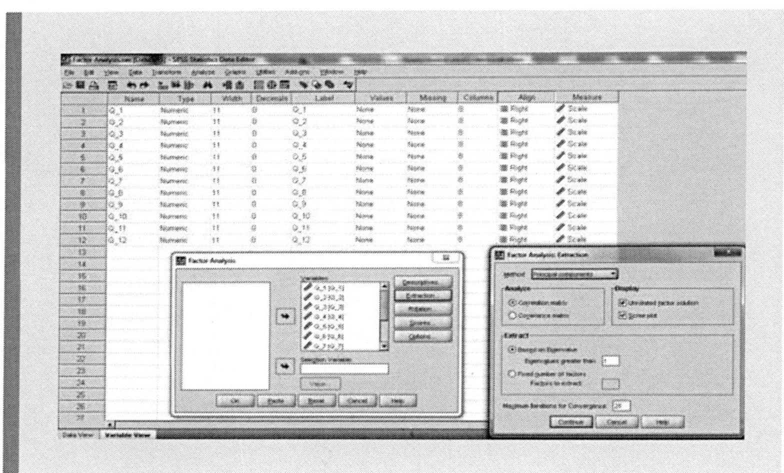

Then click 'Continue'. Once again, in the 'Factor Analysis' dialog box, go to 'Extraction' and another pop-up window will appear as 'Factor Analysis: Extraction'. In this dialog box, select 'Principal Components' as 'Method'. In the same dialog box, go to 'Display' and tick 'Scree plot' (Exhibit 18.2).

Then click 'Continue'. Once again, in the 'Factor Analysis' dialog box, go to 'Rotation' and another pop-up window will appear as 'Factor Analysis: Rotation'. In this dialog box, go to 'Method' and tick 'Varimax' (Exhibit 18.3).

EXHIBIT 18.3

SPSS Window for Factor Analysis (Step 3)

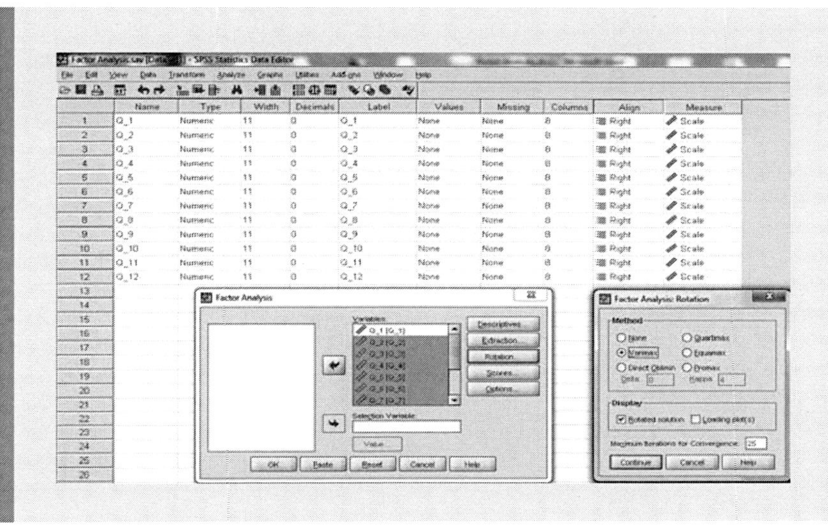

EXHIBIT 18.4

SPSS Window for Factor Analysis (Step 4)

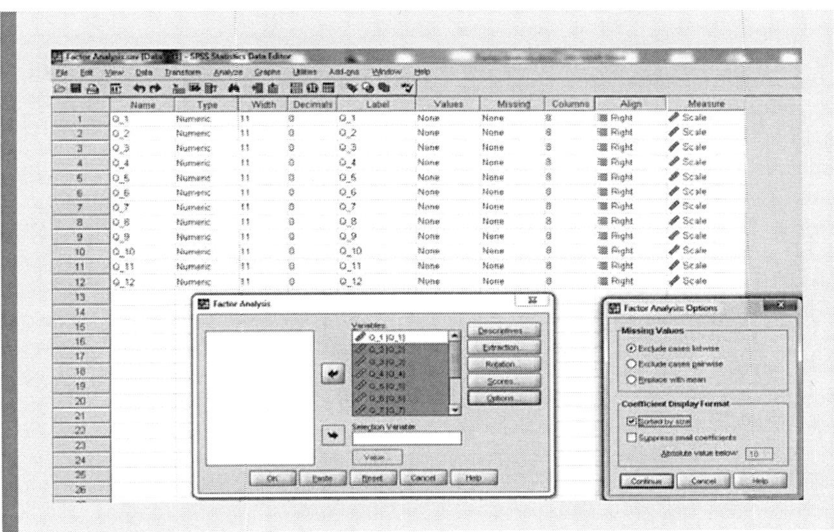

Then click 'Continue'. Once again, in the 'Factor Analysis' dialog box, go to 'Options' and another pop-up window will appear as 'Factor Analysis: Options'. In this dialog box, go to 'Coefficient Display Format' and tick 'Sorted by size' (Exhibit 18.4).

At last click 'OK'. Then, an SPSS output box will appear as shown in Table 18.1.

TABLE 18.1
Component Matrix (SPSS Output)

Component Matrix[a]			
	Component		
	1	2	3
Q 1	0.893	−0.241	−0.184
Q 2	0.892	−0.316	−0.205
Q 3	0.828	−0.318	−0.173
Q 4	0.763	−0.330	−0.111
Q 5	0.663	−.316	−0.173
Q 6	0.434	0.852	−0.106
Q 7	0.441	0.833	−0.148
Q 8	0.258	0.787	−0.102
Q 9	0.296	0.714	−0.111
Q 11	0.343	0.113	0.696
Q 10	0.578	0.055	0.696
Q 12	0.313	0.002	0.696

Source: Authors.
Notes: 1. Extraction Method: Principal Component Analysis.
2. [a]Three components extracted.

18.4.1.1. Calculation of Eigen Values and Percentage of Variance Explained by the Factors

The correlation coefficient between factor score and variables is presented through component matrix as follows. Here, the element of the matrix, called factor loading, is used to calculate eigen values for individual factor.

Eigen value for the first factor:

$$(0.893)^2+(0.892)^2+(0.828)^2+(0.763)^2+(0.663)^2+(0.434)^2+(0.441)^2+(0.258)^2+ (0.296)^2+(0.343)^2+(0.578)^2+(0.313)^2=4.387.$$

Eigen value for the second factor:

$$(-0.241)^2+(-0.316)^2+(-0.318)^2+(-0.330)^2+(-0.316)^2+(0.852)^2+(0.833)^2+ (0.787)^2+(0.714)^2+(0.113)^2+(0.055)^2+(0.002)^2=3.033.$$

Eigen value for the third factor:

$$(-0.184)^2+(-0.205)^2+(-0.173)^2+(-0.111)^2+(-0.173)^2+(-0.106)^2+(-0.148)^2+ (-0.102)^2+(-0.111)^2+(0.696)^2+(0.696)^2+(0.696)^2=1.657.$$

As expected, all eigen values are more than ‘1’ in this study.

The total variance equals 12, because there are 12 variables. Therefore, the total sum of eigen values is also 12.

$$\text{The percentage of variance explained by the first factor} = \frac{\text{Eigen value for first factor}}{\text{Total sum of eigen values}} \times 100$$

$$= \frac{4.387}{12} \times 100 = 36.558\%.$$

$$\text{Percentage of variance explained by the second factor} = \frac{\text{Eigen value for second factor}}{\text{Total sum of eigen values}} \times 100$$

$$= \frac{3.033}{12} \times 100 = 25.275\%.$$

$$\text{Percentage of variance explained by the third factor} = \frac{\text{Eigen value for third factor}}{\text{Total sum of eigen values}} \times 100$$

$$= \frac{1.657}{12} \times 100 = 13.808\%.$$

The total variance explained by three factors = (36.558 + 25.275 + 13.808)% = 75.641%.

SPSS output shows the same result, presented in Table 18.2.

TABLE 18.2

Total Variance Explained (SPSS Output)

Total Variance Explained									
	Initial Eigen Values			Extraction Sums of Squared Loadings			Rotation Sums of Squared Loadings		
Component	Total	Percentage of Variance	Cumulative Percentage	Total	Percentage of Variance	Cumulative Percentage	Total	Percentage of Variance	Cumulative Percentage
1	4.388	36.563	36.563	4.388	**36.563**	36.563	3.940	32.837	32.837
2	3.032	25.270	61.833	3.032	**25.270**	61.833	3.152	26.263	59.100
3	1.658	13.815	75.648	1.658	**13.815**	**75.648**	1.986	16.548	**75.648**
4	0.754	6.282	81.930						
5	0.566	4.714	86.643						
6	0.535	4.462	91.105						
7	0.337	2.811	93.915						
8	0.304	2.534	96.449						
9	0.237	1.973	98.423						
10	0.099	0.825	99.247						
11	0.058	0.484	99.731						
12	0.032	0.269	100.000						

Source: Authors.

Notes: 1. Extraction Method: Principal Component Analysis.

2. 75.648 per cent of the variations explained in the total data set by three factors.

TABLE 18.3
Communalities (SPSS Output)

	Initial	Extraction
Q_1	1.000	0.937
Q_2	1.000	0.890
Q_3	1.000	0.817
Q_4	1.000	0.704
Q_5	1.000	0.570
Q_6	1.000	0.925
Q_7	1.000	0.911
Q_8	1.000	0.696
Q_9	1.000	0.609
Q_10	1.000	0.822
Q_11	1.000	0.616
Q_12	1.000	0.583

Source: Authors.
Note: Extraction Method: Principal Component Analysis

TABLE 18.4
KMO and Bartlett's Test

KMO measure of sampling adequacy.		0.761
Bartlett's test of sphericity	Approx. chi-square	1,007.045
	df	66
	Sig.	<0.001

Source: Authors.

18.4.1.2. Communalities and KMO and Bartlett's Test

In Table 18.3, communalities extraction values are above the minimum level (0.5). Therefore, we will not drop any variable from this analysis.

Here, a high value of KMO test (0.761) indicates that factor analysis is fit and appropriate with the data. On the other hand, Bartlett's test of sphericity shows that significance level is less than 0.05 (<0.001) which says that variables are significantly related with each other (Table 18.4).

Another SPSS output from the example discussed is shown in Table 18.5.

There is no proper guideline, for selecting cut-off point of factor loading of variables under each factor but generally it is taken above 0.5. Also, a researcher should observe the relative values in the factor matrix. So we can say that variables with factor loading of above 0.5 create factor. In this case, all factor loadings are significant and greater than 0.50. Here, three factors are created by factor analysis. The scree plot in Figure 18.1 shows three factors, retained in this study after factor analysis.

TABLE 18.5
Rotated Component Matrix

	Component		
	1	2	3
Q_1	**0.961**	0.059	0.097
Q_2	**0.927**	0.124	0.121
Q_3	**0.897**	0.029	0.105
Q_4	**0.827**	–0.016	0.141
Q_5	**0.753**	–0.027	0.049
Q_6	0.076	**0.954**	0.098
Q_7	0.103	**0.947**	0.060
Q_8	–0.053	**0.832**	0.037
Q_9	0.012	**0.779**	0.038
Q_10	0.276	0.124	**0.854**
Q_11	0.049	0.096	**0.777**
Q_12	0.066	–0.017	**0.760**

Source: Authors.
Notes: 1. Bold values indicate demarcation of different factors through factor loading.
2. Extraction Method: Principal Component Analysis.
3. Rotation Method: Varimax with Kaiser Normalization.
4. Rotation converged in four iterations.

FIGURE 18.1
Scree Plot

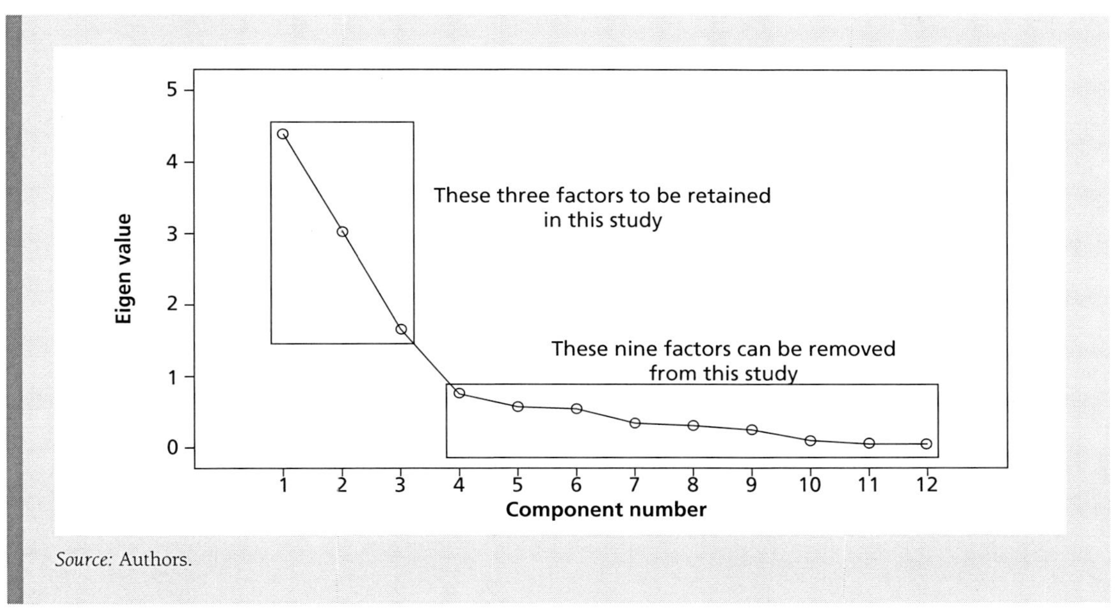

Source: Authors.

18.4.2. Identification of Factors from Factor Analysis

From rotated component matrix, three factors (explains 75.648% of the variations in the total data set) have been observed. These factors are named as per the characteristics of the grouping variables. Here, the first factor consists of Q_1, Q_2, Q_3, Q_4 and Q_5. According to the characteristics of the variables, the researcher can provide a name to the factor like 'Academic life related stresses'. Then, the second factor consists of Q_6, Q_7, Q_8 and Q_9. In this case, the researcher can provide the name 'Personal & Family life related stresses' to the factor. At last, the third factor consists of Q_10, Q_11 and Q_12. Here, the researcher can name this factor as 'Career related stresses'. Now, the researcher can easily compare the factors with a theoretical construct. If he observes that variables under the theoretical construct are same as the variables under factors after factor analysis, then it is proved that theory and the present empirical research indicate the same thing. If it is not so, then the researcher has to find out the reasons behind it and move further.

SUMMARY

Factor analysis, a multivariate method, is used to reduce a large number of variables to few controllable factors. These factors describe a major part of the variations of collected data. Factor analysis does not classify the variables as dependent or independent variables. There are two types of factor analysis: (a) EFA and (b) CFA. The basic objective of EFA is to identify the underlying structure among the items/variables and summarize the data by converting a large number of items/variables to a smaller number of factors. On the other hand, CFA follows the stages of SEM through AMOS for the hypothesized measurement model. It emphasizes on testing how well-defined variables represent factors.

KEY TERMS

factor analysis (246)
exploratory factor analysis (247)
confirmatory factor analysis (247)
communality (247)
Kaiser–Meyer–Olkin and Bartlett's tests (247)
factor loading (247)
percentage of variance explained (247)
eigen Value (247)
scree plot (247)
principal component method (247)
varimax method (248)

EXERCISES

1. What is the basic objective of factor analysis? Explain the utility of the principal component method in factor analysis.
2. What is a factor loading matrix? Explain the importance of communalities in measuring the total variance explained by the extracted factors.
3. Describe the role of the varimax rotation method in factor analysis.
4. Differentiate between exploratory and CFA.

5. Describe each of the following:
   a. KMO and Bartlett's tests
   b. Scree plot
   c. Percentage of variance explained
   d. Eigen value
6. A researcher wants to assess job satisfaction under few factors for employees in manufacturing organizations. A survey was carried out and a sample of 100 respondents was collected for this purpose. Responses were coded by assigning the following weights: 5—point scales depending upon the respondents' level of agreement towards their viewpoint (Strongly agree—5, Agree—4, Neither agree nor disagree—3, Disagree—2, Strongly disagree—1). Different variables/items of the topic are included in the questionnaire as follows.

[Please tick one box on each line according to your answer]

		Strongly Agree	Agree	Neither Agree Nor Disagree	Disagree	Strongly Disagree
Q_1	Good salary					
Q_2	Good promotional opportunity					
Q_3	Good company policy					
Q_4	Friendly colleague available					
Q_5	Good working conditions					
Q_6	Autonomy and freedom available					
Q_7	Better job scope and interesting work					
Q_8	More seniority					
Q_9	Good personality					
Q_10	Capability to handle conflict					

The collected data is presented in the following table:

Respondent No.	Q 1	Q 2	Q 3	Q 4	Q 5	Q 6	Q 7	Q 8	Q 9	Q 10
1	5	5	4	3	3	2	4	4	5	4
2	5	4	4	4	3	4	4	5	4	4
3	4	4	3	4	3	2	5	4	5	3
4	3	4	5	5	5	4	4	3	4	3
5	4	2	2	3	4	4	4	4	2	2
6	3	4	4	5	3	3	2	3	4	4
7	2	1	1	5	3	4	4	2	1	1
8	3	5	5	4	4	4	4	3	5	5
9	4	3	3	3	4	4	4	4	3	3
10	4	4	4	4	4	4	4	4	4	4
11	4	3	3	4	3	3	4	4	2	3
12	3	4	5	4	3	4	4	4	4	4

Respondent No.	Q 1	Q 2	Q 3	Q 4	Q 5	Q 6	Q 7	Q 8	Q 9	Q 10
13	5	4	4	5	4	4	5	5	2	4
14	5	4	4	5	3	4	5	5	4	4
15	5	5	5	5	5	5	5	5	4	5
16	4	4	4	4	4	4	4	4	4	4
17	4	4	4	4	4	4	4	4	4	4
18	2	3	4	1	4	4	1	1	3	2
19	3	3	3	3	3	3	3	3	3	3
20	5	5	5	5	5	5	5	5	3	5
21	4	4	4	4	4	5	4	4	4	4
22	4	4	4	4	4	4	4	4	3	4
23	4	4	4	4	4	4	4	3	4	4
24	4	4	4	4	4	5	4	4	4	3
25	4	4	4	4	4	4	4	4	2	4
26	3	3	3	3	3	3	3	3	3	3
27	2	2	2	2	2	2	2	2	2	2
28	4	4	4	4	4	4	4	4	4	3
29	4	3	1	1	2	5	3	1	3	2
30	5	4	5	5	5	5	5	5	5	5
31	3	3	3	3	3	3	3	3	3	3
32	4	4	4	4	4	3	4	4	4	4
33	3	3	3	3	3	3	3	3	3	3
34	4	4	4	4	4	4	3	4	4	4
35	4	4	4	4	4	4	4	5	5	5
36	4	4	4	4	4	4	4	4	4	4
37	5	5	5	5	5	5	5	5	5	5
38	4	4	4	4	4	3	4	5	5	5
39	4	4	4	4	4	4	4	5	5	5
40	1	1	1	1	2	1	4	3	4	4
41	3	3	3	4	4	4	4	4	3	4
42	5	5	5	5	3	3	5	4	3	4
43	4	4	4	5	4	2	5	5	5	4
44	4	4	4	5	4	4	5	5	5	5
45	2	2	2	4	3	3	4	4	3	4
46	4	4	4	4	3	3	4	4	3	4
47	1	1	1	4	4	4	4	5	5	3
48	5	4	3	5	5	3	5	4	3	4

Respondent No.	Q 1	Q 2	Q 3	Q 4	Q 5	Q 6	Q 7	Q 8	Q 9	Q 10
49	3	3	3	4	3	3	4	4	4	4
50	4	4	4	4	4	4	4	4	3	4
51	3	3	3	5	4	4	5	5	5	5
52	4	4	4	5	4	4	2	5	5	5
53	4	4	4	4	3	3	4	3	3	3
54	4	4	4	4	3	3	4	4	4	4
55	5	5	5	4	4	4	3	4	4	4
56	4	4	4	4	4	4	4	2	3	1
57	4	4	4	5	4	3	5	4	4	4
58	4	3	2	4	4	4	4	4	3	4
59	3	3	3	4	3	3	4	3	4	4
60	5	5	5	4	4	2	4	4	4	4
61	4	4	4	4	5	5	4	4	3	4
62	4	4	4	3	4	4	3	4	4	4
63	4	4	4	4	4	4	4	4	3	4
64	4	4	4	5	4	4	5	5	5	5
65	4	3	4	5	4	3	5	2	2	2
66	3	3	3	3	4	4	3	5	5	5
67	2	2	2	4	4	4	4	5	3	5
68	4	4	4	4	4	4	3	2	2	2
69	1	1	1	4	3	3	4	1	1	1
70	5	5	5	4	4	2	4	2	2	2
71	3	3	3	4	4	4	4	5	5	5
72	4	4	4	3	3	3	3	4	4	4
73	3	3	3	4	3	3	4	4	4	4
74	4	4	4	4	4	4	4	4	4	4
75	3	3	3	4	3	3	4	4	4	4
76	4	4	4	4	4	4	4	4	4	4
77	4	4	4	4	4	4	4	4	4	4
78	4	4	4	4	4	4	4	4	4	4
79	5	5	5	5	5	5	5	3	3	3
80	4	4	4	4	4	4	4	4	4	4
81	4	4	4	4	4	4	4	3	4	4
82	1	1	1	1	1	1	1	5	5	5
83	3	3	3	3	3	3	3	4	3	4
84	5	5	5	5	5	5	5	4	3	4

Respondent No.	Q 1	Q 2	Q 3	Q 4	Q 5	Q 6	Q 7	Q 8	Q 9	Q 10
85	4	4	4	4	4	4	4	4	4	4
86	4	4	4	4	4	4	4	4	3	4
87	4	4	4	4	4	4	4	4	4	4
88	4	4	4	4	4	4	4	1	3	2
89	4	4	4	4	4	4	4	4	4	4
90	3	3	3	3	3	3	3	4	5	4
91	2	2	2	2	2	2	2	4	4	4
92	4	4	4	4	4	4	4	4	3	4
93	1	1	1	1	1	1	1	4	4	5
94	5	5	5	5	5	5	5	4	4	4
95	3	3	3	3	3	3	3	3	5	3
96	4	4	4	4	4	4	4	4	4	4
97	3	3	3	3	3	3	3	4	4	5
98	4	4	4	4	4	4	4	5	4	4
99	4	4	4	4	4	4	4	4	4	5
100	4	4	4	4	4	4	4	3	5	3
101	4	4	4	4	4	4	4	5	5	5
102	3	3	3	3	3	3	3	3	3	5
103	4	4	4	4	4	4	4	3	3	3
104	4	4	4	4	4	4	4	4	4	4
105	4	4	4	4	4	4	4	3	5	3
106	5	5	5	5	5	5	5	5	3	3
107	4	4	4	3	3	3	3	3	5	3
108	3	3	3	2	2	2	2	3	4	4
109	5	5	5	4	4	4	4	4	4	4
110	2	2	2	1	1	1	1	1	5	3
111	5	5	5	5	5	5	5	4	4	4
112	4	4	4	3	3	3	3	4	4	4
113	3	3	3	4	4	4	4	4	4	4
114	5	5	5	3	3	3	3	4	3	4
115	2	2	2	4	4	4	4	4	4	4
116	1	1	1	3	3	3	3	4	4	4
117	3	3	3	4	4	4	4	4	4	4
118	2	2	2	4	4	4	4	4	4	4
119	4	4	4	4	4	4	4	3	3	3
120	5	5	5	5	5	5	5	5	5	5

Respondent No.	Q 1	Q 2	Q 3	Q 4	Q 5	Q 6	Q 7	Q 8	Q 9	Q 10
121	4	4	4	4	4	4	4	5	4	5
122	4	4	4	4	4	4	4	3	3	3
123	3	3	3	1	1	1	1	1	1	1
124	4	4	4	3	3	3	3	3	3	3
125	3	3	3	5	5	5	5	5	5	5
126	3	3	3	4	4	4	4	5	5	5
127	4	5	4	4	4	4	4	3	3	3
128	4	4	5	4	4	4	4	4	5	4
129	3	4	3	4	4	4	4	3	3	3
130	5	5	4	4	4	4	4	5	5	5
131	5	5	4	3	3	3	3	5	5	5
132	3	3	3	2	2	2	2	3	3	3
133	5	5	5	4	4	4	4	5	5	5
134	2	2	2	1	1	1	1	2	2	2
135	5	5	5	5	5	5	5	5	5	5
136	4	4	4	3	3	3	3	4	4	4
137	3	3	3	4	4	4	4	3	3	3
138	5	5	5	4	4	4	4	3	5	5
139	2	2	2	4	4	4	4	2	2	2
140	1	1	1	5	5	5	5	1	2	1
141	3	3	3	3	3	3	3	3	3	3
142	2	2	2	5	5	5	5	2	3	2
143	4	4	4	5	5	5	5	4	4	4
144	5	5	5	4	4	4	4	5	3	5
145	4	4	4	4	2	3	4	4	4	4
146	4	4	4	4	3	2	4	4	4	4
147	3	3	3	3	3	3	3	3	3	3
148	3	3	3	3	3	3	3	3	3	3
149	4	4	4	4	4	4	4	4	4	4
150	4	4	4	4	4	4	4	4	4	4

Question:

Conduct a factor analysis to identify the underlying factors and give appropriate names to those factors.

CHAPTER

19

Cluster Analysis

LEARNING OBJECTIVES

After studying this chapter, you should be able to

- Understand the importance and utility of cluster analysis in research study.
- Understand the key terms related with cluster analysis.
- Understand different methods of clustering techniques.
- Learn selection of an appropriate clustering technique for a research study.
- Interpret cluster analysis from the SPSS output.

19.1. CONCEPT OF CLUSTER ANALYSIS

Cluster analysis is a multivariate technique which creates mutually exclusive and collectively exhaustive groups with objects or entities or cases. It is also called numerical taxonomy or Q-analysis. Cases within a cluster are always homogeneous and cases of different clusters are heterogeneous, that is, dissimilar in nature. Figure 19.1 represents the situation of the objects in a population, before and after the cluster analysis.

The cluster analysis is basically used for segmenting multiple factors involved in collected data such as segmentation of markets/industries/sectors/demographic profiles.

19.2. KEY TERMS IN CLUSTER ANALYSIS

The following key terms are generally used in cluster analysis:

Agglomeration schedule: It shows the information of the cases of similar pair from the beginning stage of the hierarchical cluster analysis method and also the information about the cases of joining the similar pair at a later stage.

Cluster membership: It specifies the cluster with which a particular case/object is associated. Cluster membership depends on certain research requirements of the researcher.

FIGURE 19.1
Before and After the Cluster Analysis

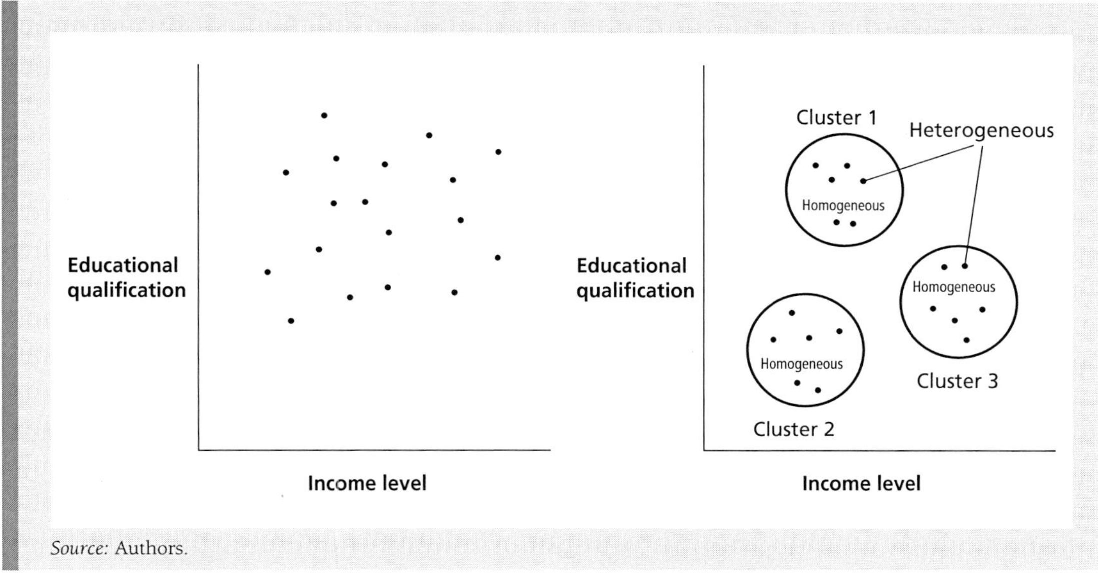

Source: Authors.

Euclidean distance: It is used for measuring the similarity of objects or cases in a population. Euclidean distance is calculated by the square root of the sum of squared of differences between variables.

Dendrogram: This tree-like graph represents the number of clusters associated with different situations. Here, the vertical axis shows the cases/objects and horizontal axis shows the inter-respondent scaled distance, ranging from 0 to 25. The interpretation is drawn from left to right of the graph depending on the relative similarities between the cases and requirement of the researcher.

ANOVA table: Here, a one-way ANOVA table represents the difference between clusters. Higher ANOVA value (F-value) means greater difference between clusters and lower value indicates lower difference between clusters.

19.3. CLUSTER ANALYSIS PROCESS

In conducting cluster analysis, the following steps are involved:

1. Problem formulation
2. Identification of metric and non-metric data
3. Establishing appropriate clustering method
4. Defining the number of clusters
5. Interpreting the clusters

The detailed explanations of the listed steps have been given in the following section with the help of an example.

19.3.1. Problem Formulation

The most important task in cluster analysis is to define and formulate the problem with the help of different variables of the research. These research variables help to execute the cluster analysis process smoothly.

Example: A researcher wants to assess the performance of PG (Postgraduate) students and reputation of the institution (a portion is taken from the example from Chapter 13, Multiple Regression Analysis and Structural Equation Modelling (SEM) by AMOS and Chapter 18, Factor Analysis). A survey was carried out and a sample of 20 respondents was collected for this purpose. In this case, only seven statements are taken for the questionnaire. These statements are rated on a 9-point scale from Strongly agree (9) to Strongly disagree (1) as follows:

[Please put the value from 1 to 9 in one box on each line according to the level of disagreement to agreement of your answer]

	Academic Life Related Concern	Strongly agree (9) to Strongly disagree (1)
AL_1 (q1)	Friendly classmates available	
AL_2 (q2)	Friendly teachers available	
AL_3 (q3)	Enjoyable classroom environment available	
	Personal & Family Life Related Concern	
PFL_1 (q4)	Mental support from the family members	
PFL_2 (q5)	Sufficient availability of pocket money	
	Career Related Concern	
CR_1 (q6)	Good job opportunity available	

Table 19.1 provides the scores rated by the 20 respondents. But cluster analysis is generally executed on more than or equal to 100 respondents/cases.

TABLE 19.1
Scores Rated by the Respondents

Respondents	q1	q2	q3	q4	q5	q6
1	9	8	9	4	4	7
2	7	7	6	2	3	7
3	8	7	9	5	4	8
4	7	6	7	3	2	8
5	8	9	8	5	5	7
6	7	7	6	2	2	8
7	8	7	8	5	4	8
8	4	5	6	8	8	4
9	4	4	5	8	8	4
10	8	9	8	5	5	7
11	4	4	5	8	8	4
12	8	9	8	5	5	7
13	4	4	5	8	8	4
14	4	4	5	8	9	5
15	4	4	5	8	8	4

Respondents	q1	q2	q3	q4	q5	q6
16	9	8	9	4	4	7
17	7	7	6	2	2	7
18	5	5	4	9	9	5
19	5	3	5	9	9	5
20	4	4	5	8	8	4

Source: Authors.

19.3.2. Identification of Metric and Non-metric Data

Now, researchers have to decide how the variables would be used in the measuring instruments. First of all, a proper scale should be identified according to the categories of subjects or cases.

19.3.3. Establishing an Appropriate Clustering Method

There are mainly two types of clustering method: (a) hierarchical method and (b) non-hierarchical method. The detailed classification is given in Figure 19.2.

FIGURE 19.2
Classification of Clustering Method

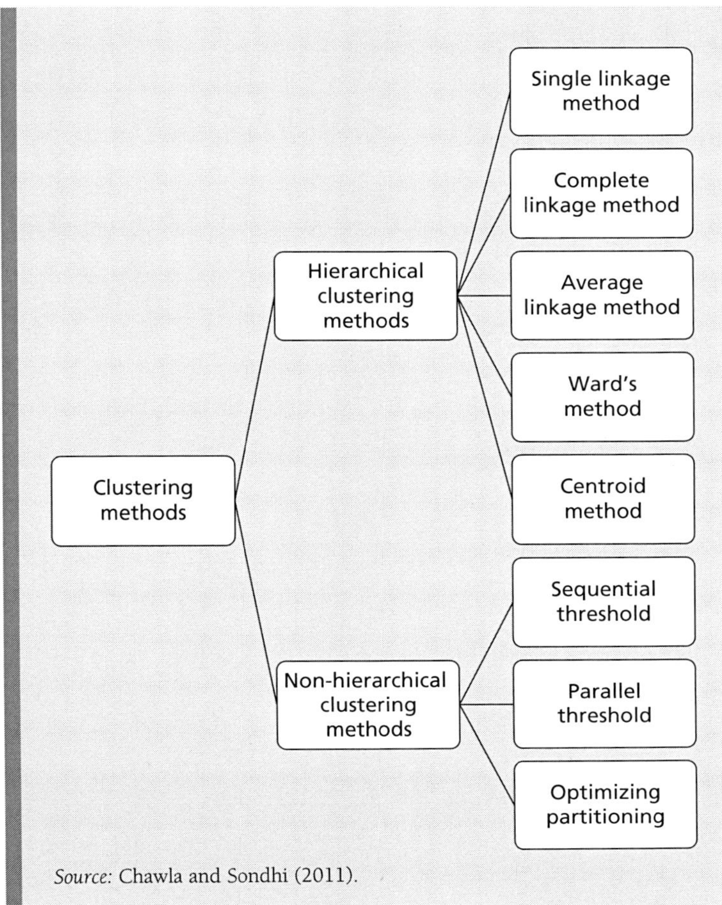

Source: Chawla and Sondhi (2011).

1. Hierarchical method

This technique deals with one big cluster containing all the cases/subjects within it, and then different individual subject clusters, as per the requirement of the researchers, are created by dividing and subdividing the big cluster. It is further classified into the following five techniques.

a. Single linkage method

Single linkage method is based on the shortest distance between two cluster elements. Basically, it is defined as the minimum distance between two closest points of two clusters. In this process, the first closest pair is included in the first cluster, then the next closest pair is added with it in the next stage and so on (Figure 19.3).

FIGURE 19.3
Single Linkage Method

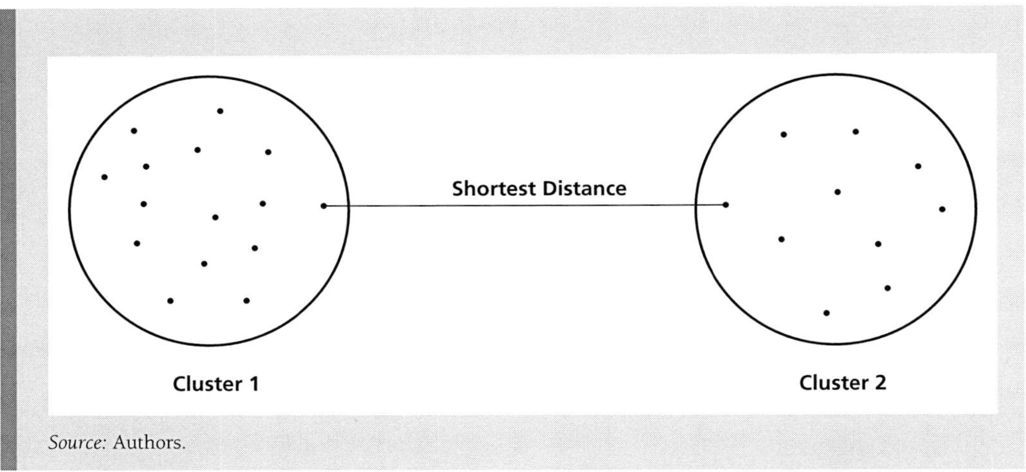

Source: Authors.

b. Complete linkage method

This method is based on the longest distance between two cluster elements, which is just opposite of the single linkage method.

FIGURE 19.4
Complete Linkage Method

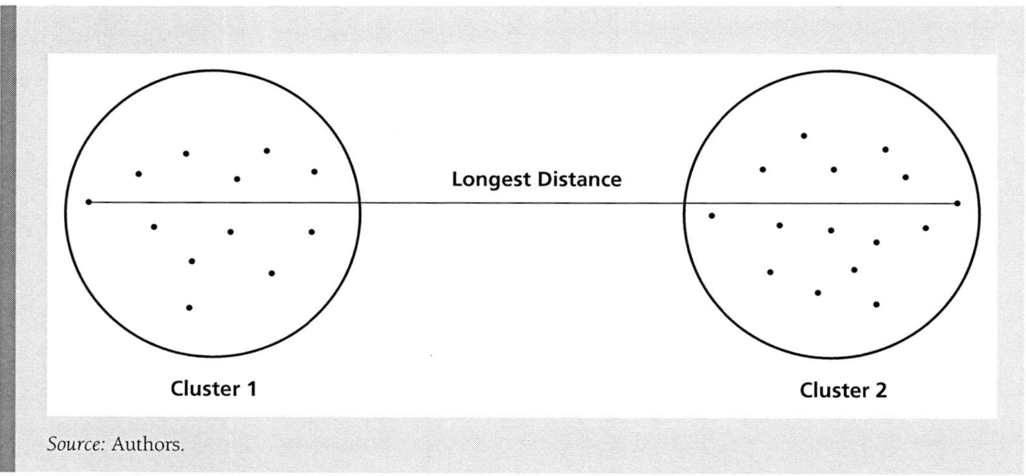

Source: Authors.

c. Average linkage method

This method is based on the average distance from all the elements of one cluster to all the elements of another cluster. In this case, the cluster contains grouping objects/cases with higher homogeneity and a small variance.

FIGURE 19.5
Average Linkage Method

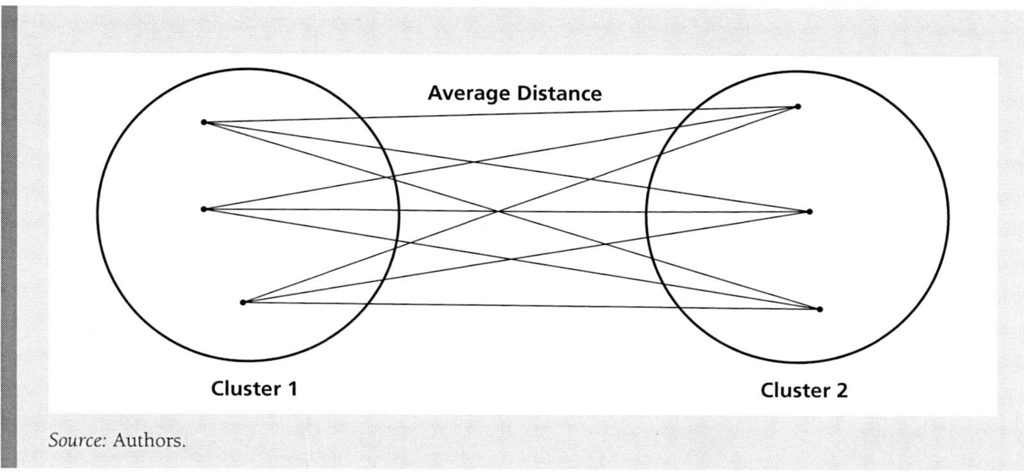

Source: Authors.

d. Ward's method

In this minimizing cluster variance method, the distance is calculated as the total sum of square deviation from the mean of a cluster where the research cases are assigned.

FIGURE 19.6
Ward's Method

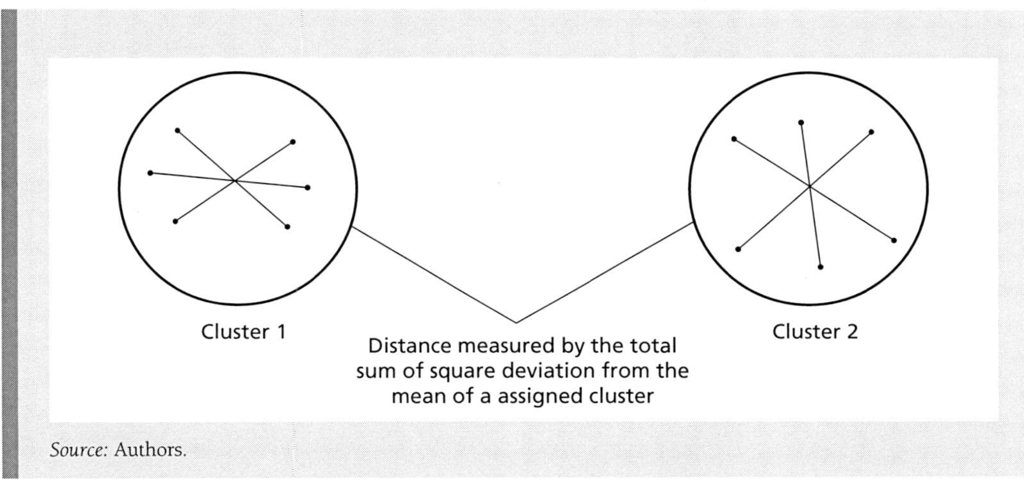

Source: Authors.

e. Centroid method

In this method, the distance is calculated as the squared distance between two cluster centroids which is actually the mean value of the clustering elements in a cluster (Figure 19.7).

FIGURE 19.7
Centroid Method

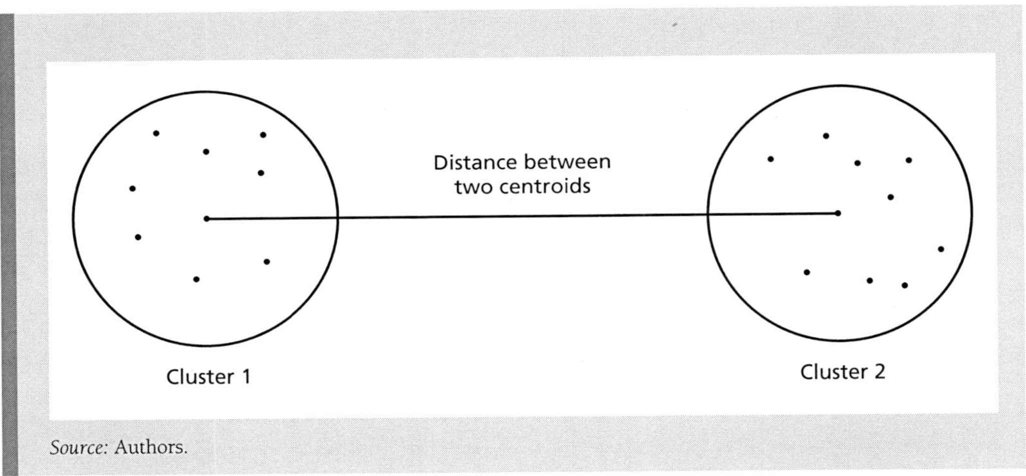

Source: Authors.

2. Non-hierarchical method

In this cluster-forming method, any element of one cluster can leave that cluster and add with another cluster. This technique begins with a pre-defined number of clusters. It is also called as K-means clustering. It is classified into the following three techniques.

a. Sequential threshold method

At first a cluster centre is chosen and all the elements with pre-defined values and associated with the cluster centre are clubbed together for the formation of a cluster. In the next step, a new cluster centre is chosen and the same method is repeated for the elements which are not still grouped together. This process is continued till clusters are formed with all the elements.

b. Parallel threshold method

Here, several cluster centres are chosen at a time and the elements with pre-defined values are grouped to the nearest cluster centre. For any cluster, pre-defined values can be adjusted to incorporate more associated elements to the particular cluster.

c. Optimizing threshold method

In this method, the overall measurement criteria can be improved and optimized by replacing the divergent elements from one cluster where the elements were initially assigned, to the other more similar cluster. Basically, it helps to optimize the homogeneity within the clusters.

19.3.4. Defining the Number of Clusters

For defining the number of clusters for this problem, we will use SPSS by applying the hierarchical clustering method (Ward's method).

After putting data and variable in the 'Data View' window and 'Variable View' window, click Analyze → Classify → Hierarchical cluster in the SPSS window. One pop-up window will appear as

EXHIBIT 19.1

SPSS Window for Hierarchical Cluster Analysis (Step 1)

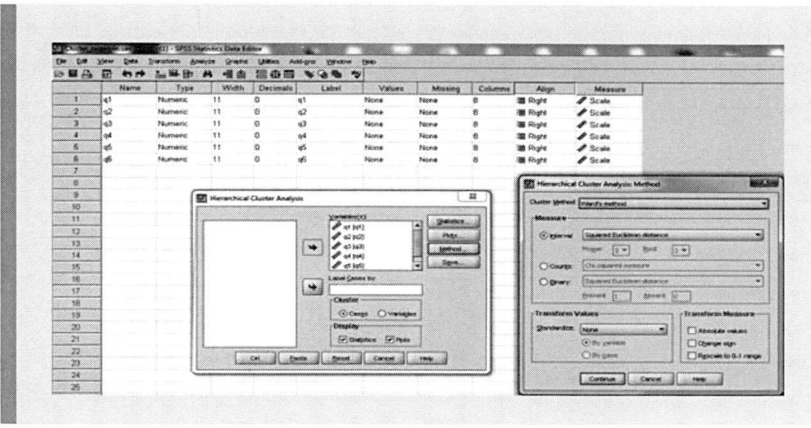

EXHIBIT 19.2

SPSS Window for Hierarchical Cluster Analysis (Step 2)

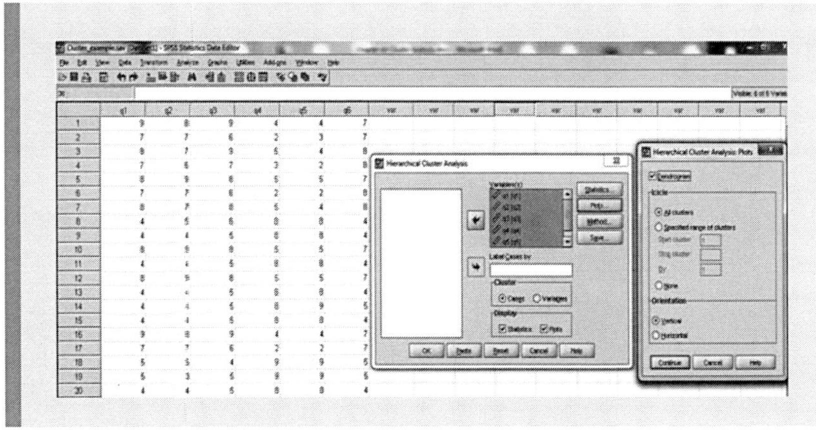

'Hierarchical Cluster Analysis'. Then send q1–q6 to 'Variables'. Then in the 'Hierarchical Cluster Analysis' dialog box, select 'Method' and a pop-up window will appear as 'Hierarchical Cluster Analysis: Method'. In this dialog box, select the 'Cluster Method' as 'Ward's method' and then go to 'Measure' and check the 'Interval' as 'Squared Euclidean distance' (Exhibit 19.1).

After that, click 'Continue'. Again, in the 'Hierarchical Cluster Analysis' dialog box, select 'Statistics' and one pop-up window will appear as 'Hierarchical Cluster Analysis: Statistics' and check 'Agglomeration Schedule'. Then, click 'Continue'. Now, in the 'Hierarchical Cluster Analysis' dialog box, select 'Plots' and one pop-up window will appear as 'Hierarchical Cluster Analysis: Plots' and click 'Dendrogram'. Then go to 'Icicle' and check 'All clusters' and in the 'Orientation' box, check 'Vertical' (Exhibit 19.2).

After that, click 'Continue'. Then click 'OK' and an SPSS output box will appear as shown in Tables 19.2–19.4 and Figure 19.8.

TABLE 19.2
Case Processing Summary

Cases					
Valid		Missing		Total	
N	%	*N*	%	*N*	%
20	100.0	0	0.0	20	100.0

Source: Authors.
Notes: 1. Squared Euclidean distance used.
2. Ward linkage.

TABLE 19.3
Agglomeration Schedule

Stage	Cluster Combined: Cluster 1	Cluster Combined: Cluster 2	Coefficients	Stage Cluster First Appears: Cluster 1	Stage Cluster First Appears: Cluster 2	Next Stage
1	15	20	0.000	0	0	3
2	1	16	0.000	0	0	15
3	9	15	0.000	0	1	6
4	11	13	0.000	0	0	6
5	10	12	0.000	0	0	7
6	9	11	0.000	3	4	12
7	5	10	0.000	0	5	17
8	6	17	0.500	0	0	10
9	3	7	1.000	0	0	15
10	2	6	1.833	0	8	14
11	14	19	3.333	0	0	13
12	8	9	5.000	0	6	16
13	14	18	7.500	11	0	16
14	2	4	10.167	10	0	18
15	1	3	14.417	2	9	17
16	8	14	20.750	12	13	19
17	1	5	28.571	15	7	18
18	1	2	77.455	17	14	19
19	1	8	488.050	18	16	0

Sudden jump in distance from stage 17 to 18 and 18 to 19. So, three clusters are formed after stage 16.

Source: Authors.

FIGURE 19.8
Dendrogram Using the Ward Method

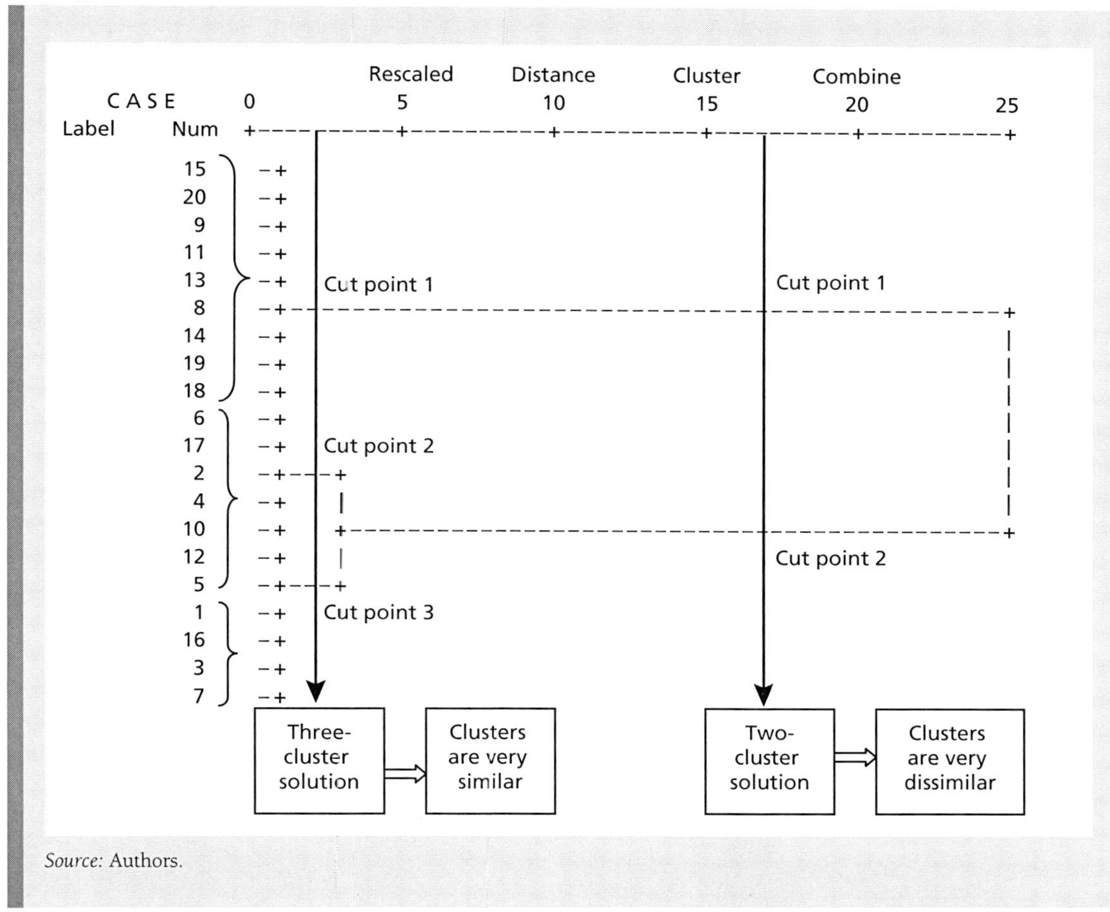

Source: Authors.

TABLE 19.4
Cluster Membership

Case	5 Clusters	4 Clusters	3 Clusters	2 Clusters
1	1	1	1	1
2	2	2	2	1
3	1	1	1	1
4	2	2	2	1
5	3	3	1	1
6	2	2	2	1
7	1	1	1	1
8	4	4	3	2

(Table 19.4 Continued)

(Table 19.4 Continued)

Case	5 Clusters	4 Clusters	3 Clusters	2 Clusters
9	4	4	3	2
10	3	3	1	1
11	4	4	3	2
12	3	3	1	1
13	4	4	3	2
14	4	4	3	2
15	4	4	3	2
16	1	1	1	1
17	2	2	2	1
18	5	4	3	2
19	5	4	3	2
20	4	4	3	2

Source: Authors.
Note: Different shades indicate cluster membership under individual cluster.

19.3.5. Interpreting the Clusters

Case processing summary describes the total number of cases, valid cases and missing cases for this problem. Then the agglomeration schedule provides the information about how the elements are being grouped in each stage. For example, cases 15 and 20 are clubbed at Stage 1 with minimum squared Euclidean distance. In the third stage 'Stage Cluster First Appears', column stage 1 is mentioned. This illustrates that case 15 that was clubbed with case 20 at the first stage is clubbed again with case 9, forming a three-case cluster for this stage. This process will repeat at the sixth stage and form a new cluster with more number of cases. Agglomeration schedule indicates a good cluster solution by showing the incidents of sudden jump. In this example, at stage 17, a sudden jump has been observed. So, stage 17 is the stopping point for the merging process of clusters and we get a three-cluster solution in this scenario. On the other hand, a dendrogram indicates a relative similarity between elements in cluster analysis. It actually determines the number of clusters derived by cluster analysis. We can get different cluster solutions by depicting an imaginary vertical line on a dendrogram. Different numbers of cluster solutions have been observed by counting the number of cut points, generated by the vertical line. Here, the first vertical line creates a three-cluster solution and the second vertical line creates a two-cluster solution. If the distance of the vertical line (from the left) increases, then dissimilarity among clusters will increase. Cluster membership ('2–5 cluster' in 'Range of Solutions' by SPSS 'Hierarchical Cluster Analysis: Statistics') indicates member under different clusters. For a three-cluster solution, elements 1, 16, 3 and 7 are the members of cluster 1, elements 6, 17, 2, 4, 10, 12 and 5 are the members of cluster 2 and elements 15, 20, 9, 11, 13, 8, 14, 19 and 18 are the members of cluster 3 in this problem.

19.4. NON-HIERARCHICAL CLUSTERING

Now, we are executing the non-hierarchical clustering technique (K-means cluster analysis) for the same problem. After putting data and variable in the 'Data View' window and 'Variable View' window, click Analyze → Classify → K-Means Cluster in the SPSS window. One pop-up window will appear as

'K-Means Cluster Analysis'. Then send q1–q6 to 'Variables'. Then in the 'K-Means Cluster Analysis' dialog box, go to 'Number of Clusters' and put the value '3' (generated by 'hierarchical cluster analysis'). After that, in the 'K-Means Cluster Analysis' dialog box, select 'Options' and one pop-up window will appear as 'K-Means Cluster Analysis: Options'. In the 'K-Means Cluster Analysis: Options' dialog box, go to 'Statistics' and tick 'Initial cluster centres' and 'ANOVA table' (Exhibit 19.3).

After that, click 'Continue'. Again, in the 'K-Means Cluster Analysis' dialog box, select 'Save' and one pop-up window will appear as 'K-Means Cluster Analysis: Save New Variable' and tick 'Cluster membership' (Exhibit 19.4).

EXHIBIT 19.3
SPSS Window for K-Means Cluster Analysis (Step 1)

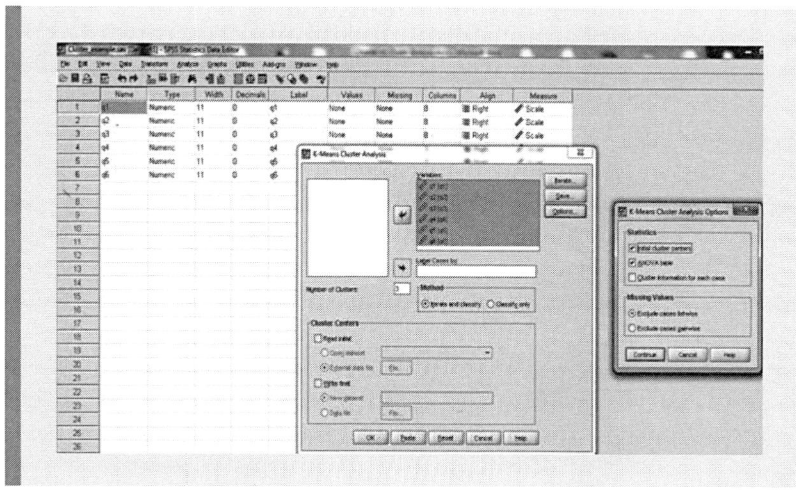

EXHIBIT 19.4
SPSS Window for K-Means Cluster Analysis (Step 2)

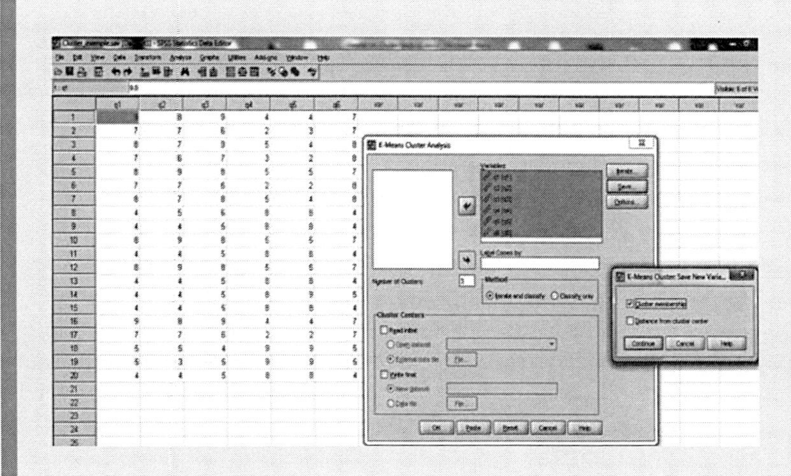

TABLE 19.5
Final Cluster Centres

	Cluster		
	1	2	3
q1	4	7	8
q2	4	7	8
q3	5	6	8
q4	8	2	5
q5	8	2	4
q6	4	8	7

Source: Authors.

TABLE 19.6
ANOVA (F-Test)

	Cluster		Error			
	Mean Square	df	Mean Square	df	F	Sig.
q1	34.108	2	0.176	17	194.306	<0.01
q2	33.227	2	0.500	17	66.485	<0.01
q3	23.243	2	0.263	17	88.509	<0.01
q4	55.733	2	0.220	17	253.730	<0.01
q5	60.643	2	0.263	17	230.928	<0.01
q6	22.786	2	0.261	17	87.468	<0.01

Source: Authors.
Note: The F tests should be used only for descriptive purposes because the clusters have been chosen to maximize the differences among cases in different clusters. The observed significance levels are not corrected for this and thus cannot be interpreted as tests of the hypothesis that the cluster means are equal.

Then, click 'Continue'. At last, click 'OK' and an SPSS output box will appear as shown in Table 19.5.

The values of 'Final cluster centres' indicate that the first cluster has high cluster centre values for variables q4 and q5, the second cluster has high cluster centre values for variable q6 and the third cluster has high cluster centre values for variables q1, q2 and q3. In every cluster, except the aforementioned high values, the cluster centre values for other variables are relatively low. The ANOVA table indicates the usefulness of the variables in cluster analysis (Table 19.6). Here, all large F-values point out that all variables are important for cluster analysis. In any case, F-values should not be close to 1. Table 19.7 represents the number of cases allocated to each cluster. If disproportionate numbers of cases are observed in different clusters, then it is a clear indication of the problem regarding the cluster analysis process. Therefore, this process and clusters containing variables should be re-examined by the researcher.

TABLE 19.7
Number of Cases in Each Cluster

Cluster	1	9
	2	4
	3	7
Valid		20
Missing		0

Source: Authors.

SUMMARY

Cluster analysis (Q-analysis) is a multivariate technique which creates the mutually exclusive and collectively exhaustive groups with objects or entities or cases. The cluster analysis is basically used for segmenting multiple factors involved in collected data such as segmentation of markets/industries/sectors/demographic profiles. There are mainly two types of clustering method: (a) hierarchical method and (b) non-hierarchical method. The hierarchical method is classified into five techniques: (a) single linkage method, (b) complete linkage method, (c) average linkage method, (d) Ward's method and (e) centroid method. On the other hand, the non-hierarchical method is classified into three techniques: (a) sequential threshold method, (b) parallel threshold method and (c) optimizing procedures.

KEY TERMS

Q-analysis (264)
agglomeration schedule (264)
cluster membership (264)
Euclidean distance (265)
dendrogram (265)
ANOVA table (265)
hierarchical method (267)
non-hierarchical method (267)
single linkage method (267)
complete linkage method (268)
average linkage method (268)
Ward's method (269)
centroid method (269)
sequential threshold method (270)
parallel threshold method (270)
optimizing procedures (270)

EXERCISES

1. What is cluster analysis? Explain the assumptions of this technique.
2. Describe cluster analysis process in detail with a suitable example.
3. Differentiate between the hierarchical and non-hierarchical method with an example.
4. Differentiate between the complete linkage method and Ward's method.
5. Differentiate between the average linkage method and centroid method.
6. Differentiate between the parallel threshold method and optimizing procedures.

7. Describe each of the following:
   a. Agglomeration schedule
   b. Dendrogram
   c. Euclidean distance
   d. Sequential threshold method
8. Hotel chain survey was carried out and a sample of 25 respondents was collected for the purpose of testing the relative importance of seven attributes regarding hotel facilities. Responses are rated on a 9-point scale with very important (9) to very unimportant (1) as follows:

	Variables	Very important (9) to Very unimportant (1)
Q_1	Price	
Q_2	Physical evidence	
Q_3	Responsiveness	
Q_4	Food taste	
Q_5	Food hygiene	
Q_6	Location	
Q_7	Menu variety	

Scores rated by the respondents:

Respondents	Q 1	Q 2	Q 3	Q 4	Q 5	Q 6	Q 7
1	7	6	7	3	2	8	7
2	7	9	8	4	5	7	7
3	9	8	9	4	4	7	9
4	7	7	6	2	3	7	5
5	8	7	9	5	4	8	9
6	7	6	7	3	2	8	6
7	8	8	8	5	5	7	8
8	7	7	6	2	2	8	5
9	8	7	8	5	4	8	8
10	4	5	6	8	8	4	5
11	4	4	5	7	9	4	5
12	7	9	8	5	5	7	7
13	4	4	5	8	8	4	5
14	8	9	8	5	5	7	7
15	4	4	5	8	8	4	5
16	4	4	5	8	9	5	4
17	8	8	8	5	5	7	8
18	4	4	5	8	8	4	4

Respondents	Q 1	Q 2	Q 3	Q 4	Q 5	Q 6	Q 7
19	7	8	7	5	5	7	7
20	9	8	9	4	4	7	8
21	7	7	6	2	2	7	6
22	5	5	4	9	9	5	5
23	8	7	8	5	5	7	8
24	5	3	5	9	9	5	4
25	4	4	5	8	8	4	5

a. How would you interpret the cluster analysis results from the SPSS output?
b. What attributes should a hotel be cautious for each of the created clusters?

CHAPTER

20

Multidimensional Scaling

LEARNING OBJECTIVES

After studying this chapter, you should be able to

- Understand the concept and usage of multidimensional scaling (MDS) in research study.
- Learn the MDS process.
- Learn to select the appropriate MDS technique for a research study.
- Study the analysis of metric and non-metric data through SPSS.
- Interpret SPSS output of MDS through mapping of different dimensions.

20.1. CONCEPT OF MULTIDIMENSIONAL SCALING

MDS is a visual display technique which plots individual or group-wise perceptions and preferences of the respondents. The graphically portrayed output of MDS (called spatial/perceptual map) is presented through the location of elements/objects on different dimensions. Basically, cluster analysis creates clusters by grouping similar objects and MDS creates some graphs where preference judgements of the elements by the respondents are examined visually and quantitatively. MDS deals with metric data (rating of respondent's choice) as well as non-metric data (ranking of respondent's relative choice). In MDS, R-square value (squared correlation) indicates the amount of variance prevailing in the MDS model. R-square value should be higher for the goodness of fit of the MDS model. On the other hand, a high 'stress' value in MDS indicates lack of model fit. MDS is one of the most effective tools where new concepts, different products, pricing, brands and so on are tested to know the preference level or acceptability of the customers on multiple dimensions.

20.2. MULTIDIMENSIONAL SCALING PROCESS

Conducting MDS involves the following steps:

1. Problem formulation
2. Identification of metric and non-metric data
3. Establishing an appropriate MDS process
4. Determining the number of dimensions for spatial mapping and interpreting the output

Detailed explanations of the listed steps have been given in the following section with the help of an example.

20.2.1. Problem Formulation

At first, we are taking 10 popular soap brands, namely Pears, Lifebuoy, Liril, Hamam, Dove, Breeze, Lux, Rexona, Dettol and Fiama. The objective of the researcher is to find out whether a new soap brand can be launched in the present market situation and what will be the positioning strategies of the new soap brand. Here, 100 respondents are taken in this survey research. The researcher should not use very small number of objects in MDS. The data collected from the respondents should be on the basis of preferences or similarity of the attributes.

Another problem will be discussed on 10 popular motorcycle brands depending on the ranking of respondent's relative choice. These brands are Hero MotoCorp, Bajaj, Yamaha, TVS Motor Company, Honda, Mahindra, Royal Enfield, Suzuki, Kawasaki and Harley-Davidson. Here, the objective of the researcher is to see whether a new motorcycle brand can be launched in the present market situation and what will be the positioning strategies of the new brand. In this case, 100 respondents are taken for collecting data.

20.2.2. Identification of Metric and Non-metric Data

In both of the examples, we have to put the input data (metric or non-metric form) in the SPSS window. Here, we want to measure the similarity and preferability among objects through graphical representation with the help of collected data using a 9-point Likert scale and ranking scale. For pair comparison and ranking among objects, the formats that have been used are shown in Tables 20.1 and 20.2.

TABLE 20.1
For Soap Brand

Pair of Soaps	Put the Value from 1 (Extremely Dissimilar) to 9 (Extremely Similar)								
Pears and Lifebuoy	1	2	3	4	5	6	7	8	9
Pears and Liril	1	2	3	4	5	6	7	8	9
Lifebuoy and Liril	1	2	3	4	5	6	7	8	9
....	.....	.....	.....	.....	.....	.....	.....	.....	.....
Dettol and Fiama	1	2	3	4	5	6	7	8	9

Source: Authors.

TABLE 20.2
For Motorcycle Brand

Rank the Brands According to Your Preferability from 1 (Most Preferable) to 10 (Least Preferable)										
Respondents	Hero MotoCorp	Bajaj	Yamaha	TVS Motor Company	Honda	Mahindra	Royal Enfield	Suzuki	Kawasaki	Harley-Davidson
1										
2										
.....	.....	.....	.....	.....	.....	.....	.....	.....	.....	.....
10										

Source: Authors.

For pair comparison, $n \times (n - 1)/2$ pairs are required to be judged by the respondents. Here, n is the number of brands that are used in the pair comparison. For 10 brands, total pairs under judgement will be 45. Both metric data (interval scale data in the example of soap brands) and non-metric data (ordinal scale data in the example of motorcycle brands) can be easily handled by SPSS software (see Tables 20.3 and 20.4).

20.2.3. Establishing an Appropriate Multidimensional Scaling Process

The MDS process depends on different types of input data such as ordinal data and interval data. Both metric and non-metric MDS procedures always produce metric outputs and provide similar results. Perceptual mapping can be drawn for individual respondents through individual-level MDS procedures. It can be also done on the basis of the average similarity rating procedure for a large number of respondents.

TABLE 20.3
Collected 'Similarity Score Data' for Different Soap Brands

Brands	Pears	Lifebuoy	Liril	Hamam	Dove	Breeze	Lux	Rexona	Dettol	Fiama
Pears	0									
Lifebuoy	6	0								
Liril	4	7	0							
Hamam	5	5	6	0						
Dove	7	4	5	6	0					
Breeze	8	2	4	5	5	0				
Lux	7	5	5	6	4	8	0			
Rexona	5	6	6	4	6	3	4	0		
Dettol	6	5	2	3	4	5	2	4	0	
Fiama	9	4	3	4	2	9	3	3	5	0

Source: Authors.

TABLE 20.4
Collected Preferable Rank for Different Motorcycle Brands from 10 Respondents

Respondents	Hero MotoCorp	Bajaj	Yamaha	TVS Motor Company	Honda	Mahindra	Royal Enfield	Suzuki	Kawasaki	Harley-Davidson
1	1	10	7	5	2	9	6	4	8	3
2	1	9	7	4	5	8	2	3	10	6
3	8	1	2	9	7	3	10	5	6	4
4	1	6	7	9	2	4	5	3	10	8
5	2	5	4	8	3	1	10	6	9	7
6	7	4	6	8	2	5	1	10	9	3
7	1	10	4	9	2	3	6	7	8	5
8	6	3	1	10	9	5	2	8	7	4
9	7	10	6	4	5	8	1	2	9	3
10	1	4	9	10	2	7	5	6	8	3

Source: Authors.

20.2.4. Determining the Number of Dimensions for Spatial Mapping and Interpreting the Output

A suitable numbers of dimensions are used for the best fit of perceptual mapping. Basically, two- or three-dimensional perceptual maps are desirable for MDS. In general cases, the desired ratio for objects and dimensions is 4:1. Therefore, at least eight objects are required for a two-dimensional map. Sometimes, many dimensions create complexity in the interpretation of a map. A researcher must have in-depth subject knowledge on the research topic to understand the underlying dimensions.

20.3. DIFFERENT MULTIDIMENSIONAL SCALING METHODS THROUGH SPSS

20.3.1. Analysis on Metric Data (for Soap Brand)

After putting data and variable in the 'Data View' window and 'Variable View' window, click Analyze → Scale → Multidimensional Scaling (ALSCAL) in the SPSS window. One pop-up window will appear as 'Multidimensional Scaling'. Then send all objects as 'Pears, Lifebuoy, Liril, Hamam, Dove, Breeze, Lux, Rexona, Dettol, Fiama' to 'Variables'. Then in the 'Multidimensional Scaling' dialog box, go to 'Distances' and tick 'Data are distances' for metric data. Then select 'Model' and one pop-up window will appear as 'Multidimensional Scaling: Model'. In this dialog box, go to 'Level of Measurement' and tick 'Interval'. Then go to 'Conditionality' and check the tick in 'Matrix' and go to 'Scaling Model' and check the tick in 'Euclidean distance'. At last, go to 'Dimensions' and input the value 2 in 'Minimum' and 3 in 'Maximum' (Exhibit 20.1).

EXHIBIT 20.1
SPSS Window for Multidimensional Scaling (Step 1)

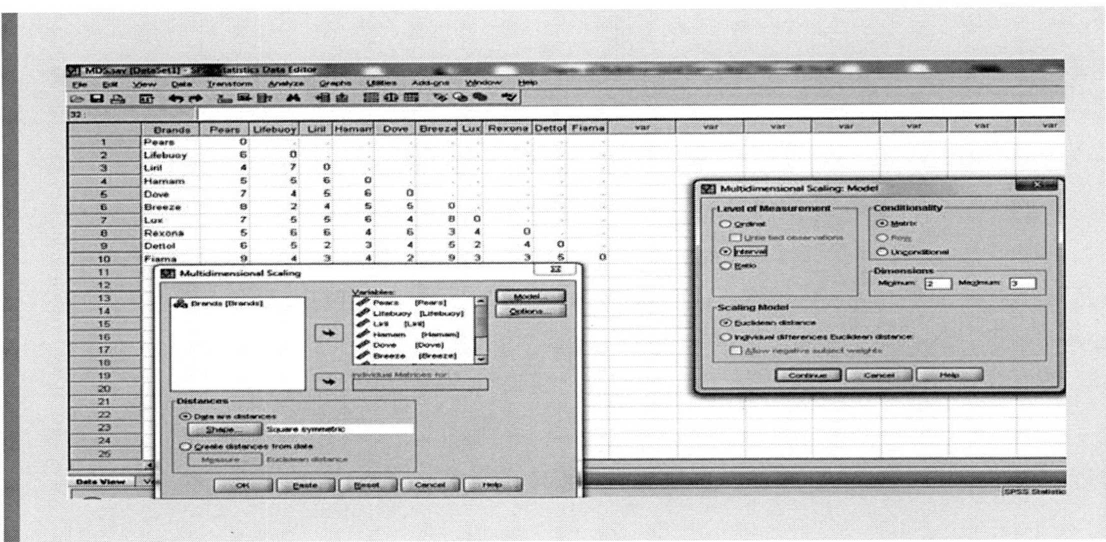

EXHIBIT 20.2
SPSS Window for Multidimensional Scaling (Step 2)

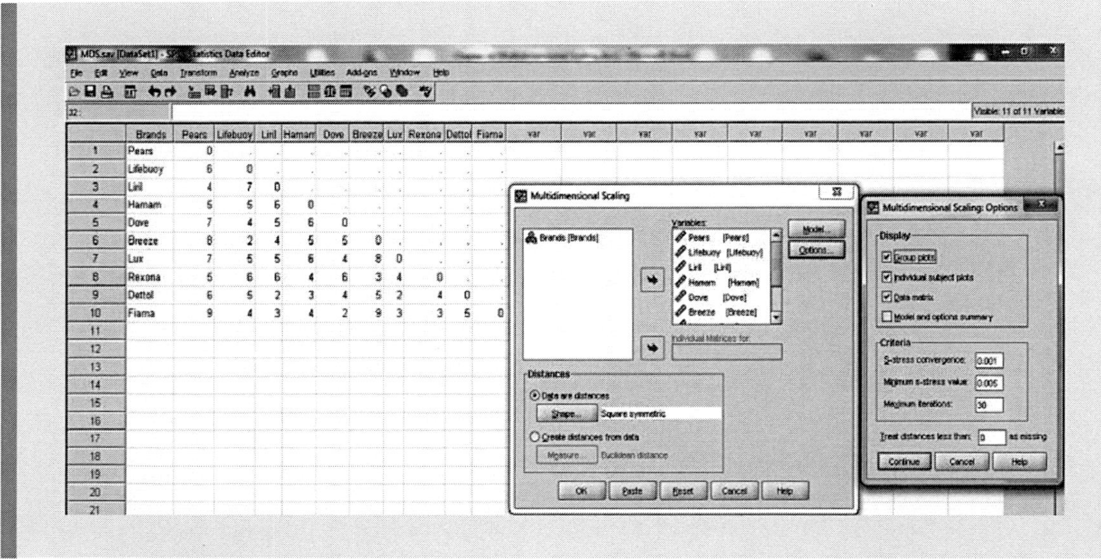

After that, click 'Continue'. Again in the 'Multidimensional Scaling' dialog box, select 'Options' and one pop-up window will appear as 'Multidimensional Scaling: Options'. Then go to 'Display' and tick 'Group plots', 'Individual subject plots' and 'Data matrix' (Exhibit 20.2).

TABLE 20.5
Stress Scores and R-square Values

Number of Dimensions	Stress Value	R-square Value
1	0.47814	0.22174
2	0.2611	0.51423
3	**0.19516**	**0.55347**

Source: Authors.
Note: Bold values indicate stress values which are closest to zero as well as R-square values which are more than 0.6 for getting models with acceptable solutions.

TABLE 20.6
Stimulus Coordinates for Three-dimensional Solution

		Dimension		
Stimulus Number	Stimulus Name	1	2	3
1	Pears	1.4346	–1.7721	0.1134
2	Lifebuoy	0.5990	1.6215	0.0295
3	Liril	0.0527	–0.9497	1.3558
4	Hamam	0.5288	–0.2979	–1.5465
5	Dove	–0.8246	0.9829	1.0153
6	Breeze	1.6219	1.2411	0.3660
7	Lux	–1.6511	–0.3519	–0.0217
8	Rexona	0.2308	–0.1022	–1.4741
9	Dettol	–0.3293	–0.7354	0.6593
10	Fiama	–1.6628	0.3636	–0.4969

Source: Authors.

Then, click 'Continue'. At last click 'OK' and an SPSS output box will appear as shown in Table 20.5.

Stress values range from 1 to 0. Here, the value 1 indicates the worst fit and 0 indicates the best fit in MDS. For the third dimension (Table 20.5), the stress value is closest to 0. Therefore, it can provide best explanation. In general cases, the R-square value must be 0.6 or more for an acceptable solution. Here, the third dimension's R-square value is closest to 0.6. So the third-dimensional model is an acceptable solution in this scenario.

In three-dimensional solutions, let us focus on grouping objects with extreme values. Table 20.6 shows that Pears and Breeze have the highest values and are closest to each other in the first dimension and Lux and Fiama have the lowest values and are nearest to each other in the same dimension. As per the customer's view for individual brand position in the market, Pears and Breeze are more related to 'pure and gentle treatment for skin' and Lux and Fiama are related to 'the beauty and glamorous world'. So we can name the dimension as 'skincare with looks', ranging from pure skin treatment to a glamorous look. In the second dimension, Lifebuoy has the highest value and Pears has the lowest value. If we observe the customer's view for individual brand position in the market, then Lifebuoy is more related to 'germ protection' and Pears is related to 'better treatment of skin'. So we can name the dimension as 'germ protection with skincare', ranging from better germ protection to proper treatment of skin. In the third dimension, Liril has the highest value and Hamam has the lowest value. If we observe the customer's view for individual brand position in the market, then Liril is more related to 'freshness' and Hamam is related to 'homeliness'. So we can name the dimension as 'freshness with homeliness', ranging from freshness to family feeling. In MDS, the uncovered space in three-dimensional mapping (Figure 20.1) can be targeted by the managers for a new soap brand.

FIGURE 20.1
MDS Three-dimensional Mapping
(Derived Stimulus Configuration and Euclidean Distance Model)

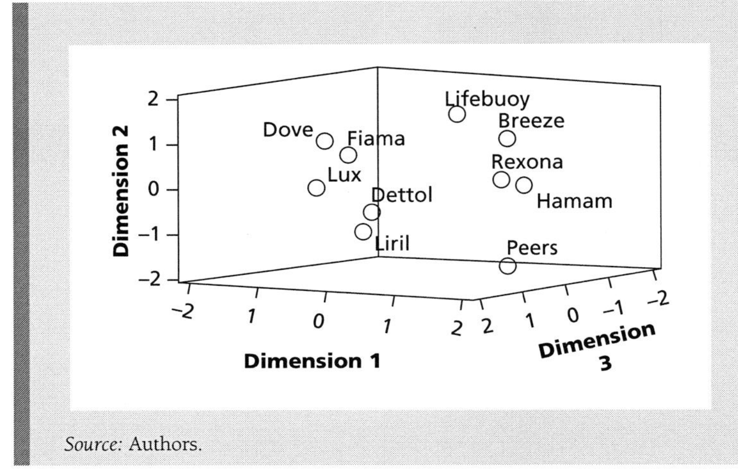

Source: Authors.

In the case of a two-dimensional solution, Table 20.5 shows the non-acceptable stress score and non-significant R-square value. Therefore, two-dimensional solution as perceptual mapping is not presented here.

20.3.2. Analysis on Non-metric Data (for Motorcycle Brand)

After putting data and variable in the 'Data View' window and 'Variable View' window, click Analyze → Scale → Multidimensional Scaling (ALSCAL) in the SPSS window. One pop-up window will appear as 'Multidimensional Scaling'. Then send all objects as 'Hero MotoCorp, Bajaj, Yamaha, TVS Motor, Honda, Mahindra, Royal Enfield, Suzuki, Kawasaki, Harley Davidson' to 'Variables'. Then in the 'Multidimensional Scaling' dialog box, go to 'Distances' and tick 'Create distances from data' for non-metric data. Then select 'Model' and one pop-up window will appear as 'Multidimensional Scaling: Model'. In this dialog box, go to 'Level of Measurement' and tick 'Ordinal'. Then go to 'Conditionality' and check the tick in 'Matrix' and go to 'Scaling Model' and check the tick in 'Euclidean distance'. At last, go to 'Dimensions' and input the value 2 in 'Minimum' and 3 in 'Maximum' (Exhibit 20.3).

After that, click 'Continue'. Again, in the 'Multidimensional Scaling' dialog box, select 'Options' and one pop-up window will appear as 'Multidimensional Scaling: Options'. Then go to 'Display' and tick 'Group plots', 'Individual subject plots' and 'Data matrix' (Exhibit 20.4).

Then, click 'Continue'. At last click 'OK' and an SPSS output box will appear as shown in Table 20.7.

EXHIBIT 20.3
SPSS Window for Multidimensional Scaling (Step 1)

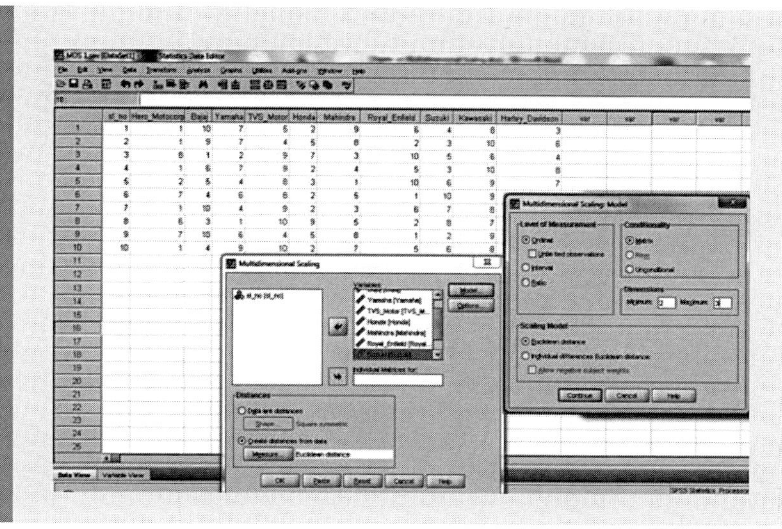

EXHIBIT 20.4
SPSS Window for Multidimensional Scaling (Step 2)

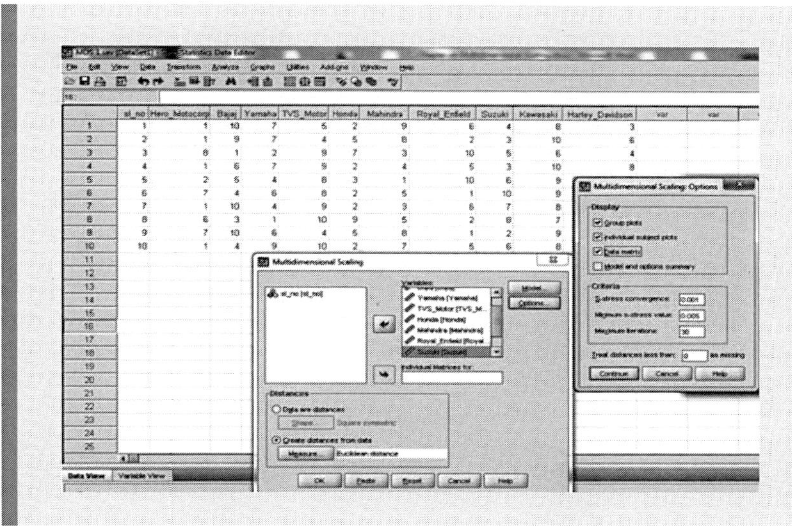

In the second and third dimension solutions (Table 20.7), the stress value is closest to 0. Therefore, both solutions can provide the best explanation for the positioning of the new motorcycle brand. Here, second and third dimension's R-square values are more than 0.6. So both models have the acceptable solutions in this case.

TABLE 20.7
Stress Scores and R-square Values

Number of Dimensions	Stress Value	R-square Value
1	0.3098	0.67633
2	**0.10948**	**0.91473**
3	**0.03507**	**0.98696**

Source: Authors.
Note: Bold values indicate stress values which are closest to zero as well as R-square values which are more than 0.6 for getting models with acceptable solutions.

Alike the previous example, let us focus on grouping objects with extreme values for two- and three-dimensional solutions. Table 20.8 shows that Hero MotoCorp has the highest value in the first dimension and Kawasaki and Bajaj have the lowest values and are nearest to each other in the same dimension. According to the customer's view on positioning for an individual brand in the market, Hero MotoCorp is more related to 'fast and sporty looking bike with powerful engine' and Kawasaki and Bajaj are related to 'wide variety bikes for average Indians'. So we can name the dimension as 'sporty bikes', ranging from fast and sporty bikes to bikes for average Indians. In the second dimension, Mahindra has the highest value and TVS Motor Company has the lowest value. As per the customer's view on positioning for individual brand in the market, Mahindra is related to 'spacious and affordability' and TVS Motor Company is related to 'style and powerful pick up'. So we can name the dimension as 'spacious with affordability and style', ranging from spacious and affordable bikes to stylish bike. In the third dimension, Royal Enfield has the highest value and Suzuki has the lowest value. According to the customer's view on positioning for individual brand in the market, Royal Enfield is related to 'hardiness of bike' and Suzuki is related to 'good mileage and performance'. So we can name the dimension as 'hardiness with performance', ranging from hardiness to mileage and performance.

TABLE 20.8
Stimulus Coordinates for Three-dimensional Solution

		Dimension		
Stimulus Number	Stimulus Name	1	2	3
1	Hero_Mot	2.1121	0.6586	–0.7217
2	Bajaj	–1.6464	1.1677	0.2661
3	Yamaha	–0.8599	0.5966	0.4952
4	TVS_Moto	–0.5793	–1.7393	–0.6381
5	Honda	1.5731	0.6300	–0.1501
6	Mahindra	–0.3951	1.3346	–0.3110
7	Royal_En	0.7120	–1.1247	1.5635
8	Suzuki	0.5714	–0.7603	–0.8451
9	Kawasaki	–1.7898	–0.6422	–0.4569
10	Harley_D	0.3019	–0.1210	0.7981

Source: Authors.

Comparing the three-dimensional solution (see Table 20.8 and Figure 20.2) with two-dimensional solution, the first two dimensions under the three-dimensional solution are similar with the dimensions of the two-dimensional solution (Table 20.9). Here, the two-dimensional solution as perceptual mapping is depicted in Figure 20.3.

In MDS, observed uncovered space in three- and two-dimensional mapping can be targeted by the managers for the new motorcycle brand.

FIGURE 20.2
MDS Three-dimensional Mapping
(Derived Stimulus Configuration and Euclidean Distance Model)

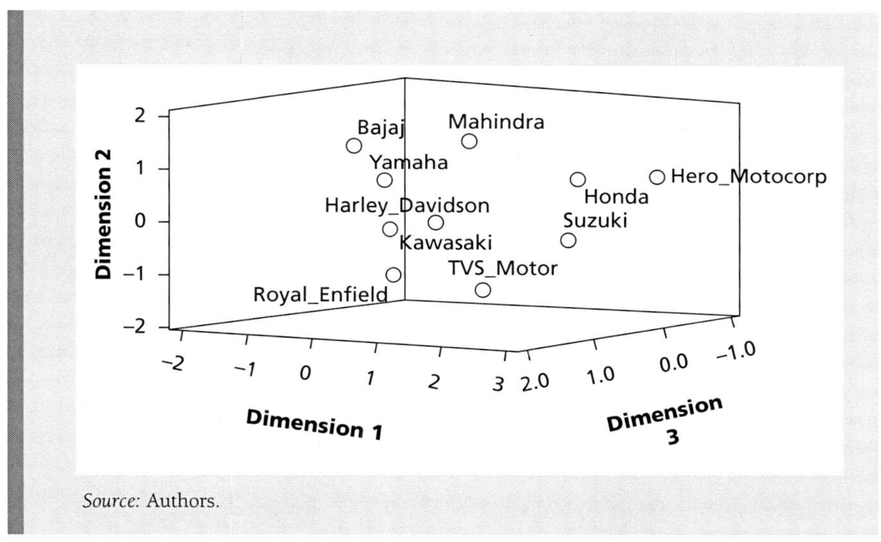

Source: Authors.

TABLE 20.9
Stimulus Coordinates for Two-dimensional Solution

		Dimension	
Stimulus Number	Stimulus Name	1	2
1	Hero_Mot	1.8617	0.8527
2	Bajaj	−1.3999	1.0005
3	Yamaha	−0.8518	0.5084
4	TVS_Moto	−0.4885	−1.5131
5	Honda	1.3836	0.4693
6	Mahindra	−0.3969	1.0528
7	Royal_En	0.9094	−1.3797
8	Suzuki	0.3874	−0.4049
9	Kawasaki	−1.6118	−0.4889
10	Harley_D	0.2068	−0.0971

Source: Authors.

FIGURE 20.3
MDS Two-dimensional Mapping
(Derived Stimulus Configuration and Euclidean Distance Model)

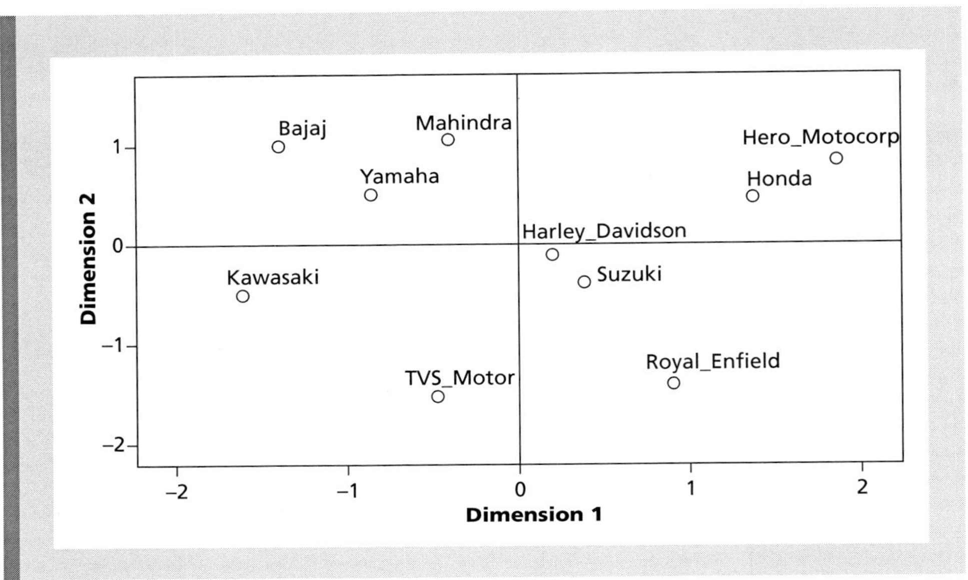

SUMMARY

MDS is a visual display technique which plots individual or group-wise perceptions and preferences of the respondents. The graphically portrayed output of MDS (called spatial/perceptual map) is presented through the location of elements/objects on different dimensions. MDS deals with metric data (rating of respondent's choice) as well as non-metric data (ranking of respondent's relative choice). Steps of implementing the MDS technique are (a) problem formulation, (b) identification of metric and non-metric data, (c) establishing an appropriate MDS process, (d) determining the number of dimensions for spatial mapping and interpreting the output.

KEY TERMS

multidimensional scaling (280)
spatial/perceptual map (280)
metric data (280)
non-metric data (280)
stress scores (285)
R-square value (285)
Euclidean distance (286)
three-dimensional solution (285)
three-dimensional mapping (286)
two-dimensional solution (289)
two-dimensional mapping (290)

EXERCISES

1. What is MDS? Explain the assumptions related with this technique.
2. Describe the MDS process with a suitable example.
3. What do you mean by 'stress' in MDS? Explain with a suitable example.
4. Define 'perceptual mapping'. How does a researcher decide on the number and labelling of different dimensions in MDS?
5. Differentiate between metric data inputs and non-metric data inputs for MDS.
6. Differentiate between R-square values and stress scores.

CHAPTER

21

Conjoint Analysis

LEARNING OBJECTIVES

After studying this chapter, you should be able to

- Understand the concept and use of conjoint analysis in research study.
- Learn the theoretical calculations of conjoint analysis in research study.
- Know the use of SPSS software in conjoint analysis.
- Interpret conjoint analysis results through graphical representation.

21.1. CONCEPT OF CONJOINT ANALYSIS

The word 'conjoint' indicates the measurement of relative values among different attributes. Basically, conjoint analysis is used to find out the respondent's most preferable attributes of any product or service. It emphasizes the relative importance of attributes of a product/service and calculates utilities in different levels under each attribute. Here, respondents are asked to evaluate all attributes of a product/service systematically, so that the preference level of attributes can be easily calculated and judged by the researcher. It follows the simple principle of constructing 'part-worth' or 'utility function' which focuses on the utility of different levels under each attribute. The relative importance of each attribute is evaluated by the ranges of part-worth under each attribute and the total ranges of part-worths. Generally, on average, six or seven attributes are used in conjoint analysis. It has a wide range of applications in different fields, specially business research and marketing.

21.2. EXPLANATION OF CONJOINT ANALYSIS THROUGH EXAMPLE

An organization wants to enter the water purifier market and finds out the most preferable attributes with various levels. First of all, for formulating the problem, four attributes and their levels are taken in this study as given in Table 21.1.

TABLE 21.1
Water Purifier's Attributes and Levels

Attributes	Level No.	Level Description
	1	7 stages
Number of purification stages	2	6 stages
	3	5 stages
	1	10 litres
Storage capacity	2	8 litres
	3	6 litres
	1	₹20,000
Price	2	₹17,000
	3	₹15,000
	1	Superior
Post-sales service level	2	High
	3	Average

Source: Authors.

21.2.1. Different Approaches to Conjoint Analysis

Conjoint analysis can be executed through two approaches: (a) pair-wise comparison approach and (b) full profile approach. In 'pair-wise comparison approach', respondents are asked to judge only two attributes at a time. In this process, all possible pairs must be considered step by step. In the case of 'full profile approach', respondents are asked to judge the complete profile with all the attributes. In the example of a 'water purifier', total six pairs can be formed for the pair-wise comparison approach as follows:

1. Number of purification stages—storage capacity
2. Number of purification stages—price
3. Number of purification stages—Post-sales service level
4. Storage capacity—price
5. Storage capacity—post-sales service level
6. Price—post-sales service level

Here, the 'full profile approach' is used for conjoint analysis in the example of 'water purifier'. Basically, it is a commonly used method.

In the water purifier's example, total 3 × 3 × 3 × 3 = 81 profiles (four attributes and three levels each) can be formed for the full profile approach.

Conjoint analysis deals with metric data (rating of respondent's choice) as well as non-metric data (ranking of respondent's relative choice). In the water purifier example, metric data is used for conjoint analysis. Here, ratings are measured using a 9-point Likert scale with '9' as 'strongly preferred' and '1' as 'not preferred' (see Table 21.2).

TABLE 21.2
Water Purifier's Profile and Rating

Profile No.	Number of Purification Stages	Storage Capacity	Price	Post-sales Service Level	Preference Rating
1	1	1	1	1	6
2	1	1	2	3	8
3	1	1	3	2	7
4	1	2	1	2	5
5	2	2	2	3	4
6	2	2	3	1	2
7	2	3	1	1	3
8	2	3	2	3	4
9	3	3	3	2	1
10	3	1	1	2	6
11	3	1	2	1	5
12	3	1	3	1	2

Source: Authors.

21.2.2. Dummy Variables for Regression Equation

Here, dummy variables are used for constructing regression equation in conjoint analysis. In this analysis, preference rating is treated as dependent variables and all dummy variables are treated as independent variables. The number of dummy variables is calculated as the number of levels under each attribute less 1. For example, if an attribute has three levels, then it can be coded in two dummy variables. Generally, dummy variables employ the value of 0 and 1 to different levels of attribute for easy interpretation, but any other values can be used. In the water purifier example, total eight dummy variables (two for each attribute) are generated for creating the regression equation.

In regression equation, dependent variable (U) measures the part-worth of the attribute level or utility of the model. The regression equation is written as follows:

$$U = b_0 + b_1x_1 + b_2x_2 + b_3x_3 + b_4x_4 + b_5x_5 + b_6x_6 + b_7x_7 + b_8x_8,$$

where b_0, b_1, b_2, b_3, b_4, b_5, b_6, b_7 and b_8 are the regression coefficients of dummy variables.

Also, x_1 and x_2 = Dummy variables for 'Number of purification stages'.
Here, x_1 = 1, if '7 stages' is selected.
= 0, otherwise.
And, x_2 = 1, if '6 stages' is selected.
= 0, otherwise.

Also, x_3 and x_4 = Dummy variables for 'storage capacity'.
Here, x_3 = 1, if '10 Litres' is selected.
= 0, otherwise.
And, x_4 = 1, if '8 Litres' is selected.
= 0, otherwise.

TABLE 21.3
Water Purifier's Data with Dummy Variables for Regression Equation

	Number of Purification Stages		Storage Capacity		Price		Post-sales Service Level		
S. No.	x_1	x_2	x_3	x_4	x_5	x_6	x_7	x_8	Preference Rating
1	1	0	1	0	1	0	1	0	6
2	1	0	1	0	0	1	0	0	8
3	1	0	1	0	0	0	0	1	7
4	1	0	0	1	1	0	0	1	5
5	0	1	0	1	0	1	0	0	4
6	0	1	0	1	0	0	1	0	2
7	0	1	0	0	1	0	1	0	3
8	0	1	0	0	0	1	0	0	4
9	0	0	0	0	0	0	0	1	1
10	0	0	1	0	1	0	0	1	6
11	0	0	1	0	0	1	1	0	5
12	0	0	1	0	0	0	1	0	2

Source: Authors.

In addition, x_5 and x_6 = Dummy variables for 'Price'.
Here, $x_5 = 1$, if '₹20,000' is selected.
= 0, otherwise.
And, $x_6 = 1$, if '₹17,000' is selected.
= 0, otherwise.

Also, x_7 and x_8 = Dummy variables for 'Post-sales service level'.
Here, $x_7 = 1$, if 'Superior' is selected.
= 0, otherwise.
And, $x_8 = 1$, if 'High' is selected.
= 0, otherwise.

Respondent's data with dummy variables is presented in Table 21.3.
Table 21.4 is used for the conjoint problem.

21.2.3. SPSS Outputs of Multiple Regression for Conjoint Analysis

From the SPSS output, we get the estimated regression equation as follows:

$$U = -1.465 + 2.675\,x_1 + 2.873\,x_2 + 3.554\,x_3 + 0.108\,x_4 + 1.331\,x_5 + 2.771\,x_6 + 0.140\,x_7 + 2.408\,x_8,$$

where $b_0 = -1.465$; $b_1 = 2.675$; $b_2 = 2.873$; $b_3 = 3.554$; $b_4 = 0.108$; $b_5 = 1.331$; $b_6 = 2.771$; $b_7 = 0.140$; $b_8 = 2.408$.

TABLE 21.4
SPSS Outputs of Multiple Regression for Conjoint Analysis

Model Summary				
Model	R	R-square	Adjusted R-square	Std. Error of the Estimate
1	0.994[a]	0.987	0.954	0.461

ANOVA[b]						
Model		Sum of Squares	df	Mean Square	F	Sig.
1	Regression	50.280	8	6.285	29.602	**0.009**[a]
	Residual	0.637	3	0.212		
	Total	50.917	11			

Coefficients[b]						
		Unstandardized Coefficients		Standardized Coefficients		
Model		B	Std. Error	Beta	t	Sig.
1	(Constant)	**–1.465**	0.992		–1.477	0.236
	x_1	**2.675**	0.403	0.612	6.641	0.007
	x_2	**2.873**	0.647	0.657	4.437	0.021
	x_3	**3.554**	0.502	0.863	7.077	0.006
	x_4	**0.108**	0.399	0.023	0.271	0.804
	x_5	**1.331**	0.341	0.305	3.904	0.030
	x_6	**2.771**	0.600	0.634	4.615	0.019
	x_7	**0.140**	0.666	0.034	0.210	0.847
	x_8	**2.408**	0.864	0.551	2.785	0.069

Source: Authors.
Notes: 1. Bold values indicate significance level and regression coefficients.
2. [a]Predictors: (Constant) x_8, x_4, x_5, x_1, x_6, x_3, x_2, x_7.
3. [b]Dependent Variable: Pref_Rating.

21.2.4. Conjoint Analysis Results and Interpretation

As we know, each coefficient of dummy variable can be expressed as the difference between different levels (concern level and base level) of part-worth (utility) of each attribute. First of all, we get the following equations for 'Number of purification stages':

$$U_{11} - U_{13} = b_1 = 2.675;$$
$$U_{12} - U_{13} = b_2 = 2.873.$$

For solving individual utility of the attributes, additional constraint equation is required as follows:

$U_{11} + U_{12} + U_{13} = 0$ (Part-worth is estimated on the interval scale and origin is arbitrary).

By solving these equations, we get the following values:

$$U_{11} = 0.826$$
$$U_{12} = 1.023$$
$$U_{13} = -1.849.$$

Then, we get the following equations for 'Storage capacity':

$$U_{21} - U_{23} = b_3 = 3.554;$$
$$U_{22} - U_{23} = b_4 = 0.108.$$

For solving individual utility of the attributes, an additional constraint equation is required as follows:

$$U_{21} + U_{22} + U_{23} = 0.$$

By solving these equations, we get the following values:

$$U_{21} = 2.333$$
$$U_{22} = -1.112$$
$$U_{23} = -1.221.$$

After that, we get the following equations for 'Price':

$$U_{31} - U_{33} = b_5 = 1.331;$$
$$U_{32} - U_{33} = b_6 = 2.771.$$

For solving individual utility of the attributes, an additional constraint equation is required as follows:

$$U_{31} + U_{32} + U_{33} = 0.$$

By solving these equations, we get the following values:

$$U_{31} = -0.036$$
$$U_{32} = 1.403$$
$$U_{33} = -1.367.$$

Then, we get the following equations for 'Post-sales service level':

$$U_{41} - U_{43} = b_7 = 0.140;$$
$$U_{42} - U_{43} = b_8 = 2.408.$$

For solving individual utility of the attributes, an additional constraint equation is required as follows:

$$U_{41} + U_{42} + U_{43} = 0.$$

By solving these equations, we get the following values:

$$U_{41} = -0.709$$
$$U_{42} = 1.558$$
$$U_{43} = -0.849.$$

For finding out the relative importance of an attributes, we need to calculate the individual range of part-worth.

Range of part-worth for 'Number of purification stages' $(R_1) = [U_{\text{Maximum}} - U_{\text{Minimum}}]$
$= [1.023 - (-1.849)]$
$= 2.872.$

Range of part-worth for 'Storage capacity' (R_2) = $[U_{\text{Maximum}} - U_{\text{Minimum}}]$
= [2.333 – (–1.221)]
= 3.554.

Range of part-worth for 'Price' (R_3) = $[U_{\text{Maximum}} - U_{\text{Minimum}}]$
= [1.403 – (–1.367)]
= 2.771.

Range of part-worth for 'Post-sales service level' (R_4) = $[U_{\text{Maximum}} - U_{\text{Minimum}}]$
= [1.558 – (–0.849)]
= 2.407.

Therefore, sum of ranges of part-worth (R) = $R_1 + R_2 + R_3 + R_4$
= 2.872 + 3.554 + 2.771 + 2.407
= 11.605.

Now, relative importance of 'Number of purification stages' = $\frac{R_1}{R} = \frac{2.872}{11.605} = 0.25.$

Relative importance of 'Storage capacity' = $\frac{R_2}{R} = \frac{3.554}{11.605} = 0.30.$

Relative importance of 'Price' = $\frac{R_3}{R} = \frac{2.771}{11.605} = 0.24.$

Relative importance of 'Post-sales service level' = $\frac{R_4}{R} = \frac{2.407}{11.605} = 0.21.$

Individual utility (part-worth) and relative importance of attributes are described in Table 21.5.

TABLE 21.5
Summarized Conjoint Analysis Result

Attributes	Level No.	Level Description	Utility	Relative Importance
Number of purification stages	1	7 stages	0.826	0.25
	2	6 stages	1.023	
	3	5 stages	–1.849	
Storage capacity	1	10 litres	2.333	0.30
	2	8 litres	–1.112	
	3	6 litres	–1.221	
Price	1	₹20,000	–0.036	0.24
	2	₹17,000	1.403	
	3	₹15,000	–1.367	
Post-sales service level	1	Superior	–0.709	0.21
	2	High	1.558	
	3	Average	–0.849	

Source: Authors.

21.3. GRAPHICAL REPRESENTATION OF PART-WORTH FUNCTIONS

As per our respondent, the relative importance assigned by him/her to the number of purification stages, storage capacity, price and post-sales service level are 25%, 30%, 24% and 21%, respectively. It has been observed that the respondent prefers six purification stages (Figure 21.1) to the other two. As expected 10 litres storage capacity (Figure 21.2) has the highest utility. Also the respondent prefers the price of ₹17,000 (Figure 21.3) to the other two levels and high post-sales service (Figure 21.4).

FIGURE 21.1
Part-worth Function for Number of Purification Stages

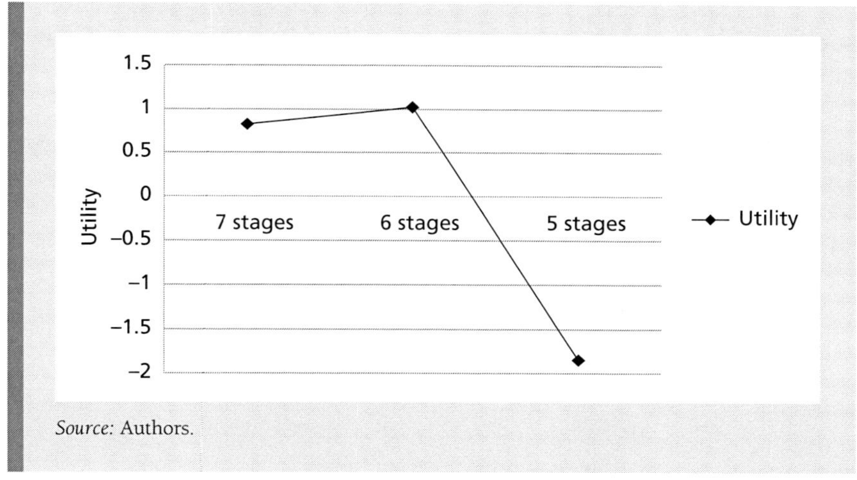

Source: Authors.

FIGURE 21.2
Part-worth Function for Storage Capacity

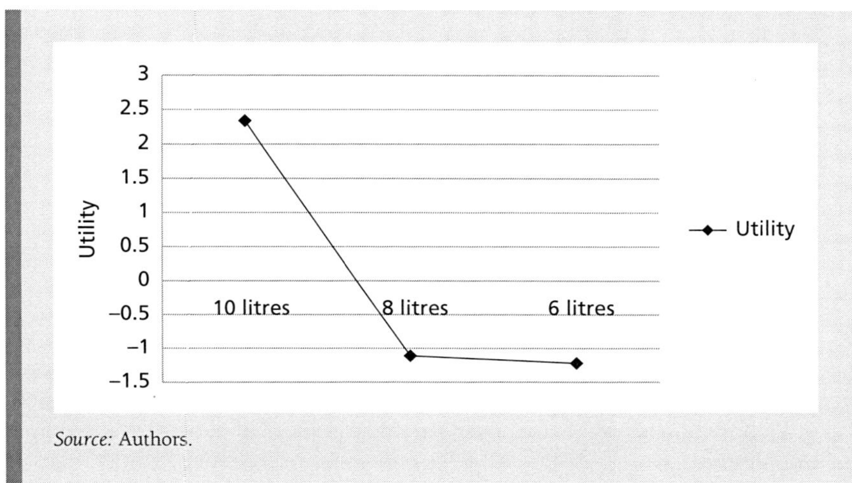

Source: Authors.

FIGURE 21.3
Part-worth Function for Price

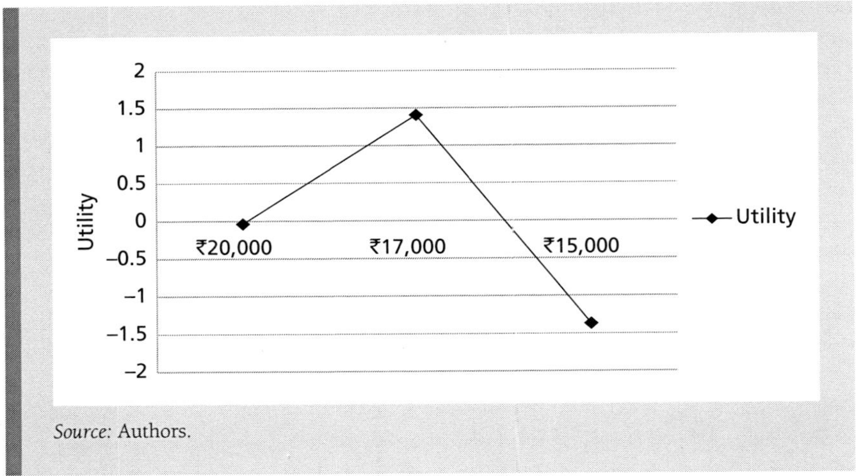

Source: Authors.

FIGURE 21.4
Part-worth Function for Post-sales Service

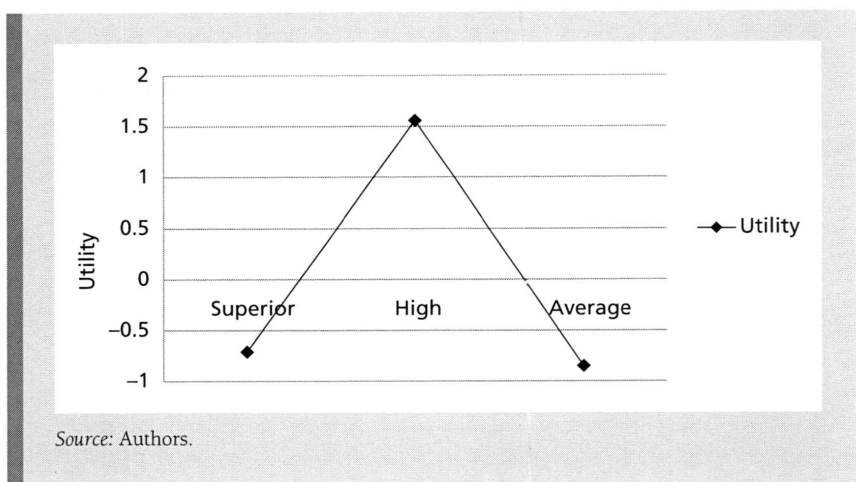

Source: Authors.

SUMMARY

Conjoint analysis is used to find out the respondent's most preferable attributes of any product or service. It emphasizes the relative importance of attributes of a product/service and calculates utilities in different levels under each attribute. The relative importance of each attribute is evaluated by the ranges of part-worth/utility function under each attribute and total ranges of part-worths. Conjoint analysis can be executed through two approaches: (a) pair-wise comparison approach and (b) full profile approach. Here, dummy variables are used for constructing the regression equation in conjoint analysis.

KEY TERMS

conjoint analysis (292)
part-worth function (292)
pair-wise comparison approach (293)
full profile approach (293)
dummy variables (294)
regression equation (294)
constraint equation (296)

EXERCISES

1. What is conjoint analysis? Explain the use of conjoint analysis in research study with an example.
2. Differentiate between pair-wise comparison approach and full profile approach in conjoint analysis with an example.
3. Explain the importance of dummy variables in conjoint analysis.
4. What do you mean by part-worth/utility function?
5. An organization wants to enter the health drinks market and finds out the most preferable attributes with various levels. Three attributes and their levels are taken in this study as given in the table that follows:

Attributes	Level No.	Level Description
Price	1	₹80
	2	₹40
	3	₹60
Availability	1	Excellent
	2	Good
	3	Average
Packaging	1	Glass bottle
	2	Plastic bottle
	3	Tetra pack
Quality	1	Outstanding
	2	Excellent
	3	Good

CHAPTER

22

Discriminant Analysis

LEARNING OBJECTIVES

After studying this chapter, you should be able to

- Understand the concept and use of discriminant analysis in a research study.
- Learn the theoretical calculations required in discriminant analysis.
- Know the use of SPSS software in discriminant analysis.
- Interpret discriminant analysis results through graphical representation.
- Learn the use of multiple discriminant analysis in research study through SPSS.

22.1. CONCEPT OF DISCRIMINANT ANALYSIS

Discriminant analysis is used to identify the variables which are relatively better in discriminating between two or more than two groups. Here, dependent variable is categorical in nature and independent variables are generally interval type. If we compare discriminant analysis with multiple regression, it is observed that dependent variable deals with metric data in the case of multiple regression but the dependent variable of discriminant analysis always deals with categorical data. In the case of independent variables, both (discriminant analysis and multiple regression) deal with metric data.

22.2. OBJECTIVES OF DISCRIMINANT ANALYSIS

The major objectives of discriminant analysis are as follows:

1. To determine the important independent variables which are relatively significant in discriminating between groups.
2. To develop a discriminant function with linear combination of independent variables for discriminating different categories under dependent variable.

3. To examine the statistical significance of the discriminant model function and check whether the significant difference exists among the groups with the help of independent variables.
4. To develop the processes for assigning new product or service whose profiles are known but group identity is unknown to one of the groups; also, discriminant analysis evaluates the correctness of classification.

22.3. DISCRIMINANT ANALYSIS MODEL

Discriminant analysis creates an equation which provides a linear combination of independent variables and helps to determine the relative importance of variables for discriminating groups on the value of the discriminant score (discussed later in this chapter). The mathematical equation of the discriminant analysis model can be presented as follows:

$$Y = b_0 + b_1 \times X_1 + b_2 \times X_2 + b_3 \times X_3 + \ldots + b_n \times X_n$$

where Y = Discriminant score, X_1, X_2, X_3, ..., X_n = Independent variables and b_1, b_2, b_3,..., b_n = Coefficients of independent variables/Discriminant coefficient.

22.4. ILLUSTRATION OF DISCRIMINANT ANALYSIS WITH EXAMPLE

Example: A soap manufacturing organization has launched a new toilet soap brand in the present market. This organization desires to categorize users into two different groups ('preferred user' and 'non-preferred user') depending on the characteristics of the consumers. A survey is conducted and all relevant data are collected from 40 users on different attributes on a 9-point scale. These attributes are (a) good cleaning power, (b) good fragrance, (c) low shrinkage, (d) low price and (e) good packaging. Collected data are shown in Tables 22.1 and 22.13 as 'analysis sample' and 'hold-out sample'. In this case, discriminant analysis is used to point out the variables which are relatively more important in discriminating between 'preferred' and 'non-preferred' users.

TABLE 22.1
Collected Data for a Soap Manufacturing Organization (Analysis Sample)

S. No.	'Preferred' (1)/ 'Non-preferred Users' (2)	Good Cleaning Power (9-point Scale)	Good Fragrance (9-point Scale)	Low Shrinkage (9-point Scale)	Low Price (9-point Scale)	Good Packaging (9-point Scale)
1	1	6	6	7	6	6
2	1	7	6	8	5	6
3	1	6	5	6	6	5
4	1	6	6	6	5	5
5	1	7	7	8	6	5
6	1	7	7	7	6	8
7	1	6	5	5	4	5

(Table 22.1 Continued)

(Table 22.1 Continued)

S. No.	'Preferred' (1)/ 'Non-preferred Users' (2)	Good Cleaning Power (9-point Scale)	Good Fragrance (9-point Scale)	Low Shrinkage (9-point Scale)	Low Price (9-point Scale)	Good Packaging (9-point Scale)
8	1	6	6	6	5	5
9	1	8	5	6	5	7
10	1	5	5	5	4	5
11	1	6	5	6	6	7
12	1	6	6	8	6	6
13	1	7	7	7	7	6
14	1	7	5	6	7	5
15	1	8	7	6	8	6
16	2	4	3	4	4	6
17	2	4	4	5	4	4
18	2	6	4	4	6	5
19	2	4	3	4	4	5
20	2	6	3	4	6	6
21	2	4	5	5	6	6
22	2	5	3	4	4	5
23	2	5	4	4	6	5
24	2	4	3	4	7	6
25	2	5	4	4	7	5
26	2	4	5	3	6	6
27	2	6	5	4	5	6
28	2	5	3	3	6	5
29	2	6	3	4	7	4
30	2	4	3	5	5	5

Source: Authors.

22.5. DISCRIMINANT ANALYSIS WITH SPSS

After putting data and variable in the 'Data View' window and 'Variable View' window, click Analyze → Classify → Discriminant in the SPSS window. One pop-up window will appear as 'Discriminant Analysis'. Then send independent variables such as 'Good cleaning power', 'Good fragrance', 'Low shrinkage', 'Low price', 'Good packaging' to 'Independents' and send groups such as 'Preference' to 'Grouping Variables'. Then click on 'Define Range' and one pop-up window will appear as 'Discriminant Analysis: Define Range'. In this dialog box, enter '1' in 'Minimum' box (Group with the first category) and enter '2' in the 'Maximum' box (Group with the second category; Exhibit 22.1).

EXHIBIT 22.1
SPSS Window for Discriminant Analysis (Step 1)

Then click 'Continue'. In the 'Discriminant Analysis' dialog box, go to 'Statistics' and another pop-up window will appear as 'Discriminant Analysis: Statistics'. In this dialog box, go to 'Descriptives' and tick 'Means' and 'Univariate ANOVAs'. Then go to 'Function Coefficients' and tick 'Unstandardized'. After that, go to 'Matrices' and tick 'Within-groups correlation' (Exhibit 22.2).

EXHIBIT 22.2
SPSS Window for Discriminant Analysis (Step 2)

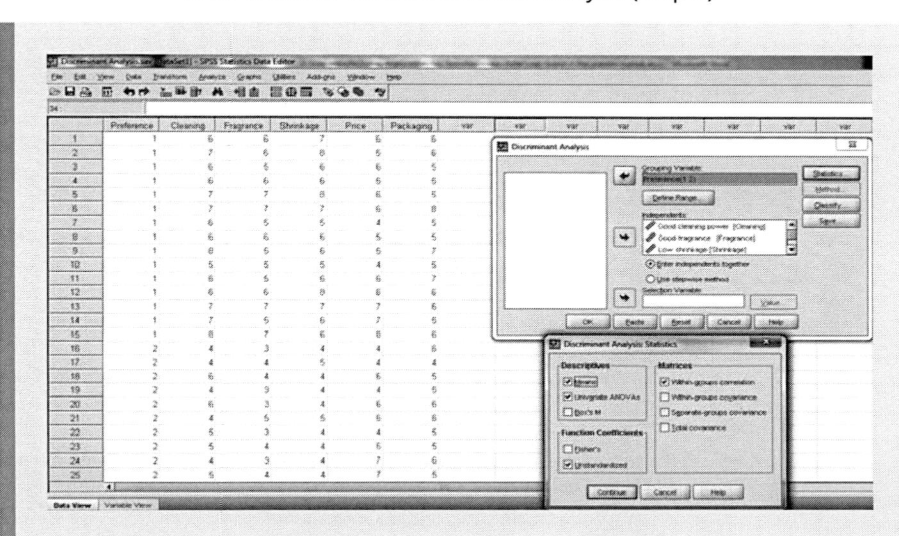

Then click 'Continue'. Once again, in the 'Discriminant Analysis' dialog box, go to 'Classify' and another pop-up window will appear as 'Discriminant Analysis: Classification'. In this dialog box, go to 'Display' and tick 'Summary table' and 'Leave-one-out classification' (Exhibit 22.3).

EXHIBIT 22.3
SPSS Window for Discriminant Analysis (Step 3)

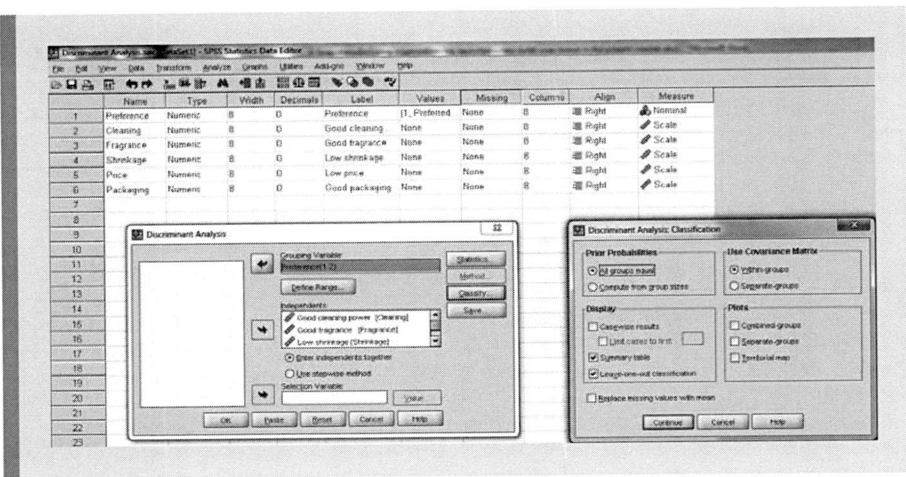

Then click 'Continue'. Once again, in the 'Discriminant Analysis' dialog box, go to 'Save' and another pop-up window will appear as 'Discriminant Analysis: Save'. In this dialog box, tick 'Predicted group membership' and 'Discriminant scores' (Exhibit 22.4).

EXHIBIT 22.4
SPSS Window for Discriminant Analysis (Step 4)

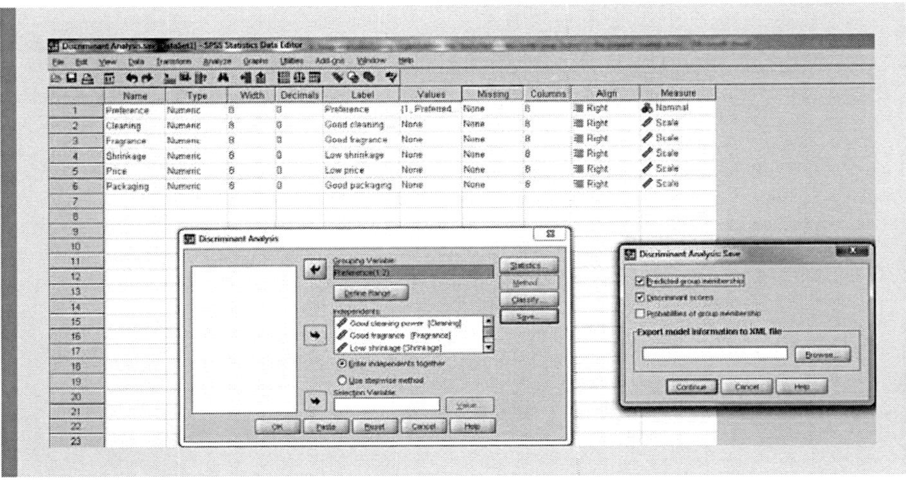

TABLE 22.2
Canonical Discriminant Function Coefficients (1)

	Function 1
Good cleaning power	0.661
Good fragrance	0.586
Low shrinkage	0.682
Low price	–0.358
Good packaging	–0.071
(Constant)	–7.721
Unstandardized coefficients	

Source: Authors.

Then click 'Continue'. At last, click 'OK' in the 'Discriminant Analysis' dialog box. Then, an SPSS output box will appear as shown in Table 22.2.

22.5.1. Unstandardized Discriminant Function and Eigen Value

In the discriminant function, unstandardized coefficients are the multipliers of the independent variables.

The estimated discriminant function can be written as follows:

$$Y = -7.721 + 0.661 \times X_1 + 0.586 \times X_2 + 0.682 \times X_3 - 0.358 \times X_4 - 0.071 \times X_5,$$

where Y = Discriminant score; X_1 = Good cleaning power; X_2 = Good fragrance; X_3 = Low shrinkage; X_4 = Low price; X_5 = Good packaging.

Discriminant score is computed by multiplying the values of independent variables by unstandardized coefficients and constant term is added with the total sum. The discriminant score corresponding to the 30 'Analysis Sample' observations can be calculated as shown in Table 22.3.

Actually, the estimation of the discriminant function indicates that the sum of squares between the groups relative to the sum of squares within the groups should be maximized. So eigen values are calculated by dividing between-groups variance by within-group variance. A large eigen value is desirable for a strong function.

Here, the eigen value is 4.203 as the desirable large value with 100% variance explained (shown in Table 22.4). Also, canonical correlation (0.899) emphasizes the correlation coefficient between discriminant score and its corresponding categories (preferred users or non-preferred users). So, $(0.899)^2 = 0.8082$, which indicates 80.82% variance between 'preferred users' and 'non-preferred users' in the discriminating model, is present because of the variations of five independent variables.

22.5.2. Group Centroids

The average value of the discriminant score for each category (preferred users or non-preferred users) is called centroid. Also, the number of groups indicates the equal number of centroids. In this example, two group discriminant analyses provide two centroids. The weighted average of all the centroids is called a 'group centroid'.

TABLE 22.3
Discriminant Score Calculations

1	Y = −7.721 + 0.661 × 6 + 0.586 × 6 + 0.682 × 7 − 0.358 × 6 − 0.071 × 6 = 1.96
2	Y = −7.721 + 0.661 × 7 + 0.586 × 6 + 0.682 × 8 − 0.358 × 5 − 0.071 × 6 = 3.66
3	Y = −7.721 + 0.661 × 6 + 0.586 × 5 + 0.682 × 6 − 0.358 × 6 − 0.071 × 5 = 0.76
4	Y = −7.721 + 0.661 × 6 + 0.586 × 6 + 0.682 × 6 − 0.358 × 5 − 0.071 × 5 = 1.71
5	Y = −7.721 + 0.661 × 7 + 0.586 × 7 + 0.682 × 8 − 0.358 × 6 − 0.071 × 5 = 3.96
6	Y = −7.721 + 0.661 × 7 + 0.586 × 7 + 0.682 × 7 − 0.358 × 6 − 0.071 × 8 = 3.07
7	Y = −7.721 + 0.661 × 6 + 0.586 × 5 + 0.682 × 5 − 0.358 × 4 − 0.071 × 5 = 0.80
8	Y = −7.721 + 0.661 × 6 + 0.586 × 6 + 0.682 × 6 − 0.358 × 5 − 0.071 × 5 = 1.71
9	Y = −7.721 + 0.661 × 8 + 0.586 × 5 + 0.682 × 6 − 0.358 × 5 − 0.071 × 7 = 2.30
10	Y = −7.721 + 0.661 × 5 + 0.586 × 5 + 0.682 × 5 − 0.358 × 4 − 0.071 × 5 = 0.14
11	Y = −7.721 + 0.661 × 6 + 0.586 × 5 + 0.682 × 6 − 0.358 × 6 − 0.071 × 7 = 0.62
12	Y = −7.721 + 0.661 × 6 + 0.586 × 6 + 0.682 × 8 − 0.358 × 6 − 0.071 × 6 = 2.64
13	Y = −7.721 + 0.661 × 7 + 0.586 × 7 + 0.682 × 7 − 0.358 × 7 − 0.071 × 6 = 2.85
14	Y = −7.721 + 0.661 × 7 + 0.586 × 5 + 0.682 × 6 − 0.358 × 7 − 0.071 × 5 = 1.07
15	Y = −7.721 + 0.661 × 8 + 0.586 × 7 + 0.682 × 6 − 0.358 × 8 − 0.071 × 6 = 2.47
16	Y = −7.721 + 0.661 × 4 + 0.586 × 3 + 0.682 × 4 − 0.358 × 4 − 0.071 × 6 = −2.45
17	Y = −7.721 + 0.661 × 4 + 0.586 × 4 + 0.682 × 5 − 0.358 × 4 − 0.071 × 4 = −1.04
18	Y = −7.721 + 0.661 × 6 + 0.586 × 4 + 0.682 × 4 − 0.358 × 6 − 0.071 × 5 = −1.19
19	Y = −7.721 + 0.661 × 4 + 0.586 × 3 + 0.682 × 4 − 0.358 × 4 − 0.071 × 5 = −2.38
20	Y = −7.721 + 0.661 × 6 + 0.586 × 3 + 0.682 × 4 − 0.358 × 6 − 0.071 × 6 = −1.84
21	Y = −7.721 + 0.661 × 4 + 0.586 × 5 + 0.682 × 5 − 0.358 × 6 − 0.071 × 6 = −1.31
22	Y = −7.721 + 0.661 × 5 + 0.586 × 3 + 0.682 × 4 − 0.358 × 4 − 0.071 × 5 = −1.72
23	Y = −7.721 + 0.661 × 5 + 0.586 × 4 + 0.682 × 4 − 0.358 × 6 − 0.071 × 5 = −1.85
24	Y = −7.721 + 0.661 × 4 + 0.586 × 3 + 0.682 × 4 − 0.358 × 7 − 0.071 × 6 = −3.52
25	Y = −7.721 + 0.661 × 5 + 0.586 × 4 + 0.682 × 4 − 0.358 × 7 − 0.071 × 5 = −2.21
26	Y = −7.721 + 0.661 × 4 + 0.586 × 5 + 0.682 × 3 − 0.358 × 6 − 0.071 × 6 = −2.68
27	Y = −7.721 + 0.661 × 6 + 0.586 × 5 + 0.682 × 4 − 0.358 × 5 − 0.071 × 6 = −0.31
28	Y = −7.721 + 0.661 × 5 + 0.586 × 3 + 0.682 × 3 − 0.358 × 6 − 0.071 × 5 = −3.12
29	Y = −7.721 + 0.661 × 6 + 0.586 × 3 + 0.682 × 4 − 0.358 × 7 − 0.071 × 4 = −2.06
30	Y = −7.721 + 0.661 × 4 + 0.586 × 3 + 0.682 × 5 − 0.358 × 5 − 0.071 × 5 = −2.05

Source: Authors.

TABLE 22.4
Eigen Value (1)

Function	Eigen Value	Percentage of Variance	Cumulative Percentage	Canonical Correlation
1	4.203[a]	100.0	100.0	0.899

Source: Authors.
Note: [a]One canonical discriminant function was used in the analysis.

TABLE 22.5
Functions at Group Centroids (1)

Preference	Function
	1
Preferred users	1.981
Non-preferred users	−1.981

Source: Authors.
Note: Unstandardized canonical discriminant functions evaluated at group means.

Table 22.5 shows the centroid values of 1.981 and −1.981 for preferred and non-preferred users, respectively. It helps to classify the individual customers into different categories. In this case, the value of group centroid is zero because the sample size (15) of two categories is the same.

Group centroid (C) = $\frac{n_1C_1 + n_2C_2}{n_1 + n_2}$, where n_1 and n_2 = sample size of different categories

C_1 and C_2 = Centroids for individual category

$$\frac{15\times(1.981)+15\times(-1.981)}{15+15} = 0.$$

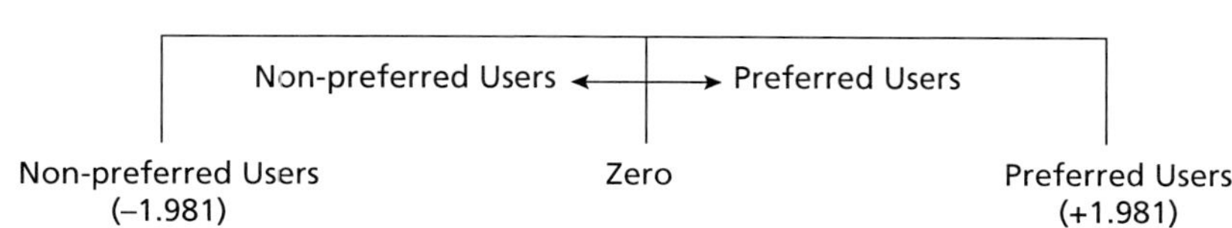

The preceding diagram depicts that the customer whose discriminant score is greater than zero is classified as 'preferred user' and the customer whose discriminant score is less than zero are classified as 'non-preferred user'. As 'Good cleaning power', 'Good fragrance' and 'Low shrinkage' have the positive unstandardized coefficient values, the high score of these attributes can classify the customers into 'preferred user'. On the other hand, 'Low price' and 'Good packaging' have the negative unstandardized coefficient values, so the high score of these attributes can classify the customers into 'non-preferred user'.

22.5.3. Descriptive Statistics and Correlation Matrix

Here, two categories (preferred users and non-preferred users) are to be compared with the help of five attributes. So mean score with standard deviation can provide us a generalized idea about the differences of categories.

Table 22.6 shows that the mean scores of all five attributes under 'Preferred users' have the higher values than the mean scores of the respective five attributes under 'Non-preferred users'. So we can say that all independent variables are useful in discriminating between two categories (preferred users and non-preferred users) in this case. As the standard deviation is high, the variability of the attribute 'Price' is also high for this example.

TABLE 22.6
Group Statistics (1)

Preference		Mean	Std. Deviation	Valid *N* (List-wise)	
				Unweighted	Weighted
Preferred users	Good cleaning power	6.53	0.834	15	15.000
	Good fragrance	5.87	0.834	15	15.000
	Low shrinkage	6.47	0.990	15	15.000
	Low price	5.73	1.100	15	15.000
	Good packaging	5.80	0.941	15	15.000
Non-preferred users	Good cleaning power	4.80	0.862	15	15.000
	Good fragrance	3.67	0.816	15	15.000
	Low shrinkage	4.07	0.594	15	15.000
	Low price	5.53	1.125	15	15.000
	Good packaging	5.27	0.704	15	15.000
Total	Good cleaning power	5.67	1.213	30	30.000
	Good fragrance	4.77	1.382	30	30.000
	Low shrinkage	5.27	1.461	30	30.000
	Low price	5.63	1.098	30	30.000
	Good packaging	5.53	0.860	30	30.000

Source: Authors.

TABLE 22.7
Tests of Equality of Group Means (1)

	Wilks' Lambda	F-value	df1	df2	Sig. (*p*-value)
Good cleaning power	**0.472**	31.338	1	28	**0.000**
Good fragrance	**0.344**	53.308	1	28	**0.000**
Low shrinkage	**0.302**	64.800	1	28	**0.000**
Low price	**0.991**	0.242	1	28	**0.626**
Good packaging	**0.901**	3.090	1	28	**0.090**

Source: Authors.
Note: Bold values indicate estimations with significance level.

Here, one-way ANOVA is executed to identify the attribute for which any significant difference exists between the mean of two categories, where 'Good cleaning power' 'Good fragrance', 'Low shrinkage', 'Low price' and 'Good packaging' are treated as dependent variables and preferred user/non-preferred user as an independent variable. The significance of the one-way ANOVA test is calculated by the corresponding *p*-values. Here, Table 22.7 shows that a significant difference exists between the mean of two categories for 'Good cleaning power' 'Good fragrance' and 'Low shrinkage' as the *p*-values are less than 0.001. The other two attributes 'Low price' and 'Good packaging' have no contribution to create the significant difference between the mean of two categories, as the *p*-values are greater than 0.05.

The 'pooled within-groups matrices' is formed by averaging all the groups' correlation matrices. It is very useful for checking multicollinearity (high correlation exists between independent variables). If the

TABLE 22.8
Pooled Within-groups Matrices (1)

		Good Cleaning Power	Good Fragrance	Low Shrinkage	Low Price	Good Packaging
Correlation	Good cleaning power	1.000	0.208	0.076	0.444	0.172
	Good fragrance	0.208	1.000	0.385	0.316	0.257
	Low shrinkage	0.076	0.385	1.000	0.092	0.112
	Low price	0.444	0.316	0.092	1.000	0.157
	Good packaging	0.172	0.257	0.112	0.157	1.000

Source: Authors.

TABLE 22.9
Wilks' Lambda (1)

Test of Function(s)	Wilks' Lambda	Chi-square	df	Sig.
1	0.192	42.057	5	0.000

Source: Authors.

correlation coefficient between two independent variables exceeds 0.75, the problem of multicollinearity is prominent in that case. In this situation, one of the two attributes should be removed for further analysis. Table 22.8 shows that all correlation coefficients do not exceed 0.75 in this example. So the problem regarding multicollinearity does not exist here.

22.5.4. Significance of Discriminant Function

As shown in the range of Wilks' lambda value is 0–1. The significance of the discriminant function increases as Wilks' lambda value decreases. Therefore, zero value is the most preferred value for Wilks' lambda. For testing the statistical significance of Wilks' lambda, a chi-square test is used. Here, the chi-square value is 42.057 with 5 degrees of freedom and *p*-value is less than 0.001. So the discriminant function is significant here at 1% level of significance (Table 22.9).

22.5.5. Standardized Discriminant Function Coefficient and Structural Coefficient

Here, the values of standardized discriminant function coefficients indicate the relative importance of the attributes in discriminating between two categories. Table 22.10 shows that 'Good cleaning power' and 'Low shrinkage' are the most important attributes in discriminating between 'Preferred users' and 'Non-preferred users' followed by 'Good fragrance', 'Low price' and 'Good packaging'.

Structural coefficients under structure matrix can be determined by the correlation between the discriminant score and each independent variable. In this example, the structural correlation coefficient between the discriminant score and the independent variable 'Low shrinkage' is 0.742, whereas the correlation with 'Good fragrance', 'Good cleaning power', 'Good packaging' and 'Low price' is 0.673,

TABLE 22.10
Standardized Canonical Discriminant Function Coefficients (1)

	Function 1
Good cleaning power	0.561
Good fragrance	0.483
Low shrinkage	0.557
Low price	–0.398
Good packaging	–0.059

Source: Authors.

TABLE 22.11
Structure Matrix (1)

	Function 1
Low shrinkage	0.742
Good fragrance	0.673
Good cleaning power	0.516
Good packaging	0.162
Low price	0.045

Source: Authors.
Notes: 1. Pooled within-groups correlations between discriminating variables and standardized canonical discriminant functions.
2. Variables ordered by absolute size of correlation within function.

0.516, 0.162 and 0.045, respectively (as shown in Table 22.11). So 'Low shrinkage', 'Good fragrance' and 'Good cleaning power' are the most important attributes in discriminating between 'Preferred users' and 'Non-preferred users' in this case followed by 'Good packaging' and 'Low price'. In both the aforementioned methods, 'Good cleaning power' and 'Low shrinkage' are the common important attributes in discriminating between 'Preferred users' and 'Non-preferred users'.

22.5.6. Classification Accuracy for Discriminant Analysis

In the classification matrix, the accurate classification is represented by the diagonal elements of the matrix. The hit ratio is defined by the corrected classified percentage of cases. It is calculated by adding the diagonal elements and dividing the sum by the total number of cases. Here, the sum of the diagonal elements is 30 (i.e., 15 + 15). So the hit ratio is 30/30 = 1, means 100%. When the size of the groups is equal, the percentage of chance classification is calculated by one divided by the number of groups. In our example, the percentage of chance classification is 0.5 (i.e., 1/2) means 50%. Generally, if the classification accuracy from the discriminant analysis is 25% greater than the percentage of chance classification, then the validity of the discriminant analysis is satisfactory. Here, 100% of original grouped cases (hit ratio = 100%) correctly classified and 93.3% of cross-validated grouped cases (hit ratio = 93.3%) correctly classified (see Table 22.12). As improvement over chance classification is greater than 25%, the validity of the discriminant analysis is satisfactory.

When the size of the groups is unequal, the maximum chance criterion and the proportional chance criterion are used to check the validity of discriminant analysis. In the case of maximum chance

TABLE 22.12
Classification Results (1)

		Preference	Predicted Group Membership: Preferred Users	Predicted Group Membership: Non-preferred Users	Total
Original	**Count**	Preferred users	15	0	15
		Non-preferred users	0	15	15
	%	Preferred users	100.0	0.0	100.0
		Non-preferred users	0.0	100.0	100.0
Cross-validated[a]	**Count**	Preferred users	14	1	15
		Non-preferred users	1	14	15
	%	Preferred users	93.3	6.7	100.0
		Non-preferred users	6.7	93.3	100.0

Source: Authors.

Notes: 1. [a]Cross-validation is done only for those cases in the analysis. In cross-validation, each case is classified by the functions derived from all cases other than that case.
2. 100% of original grouped cases correctly classified.
3. 93.3% of cross-validated grouped cases correctly classified.

criterion, randomly selected cases are assigned to a larger group to make the most of the proportion of cases correctly classified. In the case of proportional chance criterion, randomly selected cases are assigned to a group depending on the original proportion in the sample. Proportional chance criterion is calculated by the following formula:

$$C_{\text{proportional}} = (\text{Proportion of individuals belonging to Group 1})^2 + (\text{Proportion of individuals belonging to Group 2})^2$$

For 60% 'Preferred users' and 40% 'Non-preferred users', proportional chance criterion equals:

$$C_{\text{proportional}} = (0.60)^2 + (0.30)^2 = 0.45.$$

Thus, improvement over chance classification is desirable in the case of 100% and 93.3% classification accuracy.

22.5.7. Hold-out Sample Performance

The following procedure is used to check the validity of the discriminant function model. Table 22.13 represents the data regarding five attributes which help to construct the model. Here, 10 observations are utilized as a hold-out sample to test the validity of the model.

Similar to 'analysis sample', the estimated discriminant function for 'hold-out sample' is formed with the help of SPSS output.

$$Y = -13.147 + 0.696 \times X_1 + 0.534 \times X_2 + 1.248 \times X_3 - 0.524 \times X_4 + 0.\ 594 \times X_5,$$

where Y = Discriminant score; X_1 = Good cleaning power; X_2 = Good fragrance; X_3 = Low shrinkage; X_4 = Low price and X_5 = Good packaging.

TABLE 22.13
Collected Data for a Soap Manufacturing Organization (Hold-out Sample)

S. No.	'Preferred' (1)/ 'Non-preferred Users' (2)	Good Cleaning Power (9-point Scale)	Good Fragrance (9-point Scale)	Low Shrinkage (9-point Scale)	Low Price (9-point Scale)	Good Packaging (9-point Scale)	Discriminant Score (Y)
1	1	7	7	8	6	5	5.27
2	1	8	5	7	4	6	5.30
3	1	7	6	6	5	7	3.96
4	1	7	7	6	4	5	3.83
5	1	8	6	7	5	6	5.31
6	2	4	2	4	6	3	–5.66
7	2	5	3	3	7	6	–4.42
8	2	3	4	3	6	4	–5.95
9	2	5	3	2	4	5	–4.69
10	2	4	5	4	5	4	–2.94

Source: Authors.

TABLE 22.14
Canonical Discriminant Function Coefficients (2)

	Function 1
Good cleaning power	0.696
Good fragrance	0.534
Low shrinkage	1.248
Low price	–0.524
Good packaging	0.594
(Constant)	–13.147

Source: Authors.
Note: Unstandardized coefficients.

The discriminant scores corresponding to the 10 'hold-out sample' observations are mentioned in Table 22.14. It is observed that out of five 'preferred users', all five are accurately classified as their discriminant scores are greater than zero. On the other hand, out of five 'non-preferred users', all five are accurately classified as their discriminant scores are less than zero. So all the cases are accurately classified here and hold-out sample accuracy is 100%.

22.6. MULTIPLE DISCRIMINANT ANALYSIS

In multiple discriminant analysis, $(n - 1)$ discriminant functions are generated where n equals to the number of groups (more than 2) and the number of independent variables is greater than 'n'. In other words, we can say that in the case of 'n' groups and 'm' independent variables, $(n - 1)$ or 'm' (lesser value chosen) discriminant functions are generated.

22.6.1. Illustration Multiple Discriminant Analysis with Example

Example: A motorcycle manufacturing company has conducted a market survey on a newly launched motorcycle brand in the present market. This company categorizes the customers into three different groups (satisfied, neutral and dissatisfied) based on their satisfaction level on product and service quality. All relevant data have been collected from 34 customers on different attributes on 9-point scale. These attributes are (a) Affordable cost (b) Stylish (c) High mileage and (d) Good pickup. Tables 22.15 and 22.26 represent the collected data as 'analysis sample' and 'hold-out sample'. Here, discriminant

TABLE 22.15
Collected Data for a Motorcycle Manufacturing Organization (Analysis Sample)

S. No.	Satisfaction Level (Satisfied–3; Neutral–2; Dissatisfied–1)	Affordable Cost (9-point Scale)	Stylish (9-point Scale)	High Mileage (9-point Scale)	Good Pickup (9-point Scale)	Discriminant Score (Y_1)	Discriminant Score (Y_2)
1	3	6	5	5	5	0.68	–0.13
2	3	7	9	6	6	3.03	1.01
3	3	9	6	7	7	3.33	–0.17
4	3	4	6	9	9	2.40	–0.53
5	3	7	7	7	8	3.16	–0.52
6	3	5	5	5	5	0.27	–0.13
7	3	4	5	4	7	0.19	–2.01
8	3	5	4	6	4	–0.11	0.73
9	3	4	6	7	7	1.31	–0.16
10	2	5	6	4	3	–0.21	1.07
11	2	4	5	6	4	–0.16	1.06
12	2	5	5	5	1	–0.88	2.61
13	2	3	5	3	2	–1.91	0.92
14	2	5	4	6	5	0.18	0.04
15	2	4	6	5	3	–0.35	1.57
16	2	3	3	7	5	–0.72	0.22
17	2	4	5	5	4	–0.42	0.55
18	1	3	5	5	5	–0.53	–0.13
19	1	6	3	1	5	–1.05	–2.82
20	1	1	4	6	6	–1.14	–0.64
21	1	4	1	4	5	–1.79	–1.96
22	1	3	4	6	4	–0.91	0.73
23	1	4	3	3	1	–2.50	0.94
24	1	4	4	2	4	–1.54	–1.29
25	1	5	4	4	5	–0.33	–0.97

Source: Authors.

analysis is used to identify the variables which are relatively more important in discriminating between 'Satisfied', 'Neutral' and 'Dissatisfied' customers.

22.6.2. Multiple Discriminant Analysis with SPSS

After putting data and variable in the 'Data View' window and 'Variable View' window, click Analyze → Classify → Discriminant in the SPSS window. One pop-up window will appear as 'Discriminant Analysis'. Then send independent variables such as 'Affordable Cost', 'Stylish', 'High Mileage' and 'Good Pickup' to 'Independents' and send groups such as 'Satisfaction level' to 'Grouping Variables'. Then click on 'Define Range' and one pop-up window will appear as 'Discriminant Analysis: Define Range'. In this dialog box, enter '1' in the 'Minimum' box (group with the first category: Dissatisfied) and enter '3' in the 'Maximum' box (group with the third category: Satisfied; Exhibit 22.5).

EXHIBIT 22.5
SPSS Window for Multiple Discriminant Analysis (Step 1)

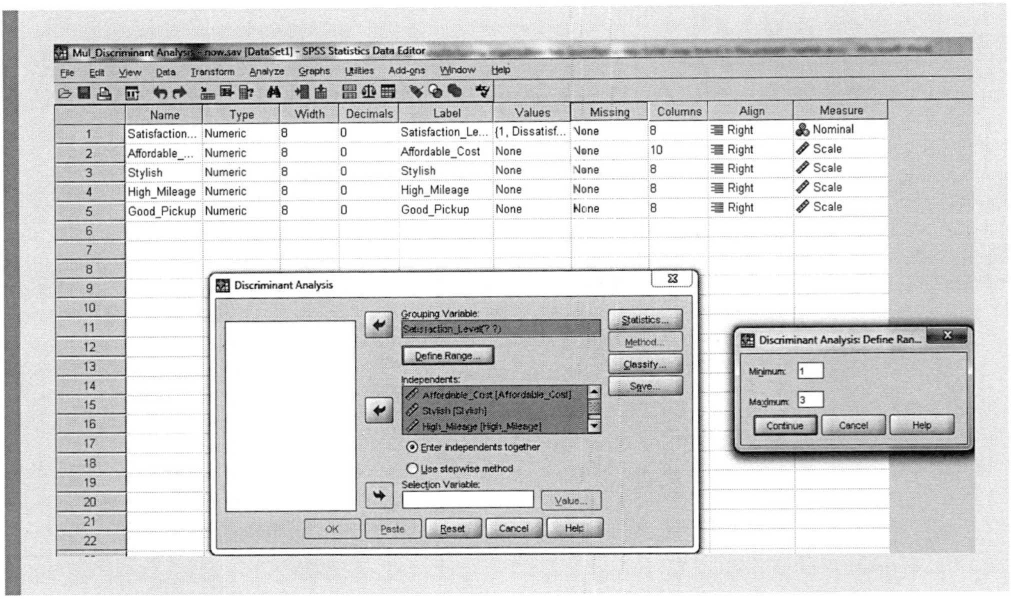

Then click 'Continue'. In the 'Discriminant Analysis' dialog box, go to 'Statistics' and another pop-up window will appear as 'Discriminant Analysis: Statistics'. In this dialog box, go to 'Descriptives' and tick 'Means' and 'Univariate ANOVAs'. Then go to 'Function Coefficients' and tick 'Unstandardized'. After that, go to 'Matrices' and tick 'Within-groups correlation' (Exhibit 22.6).

Then click 'Continue'. Once again, in the 'Discriminant Analysis' dialog box, go to 'Classify' and another pop-up window will appear as 'Discriminant Analysis: Classification'. In this dialog box, go to 'Display' and tick 'Summary table' and 'Leave-one-out classification' (Exhibit 22.7).

EXHIBIT 22.6

SPSS Window for Multiple Discriminant Analysis (Step 2)

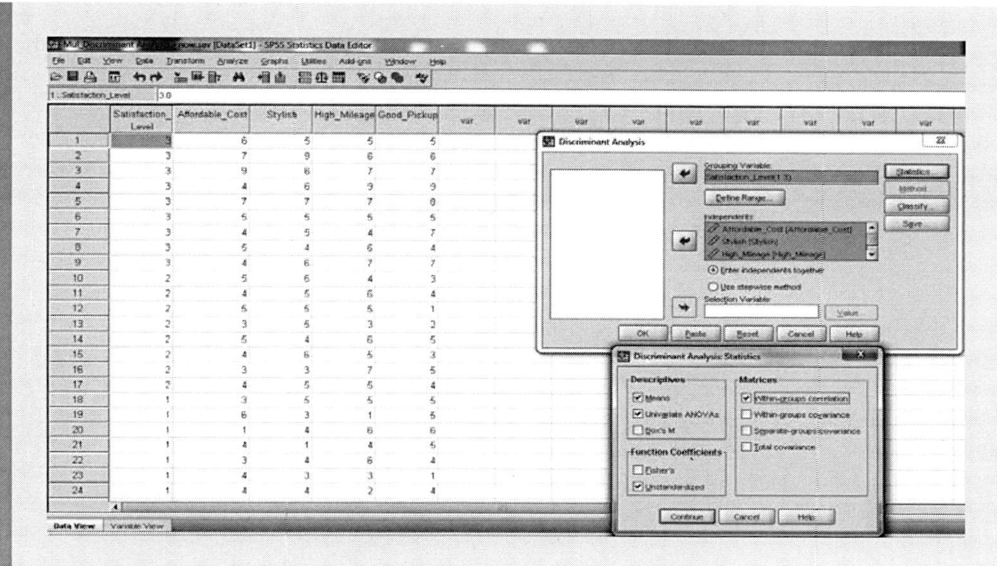

EXHIBIT 22.7

SPSS Window for Multiple Discriminant Analysis (Step 3)

Then click 'Continue'. Once again, in the 'Discriminant Analysis' dialog box, go to 'Save' and another pop-up window will appear as 'Discriminant Analysis: Save'. In this dialog box, tick 'Predicted group membership' and 'Discriminant scores' (Exhibit 22.8).

Then click 'Continue'. At last, click 'OK' in the 'Discriminant Analysis' dialog box. Then, an SPSS output box will appear as shown in Table 22.16.

EXHIBIT 22.8
SPSS Window for Multiple Discriminant Analysis (Step 4)

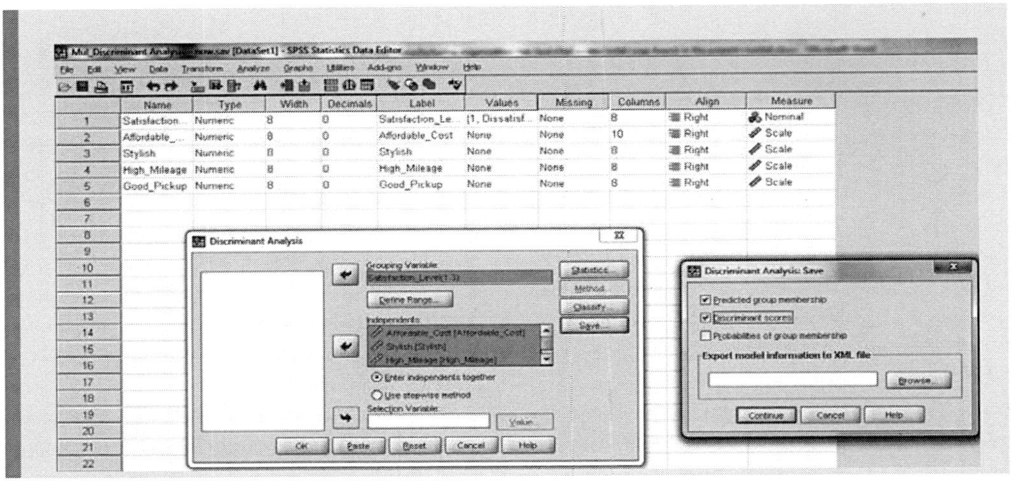

TABLE 22.16
Group Statistics (2)

Satisfaction Level		Mean	Std. Deviation	Valid N (List-wise)	
				Unweighted	Weighted
Dissatisfied	Affordable cost	3.75	1.483	8	8.000
	Stylish	3.50	1.195	8	8.000
	High mileage	3.88	1.808	8	8.000
	Good pickup	4.38	1.506	8	8.000
Neutral	Affordable cost	4.13	0.835	8	8.000
	Stylish	4.88	0.991	8	8.000
	High mileage	5.13	1.246	8	8.000
	Good pickup	3.38	1.408	8	8.000
Satisfied	Affordable cost	5.67	1.732	9	9.000
	Stylish	5.89	1.453	9	9.000
	High mileage	6.22	1.481	9	9.000
	Good pickup	6.44	1.590	9	9.000
Total	Affordable cost	4.56	1.609	25	25.000
	Stylish	4.80	1.555	25	25.000
	High mileage	5.12	1.764	25	25.000
	Good pickup	4.80	1.958	25	25.000

Source: Authors.

22.6.3. Descriptive Statistics and Correlation Matrix

Here, three categories (satisfied, neutral and dissatisfied) are to be compared with the help of four attributes. We can get a generalized idea about the differences of categories with the help of mean score and standard deviation.

Table 22.16 shows that the mean scores of all four attributes under the 'Satisfied' group have the higher values than the mean scores of respective four attributes under 'Neutral' and 'Dissatisfied' groups. On the other hand, the mean scores of three attributes (except 'Good pickup') under the 'Neutral' group have the higher values than the mean scores of respective three attributes under the 'Dissatisfied' group. So we can say that overall independent variables are responsible in discriminating between three categories (satisfied, neutral and dissatisfied) in this case. As the standard deviation is high, the variability of almost all attributes is high in this example.

Here, one-way ANOVA is executed to identify the attribute for which any significant difference exists between the mean of three categories, where 'Affordable cost', 'Stylish', 'High mileage' and 'Good pickup' are treated as dependent variables and categories with satisfied/neutral/dissatisfied group as an independent variable. The significance of one-way ANOVA test is tested by the corresponding *p*-values. Here, Table 22.17 shows that a significant difference exists between the mean of three categories for all the attributes as the *p*-values are less than 0.01 and 0.05.

As we know, if the correlation coefficient between two independent variables exceeds 0.75, the problem of multicollinearity is prominent in that case and one of the two attributes should be removed for further analysis. Table 22.18 shows that all correlation coefficients do not exceed 0.75 in this example. Thus, the problem regarding multicollinearity does not exist here.

TABLE 22.17
Tests of Equality of Group Means (2)

	Wilks' Lambda	F-value	df1	df2	Sig.
Affordable cost	**0.714**	4.409	2	22	**0.025**
Stylish	**0.582**	7.896	2	22	**0.003**
High mileage	**0.687**	5.003	2	22	**0.016**
Good pickup	**0.543**	9.251	2	22	**0.001**

Source: Authors.
Note: Bold values indicate estimations with significance level.

TABLE 22.18
Pooled Within-groups Matrices (2)

		Affordable Cost	Stylish	High Mileage	Good Pickup
Correlation	Affordable Cost	1.000	0.175	–0.287	–0.112
	Stylish	0.175	1.000	0.092	0.081
	High Mileage	–0.287	0.092	1.000	0.516
	Good Pickup	–0.112	0.081	0.516	1.000

Source: Authors.

TABLE 22.19
Wilks' Lambda (2)

Test of Function(s)	Wilks' Lambda	Chi-square	df	Sig.
1 through 2	**0.233**	29.905	8	**0.000**
2	**0.625**	9.635	3	**0.022**

Source: Authors.
Note: Bold values indicate estimations with significance level.

22.6.4. Significance of Multiple Discriminant Function

For testing the statistical significance of Wilks' lambda, a chi-square test is used. Here, chi-square values are 29.905 and 9.635 with 8 and 3 degrees of freedom, respectively and *p*-values are less than 0.01 and 0.05. So discriminant functions are significant here at 1% and 5% level of significance (Table 22.19).

22.6.5. Standardized Discriminant Function Coefficient and Structural Coefficient

Table 22.20 shows that the values of standardized discriminant function coefficients indicate the relative importance of the attributes in discriminating between three categories.

In the case as shown in Table 22.21, structural coefficients under structure matrix can be determined by the correlation between the discriminant score of any discriminant function and each independent variable.

22.6.6. Unstandardized Discriminant Function and Eigen Value

In the discriminant function, unstandardized coefficients are the multipliers of the independent variables.

TABLE 22.20
Standardized Canonical Discriminant Function Coefficients (2)

	Function	
	1	2
Affordable cost	0.572	0.000
Stylish	0.436	0.410
High mileage	0.392	0.772
Good pickup	0.434	–1.034

Source: Authors.

TABLE 22.21
Structure Matrix (2)

	Function	
	1	2
Stylish	0.608*	0.397
Good pickup	0.607*	–0.603
High mileage	0.492*	0.276
Affordable cost	0.487*	–0.035

Source: Authors.
Notes: 1. Pooled within-groups correlations between discriminating variables and standardized canonical discriminant functions.
2. Variables ordered by absolute size of correlation within function.
3. *Largest absolute correlation between each variable and any discriminant function.

TABLE 22.22
Canonical Discriminant Function Coefficients (3)

	Function	
	1	2
Affordable cost	0.403	0.000
Stylish	0.352	0.331
High mileage	0.257	0.505
Good pickup	0.288	–0.686
(Constant)	–6.223	–0.877

Source: Authors.
Note: Unstandardized coefficients.

The estimated discriminant functions using Table 22.22 can be written as follows:

$$Y_1 = -6.223 + 0.403 \times X_1 + 0.352 \times X_2 + 0.257 \times X_3 + 0.288 \times X_4$$
$$Y_2 = -0.877 + 0.331 \times X_2 + 0.505 \times X_3 - 0.686 \times X_4,$$

where Y_1 and Y_2 = Discriminant scores; X_1 = Affordable cost; X_2 = Stylish; X_3 = High mileage and X_4 = Good Pickup.

A large eigen value is always desirable for a strong function. Here, the eigen value is 1.688 as the desirable large value with 74% variance explained for the first discriminant function (shown in Table 22.23). For the second discriminant function, eigen value with percentage variance explained is not desirable.

TABLE 22.23
Eigen Values (2)

Function	Eigen Value	Percentage of Variance	Cumulative Percentage	Canonical Correlation
1	**1.688**[a]	73.8	73.8	**0.792**
2	**0.600**[a]	26.2	100.0	**0.612**

Source: Authors.
Notes: 1. Bold values indicate estimations with significance level.
2. [a]Two canonical discriminant functions were used in the analysis.

TABLE 22.24
Functions at Group Centroids (2)

Satisfaction_Level	Function 1	Function 2
Dissatisfied	–1.226	–0.767
Neutral	–0.558	1.006
Satisfied	1.586	–0.212

Source: Authors.
Note: Unstandardized canonical discriminant functions evaluated at group means.

22.6.7. Group Centroids

From Figure 22.1, it is observed that the 'Satisfied' group has the highest value on Function 1. The 'Dissatisfied' group has the lowest value on Function 1. As per the earlier discussion (Table 22.22), 'Affordable cost' and 'Stylish' attributes are strongly associated with Function 1. It means that the attributes of 'Affordable cost' and 'Stylish' of a motorcycle make customers more satisfied.

Also, it is observed that the 'Neutral' group has the highest value on Function 2. The 'Dissatisfied' group has the lowest value on Function 2. As per the earlier discussion (Table 22.22), 'Good pickup' and 'High mileage' attributes are strongly associated with Function 2. It means that the attributes of 'Good pickup' and 'High mileage' of a motorcycle make customers neutral. Even with unaffordable cost, the 'Neutral' group is more inclined towards 'Good pickup'.

FIGURE 22.1
Canonical Discriminant Functions

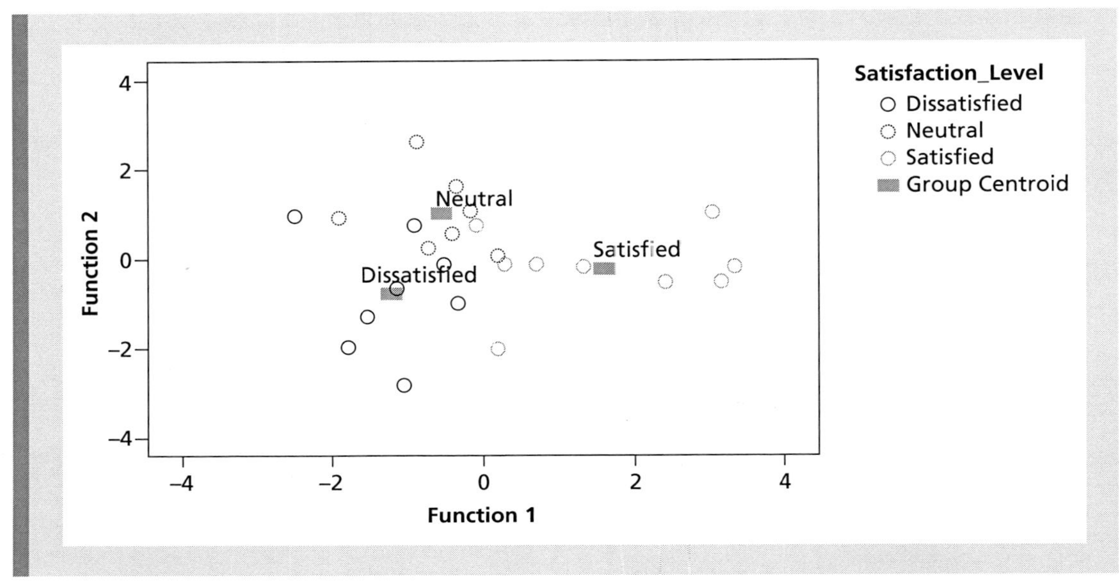

FIGURE 22.2
Territorial Map

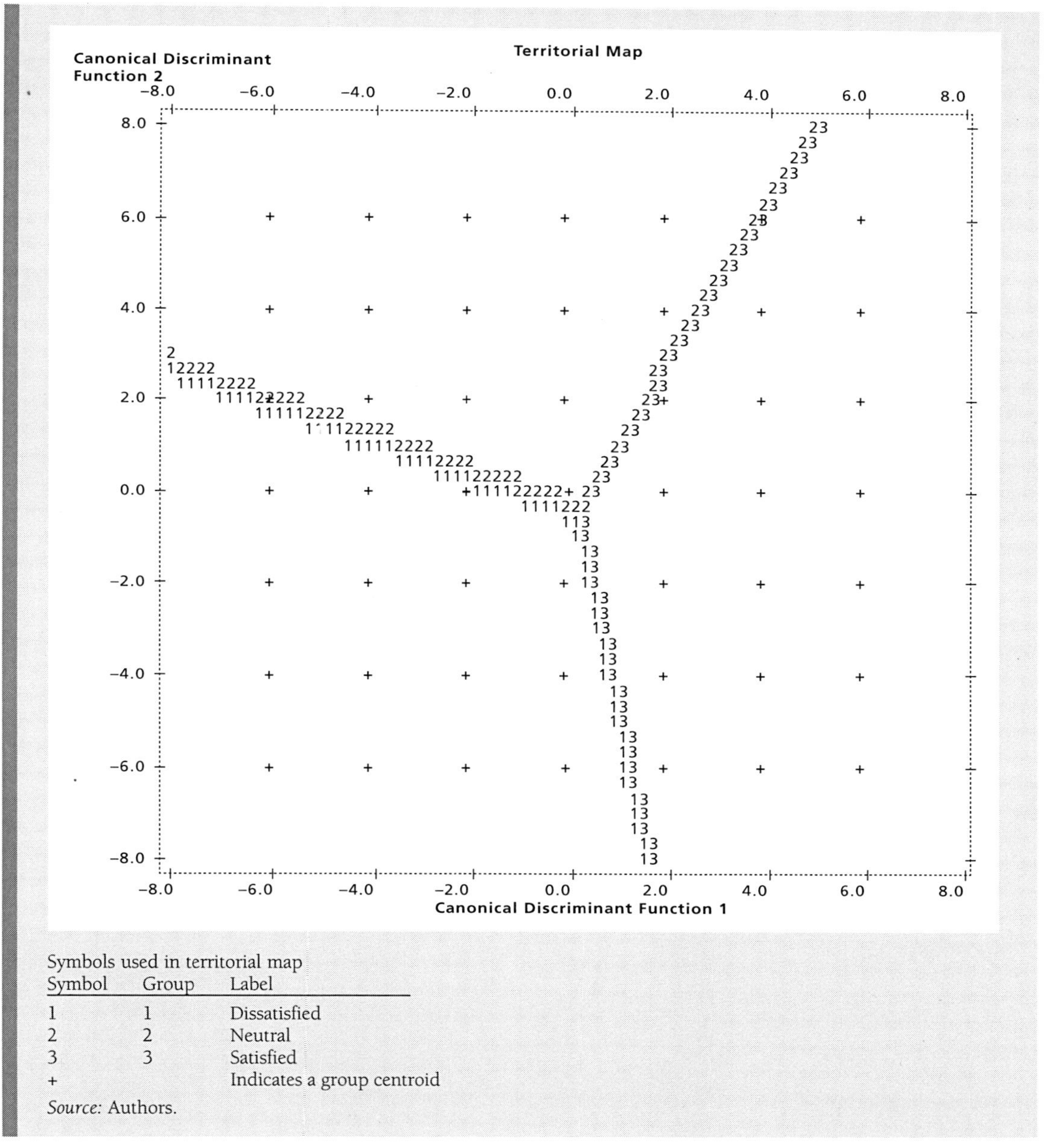

Symbols used in territorial map

Symbol	Group	Label
1	1	Dissatisfied
2	2	Neutral
3	3	Satisfied
+		Indicates a group centroid

Source: Authors.

Figure 22.2 shows the territorial map for multiple discriminant analysis. Here, asterisk denotes the group centroid in the territorial plot. Group boundaries are indicated by the scattered numbers corresponding to the individual categories. In this case, the centroid of 'Satisfied', 'Neutral' and 'Dissatisfied' groups are surrounded by number 3, 2 and 1, respectively.

TABLE 22.25
Classification Results (2)

		Satisfaction_Level	Predicted Group Membership			Total
			Dissatisfied	Neutral	Satisfied	
Original	Count	Dissatisfied	6	2	0	8
		Neutral	0	8	0	8
		Satisfied	1	1	7	9
	%	Dissatisfied	75.0	25.0	0.0	100.0
		Neutral	0.0	100.0	0.0	100.0
		Satisfied	11.1	11.1	77.8	100.0
Cross-validated[a]	Count	Dissatisfied	5	3	0	8
		Neutral	2	5	1	8
		Satisfied	1	2	6	9
	%	Dissatisfied	62.5	37.5	0.0	100.0
		Neutral	25.0	62.5	12.5	100.0
		Satisfied	11.1	22.2	66.7	100.0

Source: Authors.
Notes: 1. [a]Cross-validation is done only for those cases in the analysis. In cross validation, each case is classified by the functions derived from all cases other than that case.
2. 84.0% of original grouped cases correctly classified.
3. 64.0% of cross-validated grouped cases correctly classified.

TABLE 22.26
Collected Data for a Motorcycle Manufacturing Organization (Hold-out Sample)

S. No.	Satisfaction Level (Satisfied–3; Neutral–2; Dissatisfied–1)	Affordable Cost (9-point Scale)	Stylish (9-point Scale)	High Mileage (9-point Scale)	Good Pickup (9-point Scale)	Discriminant Score (Y_1)	Discriminant Score (Y_2)
1	3	9	7	6	7	5.49	2.52
2	3	4	6	8	9	5.42	1.17
3	3	5	6	7	7	4.63	0.71
4	2	5	4	5	1	2.09	–2.55
5	2	4	3	7	5	4.41	–1.69
6	2	4	5	6	4	2.25	–1.08
7	1	3	5	4	5	–7.75	1.43
8	1	3	1	4	5	–9.27	0.52
9	1	4	3	3	1	–7.27	–1.05

Source: Authors.

TABLE 22.27
Classification Results (3)

		Satisfaction Level	Predicted Group Membership Dissatisfied	Neutral	Satisfied	Total
Original	Count	Dissatisfied	3	0	0	3
		Neutral	0	3	0	3
		Satisfied	0	0	3	3
	%	Dissatisfied	100.0	0.0	0.0	100.0
		Neutral	0.0	100.0	0.0	100.0
		Satisfied	0.0	0.0	100.0	100.0
Cross-validated[a]	Count	Dissatisfied	3	0	0	3
		Neutral	0	2	1	3
		Satisfied	0	0	3	3
	%	Dissatisfied	100.0	0.0	0.0	100.0
		Neutral	0.0	66.7	33.3	100.0
		Satisfied	0.0	0.0	100.0	100.0

Source: Authors.

Notes: 1. [a]Cross validation is done only for those cases in the analysis. In cross validation, each case is classified by the functions derived from all cases other than that case.

2. 100% of original grouped cases correctly classified.

3. 88.9% of cross-validated grouped cases correctly classified.

22.6.8. Classification Accuracy for Multiple Discriminant Analysis

As shown in Table 22.25, the sum of the diagonal elements is 21 (i.e., 6 + 8 + 7). So the hit ratio is 21/25 = 0.84, that is, 84%. In our example, the percentage of chance classification is 0.33 (i.e., 1/3), meaning 33%. Already, we know if the classification accuracy from the discriminant analysis is 25% greater than the percentage of chance classification, the validity of the discriminant analysis is satisfactory. In this multiple discriminant analysis, the percentage of chance classification is 58% (i.e., 33 + 25). Here, 84.0% of original grouped cases (hit ratio = 84%) correctly classified and 64.0% of cross-validated grouped cases (hit ratio = 64%) correctly classified. As improvement over chance classification is greater than 58%, the validity of the discriminant analysis is satisfactory.

In the case of the classification matrix of 'hold-out sample' with nine observations (Table 22.26), 100% of original grouped cases (hit ratio = 100%) correctly classified and 88.9% of cross-validated grouped cases (hit ratio = 89%) correctly classified. As improvement over chance classification is greater than 58%, the validity of the discriminant analysis is satisfactory (Table 22.27).

SUMMARY

Discriminant analysis is used to identify the variables which are relatively better in discriminating between two or more than two groups. Here, dependent variable is categorical in nature and independent variables are generally interval type. In discriminant function, unstandardized coefficients are the multipliers of the independent variables. Eigen values are calculated by dividing between-groups variance by within-group variance. Large eigen value is desirable for a strong function. The average value of the discriminant score for each category is called centroid. The weighted average of all the centroids is called a 'group centroid'. Here, one-way ANOVA is executed to identify the attribute for which any significant difference exists between the mean of two categories. The 'pooled within-groups matrices' is very much useful for checking multicollinearity. The range of Wilks' lambda value is 0 to 1. The significance of discriminant function increases as the Wilks' lambda value decreases. In classification matrix, the accurate classification is represented by the diagonal elements of the matrix. The hit ratio is defined by the corrected classified percentage of cases. Hold-out sample is used to check the validity of the discriminant function model. In multiple discriminant analysis, $(n - 1)$ discriminant functions are generated where n is the number of groups (more than 2) and number of independent variables is greater than 'n'.

KEY TERMS

discriminant analysis (302)
standardized canonical discriminant function coefficients (312)
unstandardized coefficients (307)
centroids (307)
group centroid (307)
pooled within-groups matrices (310)
multicollinearity (310)
Wilks' lambda (311)
structural coefficient (311)
hit ratio (312)
hold-out sample (313)
multiple discriminant analysis (314)
territorial map (323)

EXERCISES

1. What is discriminant analysis? Describe the steps of executing discriminant analysis with a suitable example.
2. Explain the importance and usage of discriminant analysis in research study.
3. Differentiate regression and discriminant analysis.
4. Differentiate standardized discriminant function coefficients and structural coefficients.
5. Define canonical correlation. What is its contribution in a discriminant analysis?
6. Define Wilks' lambda. How it is used in discriminant analysis?
7. Explain hit ratio with a suitable example.

CHAPTER

23

Report Writing

LEARNING OBJECTIVE

After studying this chapter, you should be able to

- Learn the procedure of report writing.

23.1. FORMAT FOR A WRITTEN REPORT

After conducting a research, a report is written by the researcher in a very systematic and pre-defined way. A good research is diluted if it is not written or presented well by the researcher. Therefore, the report must contain all the important components.

The model format of a research report is outlined as follows:

1. Title page
2. Letter of transmittal
3. Letter of authorization
4. Table of contents
5. Executive summary
    - 5.1. Objectives of the study
    - 5.2. Methodology
    - 5.3. Results
    - 5.4. Conclusions
    - 5.5. Recommendations
6. Body of the report
    - 6.1. Introduction
    - 6.2. Research objectives
    - 6.3. Research methodology
    - 6.4. Results and findings
    - 6.5. Conclusions and recommendations
    - 6.6. Limitations of the study
7. Appendix

23.1.1. Title Page

In the title page, the researcher writes the title of the study, his/her name, designation and affiliation, month and year of the study, and the name of the client for whom the research is being conducted.

23.1.2. Letter of Transmittal

In this letter, the researcher gives a very brief description of the report to the client. It may also include some personal observation of the researcher during the study.

23.1.3. Letter of Authorization

It is a formal letter issued by the sponsoring agency through which the sponsoring agency authorizes the research-conducting agency to conduct the research. It generally includes the name of the person who is giving authority to conduct the research, nature of the research project, completion date, terms of payment and so on.

23.1.4. Table of Contents

It presents the list of topics as well as corresponding page numbers to locate the information easily. The title page, letter of transmittal, letter of authorization and table of contents are given roman numbers and Arabic numbers are assigned in other pages of the report.

23.1.5. Executive Summary

Very often, executives can only go through the summary of the report due to time constraint. Therefore, executive summary is prepared in a very precise form. It mainly contains objectives of the study, methodology, results, conclusions and recommendations.

23.1.6. Body of the Report

It represents a detailed study of the research. It mainly consists of six sections discussed as follows:

Introduction: This section mainly highlights the background of the study and its relevance in order to address a particular social problem. It connects the reader with the background of the study that led to conducting the research.

Research objectives: After finding the research gap, the researcher formulates the objectives of the research. On the basis of research objectives, research questions or hypotheses are formulated.

Research methodology: The methodology contains sample size, sampling technique, sampling frame, questionnaire, data collection, test statistic and so on. Research methodology is different from research method. Research method implies a particular technique that we are using in our research for the purpose of analysis of data but the research methodology explains the logic behind the application of a particular research method.

Results and findings: This section mainly concentrates on different statistical analysis adopted in the research and the corresponding results. All the results must be presented in a very systematic way.

Conclusions and recommendations: The conclusion is arrived at from the results and findings of the research. The researcher may accept or reject the null or alternative hypothesis with the concerned level of significance. On the other hand, recommendations are made out of the critical thinking of the researcher.

Limitations of the study: Every research has its own limitations. The researcher must mention all of the limitations of his/her study in the report so that the future researchers can start their research from the limitations of the previous research.

23.1.7. Appendix

Information which is not placed in the body of the research is mentioned in the appendix part. Generally, a researcher attaches data collection forms, statistical calculations, bibliography, any supported material and so on in this section.

SUMMARY

After successful completion of the research, a report is written. It contains the title page, letter of transmittal, letter of authorization, table of contents, executive summary, results, body of the report and appendix.

KEY TERMS

letter of authorization (328)
letter of transmittal (328)
executive summary (328)

EXERCISES

1. What is letter of transmittal?
2. What do you mean by the term letter of authorization?
3. What is the purpose of executive summary?
4. Describe the body of the report.

CHAPTER

24

APA and MLA Referencing Style

LEARNING OBJECTIVES

After studying this chapter, you should be able to

- Learn the procedure of APA citation rules.
- Learn the procedure of MLA citation rules.

24.1. APA REFERENCING STYLE

The American Psychological Association (APA) style is widely accepted in the social sciences. The following sections show some of the more commonly used APA citation rules.

24.1.1. JOURNALS, MAGAZINES, NEWSPAPERS IN PRINT FORMAT

The journal title and the volume number are in italics. Issue numbers are not required if the journal is continuously paged. If paged individually, the issue number is required and is in regular type in parentheses adjacent to the volume number.

One author

Example: Williams, J. H. (2008). Employee engagement: Improving participation in safety. *Professional Safety, 53*(12), 40–45.

Two to seven authors (list all authors)

Example: Keller, T. E., Cusick, G. R., & Courtney, M. E. (2007). Approaching the transition to adulthood: Distinctive profiles of adolescents aging out of the child welfare system. *Social Services Review, 81*, 453–484.

Eight or more authors (list the first six authors ... and the last author]

Example: Wolchik, S. A., West, S. G., Sandler, I. N., Tein, J.-Y., Coatsworth, D., Lengua, L., ... Griffin, W. A. (2000). An experimental evaluation of theory-based mother and mother-child programs for children of divorce. *Journal of Consulting and Clinical Psychology, 68,* 843–856.

Magazine article

Example: Mathews, J., Berrett, D., & Brillman, D. (2005, May 16). Other winning equations. *Newsweek, 145*(20), 58–59.

Newspaper article with no author and discontinuous pages

Example: Generic Prozac debuts. (2001, August 3). *The Washington Post,* pp. E1, E4.

24.1.2. Books, Chapters in Books, Reports and so on

One author

Example: Alexie, S. (1992). *The business of fancy dancing: Stories and poems.* Brooklyn, NY: Hang Loose Press.

Corporate author with an edition and published by the corporate author

Example: American Psychiatric Association. (1994). *Diagnostic and statistical manual of mental disorders* (4th ed.). Washington, DC: Author.

Anonymous author

Example: *Dorland's illustrated medical dictionary* (31st ed.). (2007). Philadelphia, PA: Saunders.

Chapter in a book

Example: Booth-LaForce, C., & Kerns, K. A. (2009). Child–parent attachment relationships, peer relationships, and peer-group functioning. In K. H. Rubin, W. M. Bukowski, & B. Laursen (Eds.), *Handbook of peer interactions, relationships, and groups* (pp. 490–507). New York, NY: Guilford Press.

ERIC document

Example: Shyyan, V., Thurlow, M., & Liu, K. (2005). *Student perceptions of instructional strategies: Voices of English language learners with disabilities.* Minneapolis, MN: National Center on Educational Outcomes, University of Minnesota. Retrieved from the ERIC database. (ED495903)

24.1.3. Online Journals, Magazines, Newspapers

Article retrieved from an online database

Note: Use the article's digital object identifier (DOI), the unique code given by the publisher to a specific article.

Example: Senior, B., & Swailes, S. (2007). Inside management teams: Developing a teamwork survey instrument. *British Journal of Management, 18,* 138–153. doi:10.1111/j.1467-8551.2006.00507.x

Note: Use the journal's home page URL (or web address) if there is no DOI. This may require a web search to locate the journal's home page. There is no period at the end of web address. Break a long URL before the punctuation.

Example: Koo, D. J., Chitwoode, D. D., & Sanchez, J. (2008). Violent victimization and the routine activities/lifestyle of active drug users. *Journal of Drug Issues, 38,* 1105–1137. Retrieved from http://www2.criminology.fsu.edu/~jdi/

Article from an online magazine

Example: Lodewijkx, H. F. M. (2001, May 23). Individual–group continuity in cooperation and competition under varying communication conditions. *Current Issues in Social Psychology,* 6(12), 166–182. Retrieved from http://www.uiowa.edu/~grpproc/crisp/crisp.6.12.htm

24.1.4. Other Online Resources

Online report from a nongovernmental organization

Example: Kenney, G. M., Cook, A., & Pelletier, J. (2009). *Prospects for reducing uninsured rates among children: How much can premium assistance programs help?* Retrieved from Urban Institute website: http://www.urban.org/url.cfm?ID=411823

Online report with no author identified and no date

Example: *GVU's 10th WWW user survey.* (n.d.). Retrieved from http://www.cc.gatech.edu/user_surveys/survey-1998-10/

Websites in parenthetical citations

To cite an entire website (but not a specific document within the site), it is sufficient to give the URL of the site in the text. No entry in the reference list is needed.

Example: KidsPsych is an excellent website for young children (http://www.kidspsych.org).

24.1.5. Reference Citations in Text

APA utilizes a system of brief referencing in the text of a paper, whether one is paraphrasing or providing a direct quotation from another author's work. Citations in the text usually consist of the name of the author(s) and the year of publication. The page number is added when utilizing a direct quotation.

Indirect quotation with parenthetical citation

Example: Libraries historically highly value intellectual freedom and patron confidentiality (LaRue, 2007).

Indirect quotation with author as part of the narrative

Example: LaRue (2007) identified intellectual freedom and patron confidentiality as two key values held historically by libraries.

Direct quotation with parenthetical citation

Example: Darwin used the metaphor of the tree of life 'to express the other form of interconnectedness–genealogical rather than ecological' (Gould & Brown, 1991, p. 14).

Direct quotation with author as part of the narrative

Example: Gould and Brown (1991) explained that Darwin used the metaphor of the tree of life 'to express the other form of interconnectedness–genealogical rather than ecological' (p. 14).

24.1.6. Citing Secondary Sources

When citing in the text a work discussed in a secondary source, give both the primary and the secondary sources. In the example that fcllows, the study by Seidenberg and McClelland was mentioned in an article by Coltheart, Curtis, Atkins and Haller.

Example: Seidenberg and McClelland's study (as cited in Coltheart, Curtis, Atkins, & Haller, 1993) provided a glimpse into the world.

In the references page, you would cite the secondary source you read not the original study as follows:

Example: Coltheart, M., Curtis, B., Atkins, P., & Haller, M. (1993). Models of reading aloud: Dual-route and parallel-distributed-processing approaches. *Psychological Review, 100*, 589–608.

24.2. MLA REFERENCING STYLE

The Modern Language Association (MLA) style is a widely used referencing system to achieve the following two objectives:

1. How you compile a list of reference sources at the end of your text (reference list).
2. How you refer to other authors in the body of your text (in-text citation).

The following sections show some of the more commonly used MLA citation rules.

Notation guide

REF = reference list

ITC = in-text citation

24.2.1. Book with One Author

REF: Author last name, first name. Title. Place of Publication: Publisher, Year of publication.

Example: Biswas, Debasish. The Romance of Human Resource Management. Mumbai: Himalaya Publishing House, 2013.

ITC:
(Author last name page)
(Page no.)

Example:
In another study (Biswas 120)....
Biswas has discussed (120)....

24.2.2. Book with Two or Three Authors

REF: Author(s) last name, first name and last author's first name last name. Title. Place of Publication: Publisher, Year of publication.

Example: Biswas, Debasish and Dipanjan Moitra. Management Information System. Mumbai: Himalaya Publishing House, 2016.

ITC:
(Author[s] last name and last author last name page)
(Page no.)

Example:
Others highlight a different factor (Biswas and Moitra 120)....
Biswas and Moitra (120) highlight....

24.2.3. Book with More Than Three Authors

REF: First author last name, first name et al. Title. Place of Publication: Publisher, Year of publication.

Example: Biswas, Debasish et al. Industrial Relations and Labour Welfare. Delhi: Abhijeet Publications, 2014.

ITC:
(First author's last name et al. page no.)
(Page no.)

Example:
It has been explained (Biswas et al. 125)....
Biswas (125) explains....

24.2.4. Book with a Corporate Author

REF: Organization name. Title. Place of Publication: Publisher, Year of publication.

Example: Department of Agriculture, Food and Rural Development. New Delhi: Abhijeet Publications, 2015.

ITC:
(Organization name page no.)
(Page no.)

Example:
Figures released (Department of Agriculture 125) at the time....
Figures from the Department of Agriculture (125)....

24.2.5. Book with an Editor

REF: Editors(s) last name, first name and last editor's first name last name. Ed(s). Title. Place of Publication: Publisher, Year of publication.

Example: Bag, Sudin and Debasish Biswas. Ed(s). Dynamic Evolution of Management Paradigm. Midnapore: Giri Printers, 2017.

ITC:
(Editor[s]last name page no.)
(Page no.)

Example:
Another approach (Bag100) explains....
Bag (100) explains....

24.2.6. Chapter in an Edited Book

REF: Author(s) last name, first name and last author's first name last name. "Title of chapter." Title of Collection. Ed. Editor(s) first name last name and last editor first name last name. Place of Publication: Publisher, Year of publication. Page range.

Example: Roy, Nirmal. "Problems and Prospects of Small Tea Growers." Handbook of Management Cases. Ed. Debasish Biswas. New Delhi: Kalpaz, 2017. 202–212.

ITC:
(Author[s] last name page no.)
(Page no.)

Example:
Another approach (Roy 202)....
Roy (202) writes....

24.2.7. Print Journal Article

REF: Author(s) last name, first name and last author's first name last name. "Title of Article." Title of Journal. Volume. Issue (year): pages.

Example: Biswas, Debasish. "Determinants of Customer Satisfaction." Journal of Human System Management. 36.2 (2016): 124–130.

ITC:
(Author[s] last name page no.)
(Page no.)

Example:
Another author (Roy 150) explains....
Roy (150) explains....

24.2.8. E-Journal Article

REF: Author(s) last name, first name and last author's first name last name. "Title of Article." Journal title Volume. Issue (Year): Page numbers. Database. Web. Day Month Year accessed.

Example: Roy, Nirmal. "Export of Indian Tea." Bio Publisher 6.1 (2016): 23–31. EBSCO host. Web. 5 April 2016.

ITC:
(Author[s] last name page no.)
(Page no.)

Example:
Exploring this topic (Roy 200)....
Roy (200) highlights the role....

24.2.9. Print Newspaper Article

REF: Author(s) last name, first name and last author's first name last name. "Article title." Newspaper title Day Month Year of publication, Page number.

Example: Bag, Sudin. "FDI in Retail Sector." Economic Times 10 April 2016, p. 6.

ITC:
(Author[s] last name page no.)
(Page no.)

Example:
Others (Bag 6) argue....
Bag (6) argues....

24.2.10. Online Newspaper Article

REF: Author(s) last name, first name and last author's first name last name. "Article title." Newspaper Title. Website title day Month Year of publication. Medium of publication. Day Month Year accessed.

Example: Bag, Sudin. "FDI in Retail Sector." Economic Times. The Economic Times 10 April 2016. Web. 10 April 2017.

ITC: (Author[s] last name)

Example: Others (Bag) reported....

24.2.11. Page on a Website

REF: Author(s) last name, first name (if available). "Article title." Name of site. Day Month Year of resource creation (if available). Medium of publication. Day Month Year accessed.

Example: Harris, Robert. "Evaluating Internet Research Sources." Virtual Salt. 15 June 2008. Web. 27 April 2016.

ITC: Use the first few words of the page title.

Example: According to another source (Evaluating Internet Research)....

24.2.12. Website

REF: Author(s) last name, first name (if available). Name of site. Name of institution/organization affiliated with the site (sponsor or publisher), Year of resource creation (if available). Medium of publication. Day Month Year of access.

Example: Perry, Willett. Victorian Women's Writers Project. Indiana University, May. 2012. Web. 10 February 2016.

ITC: (Author last name/Website name)

Example: According to another source (Harris)....

24.2.13. Blog

REF: Author(s) last name, first name (if available). "Posting Title." Name of site, Day Month Year of publication. Medium of publication. Day Month Year of access.

Example: Giri, Arun. "Global Warming and the Future." Jane Murphy Blog, 14 Feb 2016. Web. 13 April 2017.

ITC: (Author[s] last name)

Example: According to another source (Giri)....

24.2.14. Email Communication

REF: Sender last name, first name. "Subject Title of Email." Message to the author. Day Month Year email sent. Email.

Example: Roy, Arnab. "Re: Female Literacy." Message to the author. 26 March 2016. Email.

ITC: (Sender last name)

Example: Additional figures provided (Roy) prove....

24.2.15. Interviews

REF: Interviewee(s) last name, first name. Personal Interview. Day Month Year of interview.

Example: Roy, Manik. Personal Interview. 7 September 2016.

ITC: (Interviewee[s] last name)

Example: Additional figures provided (Roy) prove....

24.2.16. Government Agency Publication

REF: Organization name. Title. Place of Publication: Publisher, Year of publication.

Example: Department of Health & Children, Ireland. A Vision for Change: Report of the Expert Group on Mental Health Policy. Dublin: Stationary Office, 2006.

ITC:
(Organization name page no.)
(Page no.)

Example:
Figures released (Department of Health & Children 125) at the time….
Figures from the Department of Health & Children (125)….

24.2.17. Parliamentary and Legal Material

REF: Jurisdiction. Series no: Title. Place of publication: Publisher, Year.

Example: Ireland. S.I. No. 139/2011: Equality, Integration, Disability and Human Rights Order 2011. Dublin: The Stationery Office, 2011.

ITC: (Short form of title)

Example: Legislation introduced at the time (Equality, Integration, Disability 2011)….

24.2.18. Conferences

REF: Author(s) last name, first name and last author's first name last name. "Title of paper." Title of conference proceedings. Place of publication: Publisher, Year. Pages. Format.

Example: Roy, Nirmal. "Towards a Greener Ireland." Discovering Our Natural Sustainable Resources. Midnapore: Vidyasagar University, 2017. 65–69. Print

ITC: (Author[s] last name)

Example: According to another source (Roy 68)….

24.2.19. Theses

REF: Author last name, first name. "Title." Degree statement. Degree-awarding body, Year. Format.

Example: Roy, Nirmal. "Managing Human Resources." PhD thesis. Vidyasagar University, 2017. Print.

ITC:
(Author last name page no.)
(Page no.)

Example:
As argued elsewhere (Roy 155)….
Roy (155) disagrees with this….

24.2.20. Audiovisual Material

REF: Title. Dir. Director's first name last name. Film studio/distributor, year. Format.

Example: The Usual Suspects. Dir. Bryan Singer. Polygram, 1995. Film.

ITC: (Title of film)

SUMMARY

The APA style and the MLA style are widely accepted in the social sciences. They prescribe the citation rules of journals, magazines and newspapers in print format, citation rule of books, chapters in books, reports and so on, citation rule of online journals, magazines and newspapers, citation rule of other online resources, reference citations in text and citing secondary sources.

KEY TERMS

APA (330)

MLA (330)

EXERCISES

1. Write the citation rule of journals, magazines and newspapers in print format.
2. Write the citation rule of books, chapters in books, reports and the likes.
3. Write the citation rule of online journals, magazines and newspapers.
4. Write the citation rule of other online resources.
5. How would you show reference citations in text?
6. How would you cite secondary sources?
7. Describe the citation rules as per the MLA style.

Appendix

TABLE A1

Areas of a Standard Normal Distribution (Between z = 0 and a Positive Value of z)

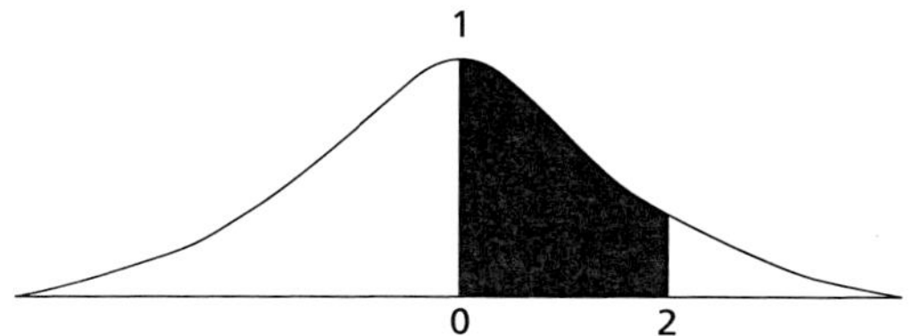

z	0	0.01	0.02	0.03	0.04	0.05	0.06	0.07	0.08	0.09
0	0	0.004	0.008	0.012	0.016	0.0199	0.0239	0.0279	0.0319	0.0359
0.1	0.0398	0.0438	0.0478	0.0517	0.0557	0.0596	0.0636	0.0675	0.0714	0.0753
0.2	0.0793	0.0832	0.0871	0.091	0.0948	0.0987	0.1026	0.1064	0.1103	0.1141
0.3	0.1179	0.1217	0.1255	0.1293	0.1331	0.1368	0.1406	0.1443	0.148	0.1517
0.4	0.1554	0.1591	0.1628	0.1664	0.17	0.1736	0.1772	0.1808	0.1844	0.1879
0.5	0.1915	0.195	0.1985	0.2019	0.2054	0.2088	0.2123	0.2157	0.219	0.2224
0.6	0.2257	0.2291	0.2324	0.2357	0.2389	0.2422	0.2454	0.2486	0.2517	0.2549
0.7	0.258	0.2611	0.2642	0.2673	0.2903	0.2734	0.2764	0.2794	0.2823	0.2852
0.8	0.2881	0.291	0.2939	0.2967	0.2995	0.3023	0.3051	0.3078	0.3106	0.3133
0.9	0.3159	0.3186	0.3212	0.3238	0.3264	0.3289	0.3315	0.334	0.3365	0.3389
1	0.3413	0.3438	0.3461	0.3485	0.3508	0.3531	0.3554	0.3577	0.3599	0.3621
1.1	0.3643	0.3665	0.3686	0.3708	0.3729	0.3749	0.377	0.379	0.381	0.383
1.2	0.3849	0.3869	0.3888	0.3907	0.3925	0.3944	0.3962	0.398	0.3997	0.4015
1.3	0.4032	0.4049	0.4066	0.4082	0.4099	0.4115	0.4131	0.4147	0.4162	0.4177
1.4	0.4192	0.4207	0.4222	0.4236	0.4251	0.4265	0.4279	0.4292	0.4306	0.4319
1.5	0.4332	0.4345	0.4357	0.437	0.4382	0.4394	0.4406	0.4418	0.4429	0.4441
1.6	0.4452	0.4463	0.4474	0.4484	0.4495	0.4505	0.4515	0.4525	0.4535	0.4545
1.7	0.4554	0.4564	0.4573	0.4582	0.4591	0.4599	0.4608	0.4616	0.4625	0.4633

(Table A1 Continued)

(Table A1 Continued)

z	0	0.01	0.02	0.03	0.04	0.05	0.06	0.07	0.08	0.09
1.8	0.4641	0.4649	0.4656	0.4664	0.4671	0.4678	0.4686	0.4693	0.4699	0.4706
1.9	0.4713	0.4719	0.4726	0.4732	0.4738	0.4744	0.475	0.4756	0.4761	0.4767
2	0.4772	0.4778	0.4783	0.4788	0.4793	0.4798	0.4803	0.4808	0.4812	0.4817
2.1	0.4821	0.4826	0.483	0.4834	0.4838	0.4842	0.4846	0.485	0.4854	0.4857
2.2	0.4861	0.4864	0.4868	0.4871	0.4875	0.4878	0.4881	0.4884	0.4887	0.489
2.3	0.4893	0.4896	0.4898	0.4901	0.4904	0.4906	0.4909	0.4911	0.4913	0.4916
2.4	0.4918	0.492	0.4922	0.4925	0.4927	0.4929	0.4931	0.4932	0.4934	0.4936
2.5	0.4938	0.494	0.4941	0.4943	0.4945	0.4946	0.4948	0.4949	0.4951	0.4952
2.6	0.4953	0.4955	0.4956	0.4957	0.4959	0.496	0.4961	0.4962	0.4963	0.4964
2.7	0.4965	0.4966	0.4967	0.4968	0.4969	0.497	0.4971	0.4972	0.4973	0.4974
2.8	0.4974	0.4975	0.4976	0.4977	0.4977	0.4978	0.4979	0.4979	0.498	0.4981
2.9	0.4981	0.4982	0.4982	0.4983	0.4984	0.4984	0.4985	0.4985	0.4986	0.4986
3	0.4987	0.4987	0.4987	0.4988	0.4988	0.4989	0.4989	0.4989	0.499	0.499

Note: Areas for negative values for z are obtained by symmetry.

TABLE A2(a)
Critical Values of F-Distribution (at 5%)

v1 v2	1	2	3	4	5	6	8	12	24	Infinity
1	161.4	199.5	215.7	224.6	230.2	234	238.9	243.9	249.1	243.3
2	18.51	19	19.16	19.25	19.3	19.33	19.37	19.41	19.45	19.5
3	10.13	9.55	9.28	9.12	9.01	8.94	8.85	8.74	8.64	8.53
4	7.71	6.94	6.59	6.39	6.26	6.16	6.04	5.91	5.77	5.63
5	6.61	5.79	5.41	5.19	5.05	4.95	4.82	4.68	4.53	4.36
6	5.99	5.14	4.76	4.53	4.39	4.28	4.15	4	3.84	3.67
7	5.59	4.74	4.35	4.12	3.97	3.87	3.73	3.57	3.41	3.23
8	5.32	4.46	4.07	3.84	3.69	3.58	3.44	3.28	3.12	2.93
9	5.12	4.26	3.86	3.63	3.48	3.37	3.23	3.07	2.9	2.71
10	4.96	4.1	3.71	3.48	3.33	3.22	3.07	2.91	2.74	2.54
11	4.84	3.98	3.59	3.36	3.2	3.09	2.95	2.79	2.61	2.4
12	4.75	3.88	3.49	3.26	3.11	3	2.85	2.69	2.51	2.3
13	4.67	3.8	3.41	3.18	3.02	2.92	2.77	2.6	2.42	2.21
14	4.6	3.74	3.34	3.11	2.96	2.85	2.7	2.53	2.35	2.13
15	4.54	3.68	3.29	3.06	2.9	2.79	2.64	2.48	2.29	2.07
16	4.49	3.63	3.24	3.01	2.85	2.74	2.59	2.42	2.24	2.01
17	4.45	3.59	3.2	2.96	2.81	2.7	2.55	2.38	2.19	1.96
18	4.41	3.55	3.16	2.93	2.77	2.66	2.51	2.34	2.15	1.92
19	4.38	3.52	3.13	2.9	2.74	2.63	2.48	2.31	2.11	1.88
20	4.35	3.49	3.1	2.87	2.71	2.6	2.45	2.28	2.08	1.84
21	4.32	3.47	3.07	2.84	2.68	2.57	2.42	2.25	2.05	1.81
22	4.3	3.44	3.05	2.82	2.66	2.55	2.4	2.23	2.03	1.78
23	4.28	3.42	3.03	2.8	2.64	2.53	2.38	2.2	2.01	1.76
24	4.26	3.4	3.01	2.78	2.62	2.51	2.36	2.18	1.98	1.73
25	4.24	3.38	2.99	2.76	2.6	2.49	2.34	2.16	1.96	1.71
26	4.22	3.37	2.98	2.74	2.59	2.47	2.32	2.15	1.95	1.69
27	4.21	3.35	2.96	2.73	2.57	2.46	2.31	2.13	1.93	1.67
28	4.2	3.34	2.95	2.71	2.56	2.45	2.29	2.12	1.91	1.65
29	4.18	3.33	2.93	2.7	2.54	2.43	2.28	2.1	1.9	1.64
30	4.17	3.32	2.92	2.69	2.53	2.42	2.27	2.09	1.89	1.62
40	4.08	3.23	2.84	2.61	2.45	2.34	2.18	2	1.79	1.51
60	4	3.15	2.76	2.52	2.37	2.25	2.1	1.92	1.7	1.39
120	3.92	3.07	2.68	2.45	2.29	2.17	2.02	1.83	1.61	1.25
Infinity	3.84	2.99	2.6	2.37	2.21	2.1	1.94	1.75	1.52	1

Notes: 1. v1 = df for greater variance
2. v2 = df for smaller variance.

TABLE A2(b)
Critical Values of F-Distribution (at 1%)

v1	1	2	3	4	5	6	8	12	24	Infinity
v2										
1	4,052	4,999.5	5,403	5,625	5,764	5,859	5,982	6,106	6,235	6,366
2	98.5	99	99.17	99.25	99.3	99.33	99.37	99.42	99.46	99.5
3	34.12	30.82	29.46	28.71	28.24	27.91	27.49	27.05	26.6	26.13
4	21.2	18	16.69	15.98	15.52	15.21	14.8	14.37	13.93	13.45
5	16.26	13.27	12.06	11.39	10.97	10.67	10.29	9.89	9.47	9.02
6	13.75	10.92	9.78	9.15	8.75	8.47	8.1	7.72	7.31	6.88
7	12.25	9.55	8.45	7.85	7.46	7.19	6.84	6.47	6.07	5.65
8	11.26	8.65	7.59	7.01	6.63	6.37	6.03	5.67	5.28	4.86
9	10.56	8.02	6.99	6.42	6.06	5.8	5.47	5.11	4.73	4.31
10	10.04	7.56	6.55	5.99	5.64	5.39	5.06	4.71	4.33	3.91
11	9.65	7.21	6.22	5.87	5.32	5.07	4.74	4.4	4.02	3.6
12	9.33	6.93	5.95	5.41	5.06	4.82	4.5	4.16	3.78	3.36
13	9.07	6.7	5.74	5.21	4.86	4.62	4.3	3.96	3.59	3.17
14	8.86	6.51	5.56	5.04	4.69	4.46	4.14	3.8	3.43	3
15	8.68	6.36	5.42	4.89	4.56	4.32	4	3.67	3.29	2.87
16	8.53	6.23	5.29	4.77	4.44	4.2	3.89	3.55	3.18	2.75
17	8.4	6.11	5.18	4.67	4.34	4.1	3.79	3.46	3.08	2.65
18	8.29	6.01	5.09	4.58	4.25	4.01	3.71	3.37	3	2.57
19	8.18	5.93	5.01	4.5	4.17	3.94	3.63	3.3	3.92	2.49
20	8.1	5.85	4.94	4.43	4.1	3.87	3.56	3.23	2.86	2.42
21	8.02	5.78	4.87	4.37	4.04	3.81	3.51	3.17	2.8	2.36
22	7.95	5.72	4.82	4.31	3.99	3.76	3.45	3.12	2.75	2.31
23	7.88	5.66	4.76	4.26	3.94	3.71	3.41	3.07	2.7	2.26
24	7.82	5.61	4.72	4.22	3.9	3.67	3.36	3.03	2.66	2.21
25	7.77	5.57	4.68	4.18	3.85	3.63	3.32	2.99	2.62	2.17
26	7.72	5.53	4.64	4.14	3.82	3.59	3.2	2.96	2.58	2.1
27	7.68	5.49	4.6	4.11	3.78	3.56	3.26	2.93	2.45	2.13
28	7.64	5.45	4.57	4.07	3.75	3.53	3.23	2.9	2.52	2.06
29	7.6	5.42	4.54	4.04	3.73	3.5	3.2	2.87	2.49	2.03
30	7.56	5.39	4.51	4.02	3.7	3.47	3.17	2.84	2.47	2.01
40	7.31	5.18	4.31	3.83	3.51	3.29	2.99	2.66	2.29	1.8
60	7.08	4.98	4.13	3.65	3.34	3.12	2.82	2.5	2.12	1.6
120	6.85	4.79	3.95	3.48	3.17	2.96	2.66	2.34	1.95	1.38
Infinity	6.64	4.6	3.78	3.32	3.02	2.8	2.51	2.18	1.79	1

Notes: 1. v1 = df for greater variance.
2. v2 = df for smaller variance.

TABLE A3
Critical Values of χ^2

	Probability under H0 that of χ^2 > chi-square						
df	0.99	0.95	0.5	0.1	0.05	0.02	0.01
1	0.000157	0.00393	0.455	2.706	3.841	5.412	6.635
2	0.0201	0.103	1.386	4.605	5.991	7.824	9.21
3	0.115	0.352	2.366	6.251	7.815	9.837	11.341
4	0.297	0.711	3.357	7.779	9.488	11.668	13.277
5	0.554	0.1145	4.351	9.236	11.07	13.388	15.086
6	0.872	1.635	5.348	10.645	12.592	15.033	16.812
7	1.239	2.167	6.346	12.017	14.067	16.622	18.475
8	1.646	2.733	7.344	13.362	15.507	18.168	20.09
9	2.088	3.325	8.343	14.684	16.919	19.679	21.666
10	2.558	3.94	9.342	15.987	18.307	21.161	23.209
11	3.053	4.575	10.341	17.275	19.675	22.618	24.725
12	3.571	5.226	11.34	18.549	21.026	24.054	26.217
13	4.107	5.892	12.34	19.812	22.362	25.472	72.688
14	4.66	6.571	13.339	21.064	23.685	26.873	29.141
15	4.229	7.261	14.339	22.307	24.996	28.259	30.578
16	5.812	7.962	15.338	23.542	26.296	29.633	32
17	6.408	8.672	16.338	24.769	27.587	30.995	33.409
18	7.015	9.39	17.338	25.989	28.869	32.346	34.805
19	7.633	10.117	18.338	27.204	30.144	33.687	36.191
20	8.26	10.851	19.337	28.412	31.41	35.02	37.566
21	8.897	11.591	20.337	29.615	32.671	36.343	38.932
22	9.542	12.338	21.337	30.813	33.924	37.659	40.289
23	10.196	13.091	22.337	32.007	35.172	38.968	41.638
24	10.856	13.848	23.337	32.196	36.415	40.27	42.98
25	11.524	14.611	24.337	34.382	37.652	41.566	44.314
26	12.198	15.379	25.336	35.363	38.885	41.856	45.642
27	12.879	16.151	26.336	36.741	40.113	44.14	46.963
28	13.565	16.928	27.336	37.916	41.337	45.419	48.278
29	14.256	17.708	28.336	39.087	42.557	46.693	49.588
30	14.953	18.493	29.336	40.256	43.773	47.962	50.892

TABLE A4
Critical Values of Student's t-Distribution

df	Significance Level for Two-tailed Test					df
	0.2	0.1	0.05	0.02	0.01	
	Significance Level for One-tailed Test					
	0.1	0.05	0.025	0.01	0.005	
1	3.078	6.314	12.706	31.821	63.657	1
2	1.886	2.92	4.303	6.965	9.925	2
3	1.638	2.353	3.182	4.541	5.841	3
4	1.533	2.132	2.776	3.747	4.604	4
5	1.476	2.015	2.571	3.365	4.032	5
6	1.44	1.943	2.447	3.143	3.707	6
7	1.415	1.895	2.365	2.998	3.499	7
8	1.397	1.86	2.306	2.896	3.355	8
9	1.383	1.833	2.262	2.821	3.25	9
10	1.372	1.812	2.228	2.764	3.169	10
11	1.363	1.796	2.201	2.718	3.106	11
12	1.356	1.782	2.179	2.681	3.055	12
13	1.35	1.771	2.16	2.65	3.012	13
14	1.345	1.761	2.145	2.624	2.977	14
15	1.341	1.753	2.731	2.602	2.947	15
16	1.337	1.746	2.12	2.583	2.921	16
17	1.333	1.74	2.11	2.567	2.898	17
18	1.33	1.734	2.101	2.552	2.878	18
19	1.328	1.729	2.093	2.539	2.861	19
20	1.325	1.725	2.086	2.528	2.845	20
21	1.323	1.721	2.08	2.518	2.831	21
22	1.321	1.717	2.074	2.508	2.819	22
23	1.319	1.714	2.069	2.5	2.807	23
24	1.318	1.711	2.064	2.492	2.797	24
25	1.316	1.708	2.06	2.485	2.787	25
26	1.315	1.706	2.056	2.479	2.779	26
27	1.314	1.703	2.052	2.473	2.771	27
28	1.313	1.701	2.048	2.467	2.763	28
29	1.311	1.699	2.045	2.462	2.756	29
Infinity	1.282	1.645	1.96	2.326	2.576	Infinity

TABLE A5
Critical Values of T in the Wilcoxon Matched Pairs Test

	Significance Level for One-tailed Test		
	0.025	0.01	0.005
	Significance Level for Two-tailed Test		
n	0.05	0.02	0.01
6	0	–	–
7	2	0	–
8	4	2	0
9	6	3	2
10	8	5	3
11	11	7	5
12	14	10	7
13	17	13	10
14	21	16	13
15	25	20	16
16	30	24	20
17	35	28	23
18	40	33	28
19	46	38	32
20	52	43	38
21	59	49	43
22	66	56	49
23	73	62	55
24	81	69	61
25	89	77	68

TABLE A6

Values for Spearman's Rank Correlation for Combined Areas in Both Tails

n	0.2	0.1	0.05	0.02	0.01	0.002
4	0.8	0.8	–	–	–	–
5	0.7	0.8	0.9	0.9	–	–
6	0.6	0.7714	0.8236	0.8857	0.9429	–
7	0.5357	0.6786	0.745	0.8571	0.8929	0.9643
8	0.5	0.619	0.7143	0.8095	0.8571	0.9286
9	0.4667	0.5833	0.6833	0.7667	0.8167	0.9
10	0.4424	0.5515	0.6364	0.7333	0.7818	0.8667
11	0.4182	0.5273	0.6091	0.7	0.7455	0.8364
12	0.3986	0.4965	0.5804	0.6713	0.7273	0.8182
13	0.3791	0.478	0.5549	0.6429	0.6978	0.7912
14	0.3626	0.4593	0.5341	0.622	0.6747	0.767
15	0.35	0.4429	0.5179	0.6	0.6536	0.7464
16	0.3382	0.4265	0.5	0.5824	0.6324	0.7265
17	0.326	0.4118	0.4853	0.5637	0.6152	0.7083
18	0.3148	0.3994	0.4716	0.548	0.5975	0.6904
19	0.307	0.3895	0.4579	0.5333	0.5825	0.6737
20	0.2977	0.3789	0.4451	0.5203	0.5684	0.6586
21	0.2909	0.3688	0.4351	0.5078	0.5545	0.6455
22	0.2829	0.3597	0.4241	0.4963	0.5426	0.6318
23	0.2767	0.3518	0.415	0.4852	0.5306	0.6186
24	0.2704	0.3435	0.4061	0.4748	0.52	0.607
25	0.2646	0.3362	0.3977	0.4654	0.51	0.5962
26	0.2588	0.3299	0.3894	0.4564	0.5002	0.5856
27	0.254	0.3236	0.3822	0.4481	0.4915	0.5757
28	0.248	0.3175	0.3749	0.4401	0.4828	0.566
29	0.2443	0.3113	0.3685	0.432	0.4744	0.5567
30	0.24	0.3059	0.362	0.4251	0.4665	0.5479

TABLE A7
Kolmogorov–Smirnov Table (Critical Values of the D_n)

n \ α	0.01	0.05	0.1	0.15	0.2
1	0.995	0.975	0.950	0.925	0.900
2	0.926	0.842	0.776	0.726	0.684
3	0.828	0.708	0.642	0.597	0.565
4	0.733	0.624	0.654	0.525	0.494
5	0.669	0.565	0.510	0.474	0.446
6	0.618	0.521	0.470	0.436	0.410
7	0.577	0.486	0.438	0.405	0.381
8	0.543	0.457	0.411	0.381	0.358
9	0.514	0.432	0.388	0.360	0.339
10	0.490	0.410	0.368	0.342	0.322
11	0.468	0.391	0.352	0.326	0.307
12	0.450	0.375	0.338	0.313	0.295
13	0.433	0.361	0.325	0.302	0.284
14	0.418	0.349	0.314	0.292	0.274
15	0.404	0.338	0.304	0.283	0.266
16	0.392	0.328	0.295	0.274	0.258
17	0.381	0.318	0.286	0.266	0.250
18	0.371	0.309	0.278	0.259	0.244
19	0.363	0.301	0.272	0.252	0.237
20	0.356	0.294	0.264	0.264	0.231
25	0.320	0.270	0.240	0.220	0.210
30	0.290	0.240	0.220	0.200	0.190
35	0.270	0.230	0.210	0.190	0.180
40	0.250	0.210	0.190	0.180	0.170
45	0.240	0.200	0.180	0.170	0.160
50	0.230	0.190	0.170	0.160	0.150
Over 50	$\frac{1.63}{\sqrt{n}}$	$\frac{1.36}{\sqrt{n}}$	$\frac{1.22}{\sqrt{n}}$	$\frac{1.14}{\sqrt{n}}$	$\frac{1.07}{\sqrt{n}}$

TABLE A8
Mann–Whitney Table (Critical Values for Various Values of Alpha)

Alpha = 0.005 (Two-tailed)

	2	3	4	5	6	7	8	9	10	11	12	13	14	15	16	17	18	19	20
2																			
3											0	0	0	1	1	1	1	1	2
4							0	0	1	1	2	2	3	3	4	4	5	5	5
5					0	0	1	2	3	3	4	5	6	6	7	8	9	9	10
6				0	1	2	3	4	5	6	7	8	9	10	11	12	13	14	15
7				0	2	3	4	5	7	8	9	11	12	13	15	16	18	19	20
8			0	1	3	4	6	7	9	11	12	14	16	17	19	21	22	24	26
9			0	2	4	5	7	9	11	13	15	17	19	21	23	25	27	29	31
10			1	3	5	7	9	11	13	16	18	20	23	25	27	30	32	35	37
11			1	3	6	8	11	13	16	18	21	24	26	29	32	35	37	40	43
12		0	2	4	7	9	12	15	18	21	24	27	30	33	36	39	43	46	49
13		0	2	5	8	11	14	17	20	24	27	30	34	37	41	44	48	51	55
14		0	3	6	9	12	16	19	23	26	30	34	38	41	45	49	53	57	61
15		1	3	6	10	13	17	21	25	29	33	37	41	46	50	54	58	62	67
16		1	4	7	11	15	19	23	27	32	36	41	45	50	54	59	64	68	73
17		1	4	8	12	16	21	25	30	35	39	44	49	54	59	64	69	74	79
18		1	5	9	13	18	22	27	32	37	43	48	53	58	64	69	74	80	85
19		1	5	9	14	19	24	29	35	40	46	51	57	62	68	74	80	85	91
20		2	5	10	15	20	26	31	37	43	49	55	61	67	73	79	85	91	97

Alpha = 0.01 (Two-tailed)

	2	3	4	5	6	7	8	9	10	11	12	13	14	15	16	17	18	19	20
2																		0	0
3								0	0	0	1	1	1	2	2	2	2	3	3
4					0	0	1	1	2	2	3	3	4	5	5	6	6	7	8
5				0	1	1	2	3	4	5	6	7	7	8	9	10	11	12	13
6			0	1	2	3	4	5	6	7	9	10	11	12	13	15	16	17	18
7			0	1	3	4	6	7	9	10	12	13	15	16	18	19	21	22	24
8			1	2	4	6	7	9	11	13	15	17	18	20	22	24	26	28	30
9		0	1	3	5	7	9	11	13	16	18	20	22	24	27	29	31	33	36
10		0	2	4	6	9	11	13	16	18	21	24	26	29	31	34	37	39	42
11		0	2	5	7	10	13	16	18	21	24	27	30	33	36	39	42	45	46
12		1	3	6	9	12	15	18	21	24	27	31	34	37	41	44	47	51	54
13		1	3	7	10	13	17	20	24	27	31	34	38	42	45	49	53	56	60

(Table A8 Continued)

(Table A8 Continued)

	2	3	4	5	6	7	8	9	10	11	12	13	14	15	16	17	18	19	20
14		1	4	7	11	15	18	22	26	30	34	38	42	46	50	54	58	63	67
15		2	5	8	12	16	20	24	29	33	37	42	46	51	55	60	64	69	73
16		2	5	9	13	18	22	27	31	36	41	45	50	55	60	65	70	74	79
17		2	6	10	15	19	24	29	34	39	44	49	54	60	65	70	75	81	86
18		2	6	11	16	21	26	31	37	42	47	53	58	64	70	75	81	87	92
19	0	3	7	12	17	22	28	33	39	45	51	56	63	69	74	81	87	93	99
20	0	3	8	13	18	24	30	36	42	46	54	60	67	73	79	86	92	99	105

Alpha = 0.02 (Two-tailed)

n1/n2	2	3	4	5	6	7	8	9	10	11	12	13	14	15	16	17	18	19	20
2																			
3		-	0	0	0	0	0	1	1	1	2	2	2	3	3	4	4	4	5
4		-	-	0	1	1	2	3	3	4	5	5	6	7	7	8	9	9	10
5		-	0	1	2	3	4	5	6	7	8	9	10	11	12	13	14	15	16
6		-	1	2	3	4	7	7	8	9	11	12	13	15	16	18	19	20	22
7		0	1	3	4	6	7	9	11	12	14	16	17	19	21	23	24	26	28
8		0	2	4	6	7	9	11	13	15	17	20	22	24	26	28	30	32	34
9		1	3	5	7	9	11	14	16	18	21	23	26	28	31	33	36	38	40
10		1	3	6	8	11	13	16	19	22	24	27	30	33	36	38	41	44	47
11		1	4	7	9	12	15	18	22	25	28	31	34	37	41	44	47	50	53
12		2	5	8	11	14	17	21	24	28	31	35	38	42	46	49	53	56	60
13		2	5	9	12	16	20	23	27	31	35	39	43	47	51	55	59	63	67
14		2	6	10	13	17	22	26	30	34	38	43	47	51	56	60	65	69	73
15		3	7	11	15	19	24	28	33	37	42	47	51	56	61	66	70	75	80
16		3	7	12	16	21	26	31	36	41	46	51	56	61	66	71	76	82	87
17		4	8	13	18	23	28	33	38	44	49	55	60	66	71	77	82	88	93
18		4	9	14	19	24	30	36	41	47	53	59	65	70	76	82	88	94	100
19		4	9	15	20	26	32	38	44	50	56	63	69	75	82	88	94	101	107
20		5	10	16	22	28	34	40	47	53	60	67	73	80	87	93	100	107	114

Alpha = 0.05 (Two-tailed)

n1/n2	2	3	4	5	6	7	8	9	10	11	12	13	14	15	16	17	18	19	20
2							0	0	0	0	1	1	1	1	1	2	2	2	2
3				0	1	1	2	2	3	3	4	4	5	5	6	6	7	7	8
4			0	1	2	3	4	4	5	6	7	8	9	10	11	11	12	13	14
5		0	1	2	3	5	6	7	8	9	11	12	13	14	15	17	18	19	20

(Table A8 Continued)

(Table A8 Continued)

n1/n2	2	3	4	5	6	7	8	9	10	11	12	13	14	15	16	17	18	19	20
6		1	2	3	5	6	7	10	11	13	14	16	17	19	21	22	24	25	27
7		1	2	5	6	8	10	12	14	16	18	20	22	24	26	28	30	32	34
8	0	2	4	6	7	10	13	15	17	19	22	24	26	29	31	34	36	38	41
9	0	2	4	7	10	12	15	17	20	23	26	28	31	34	37	39	42	45	48
10	0	3	5	8	11	14	17	20	23	26	29	33	36	39	42	45	48	52	55
11	0	3	6	9	13	16	19	23	26	30	33	37	40	44	47	51	55	58	62
12	1	4	7	11	14	18	22	26	29	33	37	41	45	49	53	57	61	65	69
13	1	4	8	12	16	20	24	28	33	37	41	45	50	54	59	63	67	72	76
14	1	5	9	13	17	22	26	31	36	40	45	50	55	59	64	67	74	78	83
15	1	5	10	14	19	24	29	34	39	44	49	54	59	64	70	75	80	85	90
16	1	6	11	15	21	26	31	37	42	47	53	59	64	70	75	81	86	92	98
17	2	6	11	17	22	28	34	39	45	51	57	63	67	75	81	87	93	99	105
18	2	7	12	18	24	30	36	42	48	55	61	67	74	80	86	93	99	106	112
19	2	7	13	19	25	32	38	45	52	58	65	72	78	85	92	99	106	113	119
20	2	8	13	20	27	34	41	48	55	62	69	76	83	90	98	105	112	119	127

Alpha = 0.10 (Two-tailed)

n1/n2	2	3	4	5	6	7	8	9	10	11	12	13	14	15	16	17	18	19	20
2																			
3		0	0	1	2	2	3	4	4	5	5	6	7	7	8	9	9	10	11
4		0	1	2	3	4	5	6	7	8	9	10	11	12	14	15	16	17	18
5		1	2	4	5	6	8	9	11	12	13	15	16	18	19	20	22	23	25
6		2	3	5	7	8	10	12	14	16	17	19	21	23	25	26	28	30	32
7		2	4	6	8	11	13	15	17	19	21	24	26	28	30	33	35	37	39
8		3	5	8	10	13	15	18	20	23	26	28	31	33	36	39	41	44	47
9		4	6	9	12	15	18	21	24	27	30	33	36	39	42	45	48	51	54
10		4	7	11	14	17	20	24	27	31	34	37	41	44	48	51	55	58	62
11		5	8	12	16	19	23	27	31	34	38	42	46	50	54	57	61	65	69
12		5	9	13	17	21	26	30	34	38	42	47	51	55	60	64	68	72	77
13		6	10	15	19	24	28	33	37	42	47	51	56	61	65	70	75	80	84
14		7	11	16	21	26	31	36	41	46	51	56	61	66	71	77	82	87	92
15		7	12	18	23	28	33	39	44	50	55	61	66	72	77	83	88	94	100
16		8	14	19	25	30	36	42	48	54	60	65	71	77	83	89	95	101	107
17		9	15	20	26	33	39	45	51	57	64	70	77	83	89	96	102	109	115
18		9	16	22	28	35	41	48	55	61	68	75	82	88	95	102	109	116	123
19		10	17	23	30	37	44	51	58	65	72	80	87	94	101	109	116	123	130
20		11	18	25	32	39	47	54	62	69	77	84	92	100	107	115	123	130	138

(Table A8 Continued)

Alpha = 0.20 (Two-tailed)

n1/n2	2	3	4	5	6	7	8	9	10	11	12	13	14	15	16	17	18	19	20
2		0	0	1	1	1	2	2	3	3	4	4	5	5	5	6	6	7	7
3	0	1	1	2	3	4	5	5	6	7	8	9	10	10	11	12	13	14	15
4	0	1	3	4	5	6	7	9	10	11	12	13	15	17	18	20	21	22	23
5	1	2	4	5	7	8	10	12	13	15	17	18	20	22	23	25	27	28	30
6	1	3	5	7	9	11	13	15	17	19	21	23	25	27	29	31	34	36	38
7	1	4	6	8	11	13	16	18	21	23	26	28	31	33	36	41	43	46	48
8	2	5	7	10	13	16	19	22	24	27	30	33	36	39	42	45	48	51	54
9	2	5	9	12	15	18	22	25	28	31	35	38	41	45	48	52	55	58	62
10	3	6	10	13	17	21	24	28	32	36	39	43	47	51	54	58	62	66	70
11	3	7	11	15	19	23	27	31	36	40	44	48	52	57	61	65	69	73	78
12	4	8	12	17	21	26	30	35	39	44	49	53	58	63	67	72	77	81	86
13	4	9	13	18	23	28	33	38	43	48	53	58	63	68	74	79	84	89	94
14	5	10	15	20	25	31	36	41	47	52	58	63	69	74	80	85	91	97	102
15	5	10	17	22	27	33	39	45	51	57	63	68	74	80	86	92	98	104	110
16	5	11	18	23	29	36	42	48	54	61	67	74	80	86	93	99	106	112	119
17	6	12	20	25	31	41	45	52	58	65	72	79	85	92	99	106	113	120	127
18	6	13	21	27	34	43	48	55	62	69	77	84	91	98	106	113	120	128	135
19	7	14	22	28	36	46	51	58	66	73	81	89	97	104	112	120	128	135	143
20	7	15	23	30	38	48	54	62	70	78	86	94	102	110	119	127	135	143	151

TABLE A9

Wilcoxon Signed Ranks Table (Critical Values for Two-tailed Test)

n	0.10	0.05	0.02	0.01	0.001
5	0				
6	2	0			
7	3	2	0		
8	5	3	1	0	
9	8	5	3	1	
10	10	8	5	3	
11	13	10	7	5	0
12	17	13	9	7	1
13	21	17	12	9	2
14	25	21	15	12	4
15	30	25	19	15	6
16	35	29	23	19	8

(Table A9 Continued)

(Table A9 Continued)

n	0.10	0.05	0.02	0.01	0.001
17	41	34	27	23	11
18	47	40	32	27	14
19	53	46	37	32	18
20	60	52	43	37	21
21	67	58	49	42	25
22	75	65	56	48	30
23	83	73	62	54	35
24	91	81	69	61	40
25	100	89	77	68	45
26	110	98	84	75	51
27	119	107	92	83	57
28	130	116	101	91	64
29	140	126	110	100	71
30	151	137	120	109	78
31	163	147	130	118	86
32	175	159	140	128	94
33	187	170	151	138	102
34	200	182	162	148	111
35	213	195	173	159	120
36	227	208	185	171	130
37	241	221	198	182	141
38	256	235	211	194	150
39	271	249	224	207	161
40	286	264	234	220	172
41	302	279	252	233	183
42	319	294	266	247	195
43	336	310	280	261	207
44	353	327	296	276	220
45	371	343	312	291	233
46	389	461	328	307	246
47	407	378	345	322	260
48	426	396	362	339	274
49	446	415	379	355	289
50	466	434	397	373	304

Glossary

adjusted goodness-of-fit index: It adjusts the GFI depending on the degrees of freedom, and the value more than 0.09 provides the best result.

agglomeration schedule: It shows the information of the cases of similar pair from the beginning stage of the hierarchical cluster analysis method and also the information about the cases of joining the similar pair at a later stage.

alpha model (Cronbach): This model emphasizes the internal consistency of a multiple-item scale depending on internal correlation.

analysis of variance: In the case of more than two populations, if a researcher wants to test the equality of means of the samples which have been drawn from the different populations, ANOVA could be used.

average annual growth rate: It is the arithmetic mean of a series of growth rates, and it is easily calculated using a normal average formula.

average linkage method: It is based on the average distance from all the elements of one cluster to all the elements of another cluster. In this case, the cluster contains grouping objects/cases with higher homogeneity and a small variance.

bar chart: It depicts the frequency. Here, the class intervals are shown in the horizontal axis and the relative frequencies are specified along the vertical axis of the graph.

binary data: These place things in one of two mutually exclusive categories—right/wrong, true/false or accept/reject.

causal research: It is quantitative in nature as well as pre-planned and structured in design.

centroid method: In this method, the distance is calculated as the squared distance between two cluster centroids which is actually the mean value of the clustering elements in a cluster.

chi-square goodness-of-fit: It ascertains the validity of the observed data by examining whether the theoretical data is similar with the observed data or not.

chi-square test of homogeneity: It is used to determine whether the proportion of a particular attribute is the same across several populations.

cluster analysis: It is a multivariate technique which creates the mutually exclusive and collectively exhaustive groups with objects or entities or cases.

cluster membership: It specifies the cluster with which a particular case/object is associated. Cluster membership depends on a certain research requirement of the researcher.

cluster sampling: This probabilistic sampling process is conducted in three steps. In the first step, population is divided by different clusters. In the second step, a simple random sampling technique is used for the selection of a random sample of clusters from population. In the third step, either all elements of each selected cluster are incorporated in the desired sample or sample of elements from each selected cluster is chosen randomly.

cohort study: It traces on sub-population over time, for example, absenteeism rates for the sales department.

communality: It describes the variance in each variable, shared with the other variables in a research study. Communality values show whether the variables/items are fit or unfit for this analysis. If the value is below 0.5, the variable should be removed from the analysis.

comparative fit index: It compares the model fit improvement of the proposed model over a model which defines no relationships among variables, and the value more than 0.09 provides the best model fit.

complete linkage method: It is based on the longest distance between two cluster elements which is just opposite of the single linkage method.

compound annual growth rate: This rate measures the return on an investment over a certain period of time. It is the mean annual growth rate of an investment over a specified period of time longer than one year.

concurrent validity: At first, researchers evaluate the collected data from the research scale. At the same time, collected data on criterion variables are evaluated. If both are shown to be valid, it is called as concurrent validity.

confirmatory factor analysis: It follows the stages of SEM through AMOS for the hypothesized measurement model. It emphasizes testing how well-defined variables represent factors.

conjoint analysis: It indicates the measurement of relative values among different attributes. Basically, conjoint analysis is used to find out the respondent's most preferable attributes of any product or service.

constant sum scales: In this scale, the respondents are asked to assign points among two or more characteristics based on their preferences, such that the total points remain the constant sum of usually 100 or 10.

construct validity: It is a validation process of construct by existing conceptual or theoretical bases through statistical analysis.

content validity: It emphasizes the adequate coverage and appropriateness of all constructs in the research study and focuses on the relevant content domain for them.

contingency coefficient: It is used when rows and columns in the contingency table become equal.

continuous rating scale: Respondents are asked to mark at a proper place on a line scale depicted with two extreme points.

continuous variable: A variable which can take up any numerical value (integral/fractional) within a certain range is called a 'continuous' variable.

convenience sampling: In this non-probabilistic sampling technique, interviewers collect the sample with convenient elements which are readily accessible.

Cramer's V: If the two variables are grouping, then we have to compute Cramer's V. It indicates the strength of relationship with chi-square test. For example, when we want to establish the degree of relationship between gender and educational status of students. Cramer's V is used when rows and columns in the contingency table are not equal. The lower limit of the Cramer's V is 0 and the upper limit of the phi coefficient is +1.

criterion validity: It deals with the appropriateness of the variables or criterion in a research study.

cross-sectional study: One-shot or cross-sectional studies are those in which data is gathered once, during a period of days, weeks or months.

Crosstabs: It is used when you want to work with two discrete/grouping/categorical variables, one in the column and another in the row.

dendrogram: This tree-like graph represents the numbers of clusters associated with different situations. Here, the vertical axis shows the cases/objects and horizontal axis shows the inter-respondent scaled distance, range from 0 to 25.

descriptive research: Descriptive research takes up the bulk of online surveying and is considered conclusive in nature due to its quantitative nature.

dichotomous questions: When a question has two possible responses, we consider it dichotomous. Surveys often use dichotomous questions that ask for a yes/no, true/false or agree/disagree response.

discrete variable: A variable which can take up only exact values and not any fractional values is called a 'discrete' variable.

discriminant analysis: It is used to identify the variables which are relatively better in discriminating between two or more than two groups.

disproportionate stratified sampling: Sample elements selected from each stratum are proportionate to relative stratum size as well as standard deviation of the elements under that stratum.

eigen value: It explains the proportion of variance described by an individual factor. It should always be greater than 1. A factor can be removed from a research study if the eigen value is less than 1.

equivalent form reliability: Researcher administers two equivalent survey-instrument forms at two different time frames.

eta: If one variable is ratio or interval and the other variable is nominal, then we calculate eta. For example, we want to establish the degree of relationship between gender and intelligent quotients of students.

Euclidean distance: It is used for measuring the similarity of objects or cases in a population. Euclidean distance is calculated by the square root of the sum of squared of differences between variables.

evaluative review: It is a type of literature review which focuses on providing a discussion of the literature in terms of its coverage and contribution to knowledge in a particular area.

exploratory factor analysis: It identifies the underlying structure among the items/variables and summarizes the data by converting large number of items/variables to a smaller number of factors.

exploratory research: Exploratory research is an important part of any marketing or business strategy. Its focus is on the discovery of ideas and insights as opposed to collecting statistically accurate data.

exploratory review: This type of literature review seeks to find out what actually exists in the academic literature in terms of theory, empirical evidence and research methods as they pertain to specific research topics and the related wider subject area.

face validity: It mainly prioritizes the subjective judgement of an item or a construct.

factor analysis: It is a multivariate method which is used to reduce a large number of variables to few controllable factors.

factor loading: It implies the correlation coefficient between the variables under a factor. The high values of factor loading (from 0.5 to 1) indicate good correlation between variables.

factorial design: Factorial design is used for one dependent variable (interval or ratio scale) and two or more independent variables (nominal scale). In this design, researchers can test the interaction between different variables.

Friedman test: It is a very useful non-parametric test which is quite similar to a randomized block design, containing ranked data (approximately χ^2 distribution). It is applicable when all blocks will be independent and there will be no interaction effect between blocks and treatments.

goodness of fit: It is evaluated with the help of different indexes. The relative χ^2 (χ^2/df) which varies depending on the sample size should be less than 3.

goodness-of-fit index: It is equivalent to R^2 which can provide the best result if it is more than 0.90.

Guttman model: This model computes Guttman's lower bounds for true reliability. It shows different reliability coefficients from lambda 1 to lambda 6 including Cronbach alpha and Guttman split-half reliability.

hierarchical method: This technique deals with one big cluster containing all the cases/subjects within it, and then different individual subject clusters as per the requirement of the researchers are created by dividing and subdividing the big cluster.

histogram: It shows the frequency of values of a variable. It gives us an idea about the distribution of the variable.

hypothesis: Hypothesis is a predictive statement of assumption or supposition to be proved or disproved by statistical means.

independent samples t-test: Detecting differences between the means of two independent groups is called independent samples t-test.

instrumental review: Literature review which seeks to find out how to conduct some research on a highly specific research problem.

inter-observer reliability: Different observers are assigned to assess the consistency of the items of the same sample through the same questionnaire.

interval scale: The distances between the points on the scale are equal.

interview method: Primary data may be collected either through personal interviews or through telephonic interviews.

judgemental/purposive sampling: In this non-probabilistic sampling technique, sample elements are purposively chosen on the basis of researcher's judgement.

Kaiser–Meyer–Olkin and Bartlett's test: This test, the measuring tool of sampling adequacy, can indicate the proportion of variations of variables for different factors.

Karl Pearson's coefficient of correlation: This is a quantitative measure of the degree of relationship between two variables. Correlation coefficient is universally denoted by 'r'.

Kolmogorov–Smirnov one-sample test: It is a non-parametric test which finds out whether there is any significant difference between an observed and theoretical frequency distribution (normal/uniform/Poisson/exponential). It is used for comparing the observed and theoretical frequency distribution on an ordinal scale.

Kruskal–Wallis test: This non-parametric test resembles with the one-way ANOVA which is a parametric test. It can be performed in interval scales as well as ordinal scale. It is based on the assumptions of independent groups.

leaf: It is the number in the first place of the value of the variable. The number of leaves tells one how many of these numbers are in the variable.

Likert scale: Likert scales are usually limited to a five-category scale, as it is often difficult to clearly display a larger number of categories.

linear regression: It is the next step after correlation. It is used when we want to predict the value of a variable based on the value of another variable.

Mann–Whitney U test: This non-parametric test resembles the t-test which compares two independent population means. In the case of an ordinal scale and doubt about the normality of the distribution, direct the researcher to execute the Mann–Whitney U test.

measures of central tendency: These are ways of describing the central position of a frequency distribution for a group of data. We can describe this central position using a number of statistics, including the mode, median and mean.

measures of spread: These are ways of summarizing a group of data by describing how spread out the scores are.

multicollinearity: When two or more than two independent variables are highly correlated to each other among several independent variables, used in the model, this condition is called multicollinearity.

multidimensional scaling: It is a visual display technique which plots individual or group-wise perceptions and preferences of the respondents.

multiple-choice scales: Researchers provide a single question with multiple alternatives. For collecting demographic or nominal type data, this scale is used.

multiple-item scale: This scale is used when researchers require evaluating people's behaviour depending on more than one attributes.

multiple regression analysis: It deals with two or more independent variables (explanatory variables) and at least one dependent variable.

normed fit index: It assumes that all latent variables are not correlated and the value should be more than 0.90.

nominal scale: Numbers and letters are used in nominal scale to identify different research entities.

non-hierarchical method (K-means clustering): In this cluster-forming method, any element of one cluster can leave that cluster and add with the other cluster. This technique begins with a pre-defined number of clusters. It is also called K-means clustering.

non-parametric test: It is basically a distribution-free test. For executing non-parametric test, it is not required to maintain any particular shape of population distribution from where the sample is chosen.

non-probability sampling: Selection of sample unit depends on the personal judgement or opinion of the researcher.

non-sampling error: It occurs due to inaccurate answers from the respondents (inability or unwillingness error), recording error by interviewers, data analysis error, questioning error, sampling frame error, respondent selection error and so on.

normal distribution (Gaussian distribution): It is used in normality test for data. One of the assumptions for most parametric tests to be reliable is that the data is approximately normally distributed.

observation method: The information is sought by the way of investigator's own direct observation without asking anything from the respondent.

one-sample sign test: It is a non-parametric test which handles basically non-metric ordinal and nominal data. In the case of one-sample test, we deal with the elements of only one sample. This test is based on basically binomial distribution.

one-way ANOVA (completely randomized design): Researchers use one-way ANOVA in the case of one dependent variable (interval or ratio scale) and one independent variable (nominal scale) with different categories/groups.

online analytical processing: Cubes procedure calculates totals, means and other univariate statistics for continuous summary variables within categories of one or more categorical grouping variables.

ordinal scale: Its entities can be arranged and ranked according to a definite order.

paired comparison scale: In this technique, respondents compare a pair of objects at a time according to some attributes. Ordinal data are observed here.

paired sample t-test: The test where the observations are made on the same sample at two different times is called paired sample t-test.

panel study: It traces on the same sample over time, for example, graduate career tracks over the period 1990–2000 for the same starting cohort.

parallel and strict parallel model: Parallel model emphasizes equal variance of all items and strict parallel model emphasizes equal means across items. It shows estimated common inter-item correlation, estimated reliability, common variance and test for goodness of fit of model.

parallel-forms reliability: Different survey-instrument forms under the same domain at same time frame are used to assess the consistency of the items.

partial correlation: In the partial correlation, we compute the degree of association between two variables keeping the third variable as control variable.

phi coefficient: If two variables are dichotomous in nature, then we have to compute the phi coefficient; for example, we want to establish the degree of relationship between gender and smoking status of students.

phi coefficient: It is used in the case of a 2×2 contingency table. The lower limit is –1 and the upper limit is +1 for the of the phi coefficient.

pictorial scale: In this scale, respondents are asked to rate the attributes on a pictorial scale from agreement to disagreement.

population element: It refers to a single member of the population.

population: It refers to the total number of units or items desired in any survey research.

predictive validity: It is established when a measuring instrument enables to predict some future events theoretically. It actually tries to correlate present and future measurements.

pretesting: Pretesting means 'testing the questionnaire on a few selected respondents' or a small sample of actual respondents with a purpose of improving the questionnaire by identifying and eliminating the potential problems.

primary data sources: These are the first occurrence of a piece of work. These mainly include (a) reports, (b) conference and proceedings and (c) theses.

principal component method: It is a commonly used method in factor analysis for reducing larger set of variables to fewer factors. It emphasizes the transformation of interrelated variables to uncorrelated factors containing linear combination of those variables.

probability sampling: It is an unbiased method. Sampling units are selected randomly in probability sampling where each population element has the fixed probabilistic chance of inclusion in the sample.

proportionate stratified sampling: Sample elements chosen from each stratum are proportionate to the relative stratum size under population.

Q sort scale: Q sort scaling is used when ranking is tiresome for the large number of rated characteristics.

qualitative classification: It is done according to attributes or non-measurable characteristics, such as social status, sex, nationality and occupation.

qualitative data: A variable differing in quality is called a qualitative variable or attribute. When we classify or categorize something, we create qualitative or attribute data.

quantitative classification: It is done according to numerical size like weights in kg or heights in cm. Here, we classify the data by assigning arbitrary limits known as class limits.

quantitative data: A variable differing in quantity is called quantitative variable, for example, the weight of a person and number of people in a car.

questionnaire method: In this method a questionnaire is mailed to the person concerned with a request to answer the questions and return the filled questionnaire. This method is most extensively applied in various researches in social science.

quota sampling: This non-probabilistic sampling process is conducted in two steps. In the first step, population is divided by different control categories or quotas. These control categories are gender, occupation, income level, age and so on.

R^2 value: It indicates how much of the total variation in the dependent variable can be explained by the independent variable.

rank order scale: In this scale, respondents are asked to rank different attributes or entities from a presented list. This scale generates ordinal data.

reliability: Reliability testing focuses on the analysis of the properties of measurement scale and its items.

root mean square error of approximation: It emphasizes that a sampling error must be less than 0.06.

rotation of factors: Rotation creates a simple structure where one factor includes high factor loading and all other factors holds low factor loading. Basically, it helps to understand the association with factor loadings with a particular factor.

run test: It is a non-parametric test to examine the randomness of the sample which is drawn from a population. Run test is based on the sequence in which the order of observations is really found.

sample: It contains some elements of the population.

sampling error: It occurs when a sample is not properly representing the population characteristics.

sampling frame: It contains properly identified population elements which are available for the researcher at any stage of sample elements selection process.

sampling unit: It is a single member of the sample.

schedule method: This method of data collection is very much like the collection of data through questionnaires, with little difference that lies in the fact that schedules (proforma containing a set of questions) are being filled in by the enumerators who are specially appointed for this purpose.

scree plot: This plot shows the optimal number of factors retained after factor analysis. Actually, it is a plot between eigen value and factor number, as per its order of extraction.

secondary data sources: These mainly include (a) journals, (b) books and (c) newspapers.

semantic differential scale: It is used to describe a person's attitude or belief towards a product, brand or organization. The respondents are asked to rate multiple items on a 5- or 7-point bipolar multiple-item scale.

simple random sampling: In simple random sampling process, every sample element is selected independently and randomly from the population.

single-item scale: A construct or a variable is measured through only one item.

single linkage method: It is based on the shortest distance between two cluster elements. Basically, it is defined as the minimum distance between two closest points of two clusters.

skewness: It measures the degree and direction of asymmetry. A symmetric distribution such as a normal distribution has a skewness of 0.

snowball sampling: In this sampling technique, at first an initial group of respondents is chosen randomly from population. In the second step, other respondents are chosen on the basis of the reference given by the initial respondents.

spatial classification: It is done with respect to space or places, for example, production of cereals in quintals in various states, population of a country according to states and so on.

Spearman's rank correlation: Spearman's rank correlation is used to determine the correlation between two series of ranks (ordinal data). The association between two ranked variable data cannot be determined by the Pearson correlation coefficient.

Spearman's rank correlation coefficient: If two variables are ordinal in nature or one variable is ordinal and the other one is ratio or interval, then we have to compute rho or spearman's rank correlation coefficient.

split-half model: This model divides randomly the items into two parts of a scale and examines the correlation between them. The main purpose of this model is to measure the reliability of the same construct into two sets.

stapel scale: Stapel scale is like the semantic differential scale with single pole and one adjective. It is constructed by placing a single adjective in the centre of an even number, generally 10, ranging from –5 to +5.

std. error: These are the standard errors for the descriptive statistics. The standard error gives some idea about the variability possible in the statistics.

stem: It is the number in the 10s place of the value of the variable. For example, the value of the variable is 31. So the stem is 3 and leaf is 1. The 3 is in the 10s place, so it is the stem.

stratified sampling: This probabilistic sampling process is executed in two steps. In the first step, population is divided into different strata. In the second step, sample elements are chosen from each stratum randomly.

structural equation modelling: It can explain the relationships among multiple variables. It verifies the interrelationship conditions, observing in a series of multiple regression equations.

systematic sampling: In this probabilistic sampling process, sample elements are selected by picking a random starting point and then choosing every *i*th element consecutively from the population.

temporal classification: It is done according to time, for example, index numbers arranged over a period of time, population of a country for several decades and exports and imports of India for different five year plans.

tertiary data sources: These are designed either to locate primary and secondary literature or to introduce a topic.

test–retest reliability: A different time frame is used to measure the consistency of items of the same sample through the same questionnaire.

Thurstone scales: In this scale, researchers choose a group of 80–100 entities pointing out different levels of favourable attitudes towards a product, brand or services under a research study.

trend study: It looks at population characteristics over time, for example, organizational absenteeism rates during the course of a year.

t-tests: These tests are used to compare two means to assess whether they are from the same population. T-tests presume that both groups are normally distributed and have relatively equal variances.

Tukey's hinges: These are the first, second and third quartiles. They are calculated in the way that Tukey originally proposed when he came up with the idea of a boxplot.

two-sample sign test: It is also a non-parametric test based on two sample observations. The process of execution is similar to the one-sample sign test. Only '+ sign' and '– sign' are determined by comparing a pair of sample observations.

two-way ANOVA (randomized block design): For one dependent variable (interval or ratio scale) and two independent variables (nominal scale) with different categories/groups, two-way ANOVA is used. The important feature of randomized block design is that each block contains an equal number of treatments.

type-I error: This error rejects null hypothesis when it is true.

type-II error: This error accepts null hypothesis when it is false.

validity: Validity focuses on the accuracy of an instrument's measurement.

Ward's method: In this minimizing cluster variance method, the distance is calculated as the total sum of square deviation from the mean of a cluster where the research cases are assigned.

Wilcoxon matched pairs signed rank test: It also resembles with the 'paired sample t-test' which is a parametric test.

Bibliography

Bajpai, N. 2011. *Business Research Methods*. Noida: Pearson India Education Services.

Chawla, D., and N. Sondhi. 2011. *Research Methodology—Concepts and Cases* (pp. 28–37 and 323–26). New Delhi: Vikas Publishing House.

Cooper, D. R., P. S. Schindler, and J. K. Sharma. 2012. *Business Research Methods*. 11th ed. New Delhi: Tata McGraw-Hill.

Field, A. P. 2009. *Discovering Statistics Using SPSS: And Sex and Drugs and Rock 'n' Roll*. 3rd ed. London: SAGE Publishing.

Fornell, C., and D. Larcker. 1981. 'Evaluating Structural Equation Models with Unobservable Variables and Measurement Error'. *Journal of Marketing Research*, 18 (1): 39–50.

Hair, J. F., R. E. Anderson, R. L. Tatham, and W. Black. 1998. *Multivariate Data Analysis*. 5th ed. Upper Saddle River, NJ: Prentice Hall.

———. 2006. *Multivariate Data Analysis*. 6th ed. Upper Saddle River, NJ: Pearson Prentice Hall.

Hair, J. F., W. C. Black, B. J. Babin and R. E. Anderson. 2010. *Multivariate Data Analysis*. 7th ed. Upper Saddle River, NJ: Prentice Hall.

Hooper, D., J. Coughlan, and M. R. Mullen. 2008. 'Structural Equation Modelling: Guidelines for Determining Model Fit'. *The Electronic Journal of Business Research Methods* 6 (1).

Iacobucci, D. 2010. 'Structural Equations Modelling, Fit Indices, Sample Size, and Advanced Topics'. *Journal of Consumer Psychology*, 20 (1): 90–98.

Kothari C. R. 2004. *Research Methodology, Methods and Techniques*. New Delhi: New Age International.

———. 2006. *Research Methodology, Methods and Techniques*. New Delhi: New Age International.

Kumar, R. 2011. *Research Methodology: A Step-by-Step Guide for Beginners*. 3rd ed. New Delhi: SAGE.

Levin, R. I., and D. S. Rubin. 2009. *Statistics for Management*. 7th ed. Upper Saddle River, NJ: Pearson Prentice Hall.

Malhotra, N. K. 2005. *Marketing Research: An Applied Orientation*. 4th ed. New Delhi: Prentice Hall of India.

Merriam-Webster. 2012. Available at www.merriamwebster.com/dictionary/metacognition (Accessed on 14 December 2016).

Naichiamas, D., and N. C. Frankfort. 1996. *Research Methods in the Social Sciences*. 5th ed. Santa Cruz, CA: Arnold.

Nargundkar, R. 2009. *Marketing Research Text and Cases*. 3rd ed. New Delhi: Tata McGraw-Hill Education.

Nie, N. H., C. H. Hull, J. G. Jenkins, K. Steinbrenner, and D. H. Bent. 1975. *SPSS: Statistical Package for the Social Sciences*. 2nd ed. New York: McGraw-Hill.

Rao, A. B. 2008. *Research Methodology for Management and Social Sciences*. 1st ed. New Delhi: Excel Books.

Schumacker, R. E. 1992. *Goodness of Fit Criteria in Structural Equations Models*. San Francisco, CA: American Educational Research Association.

Srivastava, T. N., and S. Rego. 2011. *Business Research Methodology*. New Delhi: Tata McGraw-Hill.

Young, P. V. 1960. *Scientific Social Surveys and Research*. 3rd ed. New York, NY: Prentice Hall Publications.

Zikmund, W. G. 1997. *Business Research Methods*. 5th ed. London: Dryden Press.

Index